YUGOSLAVIA IN CRISIS
1934-1941

East Central European Studies
of Columbia University

J. B. HOPTNER

YUGOSLAVIA IN CRISIS
1934–1941

COLUMBIA UNIVERSITY PRESS
NEW YORK AND LONDON

First printing 1962
Second printing 1963

LIBRARY OF CONGRESS CATALOG CARD NUMBER: 61-7174

MANUFACTURED IN THE UNITED STATES OF AMERICA

East Central European Studies
of Columbia University

The East Central European Studies, a companion series to the Studies of the Russian Institute, comprise scholarly books prepared under the auspices of the Program on East Central Europe of Columbia University or through other divisions of the University. The publication of these studies is designed to enlarge our understanding of an important region of the world, which, because of its relative inaccessibility in recent years as well as because of the linguistic problems it presents, has been somewhat neglected in serious academic study. The faculty of the Program on East Central Europe, without necessarily endorsing the conclusions reached by the authors, believe that these studies contribute substantially to knowledge of the area and should serve to stimulate further inquiry and research.

To My Parents

Foreword

It is a particular pleasure to be able to inaugurate the new series of East Central European Studies by introducing Dr. Jacob Hoptner's book, *Yugoslavia in Crisis, 1934–1941*. Dr. Hoptner's work demonstrates admirably both the importance of an understanding of events in Eastern Europe and also the qualities needed for such understanding: linguistic command, experience in the area, and, above all, a sense of the point of view from which the nations of Eastern Europe necessarily regard their domestic and external environment.

Because of its rich and new documentation, this study removes a number of prevailing misconceptions concerning Yugoslavia's foreign and domestic position under the regency of Prince Paul and the premierships of Milan Stojadinović and Dragiša Cvetković. It is of especial interest for the light it casts on the obscure and tortured events of 1940 and 1941, years that led Yugoslavia against its will into the abyss of war.

HENRY L. ROBERTS

November, 1961

Contents

INTRODUCTION

Winston Churchill hailed with great satisfaction the overthrow of the Yugoslav regency by a small group of Serb army officers on March 27, 1941. Yugoslavia, he proclaimed, had "found its soul."

In that war-torn time no one paused to question this pronouncement, and no one stopped to wonder if a poetic phrase told the whole story. In 1941 few doubted that Yugoslavia should follow Churchill's exhortations, attack the Italians in Albania, and risk savage reprisals by the overwhelming Axis force. And in 1941 no one raised his voice to ask if the goal of foreign policy is the saving of a nation's soul or the saving of the nation.

In Churchill's view at the time, the *coup d'état* in Belgrade erupted from the wrath of a people "at the betrayal of their country by the weakness of their rulers." Twenty years have passed, and it is time to test the validity of this judgment, which has colored all subsequent interpretations of Yugoslavia's prewar foreign policy.

Weighing various factors, including the dramatic events of March 27th, this study will examine the loyalties that sustained Yugoslavia's leaders in the years leading up to the war, and the choices that they faced in setting their country's political course. It will analyze policies fabricated in desperation by individuals torn between the ideal and the reality, the desirable and the practical. Yugoslavia's leaders superimposed Western political institutions on a people who lacked the common political experiences that made those institutions viable, thereby insuring the inevitability of conflict between the uncompromising adherents of theoretical institutions and the practical politicians. Of surpassing significance was the seeming inadaptability of the Serbian *raison d'état* as it was construed by certain Serb leaders to the Yugoslav idea. At every turn the harsh realities of geography, economics, military power, and civil conflict severely circumscribed political choices on all questions of both foreign and domestic policy.

The main object of the work is to examine the attempt of a small state to accommodate itself to the superior force of two neighboring powers at a time when its allies were at first unwilling and later unable to provide any help more substantial than advice. Related to this are the efforts to maintain internal peace that were made by this small country with a multinational population subject to manipulation and pressures from all sides.

In brief, we are here concerned with conflicts between and within men. The forces and influences that acted on successive Yugoslav governments; the men and their policies, the problems they faced, the solutions they sought, and the material and psychological conditions limiting their search are here examined.

The book had its origin during my tour of duty in Yugoslavia in 1946 and 1947. The extent of the devastation there was a moving experience even to one almost accustomed to the ravages that war had brought to Italy. No less appalling were the misery, malnutrition, and privation of a people who had obstinately lived through years of occupation by an alien invader. Now they were in the process of accommodating themselves to an alien social and economic system, this time imposed not by outsiders but by their own people.

Paralleling this experience was another. In my search for materials relating to the origin of the war in Yugoslavia, I at first found little that did not fall into the category of the polemical. Since the present Yugoslav government has published no systematic series of documents of the period under discussion, I set for myself the task of collecting as many primary source materials as possible from as many participants in Yugoslav political affairs as possible. The graciousness of these individuals in giving me their documents, in permitting me to use their personal papers, and in answering my many questions has made it possible to give human substance to the diplomatic documents published within the last five or six years. If contradictions exist, it is only because diplomatic documents mirror the shadow of decisions —decisions made by human beings, affecting the lives of many more human beings, subject to scrutiny and comment by still other human beings. The imperfections of the book itself are mine alone.

I am particularly indebted to H. E. Dragiša Cvetković, Milan Gavrilović, Oton Gavrilović, Radoje Knežević, Miha Krek, Vladko Maček, Časlav Nikitović, Staša Furlan Seaton, Dr. Ivan Soubbotitch,

Vl. Stakić, Ilja Šumenković, Colonel Vl. Vauhnik, and George Bakách-Bessenyey. Without help from them, and from others for whom the Yugoslav crisis had immediate personal significance, this account could not have been written.

With deep gratitude I acknowledge the warm friendship and unstinting help of Dragoš Kostić, Branko Pešelj, and the Reverend Dr. Alois Kuhar. In countless conversations with each of them I gained greater insight into the turbulent years that culminated in the events of March, 1941.

I owe a great deal also to Dr. Philip E. Mosely of the Council on Foreign Relations, for his unfailing encouragement and detailed comments on the manuscript.

Of the many others whose assistance I gratefully acknowledge I particularly mention the staff of the International Law Library of Columbia University; Dr. Paul R. Sweet and Dr. E. Taylor Parks of the historical division of the United States Department of State; E. J. Passant, librarian of the British Foreign Office; the Ford Foundation, for the fellowship which made possible the writing; the Social Science Research Council and American Council of Learned Societies for the grant in support of publication; S. Harrison Thomson, for permission to incorporate in this book certain material originally used in an article in the *Journal of Central European Affairs*; the University of California Press for permission to use economic data compiled by Jozo Tomasevich and originally published in Robert J. Kerner's *Yugoslavia;* Professors René Albrecht-Carrié, Henry L. Roberts, and Stavro Skendi for their critical reading of an early draft; Betty Scantland and Constance Nagle for their competence and infinite patience in typing the manuscript; and my wife, whose suggestions on content, logic, and style I often accepted.

J. B. HOPTNER

New York City
January 1961

ABBREVIATIONS

DBFP   Documents on British Foreign Policy, 1919–1939. Second and Third Series. London: H.M. Stationery Office.

DDI   I Documenti Diplomatici Italiani. Ottova e Nona Serie. Rome: La Libreria Dello Stato.

DGFP   Documents on German Foreign Policy, 1918–1945. Series C and D. Washington: Government Printing Office.

DIA   Documents on International Affairs. Prewar Series. London: Oxford University Press.

FRUS   Foreign Relations of the United States, 1934–1941. Washington: Government Printing Office.

IMT   International Military Tribunal. Documents presented at the International Military Tribunal at Nuremberg and now deposited in the National Archives of the United States, Washington, D. C.

JBH   Documents in the possession of the author.

NSR   Nazi-Soviet Relations, 1939–1941. Washington: Government Printing Office, 1948.

Recueil   Recueil des Traités Internationaux. Ministère des Affaires Étrangères du Royaume de Yougoslavie, Belgrade, Yugoslavia.

SIA   Survey of International Affairs. Prewar Series. London: Oxford University Press.

USMT   United States Military Tribunal. Office of the Chief of Counsel for War Crimes. Documents presented at the various war crimes trials and now deposited in the National Archives of the United States, Washington, D. C.

I

THE ROOTS OF CRISIS

The Kingdom of Serbs, Croats, and Slovenes came into existence at the end of the First World War as a product of idealistic statecraft and as a residual legatee of the Habsburg monarchy. Along with 371 square miles of Austrian and Hungarian territory, the new kingdom inherited six million subjects and some of the monarchy's domestic conflicts. With the former citizens of the Dual Monarchy, the new state numbered twelve million people with discrete historical and political experiences and with varied social and cultural backgrounds. It had to absorb and integrate seven diverse territories, each with its own legislative and administrative system. Marked differences of religious affiliation segmented it: the Serbs and Macedonians were largely Eastern Orthodox, the Croats and Slovenes largely Roman Catholic; there were Moslems among the Serbs, Moslems among the Croats. To make matters still more complex, large non-Slav minorities lived within its borders: Germans, Hungarians, and Rumanians in the Vojvodina and Croatia, Albanians in South Serbia, Italians on the Adriatic littoral.

This kingdom, devised in time of war, was a weak amalgam of peoples with contradictory and conflicting ideas of government, particularly in regard to the nature and the form of the new state. Its major internal problem in the years ahead was to make Yugoslavs out of Serbs and Croats, Montenegrins, Slovenes, and Dalmatians, Bosnians, Hercegovinians, and Macedonians—out of men and women who had lived under seven different political roofs as citizens of the independent states of Serbia and Montenegro, of the Austrian territories which are now Slovenia and Dalmatia, of the Vojvodina and Croatia-Slavonia ruled by Hungary, of Bosnia-Hercegovina administered by the Dual Monarchy, and of Macedonia, ruled until 1912 by Turkey and for the next six years by Serbia.

Although the peoples of the new kingdom shared a spirit of freedom and independence from foreign rule and alien oppressor, not all had a feeling of national unity born of a common language and the kinship of a common culture. Only the educated classes believed, and they but feebly, in self-determination as a basis for national unity. While all might agree with the romantic tenet that "a brother is a brother regardless of religion," among the uneducated there was hardly more than a passive recognition of similarities. Above all, the Yugoslav peoples shared no common political philosophy and experience out of which they could construct a new political community.

Yet, despite all the divisive forces, not a few clung to "the Yugoslav idea"—union of the Serbs, Croats, and Slovenes in one kingdom—a dream nurtured for centuries by poets and political visionaries.

In the period between 1914 and 1919 the conflict over the form of the new state had raged between two poles of political ideology. At one end of the spectrum were the centralist ideas of the powerful Radical Party of Serbia, headed by Nikola Pašić; the Radicals, once revolutionary but now accustomed to the comforts of power, held that Serbia should dominate Yugoslavia. At the other pole were the federalist ideas of the political groups that had developed in Croatia after the revolutions of 1848. In the long period of their political subordination to Hungary these groups had tried to achieve their political goals by using such techniques as passive resistance and noncooperation.

The politicians on both sides of the centralist-federalist argument carried in their heads a clear picture of what a united South Slav state should be. It was this conflict of vision that is often referred to as the Serb-Croat question. It was the Serb-Croat divergence, although primarily an internal problem, that proved crucial in the formulation and operation of the new kingdom's foreign policy.

Croat spokesmen saw the grand design of the South Slav state as including within its boundaries an autonomous Croat state. They based their image on "the rights of the historic state." Although Croatia had joined in a dynastic union with Hungary in 1102, the act was voluntary and therefore, Croat nationalists argued, Croatia had never lost its identity as a state. They held that any territory at any time owned or occupied by Croats should eventually become an autonomous Croatia within a larger constitutional monarchy. Some advanced the case for a personal union, others for a Croat republic within the monarchy.

The Dalmatian Croats and the Slovenes had no such pretensions. Long before other national groups espoused the idea of a Yugoslav state, they had led the move for unity. Only a united South Slav state could protect them from the Italians and the Dual Monarchy. Unlike the Croats, the Slovenes, separated from Belgrade by barriers of geography and language, nurtured no fear of Serb control.

The Serbs saw a united kingdom through lenses ground by their centuries-old struggle first against the Turks and later against the Austrians. They saw themselves as liberators of the Croats, even though the Croats had fought on the side of the Austrians. They felt that the Croats were in a sense their brothers, bound with the strong tie of a common language. But federalism was an alien tradition to the Serbs. Had they not survived the Turkish slaughter only because they had remained politically and militarily homogeneous? The very coat of arms of the Serbian state carried the letters that symbolized that philosophy: *Samo Sloga Srbina Spasava* (Only Solidarity Saves the Serb). Only a centralized state with the monarchy as the unifying influence could erase historic differences. Federalism was anathema, and akin to separatism.

Especially the *Prečani* Serbs (those Serbs living in the former Austro-Hungarian provinces) opposed the federalist concept. In a federal state they would become only a Serb island in a Croatian sea. In a centralized state with Belgrade the center of power they, as Serbs, would have an opportunity to share in the leadership.

This conflict over political creed and the nature of a new state came to a head during the years of the First World War. It seemed to be resolved in July, 1917, when exiled representatives of the various South Slavic groups living in Austro-Hungary met in Corfu with representatives of the Serbian government under Pašić. Here they took the first formal steps toward the creation of the Kingdom of Serbs, Croats, and Slovenes. Here they set down for the world to read their declaration that

our people constitutes but one nation, and that is one in blood, one by the spoken and written language, by the continuity and unity of the territory in which it lives, and finally in virtue of the common and vital interests

The heavy line shows the expanded German boundary of 1939.

EUROPE IN 1919

of its national existence and the general development of its moral and material life.[1]

They selected a name for the new state, designed a coat of arms, designated Serbian and Croatian as the official languages, and laid plans for the calling of a constituent assembly after the war.

But in the Corfu declaration they did not resolve the issue of federalism versus centralism. This decision they left to the constituent assembly. Meanwhile, the unity of the three nations remained more apparent than real. The Croat and Slovene leaders banded together in a United National Council with headquarters in Zagreb, the capital of Croatia. Favoring union with Serbia only after Belgrade guaranteed them measures of self-government, some Croats wanted time for further negotiations with the Serbs.

But it was too late. By the late summer of 1918 Serbian troops were crossing the Sava and Danube rivers into land abandoned only a short time before by Habsburg divisions. In the west, Italian troops were occupying northern Dalmatia, Istria, and Trieste. With Italians again on Croatian and Slovene soil, the National Council had to come to terms with the Serbs.

The Croats were propelled into continuing negotiations with the Serbs by the knowledge that Italy's claims to South Slav lands had been written into the Secret Treaty of London in 1915 by Britain, France, and Russia so that Italy would enter the war; the Soviet government had published the treaty in December, 1917. To inspire the Croat troops to fight hard against the Italians, the Austrian government was now circulating maps showing the territory Italy would obtain under the terms of the treaty. Despite this attempt to hold them true to Vienna, the Croats of the Adriatic remained the first of the "Yugoslavs," along with the Slovenes. Both rejected rule by Rome or Vienna. Both sought union with the Serbs. From the start the Slovenes believed that their distant location and separate language would save them from rigid control by the central government. Intelligent politicians, they further reasoned that they could bargain with either the Croats or the Serbs for key governmental positions and for legislation favorable to Slovenia, in return for their

[1] Pact of Corfu, reprinted in Robert J. Kerner, *The Yugo-Slav Movement* (Cambridge: Harvard University Press, 1918), p. 100.

political support. Accordingly, by October, 1918, the Croat and Slovene leaders, acting through the United National Council, proclaimed their faith in the Yugoslav idea and announced their desire to work for a united Yugoslavia.

Italian aggression had inadvertently hastened the creation of a Yugoslav state. At the same time, Serbian military strength, refreshed by victory after disastrous defeat, had psychologically assured the consolidation of political power in the hands of the Serbs, regardless of the debate over centralism and federalism.

The constituent assembly met in December, 1920. On January 1, 1921, the centralist constitution presented by Pašić received approval, largely because 161 delegates—including the Croats led by Stjepan Radić—walked out without voting. If they had remained they probably could have swayed the assembly to their view and obtained a large measure of administrative autonomy. Pašić, a politician, would have recognized the need for compromise. Radić, on the other hand, seems to have wanted all or nothing.

Once the kingdom became a reality, with the Serbs in control and the Croats leading the opposition, the government adopted a policy of centralization, eliminating many institutions of local self-government that might have proved useful in maintaining the unity of the state. Radić's policy of noncooperation quickly led to trouble. The form of the state remained an unsolved problem and the parliamentary system proved increasingly unworkable because of the absence of the Croats, overrepresentation of the Serbs, corruption, and the lack of party discipline.

The rush of military events in 1917 imposed on the Serbs, Croats, and Slovenes a false sense of unity, impelling the formation of the kingdom. In the years that followed, they grew more and more conscious of the imperative need for the long-postponed settlement of the centralism-federalism issue. By the middle of the 1930s the circumstances would be still more trying, and even tragic.

Meanwhile, tragedy was not unknown to the Yugoslav government. Radić, moved by the king's pleas for cooperation, agreed to take his seat in the parliament. There, in 1928, he and four other Croat deputies were shot down by a Radical Party deputy from Montenegro whom Radić had grievously offended.

In the constitutional crisis that followed, King Alexander resorted to dictatorial measures to achieve unity. He retained all power for himself. He could declare war or peace, promulgate laws, appoint all civil officials including the premier, the cabinet, and army officers. He held his own person inviolable and declared that he could not be held responsible or impeached for any act. He restricted freedom of press, person, association, and assembly. He abolished Yugoslavia's historic provinces and reconstructed them into nine administrative units. He dramatized his unitary outlook by transforming the cumbersome title of Kingdom of Serbs, Croats, and Slovenes into the simpler Kingdom of Yugoslavia. He dissolved all political parties of a regional character—Serbian, Moslem, or Croatian. He barred not only the formation of new parties but also the activities of those already in existence. He tried, sometimes successfully, to detach prominent politicians from their followers and to recruit them for his personal regime. Despite all of his efforts, the opposition grew. The dictatorship formally came to an end in 1931 when the king issued a new constitution, but the political effects of the dictatorship were catastrophic. Instead of achieving national unity, King Alexander had succeeded only in atomizing Serbian political life, in depriving Serbian political parties of their vigor while increasing the force and effect of those in the other provinces. After 1931 no Serbian party was strong enough to represent a large segment of the electorate. All parties splintered into small groups of politicians, with leaders but without the substance of a mass following. These leaders, with few exceptions, no longer had the power to do much more than compete among themselves for the important state posts and to bicker over their central problem: Should the Croats be suppressed or conciliated?

The reverse was true in Croatia, Slovenia, and Bosnia. Croatia's Peasant Party, united in opposition to Belgrade, grew in strength; its new leader, Vladko Maček, became the uncrowned king of Croatia. Slovenia's Populist Party, under the leadership of Father Anton Korošec, attracted thousands of new followers, as did Bosnia's Yugoslav Moslem Organization under Mehmed Spaho. The first organized Croat-Serb opposition came into existence in late 1932 when the Croat Peasant Party and the Independent Democrats jointly attacked the central government, demanding a new constitution. The following year Maček had to go to prison for his political activities, adjudged treasonous by the fearful government. Not long after his trial when three Serbian opposition leaders tried to visit him to express their political sympathy they were, in effect, taking the first step in a process that led, in October, 1937, to the organization of the United Opposition.

Although King Alexander's effort to strengthen the royal power at the expense of the people and their political parties did not solve the grave matter of internal discord, the dictatorship did permit a consistent foreign policy. In the long run, however, Yugoslavia required peace at home if it was to assure peace with its neighbors.

Along with domestic discord, Yugoslavia inherited from the Dual Monarchy a full measure of its external troubles. The Balkans had always caused trouble for the Habsburgs. In the years just before the First World War, Austria had been preoccupied with its neighbors and with the congeries of problems they created: with the very existence of Albania as a buffer state; with the nationalistic drives of Serbia, Rumania, and Bulgaria; with the ambitions of Italy. With the signing of the peace treaties, the direction of these pressures shifted from Vienna to Belgrade. Now the new Kingdom of Serbs, Croats, and Slovenes faced an irredentist Hungary and Bulgaria and an Albania which wavered between Rome and Belgrade. It faced an angry Italy that felt cheated of territory promised by the Triple Entente in the Treaty of London of April, 1915, a sullen Italy that still sought Dalmatia's harbors for the Italian navy in time of war. Now discord between Yugoslavia and Italy supplanted the prewar rivalry that had once existed, in both the Adriatic and the Balkans, between Austria and Italy.

From the outset the new state faced these problems; they were the constants of Yugoslav foreign relations.

During the early years of the kingdom the first objective of Yugoslav foreign policy was to secure the integrity of its frontiers. Its long-range objectives were to make a place for the new state in the new European order and to create a viable Balkan alliance system that would insure peace in the area and protect the Balkan states from the manipulation and intervention of the great powers.

For help in time of trouble, to whom could Yugoslavia turn? Not to Russia, sometime protector of the Serbian state; now revolutionary and revisionist, Russia was no longer acceptable to monarchist Yugoslavia. Not to defeated Germany. Not to Great Britain, whose imperial interests lay elsewhere and whose concept of European security, depending less and less on the principle of balance of power, augured weak support in the maintenance of the peace treaties. Only one power in all Europe stood firm in opposing any change in the frontiers of the southeast European states. That power was France.

In this precarious situation the young kingdom had to find allies. To counter Hungarian irredentism and prevent a Habsburg restoration, Yugoslavia joined with Rumania and Czechoslovakia in 1921 to form the Little Entente. To stave off the realization of Bulgaria's territorial aspirations, it joined with Greece, Rumania, and Turkey in 1934 to form the Balkan Entente. In the years between, Yugoslavia tried to find a place for itself in the larger European defense system by signing a treaty of friendly understanding with France.

But against Italy, the strongest and most menacing neighbor, Yugoslavia could find no sure defense. Against Italy, there were only the interlocking but restrictive ententes, the limited alliance with France, and the cumbersome machinery of the League of Nations. In their frailty they could provide little protection against the fascist powers.

It was natural that Yugoslavia, a product of war and a nation favored by the peace treaties, should have been a founding member of the League. Although collective action against aggression was a means of forwarding the League's aim of maintaining the peace, small states such as Yugoslavia, Rumania, and Czechoslovakia considered collective action neither a sufficient guarantee of peace nor a substitute for a foreign policy. Each searched for special means of solving problems peculiar to its own national existence.

While Yugoslavia sought counterweights to Italy and Hungary, Czechoslovakia looked for ways of protecting itself from Germany and Hungary, and Rumania sought defenses against the Soviet Union and Hungary. The three succession states thus had one danger in common—Hungary. All felt the threat arising from a possible Habsburg restoration, for every king of Hungary swore at his coronation to

uphold intact the rights, constitution, legal independence and territorial integrity of Hungary, the Croatian, Slavonian and Dalmatian countries, as well as to preserve the integrity and the constitution of the Croatian,

Slavonian and Dalmatian countries forming one and the same political unit with Hungary.[2]

The Yugoslavs saw in the return of the Habsburgs a double danger: a cause of war with Hungary and a source of attraction for those Slovenes and Croats who were still *kaisertreu* and thus capable of becoming foci of political disaffection.

The Little Entente was an answer to the Hungarian threat. The entente, properly speaking, first consisted of a series of treaties among Yugoslavia, Czechoslovakia, and Rumania. The first of the treaties signed between Czechoslovakia and Yugoslavia on August 14, 1920, had as its object

to maintain the Peace obtained by so many sacrifices and provided for by the Covenant of the League of Nations, as well as the situation created by the Treaty concluded at Trianon on June 4, 1920, between the Allied and Associated Powers on the one hand, and Hungary on the other.

The outstanding provision of the agreement appeared in Article I:

In case of an unprovoked attack on the part of Hungary against one of the High Contracting Parties, the other Party agrees to assist in the defense of the Party attacked.

This convention did not put a damper on the Habsburg hopes. At the end of March, 1921, Charles of Habsburg made the first of two futile attempts to regain the Hungarian throne. Both Yugoslavia and Czechoslovakia immediately concluded similar treaties with Rumania, signed in April and July, 1921. Yugoslavia also signed a military convention with Rumania in June and another with Czechoslovakia in August. After Charles's second attempt, in October, 1921, to win back his crown, Yugoslavia and Czechoslovakia transformed what was primarily a military agreement into a general political alliance. This treaty, signed on August 31, 1922, took note of the interrelated nature of the treaties and agreements of the succession states and obligated the two signatories to support each other in their international relations. Finally, more than a decade later, Czechoslovakia, Rumania, and Yugoslavia formally created the Little Entente with a pact of organization, signed at Geneva on February 16, 1933.[3]

[2] Text in Crane, *Little Entente*, p. 211.
[3] For the texts of the treaties, see League of Nations, *Treaty Series*, Vols. VI, XII, LIV, and CXXXIX.

France, the patron of the Little Entente powers, did not distribute its support uniformly. Triumphant France's primary interest was to prevent the return of a powerful German state. Undoubtedly it would have much preferred to see some kind of Danubian confederation, including Austria and Hungary, to balance German power. Although the makers of the Little Entente did not consider forming a confederation, France indicated its security interests by negotiating the Czechoslovak-French Treaty of 1924, in which both countries agreed to oppose the union of Austria with Germany and the restoration of the Habsburgs and the Hohenzollerns.

Relations between Yugoslavia and France were not so easily arranged. Not until 1927 did the two countries conclude a treaty of friendship that for a decade would remain the keystone of Yugoslav foreign policy.

It was not a simple matter for Yugoslavia to obtain a treaty of alliance with France because they differed in their attitude toward Italy. The Yugoslavs looked upon the Italians as their major enemy, a possible adversary in the Balkans. The French looked upon the Italians as a possible ally against *their* major enemy, Germany. The French sought Italo-Yugoslav cooperation against the Germans. The Yugoslavs sought French material and political assistance against Italy—a power that supported Bulgarian and Hungarian revisionism at the expense of the young Yugoslav state, that by 1927 already had its foot in Albania and the Balkans, and that clearly wanted to control the Adriatic.

Seeing itself as the conciliator between Yugoslavia and Italy, France sought a tripartite agreement with the two states. When this effort failed, the French suggested that the Yugoslavs draft something like the Czech-French agreement, but which would not contain a military convention.[4] Yugoslav Foreign Minister Momčilo Ninčić was reluctant to work on the text of an agreement of this kind. He was even more reluctant when he learned that Rumania and France were negotiating a treaty. Ninčić did not believe the time propitious to conclude a treaty with the French under these circumstances,[5] perhaps because he believed France would try to use its relation with Rumania in bargaining with Yugoslavia.

[4] Spalajković to Yugoslav foreign office, January 29, 1924. (JBH)
[5] Ninčić to Spalajković, February 1 and April 17, 1924. (JBH)

By 1926, however, the Yugoslavs and the French worked out the draft of an agreement, but as late as March, 1927, the French insisted on deferring the formalities. They gave as their excuse that it would be better to wait until Yugoslavia settled its differences with Italy; otherwise, said France, "it would look like a demonstration" against Italy.[6]

Vojislav Marinković, the Yugoslav foreign minister, became annoyed at the French evasion and instructed Spalajković to talk with Briand, then French foreign minister. The French must understand, Marinković wrote, that the real struggle was not between Yugoslavia and Italy but between Italy and France.[7] Yugoslavia was only France's advanced position in Europe. Italy wished to destroy the French system in Europe, Marinković flatly asserted, and thought it could best be damaged or destroyed by attacking Yugoslavia. Should Yugoslavia capitulate to Italy, Marinković predicted, the *status quo* in Europe would come to an end. A Yugoslav-Italian bloc joined by Hungary, Rumania, and Bulgaria would destroy the Little Entente.

France therefore must help Yugoslavia rid itself of Italian pressure. The only way to do this, in Marinković's view, would be for France and Yugoslavia to sign a security pact, deposited and made public in Geneva. Such an alliance, Marinković predicted, would put an end to the "Italian game"—a game based on the hypothesis that Yugoslavia would remain isolated from outside assistance if attacked by Italy. Italy's fallacious reasoning could lead both Yugoslavia and France into war. Once a treaty of alliance was made public, Marinković deduced, Yugoslavia could make concessions to Italy in the interests of peace, because they would not be made under duress but freely and with good will. Marinković told Spalajković that he was determined to settle the question of the treaty quickly, once and

---

[6] Spalajković to Yugoslav ministry of foreign affairs, March 28, 1927. (JBH)

[7] Mussolini told Prince Paul in 1929 that the conflict was between Rome and Paris, not between Rome and Belgrade. He said relations between Italy and France were bad because the two countries represented divergent points of view. One was parliamentary, Masonic, and democratic; the other was not. In Mussolini's view, the problem lay in the Mediterranean, in Tunisia and Syria. France, he said, always stood in the way of Italy's penetration into Abyssinia. He also believed Paris was the center of antifascism. Minute of conversation between Prince Paul and Mussolini, February 15, 1929. (JBH)

for all.[8]. The French agreed with the Yugoslavs—in principle. But the moment for signing had not yet come.

The French remained reluctant. Paternally they told Yugoslavia they believed that while the publication of a treaty with France would be a victory for internal Yugoslav politics, it would disturb Yugoslav relations abroad. This in turn would spoil the excellent disposition in high European political quarters toward Yugoslavia. This specious interpretation of Yugoslav motives drew such heavy fire from Marinković that Berthelot, secretary-general of the French foreign office, meekly agreed that France would sign the treaty in October.[9]

The Franco-Yugoslav pact of amity and understanding was finally signed on November 11, 1927, a memorable anniversary for both countries. They did not, however, conclude a military convention, as France had done in its treaties with Poland, Czechoslovakia, and Rumania.[10]

The course of negotiations indicates clearly how each country interpreted its national interest. Although he finally had his treaty with France, King Alexander was well aware that security for his country meant coming to an understanding with Italy. From November, 1930, until his murder in October, 1934, he attempted to come to that understanding.

Macedonia was the focus of conflict between Yugoslavia and Bulgaria. Although never cordial, their relations did not reach the breaking point. Both felt the tensions arising from the terrorist activities of the anti-Yugoslav Internal Macedonian Revolutionary Organization (IMRO) along their common border. Italy, vigorously supporting the Bulgarian case for the return of territory ceded to Yugoslavia by the Treaty of Neuilly, kept the pot boiling by propagandizing and by subsidizing IMRO, which had its headquarters in Sofia. From the Yugoslav point of view it was thus imperative to come to an understanding with Bulgaria. The two countries worked for *rapprochement* through quasi-governmental Balkan Conferences,

---

[8] Marinković to Spalajković, July 18 and 27, 1927. (JBH)
[9] Spalajković to Yugoslav ministry of foreign affairs, August 2, 1927. (JBH)
[10] For the text of the treaty, see League of Nations, *Treaty Series*, LXVIII, 373.

through an agreement concerning IMRO, and through state visits by the monarchs.

Through the Balkan Conferences they cooperated on such non-political projects as a chamber of commerce and industry, a medical union, and an agricultural union. A political pact was a logical result of these activities and of frequent political deliberations, but in this Bulgaria refused to participate. So long as Yugoslavia and Greece held Bulgarian irredenta, the Bulgars resisted any discussion of the Balkan pact so eagerly sought by the Yugoslavs.

Although the Balkan Conferences failed to reconcile the Bulgars to the Balkan community in general and to Yugoslavia in particular, extra-Balkan political factors were at work which would make possible a *modus vivendi* between Yugoslavia and Bulgaria. One was the pact signed in June, 1933, by Great Britain, France, Italy, and Germany. In it they agreed to consult with each other on all matters of common interest, to cooperate within the framework of the League of Nations in maintaining the peace, and together to consider ways of making the covenant of the League effective. This in effect created a directorate of Europe and as such aroused distrust in both Yugoslavia and Bulgaria.

From the beginning King Alexander saw in this pact a move by Italy and Germany to revise the peace treaties and to change the Yugoslav frontiers.[11] To prevent isolation if invaded, Yugoslavia countered on July 4, 1933, by signing a convention with the other Little Entente states and with Turkey and the Soviet Union. In it they defined various aggressive acts and asserted a state's right to defend its territories. Paragraph 5 of Article II seemed to apply specifically to Bulgaria; it defined as an aggressor a state which gave

support to armed bands formed on the territory of another state and invading the territory of another state, or refusal, in spite of the demand of the invaded state, to take all possible measures on its own territory to deprive the said bands of any aid or protection.[12]

[11] Minute of conversation between King Alexander and Guido Malagola Cappi, June 19, 1933. (JBH) Cappi was the Italian intermediary through whom the king was able to reach Mussolini privately.

[12] For the text of the treaty, see *Recueil* (1934), pp. 63-66, or League of Nations, *Treaty Series*, CXLVIII, 211.

The Yugoslav warning was clear: the Bulgarian government must suppress the IMRO raids. Fortunately, the tumultuous course of Bulgaria's domestic politics hastened the settlement of the differences with Yugoslavia. In the spring of 1934 rumors of an IMRO revolt against the Bulgarian government swept Sofia. This news stimulated a successful *coup* by two closely related groups—the Military League (composed of reserve officers) and its political arm, a group of intellectuals known as the *Zveno* (Link). The new government, desirous of friendship with Yugoslavia, immediately began interning or exiling the members of IMRO who were in Bulgaria. Within a year the Bulgars were willing to sign a protocol with Yugoslavia providing for joint measures to liquidate IMRO operations wherever found, particularly along their common border and in Macedonia.

While the foreign ministers grew acrimonious in their discussions of a larger Balkan pact—greatly desired by Yugoslavia, strongly opposed by Bulgaria—relations between the monarchs took a new turn. Alexander and Boris had never been friendly. Alexander resented both the IMRO's numerous raids into Yugoslav territory and the warm reception Sofia gave Yugoslavia's enemies. Consequently, when word came that Boris would pass through Belgrade on his way home from France and England, Alexander met his train with considerable reluctance and undoubtedly only after a strong argument from Yugoslav Foreign Minister Bogoljub Jevtić. But the brief encounter ended with great cordiality on both sides and a promise by Alexander to visit Boris in September.

Breaking ground for a Balkan alliance, Alexander visited Boris at Varna, Kemal Ataturk in Istanbul, and King Carol on a yacht in the Danube. His intentions were clear: he wanted to set up machinery for defending the Balkans. And he was willing to court Bulgaria's cooperation by offering to relinquish Tsaribrod and Bosiligrad, towns on the Bulgarian-Yugoslav frontier that Bulgaria had long coveted.[13] Bulgarian Premier Mushanov refused to consider this offer as a basis for negotiation when there was a larger stake at hand—the revision or elimination of the Treaty of Neuilly. The Bulgars stood fast to their demands for revision and the Pact of the Balkan Entente was signed

---

[13] Kosta Todorov, *Balkan Firebrand* (Chicago: Ziff-Davis, 1943), p. 253.

in Athens on February 9, 1934, by Greece, Rumania, Turkey, and Yugoslavia only.[14]

The differences between the expressed goals of the Balkan Conferences and those of the new Balkan Pact were vital. The aim of the conferences, which included Bulgaria, was to obtain mutual cooperation in solving, over a long period, a limited number of outstanding issues. The pact, which did not include Bulgaria, aimed at guaranteeing the security of Balkan frontiers against aggression by any Balkan state, alone or in league with a non-Balkan power. What the pact did not do was protect Balkan frontiers against aggression by a non-Balkan power acting alone. The Greeks insisted on this limitation, which proved only an indirect way of saying that they would not necessarily have to come to the aid of Yugoslavia if Italy alone attacked. It was purely antirevisionist—although its signatories left the door open for Bulgaria and Albania. Owing to the very nature of the pact itself, the Bulgars would not join; the Albanians, because of the Greek fear of offending Italian sensibilities and Italian power were not, despite Yugoslav efforts, invited to join.[15]

There were reasons for the absence of a warm relationship between Yugoslavia and Greece. The first was a difference of opinion over the use of the Greek port of Salonika. Serbia first used the port, then Turkish, in 1905. After the Balkan wars the creation of Albania

[14] For the text of the pact of the Balkan Entente, see *Recueil* (1934), pp. 67-68, and for the text of the protocol to the pact, see League of Nations, *Treaty Series*, CLIII, 156. King Alexander was aware, three years before the Balkan Entente, that Greece would oppose any pact which would unify the Balkan states against Italy. In view of this, he realized that only after Yugoslavia and Italy had come to a definite agreement would a lasting Balkan pact be possible. In the absence of such an agreement, he wrote his minister to France, "Yugoslavia's policy of defending the Balkans must have the full support of France." King Alexander to Spalajković, April 6, 1931. (JBH)

[15] The signatories, in effect, recognized Italian hegemony over Albania. On February 17, 1934, eight days after the signing of the Balkan Pact, A. Papanastasiou, president of the Balkan Conference, wrote to Mehmed Konica, head of the Albanian delegation, informing him of the contents of the pact. Konica replied a month later. The Albanian complained that the pact was not a nonaggression pact or a means of protection from an extra-Balkan power. He criticized Maximos, the Greek foreign minister, for going from door to door of the great powers requesting their permission to sign the pact. Maximos even asked Mussolini for his opinion whether Albania should or should not be accepted as a signatory. Richard Busch-Zantner, *Albanien. Neues Land im Imperium* (Leipzig: Wilhelm Goldmann Verlag, 1939), pp. 207-8. See also *Les Balkans* (Athens), V (March-April, 1934), 298-99.

by the great powers prevented Serbia from obtaining an alternative outlet to the sea and increased its dependence on the Greek port. From then on free and secure transit through Salonika became a principle of Serbian and then of Yugoslav foreign policy. The Greeks, however, were reluctant to grant the privilege. It was not until 1929 that they relented, and thereby settled one difference between the two countries. The question of Salonika's importance to Yugoslavia was destined to arise once again ten years later in the more tragic context of Mussolini's invasion of Greece.

The second obstacle between the two was the friendship of Greece for Yugoslavia's neighbor, Italy. The Yugoslavs held that this friendship, plus Bulgaria's attitude, made it impossible for the Balkan Pact of 1934 to become an effective instrument of defense.

As early as 1931 Alexander had viewed the Greek treaties of friendship with Italy, Albania, and Turkey as "attempts to isolate Yugoslavia by unilateral acts in the Balkans." In his opinion, these attempts were

in reality a means of weakening Yugoslavia's resistance to the Italian policy of expansion in the Balkans, especially since Greece is disinterested in the fate of Albania. It may be that Greece hopes to receive some compensation similar to that they received in the Venizelos-Tittoni agreement of 1919.[16]

The Belgrade press reflected Alexander's annoyance at the Greeks. When Greek Premier Venizelos visited the Yugoslav capital in July, 1934, he said he was hurt by newspaper reports that he had changed his policy toward Yugoslavia and had abandoned the principle of Balkan solidarity. He said he wished to remain on good terms with Yugoslavia but wanted also to make certain that Greece avoided power combinations and eventual war. In short, Venizelos made it clear that Greece intended to maintain full neutrality. He said he believed that in its relations with Italy his country would refuse any obligations against Yugoslavia, and in its relations with Yugoslavia would refuse any obligations against Italy. He said he had already

[16] Alexander to Spalajković, April 6, 1931. (JBH) In the Venizelos-Tittoni agreement of July 20, 1919, Italy agreed to support Greek claims to western and eastern Thrace and southern Albania (northern Epirus). In return Greece was to support Italian claims to a mandate over Albania and sovereignty over Valona and those ports of its hinterland that Italy would judge necessary for the defense of the region. For the text of the agreement see A.-F. Frangulis, *La Grèce et la Crise Mondiale* (Paris: Librairie Félix Alcan, 1926), II, 93-98.

rejected certain Italian proposals directed against Yugoslavia. He had, in fact, assured Mussolini that Greece would not participate in any pact against either Italy or Yugoslavia.

Venizelos told the Yugoslavs he did not oppose the Balkan Pact itself but only a liberal interpretation of Article III of the protocol, which called for solidarity of action if a signatory were attacked by a non-Balkan power acting with a Balkan state. To Venizelos this meant Italy acting with Bulgaria. He told the Yugoslavs he feared Italian power so greatly that even if an Italian army marched into Albania, Greece would remain neutral.[17]

Alexander's efforts to build a viable Balkan defense system against Italy did not preclude his trying to come to an agreement with the Duce. During the years from 1929 to 1934 he worked energetically to convince Mussolini of his friendly intentions and of his desire to see a treaty between the two countries that would permanently maintain the peace in the Adriatic. He was willing to give Mussolini all possible guarantees and concessions to obtain that end, and even considered offering Italy the facilities of the Bay of Kotor, famed deep-water naval base on the Yugoslav Adriatic opposite Italy. By this gesture, a symbol of good will and an indication of his desire for Italy's friendship,[18] Alexander hoped to convince the Duce that he was sincere in seeking a treaty requiring both countries to defend their common interests in the Adriatic against a third party.

In 1932 Alexander was willing to take upon himself the entire responsibility for negotiating the agreement with Mussolini. Not even his foreign minister, Marinković, knew anything of his ideas for strengthening Yugoslavia's ties with Italy, nor of his hope that Italy would supplant France as Yugoslavia's major ally. Nor did Marinković know that his king was willing to support Italian aims before the League.

As far as Albania was concerned, Alexander offered the following formula, which he himself prepared, as a basis for negotiation:

[17] Yugoslav foreign office memorandum, July 12, 1934. (JBH) Six years later, an Italian army headed for neutral Greece. Venizelos's successor asked for and got help from Yugoslavia.
[18] Minute of conversation between King Alexander and Guido Malagola Cappi, February 22, 1932. (JBH)

Yugoslavia, realizing the importance of the commercial, industrial and financial interests created by Italy in Albania and the development which these may undergo in the future, undertakes the obligation not to do anything which would be detrimental or damaging to these said interests.[19]

Mussolini blew hot and cold over Alexander's proposals. Alexander believed the Duce may have considered them a sign of Yugoslav weakness. He reasoned that Mussolini might, for example, have hoped that the political differences between the Serbs and Croats would explode into civil war, permitting Italy to take advantage of the resulting chaos.

If so, the Duce was wrong, Alexander told Cappi, adding that the real reason for their failure to reach an agreement lay in the fact that the Italians were greatly misinformed about the state of Yugoslavia's domestic politics:

The Croat question exists. It should be neither denied nor hidden but it is not a mortal illness for our country. We are capable of controlling it. We have all the means of doing so. When I say all the means, I am saying that I am disposed and determined to use them *all* for the good of the country.[20]

But Mussolini was unable to bring himself to the point of pursuing negotiations with Yugoslavia. To him, the Adriatic was a private waterway into the Balkans, and he was not ready to allow any country to share it with him. He made no further reply to Alexander and in May, 1934, refused to see Jevtić, who came to Rome with a secret message from the king. Alexander, sorely vexed, told Cappi that if the negotiations had not run aground they might perhaps have changed the course of European politics and prevented "many nefarious events." The murder of Alexander by the Ustaše[21] less than six months later ended Italo-Yugoslav negotiations until 1937, when they were resumed once more—this time on the initiative of Italy.

These, then, were Yugoslavia's problems as it moved into the tem-

[19] Minute of conversation between King Alexander and Guido Malagola Cappi, April 13, 1932. (JBH)

[20] Minutes of conversations between King Alexander and Guido Malagola Cappi, April 13, 1932, and June 9, 1933. (JBH)

[21] The Ustaše, under the leadership of Ante Pavelić, were terrorist Croat separatists operating out of Italy and Hungary. For a detailed description of their activities, see the League of Nations, *Official Journal*, December, 1934, pp. 1713-1840.

pestuous years leading to the Second World War. Its domestic concerns rapidly became almost inseparable from its involved relations with other countries; the reciprocal nature of its internal and external problems would soon become apparent as the kingdom sought to survive as a national entity. There were the Croats, who from the Serb point of view were a highly vocal and seemingly unassimilable national group whose political demands threatened the internal security of the state. There were all the other national groups and minorities, yearning for recognition, raising sectional voices, creating in Yugoslavia the political dissonance once the outstanding characteristic of the multinational Dual Monarchy. There were the dissatisfied neighbors—Italy, Hungary, and Bulgaria—who sought territory at Yugoslavia's expense. Yugoslavia had largely inherited these troubles from the Dual Monarchy, and fifteen years of effort had failed to ameliorate them. Their origins lay in the development of European diplomacy as a whole, and their solutions would of necessity concern the European community as a whole.

II

YUGOSLAVIA IN THE EUROPEAN ORDER, 1934-1937

The impact of the German resurrection of 1933 pervaded Europe. Trained observers began to note shifts in the continental power structure and to warn of a vengeful Germany on the march. Sir Walford Selby, the British minister in Vienna, wrote in September, 1934, that Yugoslavia was "shaking," Italy uncertain, and Poland lost to the democracies.[1] But few in Britain shared his alarm.

The French, unlike the British, were acutely conscious of the rising German strength and its possible consequences. Early in 1934, Louis Barthou, the French foreign minister, worked out his plan for a grand alliance against Hitler. He intended using both the carrot and the stick. On the one hand, France was prepared to make certain concessions to bring Germany back into the restrictive and nonexplosive confines of the League of Nations and the European order. But on the other hand, France would build a network of alliances that would hold Germany within its present borders.

Heretofore the French had limited themselves to agreements with the Little Entente countries and with Poland. Now, however, they needed military treaties with the great powers: the Soviet Union and Italy. A show of strength was the only way, Barthou argued, to reinforce the peace, to limit German ambitions, and to bring the wavering small states, such as Yugoslavia, back into the French fold.

To build a Mediterranean security system, the French needed both Yugoslavia and Italy on their side. But bringing Italy into a general Mediterranean agreement first required the resolution of long-standing differences between the two.

Franco-Italian negotiations directed, in part, toward reconciling

---

[1] Selby, *Diplomatic Twilight, 1930–1940*, p. 144.

Italy with Yugoslavia and with the other members of the Little Entente began on March 2, 1934. By the time they were over, the French had agreed to support Italy in its efforts to prevent Germany from annexing Austria and dominating Hungary. As a first step, France would bring pressure on Yugoslavia and the other members of the Little Entente to make certain of their collaboration in the alliance against Hitler. For his part, Mussolini agreed not to organize an economic bloc with Austria and Hungary and not to restore the Habsburgs. He raised no objection to the French project of arranging a *rapprochement* between the Little Entente and Austria and Hungary, insisting only that in the "best interests of peace and economic reconstruction" the Little Entente "proceed in harmony" with Italy.[2]

To the Yugoslavs, it seemed that the Italian government was planning nothing less than the disintegration of their state. They were certain that the Italians were instigating the frequent acts of violence perpetrated by Croatian separatists, including an attempt on the life of their king. They would have described as typically Italian the cynical response of Leonardo Vitetti, counselor of the Italian embassy in London, when Orme Sargent of the British foreign office suggested that Italy adopt a policy designed to attract rather than repel the Yugoslavs, so that they would not be tempted to gravitate toward Germany. Three years later Vitetti would be charged by Ciano with the responsibility of negotiating a pact of friendship with Yugoslavia. Now, however, he assured Sargent that Italy could not successfully court the Yugoslavs because Belgrade used Italophobia as cement with which to bind the Yugoslav state together. He was certain the Yugoslavs would oppose any attempt at a Franco-Italian *rapprochement*. To them, it would mean that they had been abandoned by the French and left, as Vitetti put it, to the tender mercies of Italy.[3]

This was a precise prediction of the Yugoslav reaction.

Yugoslav diplomats made no effort to hide their government's displeasure at the pressure being applied by the French to induce Yugoslavia to give benevolent consideration to Italy's economic plans.

To Belgrade, it looked as if Mussolini had combined his economic plans and political intentions. Both seemed aimed against the Little Entente in general and Yugoslavia in particular. They believed

[2] *DBFP*, II, 6, Doc. 343; and *DGFP*, C, II, Doc. 317.
[3] *DBFP*, II, 6, Doc. 360.

Mussolini was using France to tranquilize the Little Entente so that he could go about the business of forming an economic bloc with Austria and Hungary. They believed France was selfish, thinking only of its own security. Its intimate affair with Italy only strengthened Belgrade's already active distrust of France. The Yugoslavs were certain that "France would not hesitate to jettison Yugoslavia's interests" to gain Italy's support against Hitler.[4]

This mixture of impotent hatred for Italy and mounting distrust for France fed their feeling of abandonment and led their government to seek support from a great power with whom no differences existed.

Such a power was Germany. An understanding with Germany might prove to be a counterweight to Italian pressure and power now building up in the Danubian basin. The Yugoslavs undoubtedly realized they were playing a dangerous game in inviting the bear to drive out the wolf. But this was hardly a novel approach. This was old-fashioned Balkan diplomacy, last demonstrated barely thirty years before by Serbia in its efforts to escape from the Austro-Hungarian snare.

The French disregarded the Yugoslavs' bitter aspersions on their character and motives, openly expressed in all the foreign offices of Europe. They proceeded to carry out the promises they had made to Mussolini and to build their own political and military fences.

With that purpose in mind, Barthou went in June, 1934, to Belgrade, a major port of call on his tour of east European capitals. In a series of conversations he impressed on King Alexander the importance of better relations between Yugoslavia and Italy. To his surprise and delight the king, who he knew had begun to look to Germany[5] for assistance against Italy, readily agreed to continue their conferences in Paris in a few weeks.

---

[4] *DGFP*, C, II, Docs. 316 and 318.

[5] On October 26, 1934, Franz von Papen, then the German minister in Vienna, reported to Hitler the contents of a message delivered to him by the Yugoslav minister. In it King Alexander announced: "I am travelling to Paris because I have an alliance with the French and because we have a number of interests in common, but irrespective of all that might be said in Paris, I shall never take part in a coalition to settle Central European affairs, if it does not include Germany." In view of the discussion in France for a reconciliation between Rome and Belgrade, Papen found the king's statement "most interesting." *USMT*, Doc. NG-2416. For King Alexander's views in June, 1933, see *DGFP*, C, I, Doc. 279.

After Barthou's visit, Alexander told his foreign minister, Bogoljub Jevtić, that in the interests of peace he was eager to go as far as possible to accommodate Italy. While he did not wish to hinder the French policy of *rapprochement* with Italy, he felt it his duty to obtain from Mussolini strict guarantees of the integrity of Yugoslav territory. As a matter of fact, he sought an agreement that would go beyond that. Fearing that Italian influence in both Austria and Albania would place Yugoslavia in a Roman pincers, he wanted an accord with Mussolini that would defend Austria's independence, make Albania independent of both Yugoslavia and Italy, and obligate Italy to respect Yugoslavia's frontiers. The agreement, however, must not separate Yugoslavia from its allies—France, Rumania, and Czechoslovakia. Alexander wistfully expressed the hope that Mussolini would also make some gesture on behalf of the Slovene and Croatian minorities living on Italian territory by permitting them to have their own schools and to publish in their own language. This would siphon off the complaint of the Slovenes that Belgrade had abandoned them.

In return for an agreement of this kind, Yugoslavia would give Italy many economic concessions, particularly the timber and timber products that Italian industry greatly needed.[6]

These were Alexander's political objectives. But, like Barthou's grand design, they were never realized. Both men were assassinated in Marseille by the Ustaše on October 9, 1934—the day Alexander arrived in France to continue his negotiations with the French foreign minister.

In his will, Alexander named his cousin, Prince Paul, as the first of three regents to govern until the autumn of 1941, when Alexander's son Peter would come of age. The other two were Radenko Stanković, the minister of education, and Ivan Perović, the governor of Croatia.

On assuming his task Prince Paul had only a limited knowledge of the political problems of Yugoslavia, for he had lived abroad during the kingdom's formative years. Because his major interests lay in the arts rather than in the maze of Yugoslav politics, he came to his post with few contacts among the politicians and with no political counselors. As a person, he differed markedly from King Alexander, a

[6] Eylan, *La Vie et la Mort d'Alexandre 1er*, p. 183.

dynamic and dominant personality. In contrast, the Prince Regent was an introspective man who believed compromise the essence of government. He, far more than Alexander, was Yugoslav rather than Serb in outlook, and considered the ceaseless quarrels among Yugoslavia's various national groups as wasteful and debilitating to the country as a whole. If untutored in the ways of Yugoslav politics when he came to the regency, he soon grew knowledgeable, and although he devoted himself mainly to the problems of foreign policy he quickly learned the intimate relation of internal to external affairs.

In its broadest outline his domestic policy was to liquidate the heritage of the Alexandrine dictatorship—the centralism, censorship, and military control—and to pacify the country by solving the Serb-Croat problem. This dispute, he was convinced, would have to be resolved within the framework of the 1931 constitution. True, this constitution insured Serb hegemony by granting to the king even wider powers than he had had before, and established a senate nominated by the king and a lower chamber elected under laws that precluded the existence of a healthy party system. This was not, to Prince Paul's way of thinking, the best possible constitution for the country. But he often reminded himself and others that he was only a regent, a caretaker who should return the state to the reigning house in the same constitutional condition in which he had received it. Prince Paul held that only the king could take the responsibility for substantial changes in the constitution. He resolved therefore to withstand all pressures for modification.[7]

The death of King Alexander had a markedly unifying effect on Yugoslav life as the people drew together in the face of external danger.[8] Their new government immediately sought to bring a case

[7] His resolve was strengthened by the lack of agreement among four experts on Yugoslav constitutional law whom he asked to answer certain questions: Was it possible to change the 1931 constitution under the regency? Could a parliamentary monarchy be instituted, the powers of the central government be limited, and the civil list be reduced, without limiting the king's rights and privileges as guaranteed by the constitution? All four jurists agreed that the regency was fully empowered to propose and initiate constitutional changes. They did not agree, however, on whether the suggested changes would limit the king's rights as defined and guaranteed by the constitution. Minister of Interior Korošec to Minister of Court Antić, January 16, 1937, with opinions by Professors Jovanović, Ilić, Kostić, and Krbek. (JBH)

[8] *DGFP*, C, III, Docs. 263 and 264.

against Italy and Hungary, charging complicity in the murder of the king. The Yugoslavs accused both countries of harboring the murderers, known Croat terrorists. In calling for an investigation by the council of the League of Nations, the Yugoslav government noted that the Yugoslav people had maintained their dignity and calm in the face of their king's murder only because they believed "in the efficacy of the League of Nations, the guardian of peace and of the international morality on which peace depends."[9]

Action against Italy by the League was stopped by the British and the French. It was one thing to bring the Ustaše murderers to trial in a French court or even to rail against the Hungarians in the League. But it was quite another to arraign Italy before the world, even though Ustaše leaders were hiding in Italy and being protected by Italy. Speaking for Britain, Foreign Secretary Sir John Simon told Djurić, the Yugoslav minister in London, that if Yugoslavia insisted on pressing its case against Italy and Mussolini decided to go to war on that account, England would not help the Yugoslavs. In Geneva, Anthony Eden, then minister for League of Nations Affairs, said the same thing to Constantin Fotitch, Yugoslav delegate to the League (and later minister in Washington). And in Paris, Barthou's successor, Pierre Laval, took the same position.

The debate in the council that began on December 7, 1934, with Yugoslavia's complaint against Hungary for harboring Alexander's assassins broadened into the issue of the revision of the peace treaties. On one side stood the foreign ministers of the antirevisionist countries: Jevtić for Yugoslavia, Beneš for Czechoslovakia, Titulescu for Rumania, Rüstü Aras for Turkey, Laval for France. Baron Aloisi of Italy and Tibor Eckhardt of Hungary represented the revisionists. But regardless of the extensive Yugoslav documentation, regardless of questions of justice and morality, nothing decisive could come out of these debates. It was imperative for France that Italy not be embarrassed. It was imperative that France itself avoid being placed in a position where it had to vote for censure of Italy, for the French were on the point of discussing a common foreign policy with Italy, perhaps even of reaching agreement.

With the assistance of Laval and Aloisi, Eden presented a com-

[9] Walters, *History of the League of Nations*, II, 602.

promise resolution to the council on December 10. It denounced terrorism and held that the Hungarians were derelict for harboring Ustaše and permitting them to operate a training camp for saboteurs and border raiders. By failing to suppress these illegal activities, Eden pointed out, Hungary had made it possible—even easy—for the murderers of Alexander and Barthou to accomplish their purpose.

The council adopted the resolution as presented. It made no move to censure Italy, to assess damages against either Italy or Hungary, or to press prosecution of the king's assassins.

The Yugoslavs were bitter. Their king had been murdered and the chief perpetrators of the crime had escaped punishment. Italy, which had also provided a haven for the murderers, had escaped even verbal censure. The League had failed to act as "the guardian of peace and of the international morality on which peace depends." Yugoslavia bordered two countries for which political terrorism and murder were, ostensibly, instruments of national policy. And Yugoslavia's closest friends, France and Great Britain, had permitted no redress of a grievous wrong.

Yugoslavia felt isolated both diplomatically and militarily. It could count on no one—neither on the great powers nor on its allies in the Little and Balkan Ententes. No country was committed by treaty to aid Yugoslavia in a war against Italy. To breach this wall of indifference became a matter of immediate concern for the Yugoslav government.[10]

Above all, Yugoslavia felt it had to rekindle its warm ties with France. It had to convince Laval both of Yugoslavia's value as an ally in eastern Europe and of Yugoslavia's intention of doing nothing that would hamper *rapprochement* between France and Italy. In return, Yugoslavia hoped Laval would convince Mussolini, when he

---

[10] German Minister Viktor von Heeren warned his country of French attempts to poison German-Yugoslav relations. He urged the foreign office to avoid "making demands on Yugoslavia which, for compelling reasons of her position in international politics, she can either not comply with at all, or the fulfilling of which . . . would . . . cause difficulties . . . . However much the tide of popular favor may be running against France in Yugoslavia and towards Germany, and however much the Prince Regent himself may be disposed to incline towards Britain rather than towards France, it will hardly be possible in the near future for such sentiments to find expression in practical politics." *DGFP*, C, III, Docs. 263 and 264.

saw him in January, that he should respect the integrity of Yugoslav territory.[11]

Unenthusiastic at first, Laval came around to this point of view after a long conversation with the Yugoslav minister, Spalajković. In Rome, he had no little difficulty in persuading Mussolini to reverse his revisionist stand. The Duce feared the shift would react against his personal prestige. But Laval had a telling argument. If Mussolini did not withdraw his support of Hungary's revisionist claims—in fact, if he did not abandon Hungary altogether—he would see the bulk of the Yugoslav army mobilized along the Croatian and Slovenian frontiers. Furthermore, said Laval, the Yugoslavs had made it clear to him that they would leave the side of France and join with Poland and Germany if Italy did not show that it entertained no expansionist desires on the eastern shores of the Adriatic.[12]

Even more abhorrent to Mussolini than the thought of becoming an antirevisionist spokesman was the idea of recognizing, however indirectly, the existence of the Little Entente. He was willing to negotiate with France on the question of Central Europe but he was most unwilling to consult with two of France's allies: Yugoslavia and Rumania. In the end, however, he promised Laval that he would tell the Little Entente ministers in Rome that both Italy and France had agreed to respect the frontiers of Rumania and Yugoslavia.

Laval and Mussolini decided that peace in eastern Europe could be made certain only after Hungarian-Yugoslav and Italo-Yugoslav differences were resolved and the independence of Austria was assured. Both men drew up their master plan in a joint memorandum which they circulated to the interested Danubian states: Germany, Austria, Hungary, Czechoslovakia, and Yugoslavia. In the memorandum they called on these states, with Italy, to sign a convention wherein each would promise to respect the territorial integrity of the others. Later,

[11] Two weeks after King Alexander's death Mussolini told Kánya, the Hungarian foreign minister, that the most difficult issue to be discussed in the coming talks with Laval was the "reconciliation with Serbia." He did not know what ideas France held on the subject nor what was expected of him. He did not intend to change his attitude toward the Little Entente, nor his revisionist ideas. Tensions between Yugoslavia and Italy were on the increase. There could be no question of the extradition of Pavelić, the Croatian terrorist and leader of the plot against the late king, because the French had never extradited anyone who organized an attempt against the Duce's life. *USMT*, Doc. NG-2416.

[12] *FRUS*, I (1935), 175.

the convention would also be open to France, Poland, and Rumania. Each state would agree not to interfere in each other's domestic affairs, not to foster agitation or propaganda, and not to violate the territorial integrity of any of the contracting parties or change their social or political regimes by force.

Reactions from the interested governments were not approbatory. At best they were bleakly cooperative.

The Germans quietly rejected the whole idea. They knew what it would mean for their interests in Austria. Their negative reaction sowed enough doubts in the minds of other government leaders to chill the Franco-Italian project. Hungary might participate, but only out of consideration for Italy. Poland refrained from stating its position and preferred to wait to see what the Hungarians would do. Yugoslavia's assistant foreign minister, Purić, told Heeren that only out of consideration for their relationship to France would the Yugoslavs participate. The Austrians wanted no protectorate of any kind.

In the persons of Sir John Simon, then foreign secretary, and Eden, by now lord privy seal, the British, who were never officially consulted as an "interested state," told Hitler that their government was not bound to any formula in matters of foreign policy. They were therefore in a position to ascertain whether a European security system could be set up that would seriously consider the German views. After Eden recalled for Hitler the negotiations in Geneva following the murder of King Alexander, both the Germans and the British agreed how difficult it was to define satisfactorily the concept of nonintervention into the affairs of other states. Sir John promised Hitler that he would work on the problem of definition. His government, the British foreign secretary added, did not greatly favor a Danubian pact.[13]

Yugoslavia reacted to the meeting between Laval and Mussolini with restrained satisfaction. The communiqué released by the permanent council of the Little Entente on January 11, 1935, stated that "the three Ministers of Foreign Affairs have manifested their satisfaction at the results of the negotiations" and that "they have decided to collaborate with all the interested powers to put the principles of the Rome agreements into practice with the most sincere spirit."

[13] *DGFP*, C, III, Docs. 405, 408, 409, 411, 518, 520, 528, 530, and 555.

But, the communiqué went on, they would be "careful at the same time to safeguard both their national interests and the general interest." [14]

Nine days later, the permanent council of the Balkan Entente issued its communiqué, which likewise expressed the hope that France and Italy would successfully carry out the Rome agreements and take due account of the interests of all the countries desiring the consolidation of peace in central and eastern Europe. [15]

If the results of the talks between Laval and the Duce proved a disappointment to the Yugoslavs, they did not immediately show it. However, future events—Italy's invasion of Ethiopia and Germany's march into the Rhineland—sharply pointed out the deficiencies of the League of Nations as a protector of small states and of the *status quo*. The behavior of the great powers warned the Yugoslavs that they must seek new means of insuring their own security against an aggressor.

Laval, in his conversations with Mussolini, had pledged that the French government would give Italy a free hand in satisfying its ambitions in East Africa, but the British government equivocated. [16] On the one hand, bowing to public opinion, it supported the covenant and the principle of collective action against an aggressor. On the other, it tried to advance the national interest by direct diplomatic negotiations with Italy.

Adherents of the second course based their judgment on "stark and ineluctable facts." Hitler was growing stronger. The Japanese were becoming increasingly aggressive. Britain was not strong enough to resist both. It therefore needed Italy as an additional counterweight to the German power. [17]

[14] *DIA*, I (1935), 24.
[15] *DIA*, I (1935), 25.
[16] *Francia, Situazione politica nel 1935*, p. 16. Captured Italian foreign office archives (microfilm, container number 1291 in the National Archives, Washington). See *FRUS*, I (1935), 175.
[17] A report on British imperial interests in East Africa spelled out the theoretical basis for the opposition to the anti-Italian policy of the League. The Italian embassy in London obtained a copy of the report and published it. The report, by an interministerial commission headed by Sir John Maffey, admitted the existence of a Laval-Mussolini agreement on Ethiopia and expressed the opinion that an

A formidable body of pro-League public opinion opposed this view. Stanley Baldwin and a new government had come into office pledged to support the League. Sir Samuel Hoare (later Viscount Templewood) was well aware that the voice of the people did not necessarily dictate the proper directive for handling the growing crisis. Although a number of his advisers warned that the League was "practically dead" and that "it was no good trying to revive it," Sir Samuel disagreed. He insisted that life could be infused into the League. Mussolini could be deterred from bringing down both the League and the peace.[18]

For Sir Samuel, support of the League was a way of resisting German aggression. He believed Laval, with his quick and versatile mind, would readily see and support the necessity of bringing the Italians on their side to stop Hitler. At the same time, Hoare would avoid provoking Mussolini into hostility, even with the Ethiopia matter on the League agenda. Italy was needed as an ally. Sir Samuel was willing to see Italy expand into African wastes but was not willing to go so far as Laval in giving the Duce a completely free hand in empire-building.

Meanwhile, life also had to be infused into the Yugoslav government. At the time of King Alexander's death many Yugoslavs had expressed the hope that a united government representing all democratic parties would come into being to resist the danger from abroad. But the premier, Uzunović, had reconstructed his cabinet along the old one-party line of Serb hegemony. It included Jevtić, who as foreign minister had argued Yugoslavia's case against Hungary before the council of the League of Nations. He was friendly to the anti-government parties, however, and soon resigned, as did the rest of the cabinet. The regents then asked Jevtić to form a new government.

Italian conquest of Ethiopia would not affect any British interest. In some respects, Italian control would be advantageous for Britain, the report pointed out. British interests would be threatened only if Britain and Italy were at war, and that was improbable, according to the commission. The New York *Times*, February 20, 1936.

[18] Templewood, *Nine Troubled Years*, pp. 153 and 166. One of Britain's more active opponents of sanctions against Italy was Leopold Amery (later secretary of state for India), who argued that "he was not prepared to send a single Birmingham lad to his death for Abyssinia." Winston Churchill, *While England Slept* (New York: G. P. Putnam's Sons, 1938), pp. 225 and 230. Six years later Amery was appealing to the Serbs to go to their deaths for Britain.

Unfortunately, he was not able to maintain his political balance for long because of pressure from two sets of forces: one demanding that he liberalize the government, the other that he return to the methods of King Alexander's dictatorship. To avoid making the all-important decision, the Jevtić government dissolved the parliament and called for an election.

All the major parties except the Slovene Populists participated in that May, 1935, election. Maček, newly released from prison, headed a Croat-Serb coalition ticket organized solely for the election with no thought for future joint political operations. Despite a controlled press, open balloting, and police interference, the *ad hoc* ticket won some 40 percent of the votes. Under the electoral law, which was heavily weighted in favor of the government, this showing gave the opposition only 67 out of 373 seats and its members once more boycotted the parliament.

Although the Croats criticized the handling of the election (their criticism received marked attention from Prince Paul), there was no sharp internal crisis until one of Jevtić's Croatian colleagues accused Maček and his Peasant Party of secretly sympathizing with the murderers of Marseille. Thereupon three Croatian ministers resigned, along with two Serbs, Minister of War General Živković and Finance Minister Milan Stojadinović.

In early June, Prince Paul asked Stojadinović to survey the possibilities of forming a new government.[19] In the next two weeks the man who was to be the new prime minister talked with the leaders of the National Radical Party, the Slovene Populist Party, and the Yugoslav Moslem Organization. All agreed that the May election had not lessened Yugoslavia's internal tension, that the Jevtić government lacked the country's confidence, and that a new government with the proper authority, with the confidence of the people, even with Maček in the cabinet, should come into being.

The new government, Stojadinović reported to Prince Paul, should begin to organize a new political party combining all the pro-govern-

---

[19] Nevile Henderson, then British minister in Belgrade, claimed that Stojadinović owed much of the success of his political career to him (Henderson, *Water under the Bridges*). This may be true since Henderson's advice carried some weight in Yugoslav court circles. In addition, Stojadinović had numerous British banking connections.

ment elements under the title of the *Jugoslavenska Radikalna Zajednica* (Yugoslav Radical Union). Its executive committee should include Aca Stanojević, the octogenarian head of the National Radical Party, Milan Stojadinović also of the Radicals, Father Korošec of the Slovene Populist Party, and Mehmed Spaho of the Yugoslav Moslem Organization.[20]

Prince Paul agreed with these suggestions, and on June 23d the regents officially asked Stojadinović to form a cabinet which would introduce liberal reforms and ease political tensions. Stojadinović's first act was to appoint Father Korošec as minister of the interior and Spaho as minister of communications. For himself he retained the portfolio of minister of foreign affairs.

At first the leaders of the opposition neither vigorously opposed these changes in the government nor offered to participate.

Unlike the British, the new Yugoslav government was united in its determination not to mollify Italy. It was unaware of Whitehall's increasing doubts and misgivings about the value of the League of Nations and of sanctions, and had no inkling that Britain viewed Italy as a prospective ally. As a matter of fact, the Yugoslav council of ministers declined, in principle, any support of Italy in its venture in Abyssinia and went on record as "prepared to join those forces which support the League of Nations." As a final touch, the council reaffirmed Yugoslavia's ties with the Little Entente, the Balkan Entente, and France. These were the pillars of its foreign policy. Yugoslavia and its allies, the council maintained, must orient their policy to the European policy of the British. On the mistaken assumption that they were following Britain's course, the Yugoslavs rejected overtures made by Italy for a settlement of their differences. As a first step Italy asked the Yugoslavs to press Turkey to give up its right to fortify the Dardanelles. The Yugoslavs refused on the grounds that the request was irrelevant. Then the Italians asked for a guarantee of their economic interests in Albania. The Yugoslavs countered that they could offer the guarantee only if Italy renounced all political influence in the Balkans.[21]

---

[20] Stojadinović memorandum on the formation of the JRZ, June 18, 1935. (JBH)
[21] The minutes of the July 17, 1935, meeting of the Yugoslav council of ministers appeared in the *Stajerski Gospodar* (Styrian Economist), Ljubljana, October 3, 1942.

The fact that the League was facing a crisis did not deter the French from continuing to hold military conversations with Italy. As a matter of fact, they had been talking with the Italians since 1933 about creating an Anglo-French-Italian entente. Now, in January, 1935, they were happy to entertain a proposal from the Italians that their two armies cooperate in case of German aggression against Austria. The French supreme military committee also approved General Gamelin's plan of placing a French army corps between the Italian and the Yugoslav troops in case of war, to act primarily as a bridge between the two unfriendly forces during the drive into Austria where they would link up with the Czechs. Gamelin's overall strategy was to eliminate friction between Italy and Yugoslavia, two prospective allies of France. That accomplished, he would bring into action against Germany the other states of the Little Entente—Rumania and Czechoslovakia.[22]

After conversations with Italy's Marshal Badoglio in June, 1935, Gamelin told the chiefs of staff of the Little Entente (including Yugoslavia's General Marić) that he had signed nothing during his trip to Rome. The Italians, he reported, had verbally promised to fulfill all their military obligations to France, to demilitarize the border with France, in case of war against Germany to permit French troops to cross Italy for operations in Austria, and in case of war in Africa to leave an army in Europe. The Rumanians, Badoglio and Gamelin had agreed, would enter Austria through Hungary for action against Germany.

To obviate any political deterrent to Yugoslavia's participation in military operations in Austria, Italy had also agreed to improve its relations with Yugoslavia.[23]

General Marić questioned Gamelin's assertion that he and Badoglio had signed no agreements. For all these Italian promises, he argued, the French must have promised something in return. His doubts had some justification. Gamelin writes in his book that he and Badoglio did sign a *procès-verbal*, although he reveals no French promises.[24] They were not now necessary; the French had done their share six months before when Laval promised Mussolini a free hand in Ethiopia.

[22] Gamelin, *Servir*, II, 163-64.
[23] Unsigned report to Prince Paul, July, 1935. (JBH)
[24] Gamelin, *Servir*, II, 171.

Gamelin asked his Little Entente allies to seek a demilitarized zone on the other side of the Dniester River and in return to grant passage to Soviet troops through northern Rumania. He also recommended that they urge England to grant Italy all it asked for. Italy had to find room for expansion, Gamelin asserted, and could find it only in Africa.[25]

Behind the scenes in Yugoslavia, government leaders began to doubt the wisdom of denying support to Mussolini in his African adventure, despite an offer from Göring of protection against Italy.[26] In a conversation with President Lebrun, Yugoslav Minister Spalajković pointed out that if Italy decreased the number of its troops stationed in Europe, the "entire burden of maintaining the *status quo* and the peace in Central Europe would fall on Yugoslavia." Perhaps, as Laval argued, the best solution for France and Yugoslavia would be to give Italy enough concessions in Abyssinia to keep Mussolini busy there for at least half a century. This would mean peace in the Balkans. But, said Spalajković, they would have to bring England around to this point of view. The president of France agreed.[27]

Yugoslav Prime Minister Milan Stojadinović also advised giving Italy concessions in Ethiopia. Laval's reluctance to take a stern attitude and a militant position in favor of collective security led Stojadinović to urge that the Yugoslav council of ministers shift its position. He called for a policy "as wise as serpents and as harmless as doves," for Yugoslavia alone could neither save nor destroy Mussolini. He asked:

Who can tell what the policy of a post-Mussolini Italy will be? In what direction will a rapidly multiplying people expand? I prefer to see them going to Abyssinia rather than to the Balkans. So long as France does not

[25] Unsigned report to Prince Paul, July, 1935. (JBH)

[26] Stojadinović to Prince Paul, June 12, 1936. (JBH)

[27] Spalajković to Prince Paul, July 31, 1935. Lebrun explained why France had been, and still was, eager for Italy's friendship. Before the Rome Agreement of January 7, 1935, French and Italian troops had faced each other across their common frontier. Now France no longer had to worry over its security problem in the Mediterranean or on its southern border. Italy was sending to Africa the troops once stationed on the French border. This released for front-line duty the French troops who were now manning the border or serving in Tunisia and secured French communication lines with Algeria, Tunisia, and Morocco against danger from Italy.

decide to which side it will go, we have no reason to run out ahead of the great powers.[28]

As the summer of 1935 drew to a close, Sir Samuel Hoare elaborated the British position in a speech before the League assembly. It was a stirring speech. It gave the League a lift it had not had in years. It was a plea for peace and defense of the small nations. It was a passionate statement of the British belief in the principles of the League. It heavily stressed England's stand for the collective maintenance of the covenant in its entirety, and particularly for steady and collective resistance to all acts of unprovoked aggression.[29]

Talk of sanctions increased, especially among the small powers. Less than a month later, on October 3d, the Italian army invaded Ethiopia. On October 7th, the League declared Italy an aggressor. On October 11th, the League voted to impose sanctions. That day the members of the sanctions conference agreed to stop all arms exports to Italy. On October 14th, they agreed to prohibit all loans and credits to Italian firms and to the Italian government. The matter of prohibiting imports from Italy was troublesome. If Italy refused to buy from sanctionist states (and Yugoslavia was a sanctionist state), they would face widespread unemployment and a heavy deficit. Nevertheless, states such as Yugoslavia which had the most to lose did vote for sanctions. Undoubtedly they wished to go beyond financial and economic penalties, for they saw in the application of Article XVI of the covenant a means of preventing aggression against their own countries. The Yugoslavs began to realize that sanctions against Italy for aggression in Africa might prevent later Italian aggression in the Balkans.

As part of the League's procedure, the assembly set up a planning body known as the coordination committee. (Most of the committee's work devolved upon a still smaller group—the committee of 18—of which Yugoslavia was a member). At a meeting of the coordination committee on November 2, 1935, Van Zeeland, the Belgian representative, moved that the group entrust to the British and French delegates the search for a solution to the Italo-Ethiopian question. Many members of the committee became suspicious, sensing back-

---

[28] Stojadinović to Prince Paul, September 20, 1935. (JBH)
[29] Templewood, *Nine Troubled Years*, p. 170.

stage action among the principals, and the motion died. The delegates had good grounds for their suspicions. The British and French foreign offices had been working for many weeks on a plan that would satisfy Italy. As Hoare explained to the House of Commons, Britain was pursuing the "double policy of negotiation with Italy and loyalty to the League."[30]

But something went wrong. The plan Hoare and Laval worked out for the League's approval reached the public before it reached the League.

The news, leaked by the French, that Hoare and Laval had agreed to a partition of Ethiopia for Italy's benefit whipped up a political whirlwind in Britain. It blew Hoare out of office, blew Eden in as his successor, and left Prime Minister Baldwin shaken and bewildered. That Hoare considered this agreement a prerequisite to securing Italy within the Anglo-French camp meant little to the British voter. That the agreement was designed to resist German aggression meant just as little to the millions who supported Lord Cecil and his League of Nations Union's peace ballot. For these millions, the life of the League and the honor of Britain were at stake. They saw this assault on British rectitude as the work of foreigners, unwashed and un-scrupulous Frenchmen and Italians with little understanding of the tidy, sturdy Germans. It was the diplomats, the public believed, who prevented the League from acting as a guardian of the peace.

Faced with mass stereotypes of this kind, the British government could not tell Britons the facts of life, especially when the next election might hinge on the issue of peace or war. When public opinion was swelling against France and Italy and for Germany and Ethiopia the British could not be told that Hoare's dismissal meant they might not have another chance to come to an understanding with Italy. Of great import was the considerable possibility of an Anglo-Italian war if public opinion had its way. And a war in Europe at a time of tension in the Far East was the last thing for which the military establishment was prepared. Common sense indicated, Neville Chamberlain asserted, that the League had assumed a task it could not fulfill. Since sanctions involved the risk of war it would be wiser, said Britain's future prime minister, "to explore the pos-

[30] Templewood, *Nine Troubled Years*, p. 177.

sibilities of localizing the danger spots of the world and trying to find a more practical method of securing peace by means of regional arrangements ... which would be guaranteed only by those nations whose interests were vitally connected with the danger zone."[31]

It was under these circumstances that the British raised the question of Yugoslavia's intentions in case of outright conflict between England and Italy. Yugoslavia pledged itself to support the covenant.

The Hoare-Laval episode had particular significance for the small powers and took the heart out of their effort to apply sanctions against Italy. Here was Hoare, spokesman for a great power, urging concerted action against the aggressor and at the same time contriving a peace settlement that could benefit only the aggressor. Ironically, on the very day that Hoare and Laval worked out their scheme, Sir Ronald Campbell, the British minister in Belgrade, told Stojadinović that Hoare feared Yugoslavia was hesitating in its collective function with the other small states of preserving the League of Nations and the peace.[32]

From the Yugoslav point of view there was much merit in stopping Mussolini. There was equal merit in permitting the Italians to become so preoccupied in Ethiopia that they would have little time or energy to become involved in the Balkans. But there was nothing to be gained by publicly talking of stopping Mussolini and then doing nothing effective to stop him. This was a double policy in a respect unrecognized by Whitehall, the Yugoslavs argued.

An *aide-mémoire* from the British improved their state of mind none at all. The British government wished to know when and to what extent Yugoslavia could aid Britain militarily. It also asked the Yugoslavs to tell Rome that in case of an Italian attack on Great Britain, the Yugoslavs would stand with the British. Such a declaration, the British believed, would help to end the war in Ethiopia.[33]

The Yugoslav government, Stojadinović replied, was in complete

---

[31] *DIA*, II (1935), 487-89. Winston Churchill was the first to propose abandoning the sanctions. Neville Chamberlain elaborated the idea in his diary: "The League had failed to stop the war, or to protect the victim, and had thereby demonstrated the failure of collective security." Keith Feiling, *Life of Neville Chamberlain* (London: Macmillan, 1947), p. 295.

[32] Stojadinović to Prince Paul, December 9, 1935. (JBH)

[33] The Italians had the same fear of war. Stojadinović described the Italian

accord with the British and French governments in the application of sanctions against Italy. It would faithfully carry out all the obligations imposed by Article XVI of the covenant. On military questions, the government could not answer until the general staffs of Britain and Yugoslavia exchanged views. As to the proposed declaration to Rome, the time for such an act was not opportune because the "combined efforts of the British and French governments are being felt in a friendly solution of the Italo-Ethiopian conflict." Elaborating on Yugoslavia's position, Stojadinović told the British minister:

We have followed English and French advice and have considerably improved our relations with Italy in recent months. A step of this kind, by us, would spoil all this work and expose us to the subsequent vengeance of Italy. Who would then defend us from Italy? Furthermore, we cannot make such a statement without consulting the states of the Balkan Pact.[34]

Mussolini knew he could not count on Yugoslavia to come to Italy's defense, Stojadinović assured Campbell. As his final argument for delaying a declaration to Rome, he reminded Campbell of the half-million Yugoslavs in Italy, on the Adriatic islands, in Fiume and Zadar. They would weigh heavy in the balance when the time came for the Yugoslavs to decide whether they were "pro or contra Italy."[35]

Consultation with the states of the Balkan Pact was a matter of tactics. Stojadinović believed that the Greeks and the Turks as well as the Czechs and Rumanians should know what Yugoslavia was doing. Italy would attack Yugoslavia "out of vengeance and fury," perhaps with the assistance of Austria and Hungary, which bordered "the militarily unprotected and richest regions" of Yugoslavia. The Little Entente allies must be ready to play their part, if necessary, in protecting Yugoslavia from Hungary, Austria, and Bulgaria. "We are not hesitating," Stojadinović told Campbell, "but we need to be cautious, for when it comes to fighting we will certainly be among the best of fighters, as we have been in every war." Greece and

---

minister in Belgrade, Viola di Compalto, as looking quite gloomy because of England's attitude. The Italians did not expect such resistance. "Who knows," Di Compalto said, "the British may even bombard Naples one day." Stojadinović to Prince Paul, September 20, 1935. (JBH)

[34] Stojadinović to Božidar Purić, Yugoslav minister in Paris, December 15, 1935. (JBH). Purić is also spelled Pouritch.

[35] Stojadinović to Prince Paul, December 9, 1935. (JBH)

Turkey would not be risking as much as would Yugoslavia, he pointed out; that was why it was easier for them to reply to Britain's *aide-mémoire*. "We weigh each obligation and once we accept it we fulfill it."

In a letter to Purić, the Yugoslav minister in Paris, Stojadinović expressed the opinion that a Yugoslav *démarche* in Rome would be useless unless France agreed to support it:

We must be protected against Italy not only by Britain but by France, in view of the fact that we border on Italy. Laval should be kept informed on developments in this question. We must not risk our armed forces too soon, when nothing is certain. There is always time to enter the conflict with our army of a million and a half. We must do nothing without the agreement of the states of the Balkan Pact and we must have France on our side.[36]

It remained for the Yugoslav general staff to set the tone and upper limits of Yugoslavia's foreign policy for the next five years, regardless of what promises the foreign office made to Great Britain.[37] The generals held in little regard any promises that Britain might give regarding reciprocal support.[38]

The general staff warned that Yugoslavia must not enter into any military action against Italy, considering the superiority of the Italian forces:

England does not offer us any assistance, either on land or on the sea. France is not obliged to aid England in any action in which England may be involved on land. The French have said nothing whatsoever about this to us. Actually, they show us a particularly unobliging attitude as far as rearmament is concerned.

Furthermore, said the generals, Yugoslavia should not get further involved in any action against Italy either by force of arms or by invoking new sanctions, since the Italians might retaliate.

The general staff urged the foreign office to take the position that:

[36] Stojadinović to Purić, December 15, 1935. (JBH)
[37] *DIA*, II (1935), 304-9.
[38] On July 27, 1936, Eden told the House of Commons that Italy had assured Yugoslavia that it had never contemplated, nor was it contemplating, any aggressive action against Yugoslavia because of its past sanctionist policy. Consequently, there was no longer any need for assurances of mutual support. *DIA*, II (1935), 315.

In an eventual military action against Italy we would have to stand aside in the beginning. We could join the action only after sufficient French forces enter action on land. And even then we should not act rashly but should wait for the best possible moment before involving ourselves.

Yugoslavia, the general staff believed, was in a "serious and quite dangerous position." The government must take into account, the generals warned, that Yugoslavia alone "may be subject to an act of aggression by Italy because we participate in the sanctions." They asserted that the security of the country required that the government take the following steps:

Pass emergency credits of 400 million dinars ($8,000,000) for war material. Request war material, financial aid and naval assistance from England, at least for the period of our mobilization and concentration. Determine the attitude of the states of the Little Entente and the Balkan Pact. Avoid all provocations against Italy.

Regarding mutual assistance, the general staff proposed clearing up the question of whether or not Yugoslavia would move against Italy if Italy attacked another sanctionist power or if the League decided to apply further sanctions. If the League acted, the general staff proposed a series of steps:

Determine the attitude of Rumania, Czechoslovakia and Greece in order to obtain gasoline from Rumania and munitions and war material from Czechoslovakia. Determine precisely the attitude of Turkey and watch its actions toward Bulgaria. Clarify with England the French attitude toward the use of its troops. Insist that the British, either alone or with France, extend us loans and material. Insist that the British or the League of Nations indemnify us for damages and war material expenses in case we become involved. Avoid provoking Italy.

This, then, was the advice of Yugoslavia's generals.[39]

The general staff's arguments impressed Secretary-General Martinac of the Yugoslav ministry of foreign affairs. He agreed with the generals' conclusion that Yugoslavia was in a "serious and dangerous" position, and urged Yugoslav representatives abroad to be most circumspect. He was particularly concerned about those in Rome

[39] Vl. Martinac, secretary-general of the Yugoslav ministry of foreign affairs, to Minister of Court Antić, February 25, 1936. (JBH)

and Geneva. The reports from Dučić, in Rome, indicated he was unfriendly toward Italy. As to the Yugoslav representative in Geneva, he should avoid serving as *rapporteur* on any question connected with the sanctions and avoid discussing the sanctions.

The memorandum prepared by the general staff for the foreign office expressed in only general terms how weak Yugoslavia really was. It was the reply to the British *aide-mémoire* of December, 1935, that pointed up the many difficulties facing Yugoslavia's defense system. A close look at that defense system raised certain questions: Could the Yugoslavs move a man, ship, or plane to assist a Britain attacked by Italy? More important, could Yugoslavia defend itself against an aggressor? The Yugoslav reply to the British *aide-mémoire* observed that their navy was small and "not sufficient even for the security of the Adriatic coast, particularly in view of its great length." At best, the navy could be used for raids in the Adriatic, for reconnoitering and minor defense operations. Admitting that on the sea the Kingdom of Yugoslavia was powerless, the memorandum assumed the main action would be on land, where the position was "perilous."

In front is Italy with considerable forces mobilized and a highly developed railway system making possible quick concentration of troops. Italy could count on the support of Albania, Bulgaria, Hungary and Austria.

The peril would be especially great if France were not to take part with strong land forces, since Italy was in a position to "throw herself upon the Kingdom of Yugoslavia even before Yugoslavia could prepare itself for action." [40] The Kingdom of Yugoslavia would be obliged "to exert, right from the beginning, all its strength to mobilize the maximum of its forces." Mobilization would be hampered by "palpable deficiencies in military equipment, particularly in tanks, antitank equipment, gas masks, munitions and planes." If it were not given assistance in time, Yugoslavia would not be able to overcome these deficiencies "in the present financial crisis which is rendered worse still by the application of economic sanctions." [41]

[40] Delbos, Blum's foreign minister, told Purić in 1936 that if it were only a matter of fighting Italy alone, "France herself could easily and quickly do it and have it over," but if they had to fight both Germany and Italy, "we must wait for English rearmament . . . we need British divisions." Purić to Antić, November 27, 1936. (JBH)

[41] Yugoslav foreign office memorandum to British foreign office, undated. (JBH)

The Hoare-Laval plan for the partition of Ethiopia signaled the death of the League of Nations as an instrument of collective security. It also gave Adolf Hitler a green light to proceed with his plans for retrieving German territory lost as a result of the First World War. On March 7, 1936, the German chancellor turned these plans into a grim reality by sending his troops into the demilitarized Rhineland.

The French, who could have moved against this hundred-mile advance of the German frontier, and maintained intact their strategic connections with the Czechs and the Russians, did not do so. They ascribed their failure to act to lack of British cooperation.

The British, on the other hand, believed that both the French and the Germans were bluffing and that they could negotiate with Hitler. This, they thought, was the realistic approach. They were certain that since Germany's military leaders were conservative and, like the British and the French, did not want war, the French ought to refrain from taking a legalistic stand on Hitler's occupation of the Rhineland.[42]

But while Britain argued for negotiation, the Soviet Union and the states of the Little Entente pressed France to resist with force, since in this case the use of force had the approval of international treaty. In Germany's unimpeded occupation of the demilitarized zone they saw an act negating any French promise of assistance against German aggression.

Alexis Léger, secretary-general of the French ministry of foreign affairs, said the German move placed "a Chinese wall across Europe," a wall barring France and England from central and eastern Europe, putting the succession states at the mercy of Germany. He feared that the Rhineland episode would result in the abandonment of all ideas of collective security and that henceforth the states of central and eastern Europe would have to fend for themselves. It seemed clear that the Little Entente would have to look to Germany as the great power in the area.[43]

Speaking "with cold passion," French Foreign Minister Flandin expressed the same view to an impressed but unyielding Britain. The European situation was now completely changed, he stressed, and

[42] *FRUS*, I (1936), 236.
[43] *Ibid.*, p. 268.

Hitler's occupation of the Rhineland necessitated a "fundamental reorientation of French policy." They had thrown away the last chance of saving central and eastern Europe from German domination. France would now have to make the best terms with Germany that it could get, and leave the rest of Europe to its fate.[44]

Yugoslavia had reservations about imposing sanctions against Germany. Its experience with the sanctions against Italy had proved fruitless. Although Stojadinović realized the extreme gravity of the European situation, he remained optimistic, hopeful of a peaceful solution. With Turkish Foreign Minister Rüstü Aras he formulated joint views on the Rhineland problem. Peace in Europe had to be preserved at all costs, they agreed. But if France became a victim of unprovoked German aggression, they must go to its aid. They hoped the great powers would reach an agreement through peaceful negotiations. They decided that neither Yugoslavia nor Turkey would participate in economic sanctions against Germany, for that would only mean economic ruin for both countries. At the same time, however, they had to make Germany realize that treaties could not be lightly regarded. Otherwise, they knew Bulgaria or Hungary might also be tempted to violate peace terms.[45]

In a lesser manner, Austria followed Germany's example by establishing a conscript service in violation of the Treaty of St. Germain. The Yugoslavs did not fear the Austrian military build-up as a threat to themselves or to the Little Entente. Nor did they see it as Vienna's defense against the Nazis for they had already gone on record as predicting that Austria would one day become part of Germany, either by voluntary political or economic union or by conquest. What they did fear was that Italy, in trying to reinforce its shaky position in central Europe, had put the Austrians up to it and, even worse, that as a consequence the Hungarians would shortly follow suit.[46]

In its relations with Austria, Yugoslavia always had to reckon with the specter of a Habsburg restoration. Fearing the attraction it might have for a significant number of Croats and Slovenes, the Stojadinović government opposed all legitimist propaganda in Austria. A restoration

---

[44] Robert Boothby, *I Fight to Live* (London: Victor Gollancz, 1947), pp. 136-37.
[45] Stojadinović to Prince Paul, March 11, 1936. (JBH)
[46] *FRUS*, I (1936), 289.

would lead only to conflict, with grave consequences to the peace of all Europe.[47]

At this juncture, the Austrians tried without success to strike a bargain with the Yugoslavs. French Minister of Foreign Affairs Flandin told Prince Paul in Paris of his conversation with Starhemberg, one of Austria's more opportunistic politicians, an organizer of Austrian fascism although unsympathetic to German national socialism. Starhemberg said he was willing to promise not to bring back the Habsburgs before consulting the Yugoslavs. But, he added, he would consult them only if they would guarantee the integrity of Austria.[48]

Yugoslavia, which also had the problem of countering Hungarian propaganda among its Hungarian minority, was willing to come to an understanding with Hungary provided Hungary relinquished its interest in the minority. Hungary, which could not make such a move because Rumania and Czechoslovakia might expect a similar concession, feared the power of the Little Entente and decided to put its trust in Italy if the Little Entente mobilized.[49]

The tie between Hungary and Italy was an old story to the Yugoslavs. Ever since 1928 they had seen ample evidence of Italy's meddling in central European politics. Consequently, when Hermann Göring sent Hjalmar Schacht, German minister of economic affairs, to Belgrade in June, 1936, with an offer of help, the Yugoslavs felt a deep sense of relief.[50]

And now, Stojadinović reported to Prince Paul, Germany was

---

[47] *SIA* (1936), p. 510. In 1936, Yugoslavia's position on Austria was little different from King Alexander's in 1931. He believed any attempt to restore the Habsburgs would lead to the destruction of the Little Entente, the growth of Italian strength, and Germany's going off into the "Russian adventure." King Alexander to Spalajković, April 6, 1931.

[48] Minute of conversation between Prince Paul and Flandin, February 4, 1936. (JBH) The French would agree to defend Austria only if Yugoslavia and Italy did so. Before that could happen, Flandin told Prince Paul, "it is necessary that Mussolini get out of his Ethiopian adventure without diminishing his prestige." Meanwhile, Starhemberg promised the British that he would not bring back the Habsburgs and would tell Archduke Otto, the pretender to the throne, to take a trip around the world.

[49] Ciano, *L'Europa*, pp. 65-66.

[50] Göring at this time was president of the Reichstag, minister-president of Prussia, and Reichsminister for air, commander-in-chief of the Luftwaffe and commissioner for the four-year plan. It is not clear in what capacity he addressed Stojadinović.

willing to furnish us complete security against Hungary and Italy. At the present time (Mussolini's megalomania and the chaos in France) this offer appears unusually important for us. [that is why I think that conversations in this direction] [51] For peace in our country and to secure Yugoslavia's future, we must as soon as possible obtain insurance [a safe protection] [51] against Italy.[52]

By October, 1936, Germany had taken on the double task of supporting Yugoslavia against Italy and Hungary while acting as mediator between Yugoslavia and Italy. Hitler urged Ciano to arrive at a solid understanding with Stojadinović on the points at issue and at the same time to press the Hungarians to direct their irredentism against Czechoslovakia rather than Yugoslavia.[53]

Less than a month later, Ciano found on a visit to Budapest that relations between Hungary and Yugoslavia were improving and that cordial agreement might even be possible. Kálmán de Kánya, the Hungarian foreign minister, favored Italy's suggestion of a *rapprochement* with Belgrade. He thought, however, that the whole project would have to be approached with "extreme vigilance." The Hungarians found that Stojadinović, while eager to reach an understanding with de Kánya, was not willing to define his terms with any precision. He intended, the Hungarians believed, to continue "to have his fingers in a large number of pies." [54]

As the Yugoslavs maneuvered Germany into position as a barrier between themselves and the Italo-Hungarian threat they worried about the course France might take as a result of the episodes in Ethiopia and the Rhineland. If the French changed their policy of collective security, or faltered as the mainstay of that policy, there would be serious consequences for the states of the Little and the Balkan Ententes. If the policy itself disintegrated, as clearly seemed possible, then France would have to make bilateral treaties of alliance

[51] Bracketed portions were deleted by Stojadinović.

[52] Stojadinović to Prince Paul, June 12, 1936. True, a few months earlier, in February, Viktor von Heeren, the German minister in Belgrade, had told Prince Paul that Hitler promised that "no matter what the future policy of Germany will be, one of its principles will be a strong and independent Yugoslavia." Minute of conversation between Prince Paul and Heeren, February 27, 1936. (JBH)

[53] Ciano, *L'Europa,* p. 97.

[54] Ciano, *L'Europa,* pp. 107-8.

with other countries, particularly with Italy. That in turn would. as a Yugoslav official pointed out, "put an end to the alliance between France and the Little Entente countries and eventually leave Yugoslavia face to face with a militant and well-prepared Italy."[55]

If France's internal and external policies disconcerted the Yugoslavs, Britain's foreign policy irritated them. It seemed purposeless, drifting. In an attempt to fathom its mystery, Purić had a long talk with Eden in Geneva,[56] in the "somewhat worn-out premises of the Carlton Hotel right next to the new League of Nations building." As if to establish the warmth of their relationship, a genial Eden noted that "Yugoslavia and England are drinking cocktails, and sidecars at that." Then, in an abrupt change of mood, he suddenly asked Purić if he thought Italy was going to leave the League. Purić replied that he believed the Italians had made good use of France and Laval to get Ethiopia. Now they no longer needed the League. But, he added, if they remained as shrewd as they had been and "if we remain as naïve as we have been up till now," they will withdraw their delegate but always keep the door open. "But," Purić added, "they are hurrying toward Berlin."

Eden said he thought the situation would change once the Italians left. But he wondered what the sanctionist powers could do when the council of the League met again in June. Purić argued for an understanding with France. "Blum is for complete collaboration with England," he pointed out. "He fears only that England might yield. He is against Mussolini and will work with the Little Entente and Balkan Pact states and with the Soviets."

"How far with the Soviets?" Eden interrupted.

"As far as need be," Purić replied. It would soon be impossible to reverse France's drift away from the League, he predicted. "France is slipping away from us. We must reach an agreement. It should be easy because France too wants it. We must therefore make use of that fact."

Eden was pessimistic. "You cannot believe to what extent public opinion in England is against France," he told Purić. "If you asked ten average Englishmen whether they are for Germany or France, nine will answer that they are for Germany."

[55] *FRUS*, I (1936), 289-90.
[56] Purić to Stojadinović, May 15, 1936. (JBH)

Purić resented Eden's skepticism regarding an agreement with France. "Public opinion and the average citizen have nothing to do with the matter," he fumed. "Foreign policy is carried out by governments. Whenever a government is weak and does not know what it wants, public opinion and average citizens get involved in foreign affairs. Fascism and Nazism are strong because we are weak and indecisive," he snapped. "Once England reaches an agreement with France, the war that is now being lost in Abyssinia can be won. Once France is won over to our side, we can dictate conditions to Mussolini through the League. If Mussolini should not accept, we can extend the sanctions and perhaps close the Suez Canal. Mussolini would not go to war against England, France and the League. It would ruin him completely. It is better for us all to go to war while we are all together, rather than later on and each one by himself."

In France a change of government always comes at the wrong time, Eden mused. Then, with a shrug, he met Purić's arguments:

Even if we were to win over France, we no longer have Ethiopia. I do not want war. Ethiopia is a question for the League of Nations, and whatever the League decides I will accept.

Purić was exasperated. "The League of Nations will agree to anything England decides." he retorted. "But you must know what you want."

Eden replied softly, as if speaking only to himself. "That is something I would like to know too," he murmured.

"The real question," Purić went on, "is not about Abyssinia, which nobody is concerned about, but who is to be master of the Mediterranean."

The comment seemed to shake Eden. "Is that a factor?" he asked.

Purić observed that the question had arisen in the events of the previous October and that it had been answered in favor of Mussolini.

Eden defended himself energetically. Britain was not afraid of Italy, he told Purić.

Even alone it could fight a war against Italy. Britain is always Britain and her prestige is great. But England does not want war. There is no need to exaggerate. Italy is exhausted economically and financially. She will be busy for years organizing Ethiopia. The English have a colonial empire and colonial experience and they know this well.

Purić responded that the British colonial experience was worth
nothing now because it belonged to a time of swords and single-bullet
rifles. Mussolini, with his air force and motorized troops, had upset
all the British forecasts. There was no reason why Mussolini could
not use Ethiopian troops equipped "with a uniform with gold buttons,
a rifle and five lire a month pay" to fight and die for him. This was
the last moment to take a determined stand and to profit by the
change in the French government. "Otherwise," Purić told Eden,
"you will lose France, France will lose England, and the rest of us
will be forced to make the choice between Berlin and Rome, if not
Moscow."

Eden could not take this seriously. Did Purić really believe Mussolini might become dangerous for Britain in Africa and for Yugoslavia
in the Balkans?

Not only did he believe it, said Purić; he was convinced of it.

Perhaps you may not be ready for war. We are even less ready. Yet I
would prefer that my country go to war with Italy now, while we can be
together with England, France and the League of Nations rather than later
on when each of us will be alone. Thanks to Laval and Flandin, France is
isolated and no one will come to its assistance. The new French government wants to remedy this. Unless you take the initiative, England will be
alone. We have all been for England because England is the guardian of
peace and order. But if you go on as you are doing now, the future of the
British Empire is questionable. Either you rejuvenate and strengthen it in
the Mediterranean or you will lose it once and for all.

"No one in London wants war," Eden insisted.

"We want it even less," Purić said tartly. "But does anyone in London believe that with these words the empire that holds half the world
can be preserved?" An agreement with France would enable England
to dictate peace terms to Mussolini, Purić reiterated. "To be successful, we must be determined, be ready for everything and even risk
war," he went on. "There is no need to fear Germany. After all,
the most Germany could take would be Austria, and someday it will
take that anyway."

Eden replied that he was not worried about Germany. He was
convinced, he said, that Germany would always prefer friendship

with England to friendship with Italy.[57] "England is slow," he said, "but she always wakes up in time."

Purić would have none of this. "It is more difficult to carry out a decision now than it was in the nineteenth century," he said. "Now there is need for speed. If England," he concluded, "can afford to be indecisive for a relatively long time, other countries, even against their will, will find themselves forced to form combinations, make alliances and reach agreements without England, and if need be even against England."

Their conversation had lasted an hour and a half. Eden thanked Purić for his sincerity and frankness, but could tell him nothing, could promise him nothing, could undertake no obligations for future action. He must think much about all this, he said, and talk with many people in London as well as with the dominions.

In his analysis of the conversation, Purić wrote Stojadinović that he believed "certain circles in London have given up... and liquidated the agreement with France. Preliminary conversations with Germany have begun. France might remain alone or with Italy, which is even worse than alone." The English, he pointed out, "are confused on the one hand by a new government in France and on the other by Austen Chamberlain's discovery that Germany remains the principal danger. Because of this, there is need to mediate for Britain between France and Italy," Purić concluded.[58]

Faced with an England ambivalent toward Italy, a France eager

[57] Heeren told Prince Paul that "Hitler would like to go with England, but if that is impossible, he will march with Italy. In this there is no sentimentality but *realpolitik*." It was Prince Paul's opinion that the Germans were strengthening their ties with Rome. Minute of conversation between Prince Paul and Heeren, February 27, 1936. (JBH)

[58] Purić to Stojadinović, May 15, 1936. (JBH) During a visit to Yugoslavia in 1936, R. W. Seton-Watson, British historian and long a friend of the Yugoslavs, told Miša Trifunović, an anti-Stojadinović politician, that he was "almost" an official representative of the British foreign office. In his opinion, England's principal aim was "to clear up" things with Italy. Toward that end, England had an arrangement with France and was bringing Germany into the "combination." England would compromise on many issues with Germany, he said, because it had a plan for a common front with Germany against Italy. This plan was to be implemented within six months, he told Trifunović, and England needed a strong Yugoslavia in the "combination." Prerad Preradović to Minister of Court Antić, October 17, 1936. (JBH)

for Italy's friendship, Yugoslav foreign policy slowly shifted from its long-time position in the French security system to the neutrality assumed two years before by Poland and later by Belgium.

As a defense against Hungary the Little Entente was a useful instrument of Yugoslav foreign policy. But it was useless against Italy, the greater threat. The problem was to negotiate with Italy in such a way as to isolate Hungary. Yugoslavia's evolving relationship with Germany impelled the rejection of any appeals for aid from France or Czechoslovakia if Germany attacked either of them, or both.

For the same reason Yugoslavia valued its relationship with the Balkan Pact states, particularly Greece and Turkey, since they too sought to avoid any commitments to Czechoslovakia.

The question of meeting possible Italian aggression in the Balkans arose in the May, 1936, meeting of the permanent council of the Balkan Entente. Stojadinović reported that Premier Metaxas of Greece "made a very good impression. He is frank, like a soldier, and well disposed toward Yugoslavia." However friendly Metaxas might be, Greece could not accept any obligations directed against Italy unless Yugoslavia had England's support. Without that, Greece remained sympathetic but neutral. The Yugoslav delegation had no quarrel with this position but asked the Greeks for their definition of neutrality—in writing. They complied, leaving Stojadinović with the impression that they feared Italy a great deal and were "heart and soul against her." [59]

The communiqué released after the meeting reemphasized the Greek approach to the Balkan Pact as interpreted by the protocol. [60]

The meeting of the permanent council of the Little Entente followed close on that of the Balkan Entente. Before the meeting Eduard Beneš, Czechoslovakia's president and chief delegate, submitted four proposals: for common national holidays, regular meetings of heads

---

[59] Stojadinović to Prince Paul, May 11, 1936. (JBH) The Greek reply to Yugoslavia's request appears in Papagos, *Battle of Greece, 1940–1941*, pp. 37-38.

[60] According to one observer of the meeting, the states of the Balkan Entente realized after Ethiopia that the small powers could no longer depend either on the League of Nations or on a great power for protection. The meeting reaffirmed the Greek position that the Balkan Entente states had to defend each other only if Bulgaria went to war against any of them. They did not regard Albania, Italy's bastion in the Balkans, as a Balkan state. G.E.R. Gedye in the New York *Times*, June 6, 1936.

of states, common efforts toward rearmament, and a unified army command. As to the first, Stojadinović believed an increase in the number of holidays would only reduce their importance; the best thing to do, he suggested, was "to limit ourselves to special lectures in the schools about the allies on such days." In principle, Stojadinović believed regular meetings of chiefs of state were of value, but he recommended that the time and place of the meetings not be set in advance. He was more enthusiastic over Beneš's armament proposal. For example, he foresaw that Yugoslavia could ask Rumania to place at its disposal sixteen million kilograms of aircraft gasoline and nine million kilograms of automobile gasoline. Yugoslavia would deliver copper and iron to Czechoslovakia, which in turn would deliver war material to Rumania in payment for the gasoline delivered to Yugoslavia. Stojadinović also suggested that Rumania and Yugoslavia work out a bilateral treaty on the delivery of Rumanian gasoline to Yugoslavia or on the exploitation of a Rumanian oil well. As to Beneš's proposal of a unified command, Stojadinović agreed with it in principle but thought "nothing concrete should be fixed." Instead, he believed they should make an agreement on a unified command only when they knew the location of the principal theater of war and then they could decide whom to appoint.[61]

The communiqué from the meeting summarized international developments since 1919 appealed for international understanding and peaceful collaboration, and asserted that the allies would take measures in common to defend their "national patrimony."[62]

Meanwhile, Prince Paul had traveled to Bucharest for a meeting of the heads of the Little Entente countries. He did so at the urging of Stojadinović, who stressed that the trip would "be a manifestation which can be useful, especially at a time when Italy is holding her head too high. It will be good for the world to see that Yugoslavia is not alone."[63]

The permanent council of the Little Entente met again in Bratislava in September. Marked difference of opinion and outlook—between Czechoslovakia on the one hand, Rumania and Yugoslavia on the other—appeared almost at once. The new Yugoslav policy of doing

[61] Stojadinović to Prince Paul, June 5, 1936. (JBH)
[62] DIA (1936), pp. 349-51.
[63] Stojadinović to Prince Paul, May 20, 1936. (JBH)

everything to avoid complications with Italy also became evident to all. Stojadinović was heeding the advice of the Yugoslav general staff.[64]

The dissension at Bratislava arose out of Beneš's efforts to convert the Little Entente system into an alliance for mutual defense against attack from any quarter. Developments in Germany had alarmed the Czechs, who wanted help from the Yugoslavs and the Rumanians in case of a German attack. The Rumanians refused to help anybody —neither Czechoslovakia in case of a Nazi invasion nor Yugoslavia in case of an attack by Italy. There were further differences between the Czechs on the one hand and the Rumanians and Yugoslavs on the other concerning the possibility in Austria of a Habsburg restoration. The Czechs preferred a restoration to an *Anschluss*. The Rumanians and the Yugoslavs were reconciled to the inevitability of an *Anschluss* but bitterly opposed the return of the Habsburgs.

The three states also argued about their policies toward the Soviet Union. The Czechs had a treaty with the Soviet Union. The Yugoslavs were unalterably opposed to recognizing the Russians. And although the Rumanians once had liked the idea of an alliance with Russia along the lines of the Franco-Soviet treaty, they now strongly opposed it.[65]

The communiqué from this meeting indicated another departure in the outlook and procedures of the Little Entente. Heretofore the statute of the Little Entente forbade any member from entering into political treaty relations with a non-Entente state except with the consent of the other Entente states. In 1935, Czechoslovakia signed a pact with the Soviet Union, apparently without consulting Yugoslavia and Rumania. The communiqué indicated that the Entente, this precedent at hand, had approved the principle of treaties between

[64] In May, 1936, Stojadinović told Polish Foreign Minister Beck that although the tensions between Italy and Yugoslavia were being ameliorated, the fundamental problem remained. Germany was a threat to Yugoslavia, although not so direct nor so menacing a threat as Italy. Yugoslavia would not go to war in case of an *Anschluss*. Stojadinović made no attempt to hide from Beck his aversion to Beneš's anti-German policies. The Little Entente was not only a traditional alliance system for Yugoslavia but, under certain circumstances, a very advantageous one. On the other hand, Stojadinović told Beck he could not envision the Serbs rescuing the Czechs from an attack by Hungary. They would end up "chasing the Hungarians into the Carpathians." Beck, *Dernier Rapport*, p. 120.

[65] *FRUS*, I (1936), 369.

bordering states as well as regional agreements.[66] In everyday language, this meant the Little Entente accepted the precedent set by the Czech treaty. Moreover, the Yugoslavs could now seek an accord with the Italians, the Germans, or even the Hungarians without violating the letter of the Little Entente agreements.

Here, with the Bratislava meeting, began the disintegration of the Little Entente. No longer was there the focus of a common defense, of a common interest. What was now common to all was the drive for national security, each in its own way. And in its own way the Bratislava meeting of the Little Entente reflected the fate of the League after the eruptions in Ethiopia and the Rhineland.

For years France had consistently refused Yugoslavia's request for a treaty of mutual assistance, on the grounds that it would bar a reconciliation with Italy.

In June, 1936, Rumanian Foreign Minister Titulescu suggested that France review Barthou's 1934 plan for a pact of mutual assistance with Germany and the Little Entente. It is doubtful if the Germans would have accepted it, but they were never offered the opportunity. France rejected the idea for the same reason it had given Yugoslavia.

A month later, during the session of the League council, the Little Entente states raised the question once more. The Yugoslav representative pointed out the overriding feature of the plan—it would be more advantageous to France and Czechoslovakia than to Yugoslavia. The French did not reply until October and once again their answer was no.[67]

But in November—two months after the Bratislava meeting—the French had a change of heart and admitted that the Czechs were responsible in part for this reversal of policy. In any event, on November 2d and 13th the French delivered two *démarches* to the Yugoslav government. The core of the notes concerned "the manner in which the solidarity between France and the Little Entente could be reaffirmed and defined." The French government offered to enter into pacts of mutual assistance with Yugoslavia, Rumania, and Czechoslovakia—provided that the governments of those countries would expand their obligations for common defense, now limited to

[66] *DIA* (1936), pp. 352-53.

[67] Robert Dell, *Geneva Racket* (London: Robert Hale, Ltd., 1941), pp. 253-54.

defense against Hungary and Bulgaria, in a pact providing for mutual assistance against attack from any quarter. Such a treaty, the French assured the Yugoslavs, would contain only a general reference to existing pacts between France and each of the states of the Little Entente. Therefore there was no reason for Belgrade to fear that a "thorn would be placed in the side of any state."[68]

Now it was the Yugoslavs who refused to enter what Stojadinović termed the "Paris-Moscow bloc." Turning down the French proposal, he stressed to Prince Paul that both Sir Ronald Campbell and Heeren approved Yugoslavia's avoidance of "the French embrace."[69] In a more polite form he explained to Delbos that while his country was unable to accept such a pact at that time, the government would take the matter under advisement. He pointed out that Yugoslavia had no desire to disturb its present relations with Germany and Italy.

Nevertheless, the French persisted. Although their conversations with the Yugoslavs were supposed to be secret, the facts were soon known and quickly spread by the more gossipy members of the diplomatic corps in Paris. The Poles told the Americans that the Rumanians had told them they would not accept the French offer. In rejecting the proposal the Rumanians had put the onus of their refusal on the Yugoslavs; although they themselves were ready to accept the proposal, they were certain the Yugoslavs would reject it.[70] The Yugoslavs indeed had other plans, plans for obtaining the answer to their big political question: What kind of protection against Italy could they find?

During these months that the French were urging the Yugoslavs to sign a treaty of mutual support, the Italians were also wooing them. With the signing of an economic and financial agreement in September, the stage had been set for an Italo-Yugoslav *rapprochement*. The Germans too had been active in pushing Italy into a pro-Yugoslav policy.[71] An agreement with Yugoslavia, Hitler told Ciano, would accomplish two ends: it would prove of inestimable propaganda value against communism and would lure the Yugoslavs from British

[68] French legation, Belgrade, to the Yugoslav ministry of foreign affairs, January 18, 1937. (JBH)
[69] Stojadinović to Prince Paul, November 11, 1936. (JBH)
[70] *FRUS,* I (1936), 383 and 389.
[71] Ciano, *L'Europa,* p. 90.

influence. Mussolini responded to Hitler's recommendations with a speech in Milan on November 1st. There he referred to a speech he had made two years earlier in which he had held out "the possibility that cordial friendly relations . . . could be established" between Italy and Yugoslavia. Now, he added, new conditions of a political and economic character made it possible "to place on a new basis of concrete friendship the relations between the two countries."[72]

The Yugoslav reaction was direct. Prince Paul told the Italian minister, Indelli, that his feelings, which coincided with his political conviction, had never varied. He had years ago given proof of his good will.

Unfortunately, Italian policy of late and the tragic events of October have sown a great distrust in our people. Above all, there is need to inspire confidence and to prove that Italy does not wish to undermine the foundations of the state by terrorism or other illegal means. Will Mussolini be sufficiently wise as to realize this and admit it? Is it in Italy's interest to have a strong Hungary pushing to the Adriatic? A Hungary which sooner or later will go with Germany, as it always has in the past? Or is it better for Italy to maintain a policy of friendship with its eastern neighbor which is complementary to Italy from an economic point of view? Especially since both countries see the same danger on the horizon?

The negotiations between Mussolini and the late King Alexander should serve as a basis for an agreement. Perhaps the fact that they negotiated behind the backs of their ministers of foreign affairs accounts for their failure. The Yugoslav drive is toward the Aegean, but we do not have the least desire for Salonika. On the contrary. The possession of this port would not enrich us in any way.[73]

Were the French aware that the Italians were cracking their treaty system? Certainly by mid-December they were beginning to recognize that Yugoslavia would never accept any proposals for mutual assistance.

By January, 1937, the French were certain of it. Stojadinović had rejected the mutual assistance pact. He wrote Purić that Yugoslavia's rejection of the pact did not sit well with the French. Nevertheless, they should understand that:

We must not provoke either the Germans or the Italians. After the signing

[72] DIA (1936), p. 345.
[73] Undated minute of conversation between Prince Paul and Indelli. (JBH)

of the Anglo-Italian declaration in Rome,[74] and the improvement of Franco-Italian relations, it is probable that the French government will be less insistent about the pact. It must be clear to every Frenchman that the Czechoslovak guarantee is less interesting to us than Italy's, especially now that we have England's. And without any obligation on our part.[75]

Stojadinović cautioned Purić against the idea that relations with France were deteriorating, and instructed him to tell French Premier Léon Blum that Italy, with whom the Yugoslavs had in the past experienced so many difficulties, had "lately begun to make overtures toward us," and to cite Mussolini's Milan speech as evidence. The Italians, Stojadinović continued, wanted to "liquidate" all controversial questions.

We will carefully examine whether or not they really wish to liquidate these questions in order to create a better atmosphere. We are now in the process of examining the possibility of creating a new atmosphere in the Adriatic.

Stojadinović asked Purić to pass this information on to Blum to "inform him about the principal question in our foreign policy and to obtain his opinion of Italy's new attitude toward us." Blum was to consider the information as most secret. Only later on and if necessary, said Stojadinović, "will we inform him officially, along with the Quai d'Orsay."[76]

Yugoslav foreign policy under the regency did not markedly shift from the course set by King Alexander. Its goals were not altered. To achieve stability and peace at home the Yugoslavs would have to

---

[74] The Anglo-Italian Agreement (the Gentlemen's Agreement) of January 2, 1937, guaranteed the *status quo* in the Mediterranean.

[75] Stojadinović to Purić, January 10, 1937. (JBH)

[76] Stojadinović to Purić, January 10, 1937. (JBH) In a conversation with William Bullitt, the American ambassador, Purić likened the French proposals to an experimental serum and the Little Entente to the rabbit into which France would inject the serum. He thought the Quai d'Orsay should make a mutual assistance pact with England, not experiment on her friends. Germany and Italy were certain to ask the aim of the pact. The answer was obvious. It was Yugoslavia's firm policy to avoid any situation which could give rise to conflict, Purić told Bullitt. His country refused to enter any treaty system that bound Czechoslovakia and France to the Soviet Union. As Slavs, the Serbs got along well with the Russians, but they were determined to have nothing to do with the Bolshevik government, Purić emphasized. *FRUS*, I (1937), 69-71.

achieve stability and peace in international relations. This political equation could be solved only by a settlement with Italy.

It was Italy that disturbed the domestic tranquillity of Yugoslavia. Italy, the major enemy power, touched upon and reached into Yugoslavia from every point of the compass: from the north through Austria and Hungary, where Italian propaganda infected dissident Slovenes and Croats; from the east, where Italy supported those Bulgarians who dreamed of revenging the defeats of the second Balkan war and the world war by retaking Yugoslav Macedonia; from Albania in the south, where Italy the protectress could take but one step and be across the Yugoslav threshold; and from the west, where Italian enclaves penetrated the Yugoslav coast, and only a hundred miles beyond lay Italy itself.

To eliminate the Italian menace the Yugoslavs had always had the following choices: they could go to war with Italy (as they would have done if Italian troops had crossed the Brenner into Austria to "maintain order" against local Nazis following the murder of Austrian Chancellor Dollfuss); they could continue to seek an understanding with Italy; they could seek the support of a strong power now outside their present alliance system; and they could limit themselves to their present alliance system.

The first of these choices was out of the question from the beginning because Yugoslavia had no desire to be branded an aggressor by the League of Nations; also, the other members of the Little Entente were not bound to come to Yugoslavia's aid in case of war with Italy. King Alexander had followed the second course and had sought an agreement with Italy. Simultaneously he had made overtures to Germany as a balance against Italy. Now, near the end of 1936, the Yugoslav government saw no one to turn to.

France, the preponderant European power, seemed to be losing its vigor. Whether or not this was the case, France had never firmly supported Yugoslavia against Italy because it needed Italy to limit German ambitions. London too flirted with its onetime ally, Rome, but actually yearned for marriage with Berlin. Thus it seemed to Yugoslavia that it could easily be isolated from the mainstream of European affairs and that its position as an independent power could be made increasingly precarious.

The experience of the last two years had dissipated still another illusion for the Yugoslavs. From the time of the assassination of King Alexander to the German remilitarization of the Rhineland the great powers had failed the lesser states and the principle of collective security. The small states had discovered that the League of Nations was only a forum, not a supernational body with the will and the power to act independently of the great powers.

In early 1938, Prime Minister Neville Chamberlain described the League as a sham and concluded that the small nations should not delude themselves into thinking it could protect them from aggression.[77]

The Yugoslav government had come to that conclusion two years earlier. Logically, the next step was to strike out independently in international affairs, to make no new commitments to any state or alliance system until a settlement with Italy could be reached. Even then, no commitments could be made that might jeopardize that agreement.

---

[77] *Hansard,* CCCXXXII (February 22, 1938), cols. 226-27.

III

THE ACCORDS
OF NEUTRALITY

"French political and newspaper circles are not used to independent action by our state on questions of foreign policy," wrote Premier Stojadinović to the Yugoslav minister in France, Božidar Purić, on March 16, 1937. By then, Yugoslavia and Italy were well into negotiations for a pact of friendship.

Stojadinović's acid comment on French criticism of his policy toward Italy seemed harsh words for an ally. But harsher phrases were still to come. Stojadinović saw French policy as vacillating and weak, and he felt compelled to find a new way for Yugoslav foreign policy, a way unencumbered by restrictive alliances.

"After all," he observed, "today the Kingdom of Yugoslavia means more than the prewar Serbia."[1]

By March, 1937, the European democracies were in full diplomatic retreat. The small powers had assessed their alliances, and, as in Yugoslavia's case, had found them wanting. A year before, Hitler had marched into the Rhineland. To this challenge Britain had responded with nothing more vigorous than Stanley Baldwin's plea for friendship between France and Germany. Although France had lost no time in protesting Hitler's violation of the Versailles and Locarno treaties, Pierre Laval had actively hampered efforts by the League of Nations to halt Italy's aggression against Abyssinia.

Britain, its imperial interests threatened when Mussolini successfully invaded Ethiopia, had sought security in the Mediterranean by means of a pact with Italy, the Gentleman's Agreement of January, 1937. To the small powers of Europe, the pact seemed to climax the series of diplomatic retreats that had begun almost a year before

[1] Stojadinović to Purić, March 15, 1937. (JBH)

when the great powers permitted Hitler his unimpeded march into the Rhineland.

To Yugoslavia, Britain's policy toward Italy pointed the way. Just as Britain needed security in the Mediterranean and sought it in friendship with Italy, Yugoslavia needed security in the Adriatic and on its Albanian border and would seek it in a similar pact with Italy. To Stojadinović, this course seemed to offer his country more protection than that deriving from Yugoslavia's long-time position in the fragile French security system.

But to France, independent action by Yugoslavia was heretical. And to Dr. Eduard Beneš, president of Czechoslovakia, Yugoslavia's new policy augured the disruption of the Little Entente. To him, he disclosed later, it meant that Prince Paul, chief regent of Yugoslavia, and Mussolini were conspiring to destroy central Europe.[2]

The signing in late September, 1936, of an economic and commercial agreement between Italy and Yugoslavia gave Stojadinović his first opportunity to speak out in favor of "the development of relations between Italy and Yugoslavia" and to look forward to "a new period of collaboration."[3]

A few weeks later, in a speech at Milan, Mussolini took friendly note of this gesture.

His speech had repercussions. Stojadinović reported to Prince Paul that Sir Ronald Campbell, Britain's minister to Yugoslavia, became "a bit excited because of Mussolini's cordiality toward us. I soothed him and told him not to worry." Viktor von Heeren, Berlin's minister in Belgrade, told Stojadinović that the Germans "really believe in the sincerity of Mussolini's offers" to Yugoslavia, and urged him "not to reject this offer lightly." Foreign Minister Ciano had assured the Germans "that Italy has an absolutely honorable and sincere intention of improving her relations with Yugoslavia."[4]

Both Ciano and Germany's Neurath spoke only of Yugoslavia, Heeren told Stojadinović, and their governments desired nothing but the best of relations with Yugoslavia. Heeren's own attitude was unusually friendly and "more than ordinarily well disposed," Stojadinović noted.

[2] Beneš, *Memoirs*, p. 31.
[3] Ciano, *L'Europa*, p. 113.
[4] Stojadinović to Prince Paul, November 11, 1936. (JBH)

In short, he reported to Prince Paul, both Germany and Italy wanted an agreement.[5]

Sometime in December Ciano approached Jovan Dučić, the Yugoslav minister in Rome, to propose a meeting with Stojadinović.[6] The Yugoslav answer was "written in a great many nice words," Stojadinović wrote Prince Paul. So far as a meeting with Ciano was concerned, he reported, "I have said that the best thing is first to prepare the terrain, clear up all the controversial questions, and then have the meeting at the end." Ciano "gave an enthusiastic reply to our minister. They are willing to go along with us to a complete agreement, and even further..." The Italians were willing to clear up all the controversial questions at once. They proposed that the Yugoslavs send four delegates—two to negotiate on economic matters and two on political matters.[7]

Stojadinović suggested Rome as the meeting place and, Ciano noted, urged that both parties maintain the "utmost reserve."[8]

By the end of 1936, Ciano received further word from Dučić: Yugoslavia would be represented by Milivoje Pilja, a high official of the ministry of commerce, who would conduct negotiations concerning a new economic agreement, and by Dr. Ivan Subbotić, a seasoned diplomat, Yugoslavia's representative to the League of Nations and later minister to the Court of St. James's, who as minister plenipotentiary would speak for his country on political matters.[9]

Subbotić, summoned by Prince Paul from his post in Geneva, first made an unpublicized trip to Rome without Pilja to find out whether or not a viable agreement with the Italians was possible. Reluctant to go, Subbotić had insisted that he was not the man to undertake this delicate mission. After all, he had the reputation of being pro-League of Nations and was involved with the task of levying sanctions against Italy. But Prince Paul was persuasive. Subbotić had never been in direct conflict with the Italians, he pointed out, and since he had served with the south Balkan department of the Yugoslav foreign office he had the proper background.

[5] Stojadinović to Prince Paul, November 11, 1936. (JBH)
[6] Ciano, L'Europa, p. 114; the exact date is uncertain, but it is known that Ciano received the reply on December 18.
[7] Stojadinović to Prince Paul, December 24, 1936. (JBH)
[8] Ciano, L'Europa, p. 114.
[9] Ciano, L'Europa, p. 115. Subbotić is also spelled Soubbotitch.

Early in January Subbotić went to Italy, ostensibly for a skiing vacation. In Rome he twice met for long conversations with the men who were to represent Italy in the formal negotiations: Gino Buti, director-general of European and Mediterranean affairs, and Count Leonardo Vitetti,[10] director-general of general affairs, both of the ministry of foreign affairs. After a week in Rome Subbotić returned to Belgrade with a favorable report, and on January 14th went back to his post in Geneva. In late February Stojadinović recalled him to Belgrade to prepare for the formal negotiations.

The premier instructed him to show "intense interest and the wish to achieve results," but cautioned that

no concessions should be made simultaneously on all points of disagreement. Yielding should be linked with concessions made by the Italians on other points ... there are four fundamental questions so far as you are concerned: the pact, Albania, the terrorists and the minorities.[11]

Subbotić arrived in Rome the second time with an agenda of eight items: the political pact itself; agreements to be reached concerning Albania, the Ustaše terrorists living in Italy under Italian protection and on Italian subsidies, the Yugoslav minorities living under Italian rule, the Mahovljani (250 families resettled in Bosnia by the Austrians and regarded as Yugoslav nationals by Belgrade and as Italians by Rome), Italian optants in Dalmatia; clarification of the St. Margherita and Nettuno conventions; and resolution of the problem of compensation arising out of the agrarian reform in Dalmatia.

The negotiations were carried on, not at the foreign office in the Palazzo Chigi, but in an out-of-the-way wing of the ministry of the interior.

Subbotić did not meet Ciano until March 3, 1937. By then he had nothing but praise for the progress of the negotiations. He was certain, he told Ciano, that only positive values would be achieved when their pact was announced to the world. Particularly it would indicate that the "two nations are desirous of friendly relations and cooperation and seek to avoid hostility and litigation."[12]

---

[10] As if symbolizing the continuity of diplomats, Count Vitetti was, in 1958, Italy's permanent representative to the United Nations.

[11] Stojadinović to Subbotić, March 12, 1937. (JBH)

[12] Subbotić to Stojadinović, March 6, 1937. (JBH)

But the shadows of "hostility and litigation" hovered, Subbotić emphasized. Croatian terrorists—King Alexander's murderers—were living in Italy and plotting the disruption of the Yugoslav state. Subbotić pointed out that the Yugoslavs had even heard that the Ustaše leader, Ante Pavelić, was making stealthy trips abroad, unhindered by the Italians. He described to Ciano the sobering effect of this news. Stojadinović, he observed, was worried about the future of Italo-Yugoslav relations so long as the Italians took no steps toward controlling Ustaše agitation. It was only "that great faith in the need for friendship between the two countries ... that has prevented those in charge in Belgrade from leaving the path they have begun to follow."

Nevertheless, said Subbotić, his premier had confidence in Ciano. He assumed Ciano would forbid, categorically and unequivocally, further terrorist activity and freedom of movement. Such a step was necessary, the Yugoslav minister continued, "if you wish to place our common relations on a new basis." If the Yugoslav government insisted on the liquidation of the terrorists, it was not because the Yugoslav leaders feared further crimes against the country.

We are strong enough to wrestle with this band of criminals. And even if we ourselves were not strong enough for it, we could find countries who can hardly wait to help us. It is up to you, Count Ciano, and your government to take the initiative and put an end to this state of affairs. You must realize that if you wish to place our common relations on a new basis, then terrorist action must definitely cease ... and the whole world must know that it has ended.

Subbotić reported that he expounded his government's position "quietly, without anger and in a very friendly and serious tone." He said he would not attempt to appeal to Ciano's morality and decency but rather to his political sense. It was impossible for Yugoslavia and Italy to "create new relations" if there existed "even the smallest uncertainty on the future of the terrorists and if the news of Pavelić's comings and goings keeps appearing all the time." [13]

Ciano listened carefully but impatiently, fretfully. He responded, Subbotić noted, as if such news should never come to his attention

[13] Subbotić to Stojadinović, March 6, 1937. (JBH)

for it was all too unpleasant. Finally he interrupted the Yugoslav's complaints by a nervous gesture of his hands.

No, no... all this is untrue. Pure invention by perjured informers.... Tell Dr. Stojadinović that I myself, Count Ciano, have given you my word of honor that all the terrorists have been under police surveillance for months. Virtual prisoners....

It was untrue, he insisted, that Pavelić had been away. On the contrary, the Italian police had prevented him from all political activity.

He is furious. He keeps sending me messages blaming me for Italy's having abandoned the Croatian cause. I do not even answer him. I have no interest in him or his kind. I am fed up with them. They keep quarreling among themselves.... But I cannot deliver them to you. This is by no means a complex question. It is a minor matter.... We are strong enough for much greater things.

Subbotić was neither mollified nor easily turned from his task. Although, he conceded, Ciano's attitude was laudable, he suggested Italy give Yugoslavia "visible and tangible proof" of what the Italian government should do, such as ordering its police to collaborate with Yugoslav police in controlling Pavelić.

Ciano ignored this suggestion and asked only that Stojadinović have faith in him. As further proof of his motives, he reached for the telephone and called the chief of police:

Yes, Ciano speaking. How are things with the Croats? Are they quiet and under control? I don't care. Strengthen the guard.

Replacing the receiver, he turned to Subbotić and asked him to tell Stojadinović that

I personally and in your presence renewed the order. The police chief tells me Pavelić keeps on complaining all the time, while the others are quiet. Tell Mr. Stojadinović to have confidence in me. After all, I have denied all this before through Mr. Indelli.

If the Yugoslav premier lacked confidence in Ciano, he himself would not be in Rome, Subbotić replied reassuringly. But, he added, it was necessary for Ciano to demonstrate that this confidence was well placed not only, in this way, through me, tete-à-tete so to speak, but also in a way which could be used against those circles critical of a policy of close cooperation with Italy.

Would Ciano supply Subbotić with a message to that effect for his prime minister?

Ciano replied by urging Subbotić to report that Italy would "permit no terrorist activity, that Pavelić, like the others, is under the strictest surveillance." [14] Furthermore, Ciano promised, once political matters were settled, he would completely liquidate the terrorist organization; it would be, he emphasized, just a "matter of a few orders issued over a telephone." Adding that he would include a paragraph to that effect in the treaty, he repeated:

All the news about the terrorists' action is untrue. We want to cooperate with you and not to weaken you. I wish an alliance to materialize between us; if it is not possible immediately, then at least we must keep moving in that direction.

In his interview with Subbotić, Ciano revealed his anxieties, his concern over Italy's weakness and Germany's strength, his desire to see his country powerful, his carefully articulated realization that Italy had neither the substance to create power nor the ability to sustain it. He was fearful of the future—and of Germany.

I am a friend of Germany but—between us and confidentially—Germany is not only a dangerous adversary to her enemies but a difficult friend to her friends. It is not that I think we should organize ourselves against Germany, but still one should keep in mind that both our—your—position with respect to Germany will be improved if we are together. Our 42 million and your 15 million will mean more together than separately. Do not misunderstand me. I do not mean we should turn against Germany, but we should—between us—organize our collaboration with her.

Only a few months before, in the Axis Protocols, Mussolini had proclaimed his unity of faith with the Nazis. Little wonder that Subbotić listened with some astonishment to Ciano's candid avowals.

Ciano's attitude toward Germany was directly related to impending events in Austria. It was going to be just as impossible to prevent an

[14] Subbotić to Stojadinović, March 6, 1937. (JBH)

Anschluss as to restore the Habsburgs. That, he insisted to Subbotić, "must be kept in mind" as they discussed common problems.

He was particularly proud, he confided, of Italy's work in Spain.

Have you seen how well and elegantly we performed the Malaga operations?... Important things are underway in Spain and before long the game there will be won. That is how I work! When I decide to do something, I apply myself to it entirely and I succeed!

Subbotić prodded the fires of Ciano's ego. The Italian was, he agreed, "colossal." "Energy beamed" from him. Ciano responded to these observations by "smiling with satisfaction and admiring himself," and went on:

That is why Göring and I understand each other so well. We analyze a situation, think a bit, and within five minutes make our decision. And then we act.

Suddenly Ciano stopped speaking of himself and turned to the drafts of the texts. Did Subbotić, he asked, bring drafts with him? Subbotić said he had a draft on the question of Albania but did not have it with him. It seemed to him, he added, that the two of them agreed in principle that they were both for Albanian independence, would do nothing which could affect that independence, and would even collaborate to preserve it. Ciano completely agreed. To Subbotić's reminder that they had several other questions to discuss, he was indifferent to all but the political pact. He was unhappy with the Yugoslav draft. To him, it seemed "meager" and "pale." Subbotić, on the other hand, objected with equal vigor to parts of the Italian draft. Ciano shook off Subbotić's objections and referred the matter to his staff for arbitration. "If something gets stuck," he pointed out, "I personally will always be at your service. You can come to me whenever you wish."

Ciano then raised the question of military clauses. What he would like to see, he said, was a protocol in which they agreed not to arm against each other. Subbotić parried by asking if he meant naval rearmament. Ciano was specific:

No, not the naval one, but on land. That is, we will no longer build new fortifications on our borders.

Again Subbotić countered:

You wish that along the border there be created some sort of demilitarized zone in which no new fortifications will be built and existing ones destroyed?

Ciano had not expected this question. He really did not intend to go so far as that, he said:

It will be difficult to destroy existing ones. I did not mean that. The main thing is not to build new ones. We could not only build new roads and agree not to increase units already stationed on our common borders. Perhaps even decrease these units.

Since Subbotić was not prepared to talk on military matters, Ciano was willing to postpone discussion of them. He concluded their conference by accepting Stojadinović's invitation to visit Belgrade at the end of March.[15]

Within three days after his interview with Ciano, Subbotić and the Italians were able to draw up a joint working draft and to send to Stojadinović a comparative review of the original treaty drafts.

Subbotić raised serious objections to a number of clauses in the Italian draft.[16] For example, the preamble expressed the principle that respect for the *status quo* "relative to the national sovereignty of territories in the basin of the Adriatic Sea is an essential condition" of Italo-Yugoslav collaboration. To the Italians this meant that neither they nor the Yugoslavs would violate the integrity of Albania. Furthermore, said the Italians, this guarantee should appear not only in the pact itself but also in the separate agreement on Albania. Subbotić found all this unsatisfactory because the guarantee would cover the Italian occupation of Saseno, an island off the coast of Albania whose status was in question.

The Italians accepted his objection and countered with a formula identical to that of the Anglo-Italian Gentleman's Agreement. "Such

[15] Subbotić to Stojadinović, March 6, 1937. (JBH) Subbotić was under instructions to make Ciano "aware that the meeting of the Little Entente will begin on April 1st in Belgrade and that Mr. Beneš will arrive on April 5th. Do not make any tangible proposals . . . state the facts and leave it up to the Italians to choose a date for themselves." Stojadinović to Subbotić, March 12, 1937. (JBH)

[16] Subbotić to Stojadinović, March 6, 1937. (JBH)

a rendition," Subbotić reported, "would be acceptable only after a declaration on Albania has been agreed upon."

The Italians' aim of isolating Yugoslavia from the French security system was apparent in the second article of their draft. Subbotić "rejected energetically" their suggestion that the two states promise "not to enter into any understanding with third powers which might be directed against the security of one of them."

When the Italians insisted that Subbotić transmit the article to Belgrade, he did so, but with a strongly unfavorable recommendation.

I said I would transmit it to you. I not only refuse to recommend... it but I oppose it at any cost... even in the interest of our future friendship.

The text is dangerous and can only become a source of misunderstanding. The formula that "which could be directed against the security of the other...." is vague and arbitrary.

This phrase, he argued, would prohibit a customs union or a trade treaty with a third state. "If we persist, they will agree to delete this clause and will sign the treaty without it," he told Stojadinović. The Italians also demanded that the agreement be so written as to have "no connection whatsoever with any multilateral treaty and particularly with the pact of the League of Nations or even with the Kellogg-Briand Pact." The agreement must be purely bilateral. Behind this approach, Subbotić reasoned, "are concealed their dissatisfactions with the League of Nations, collective security and peculiar political conceptions."[17]

Stojadinović had felt the treaty should refer to the Kellogg Pact. "It would be beneficial because of British sensitivity," he observed, and without it "the treaty would have an entirely bilateral character, which is neither in harmony with our overall policy of collective security nor with our prior international obligations."[18] However, the Italians, who did not want an article in which they would reject war as an instrument of national policy, acceded to Yugoslavia's demand only after a sentence alluding to the Kellogg Pact was deleted.

Stojadinović thus supported Subbotić's contention that what the Italians wanted was "a purely bilateral treaty, a self-contained pact.

[17] Subbotić to Stojadinović, March 6, 1937. (JBH)
[18] Stojadinović to Subbotić, March 12, 1937. (JBH)

This is the point of view of the Germans and of those states which are opposed to the League of Nations."[19]

Even more disturbing to the Italians was an article introduced by the Yugoslavs that called for the two countries to agree "that nothing in the present treaty . . . be considered contrary or detrimental to the existing international obligations of the two states." For many hours the negotiators debated this issue. Buti and Vitetti rejected the Yugoslav recommendation, Subbotić reported,

because they cannot recognize all our previous international agreements as being above this treaty because, they claim, they do not know all of them. Tomorrow may show that we do have secret treaties with other states.

They asked Subbotić what his country expected to obtain with this clause.

I answered that we intended to make clear that this treaty should not be regarded as contrary to the pact of the League of Nations. We do not use this formula because of them. We realize they do not have good relations with the League of Nations. On the other hand, we do not want to offend the League.

They compromised by adding to Article VI the phrase "these obligations being public." To avoid a negative reaction, Subbotić reported that he was impressed by the Italians' eagerness to conclude the treaty, by their willingness to make a great many concessions, and by their concern that Germany was "drawing us too close to her," which seemed, he added, to "worry them much more than England's power of attraction."

The Ustaše ringleaders had taken refuge in Italy after the murder of King Alexander in October, 1934. Control of the regicides and the liquidation of their organization were high on the list of items for negotiation.

Subbotić had brought up the matter of the Ustaše during his January visit with Buti, who proposed that Indelli, the Italian minister in Belgrade, issue a statement emphasizing that

[19] Although the Yugoslavs did not succeed in placing the reference to the Kellogg Pact in the final accord, Stojadinović directly alluded to it and other multilateral agreements in his speech immediately following the signing of the Pact of Belgrade. *Corriere della Sera*, March 26, 1937.

whatever the outcome of the negotiations, the terrorist organization will be liquidated and a halt put to their activities in order that these individuals . . . can no longer exercise in any form whatsoever an activity detrimental to the state of Yugoslavia.[20]

A month later Ciano had not yet approved the statement for delivery. Up to March 6th the Yugoslavs had only Ciano's word that the terrorists were in no position to act. Buti, however, was optimistic. He proposed that the Yugoslav and Italian police establish contact in order to agree on a method of liquidating the Ustaše organization. In his opinion, Italy would neither extradite nor try them, but would permit certain Yugoslavs to return home provided the Belgrade government approved. With respect to other Yugoslavs, the Italians would decide "whether it is better to send them to the colonies or to keep them in Italy under surveillance."

Subbotić, however, insisted on having the names of the terrorists. He argued that even if the Italians regarded these dangerous criminals as mere political *émigrés* the delivery of the list of names would not represent an infraction of the right of asylum. On the contrary, it would be simply a matter of supplying information to the Yugoslav government.[21]

The melancholy fact remained that this proposal was conditional since it first had to have Ciano's approval and then Yugoslavia's. But so far, the only text Ciano had approved was that which ultimately became Article IV of the pact.[22]

Subbotić neither accepted nor rejected Buti's suggestion that there be police cooperation against subversive elements. Certainly the suggestion, he wrote Stojadinović, should not be accepted for the time being. It was all too possible that the Yugoslavs would receive "a sheet of paper containing a text behind which the Italians could hide," instead of the liquidation of the Ustaše organization that they sought. It was more important, he emphasized, that the Italians

[20] Subbotić to Stojadinović, March 6, 1937. (JBH)
[21] Subbotić to Stojadinović, March 6, 1937. (JBH)
[22] "The High Contracting Parties promise not to tolerate on their respective territories or assist in any way any activity directed against the territorial integrity or established order of the other Contracting Party or which is of such a nature as to be prejudicial to the friendly relations between the two states." This text, apart from minor editorial changes, was identical to that proposed by the Yugoslavs.

liquidate the terrorist organization and inform us by placing our police in contact with their police for the purpose of receiving that information. To go further would be to take upon ourselves the responsibility for the efficiency of this liquidation.

He sensed, nonetheless, that the Italians were "really linking the question of liquidation with the signing of the treaty."

It was not until March 11th that Ciano sent down his text on the means of handling the question of the terrorists. Subbotić received a note from Buti and Vitetti informing him that

His Excellency, the Minister of Foreign Affairs of Italy, is ready to dispatch to the Italian minister in Belgrade an instruction to make the following declaration to the Yugoslav minister of foreign affairs. The declaration will be in verbal form. His Excellency may use its first paragraph confidentially and discreetly; the remaining portion of this declaration, however, must remain absolutely secret:

I. In any case, and independently of the results of current negotiations, the existence of all organizations, as well as the activity of persons, directed against the territorial integrity and public order of the Yugoslav state, are now, and will be in the future, interdicted.

II. Pavelić, Kvaternik and other leaders will be interned.

III. It will be made impossible for these leaders, as well as any other persons, to develop any activities whatsoever, and the leaders will be prevented from having contact with other men and with foreign countries.

IV. A certain number of these men will be deported in small groups or individually as laborers to Italian colonies.

V. The Italian police will inform the Yugoslav police of the place(s) where the above-mentioned persons are interned or confined.

VI. The Italian police will inform the Yugoslav police of the names of those who wish to return to Yugoslavia.

VII. An officer of the Yugoslav police will be accepted to establish contact with the Italian police in connection with the above matter.[23]

[23] Eugen Kvaternik, who served Pavelić in 1941 as chief of Ustaše security forces, in 1955 accused Mussolini of maltreating the Croat separatists. He said that six weeks after the murder of Alexander, the Italians interned all the Ustaše but Pavelić on the island of Lipari. Pavelić they allowed to live in semi-confinement in Siena on an Italian subsidy of 5,000 lire a month. Kvaternik claims that when the representative of the Yugoslav police, Vladeta Miličević, arrived in Italy, Italian persecution of the Ustaše grew worse. Eugen Kvaternik, "Riječi i Činjenice" ('Words and Facts'), *Hrvatska Revija*, Buenos Aires, V (March, 1955), 56-59.

Later, during negotiations, the phrase "public order" was replaced by "established order" so as to cover crimes against individuals "who are representatives of the supreme order of the state." The Italians rejected Subbotić's phraseology "against the life of the sovereign and of the high representatives of the state" as too embarrassing.

The Yugoslavs were adamant. Subbotić demanded that the idea of interdicting activity against "public order" include the idea of crimes against "high personalities" as well. The Italians finally acceded and the three negotiators drafted the following note, subject to the approval of Ciano and Stojadinović:

At the moment of signing this agreement, the two ministers of foreign affairs will exchange the following declaration:

By the expression, "established order," used in Article 5 signed today, is to be understood all activity against the lives of the chiefs of the two states, members of the two royal families, leaders or members of the government as well as representatives of public authority.[24]

Later that evening (March 17) Ciano sent word to the negotiators that he accepted the note provided it was not to be a public declaration but a verbal statement. He proposed a change in the preamble:

At the moment of the signing of the treaty, the two ministers of foreign affairs will give the following verbal assurances, which are destined to remain secret . . .

Subbotić saw his opportunity to press for more concessions. He insisted that the statement prohibiting crimes against "high personalities" be made an annex to the treaty. The Italians were reluctant. Writing to Stojadinović, Subbotić pointed out: "They do not want this to be made public in order not to make it appear that they admit their guilt in the death of the late king."

So far as secrecy was concerned, Ciano agreed, if it were requested of him at the time of the signing of the pact, to permit release of the statement to a restricted group of "party leaders and friendly ambassadors," but not to the press.[25]

This procedure obtained.

---

[24] Subbotić to Stojadinović, March 17, 1937. (JBH)
[25] Subbotić to Stojadinović, March 17, 1937. (JBH)

In 1920 the Italo-Yugoslav Treaty of Rapallo had recognized Italian control of territories inhabited by a large number of Croats and Slovenes, variously estimated at between 450,000 and 600,000, who lived in the area known as the Julian March. Since Italy had signed no treaty with Yugoslavia guaranteeing the rights of the minority, the Fascist process of transforming Slavs into Italians, especially after 1928, had been a constant source of irritation to Yugoslav public opinion. In raising the question of the minorities, Stojadinović hoped to obtain a settlement that would create on the Yugoslav borders an "atmosphere of sincere friendship and complete confidence." The people in the borderzone, he wrote, must be satisfied "and given the minimum conditions for their cultural development."[26]

Stojadinović's instructions were adroitly drafted. He urged Subbotić to keep in mind the "high sensitivity" of the Fascist regime, "but," he emphasized, "do not withdraw our demands." He told Subbotić to point out to the Italians that "we do not wish to meddle in their internal affairs," that the settlement of the minority problem would be "a visible proof of improved relations between our two countries," and a trifling matter for a state with the "reputation of a great power and whose internal regime is sound." He wrote Subbotić:

We do not expect an international obligation, but only an internal act. An act made on their own initiative which would secure for our co-nationals who are Italian nationals the rights given the German minority in the Tyrol.[27]

Faced with the Yugoslav request, the Italians responded with their standard opening move in diplomatic chess. They offered the Yugoslav government a verbal declaration, to be delivered by Indelli on the day of the signing of the pact. The statement, they said, would assure the Yugoslavs that the Italian government would examine "with good will the requests made by Slovene or Serbo-Croat-speaking Italian citizens concerning private education and the performance of religious services in those languages."

This time Subbotić not only pressed for more concrete promises but made proposals himself. Assuring the Italians that his government had neither subversive nor irredentist intentions, he suggested that

[26] Stojadinović to Subbotić, March 12, 1937. (JBH)
[27] Stojadinović to Subbotić, March 12, 1937. (JBH)

keeping the minorities satisfied would strengthen the friendship between two states. Permitting the minority the privilege of publishing books and calendars in their own language, allowing them to inscribe their tombstones in the mother tongue, allowing them to import Yugoslav newspapers, and amnestying certain individuals would produce, Subbotić observed, "a fine echo and popularize the treaty among our minority as well as our people." [28]

This barrage of demands, interlarded with appeals to vanity, obtained from Ciano a promise to send a personal letter to Stojadinović, a promise fulfilled:

Mr. President: I have the pleasure to inform you that prior to my leaving Italy to visit you, my government, on my suggestion, issued instructions to the competent Italian authorities to examine with good will the requests of Italian subjects concerning private education in the Slovene and Serbo-Croat languages as well as performance of religious rites within the framework of existing laws. . . .

I may add that our authorities will consider the publication of books and of one or more newspapers and other cultural manifestations in the same languages.

In his report to Stojadinović, Subbotić pointed out that the phrase "other cultural manifestations" covered associations of minorities and that in their discussions the Italians had been quite explicit in stating that the scope of application of the letter would depend on the political relations between the two countries. [29]

Of Albania, Alexander of Yugoslavia had said, "I would not want it as a gift." [30]

He was willing to guarantee, "together with Italy, the integrity, the freedom and the independence of Albania in the broadest way Italy may wish." Willing to see for Albania the formula of neutrality designed for Belgium, Alexander felt certain Rumania and Czechoslovakia would join him. Even England, he noted, "has made me

[28] Subbotić to Stojadinović, March 21, 1937. (JBH) Both Stojadinović and his minister of the interior, Dr. Korošec, agreed to accept this proposal, "since nothing much better was possible." Memorandum from Stojadinović to Prince Paul, March 22, 1937. (JBH)

[29] Subbotić to Stojadinović, March 21, 1937. (JBH)

[30] Minute of conversation between King Alexander and Guido Malagola Cappi, May 24, 1931. (JBH)

understand, through her minister, that she would look upon our agreement with Italy with satisfaction." [31]

The Yugoslav regency had inherited the attitude toward Albania that had been expressed in 1932 by King Alexander. Five years later, in 1937, Subbotić told Ciano substantially the same thing: "We are both for Albanian independence; we will do nothing which could affect that independence and we will even collaborate to preserve that independence." [32] Ciano agreed. The statement reflected Stojadinović's preliminary instruction, later elaborated to insist on this formula until "it appears that negotiations will break down because of common support for Albanian independence." Merely to agree, wrote Stojadinović, that Albanian independence is a goal of the foreign policy of the two states is not precise enough. "Italy can always say that her Albanian policy is a defense of Albania against her Balkan neighbors," he pointed out. To sign such a tenuous agreement would mean that Yugoslavia gave approval to Italian policy in Albania. The Yugoslavs would be guaranteeing "an independence which in reality no longer exists," he said. [33] The declaration that would suit Yugoslavia's requirements, Stojadinović held, was one that yielded no approval of the Italian regime in Albania. On the contrary, it would permit a "realistic revision of the already existing situation."

The best he could hope for was a declaration that would "represent an open door, a new platform which would gradually lead to a partial revision of the present state of affairs." The declaration he wanted, while not excluding "all of the privileges the Italians have gained in the Adriatic," would at the same time provide the Yugoslav government "with an instrument it can use—at the proper political time—to remove all situations which might threaten our vital interests." A declaration of this kind would "foresee direct discussions for the removal of such situations, regardless of whether or not they existed prior to this declaration or arose after it. Italy could not refuse to hold these discussions without damaging the letter and the spirit of the agreed text."

[31] Minute of conversation between King Alexander and Guido Malagola Cappi, February 22, 1932. (JBH)

[32] Subbotić to Stojadinović, March 6, 1937. (JBH)

[33] Stojadinović to Subbotić, March 12, 1937. (JBH)

If it were not possible to conclude such an agreement, Stojadinović decided, then "it would be better to exclude this problem from our negotiations rather than compromise our future juridical position in the Albanian question."[34] With these instructions in mind, Subbotić proceeded further into the negotiations on Albania.

But as the conversations went on, he found the Italians reluctant to go beyond a statement of principles. He told them that the Albanian question was of capital importance to the Yugoslavs. A superficial solution would lead only to new misunderstanding. He referred to Ciano's earlier assertion that Italy sought a realistic long-term agreement with the Yugoslavs on this question. Subbotić then urged Buti and Vitetti to put this concretely, in a declaration and in deeds in Albania itself. He appealed to their sense of logic. Since they agreed with him in principle, he noted, certainly their position on Albania must clearly be adapted to that position. Pointing out to Buti and Vitetti how contradictory their position would otherwise be, he urged them to accept his version of the declaration, which called on both states to promise not to seek any special or exclusive political and economic advantage which might, directly or indirectly, compromise the independence of Albania. Should a situation arise "incompatible with these principles," the two states would "proceed in a most amicable spirit to a common examination of that situation and will concentrate on it to cause it to disappear without delay."[35]

The Italians flatly rejected the Yugoslav version. They offered instead their own in the form of two letters to be exchanged when the pact was signed. In the letters, identical in content, both governments would agree that the sovereignty and independence as well as the inviolability of the Albanian frontiers were "indispensable to the maintenance of peace, stability and security in the Adriatic basin" and that both would examine such "situations which could be in opposition to their interest in respect to the independence of Albania."[36] An amendment suggested by Subbotić merely paraphrased his earlier text. The Romans, proving themselves as wily as the man from Belgrade, rejected it. They argued that the paragraph was superfluous because the idea was already contained in the

---

[34] Stojadinović to Subbotić, March 12, 1937. (JBH)
[35] Subbotić to Stojadinović, March 11, 1937. (JBH)
[36] Subbotić to Stojadinović, March 11, 1937. (JBH)

agreement and was dangerous because it would provoke constant disagreement.

When Subbotić tried to obtain concessions on the declaration by raising the matter of placing one or two Yugoslav military instructors with the Albanian army, so that it "could be seen that the army is not subject to Italian influence alone," the Italians rejected the demand. They also refused to promise not to build, finance, or construct new fortifications without preliminary agreement with Yugoslavia. In a report to Stojadinović on March 17th, Subbotić said Buti argued that if the Italians acceded to this request, the Yugoslavs could then demand the withdrawal of the Italian bank in Albania, the various economic privileges now enjoyed by Italy, the Italian military instructors with the Albanian forces. No, Buti contended, the Yugoslav amendment was "too broad, not only in style but in ideas." The Italians saw their position in Albania "as one which would remain unchanged even after our agreement, since it subverts neither Albanian independence nor Yugoslav integrity," Subbotić reported.

He went to great lengths to explain to Buti that what concerned his country most was not Italy's economic interest in Albania as such but the probability that Italy might be in a position to create a military stronghold aimed at Yugoslavia. Subbotić reported to Stojadinović that:

They keep on saying that we must trust them, that everything depends on political relationships. I said we cannot recognize their exclusive right to defend Albanian independence.

They replied that the defense of Albania does not mean defense from Yugoslavia and Greece but from some other power—Great Britain.

In response to their argument, Subbotić was equally direct. He told the Italians that the Yugoslav amendment was not related to concessions and such minor matters. It was related more, he said, to the nature of principles and other important subjects. For example, the Italians could very well take over Albania's postal and telegraph services and railroads. Overnight they could appoint Italians as technical experts to all Albania's ministries. Was it not true, he asked, that the Italians "have instructors everywhere—save in the police force—and that the army is clothed in Italian uniforms?"[37]

[37] Subbotić to Stojadinović, March 11, 1937. (JBH)

But the Italians stood in Albania, and they would not be moved. On March 19th, Subbotić had a "lengthy argument" with Ciano. Ciano too completely rejected the Yugoslav version because it would bring up for discussion all the privileges Italy had already gained. Ciano proposed instead to establish a policy for the future.[38] Two days later Buti offered Subbotić a choice of three texts. The Yugoslavs accepted that version in which both contracting parties promised henceforth

not to seek any special or exclusive advantage of a political order or of an economic or political nature such as to compromise directly or indirectly the independence of Albania and ... to jointly proceed to a friendly examination of all situations which could arise and which would be incompatible with the intentions expressed above.[39]

The Yugoslav government accepted this because it avoided any written declaration on their part and related only to the future.[40]

The Italians were willing to settle the Mahovljani question by verbally declaring, either in Rome or through Minister Indelli in Belgrade, that:

The Yugoslav Government, having brought to the attention of the Italian Government the difficulties which arise from the determination of citizenship of certain inhabitants of Mahovljani and having expressed its desire that these difficulties be solved, the Government of Italy declares itself ready to take into consideration this wish of the Yugoslav Government in order to bring about a gradual and satisfactory elimination of the above-mentioned difficulties.

Buti interpreted this declaration as indicating that Italy was not really interested in the Mahovljani and would make no difficulties if Yugoslavia transferred them over a period of three years to exclusively Yugoslav citizenship. Italy would accept those who did not wish Yugoslav citizenship. Buti stipulated only that the Yugoslavs carry out the process without "gross and sensational intervention by the local authorities, the press or public opinion."[41] Stojadinović finally

---

[38] Subbotić to Stojadinović, March 19, 1937. (JBH)
[39] Subbotić to Stojadinović, March 21, 1937. (JBH)
[40] Stojadinović to Subbotić, March 22, 1937. (JBH)
[41] Subbotić to Stojadinović, March 11, 1937. (JBH)

accepted the Italian recommendation and the negotiators apparently postponed the minor questions.[42]

By March 22d the texts were complete. Ciano notified Stojadinović that he would arrive in Belgrade on the 25th.[43]

And so it was. Signatures were affixed as Ciano declared that the political and economic agreements meant "peace and security" between the two countries, and as Stojadinović agreed that they were "an instrument of peace between neighbors."[44] But each saw the accords as strategic measures in the defense of his own country and in the advancement of its interests.

Privately both men spoke frankly of their plans. The Yugoslav did not hesitate to reveal his criticism of French foreign policy, past, present, and future. Recalling Gamelin's conversations with the military staffs of the Little Entente two years earlier about possible operations against Germany and Hungary, he confided that henceforth there would be no further alliances of any kind between France and Yugoslavia. He was ready, he asserted, for a verbal clash with the French and was well prepared for their charge of selfishness. "The French always accuse anyone of selfishness who is not prepared to let himself be killed for them," he complained.

The two men wandered over many fields: Austria, Germany, the possibility of an agreement between Hungary and Yugoslavia, Rumania, Albania (about which Stojadinović said little) and England. Stojadinović said he set no store by the League of Nations and was proud of never having visited Geneva. It was only because of the pressure of public opinion that Yugoslavia belonged to the League, he disclosed.

[42] Stojadinović to Subbotić, March 22, 1937. (JBH)

[43] The plans called for Ciano to fly to Belgrade; after the ceremony of the signing of the pacts the Italian aircraft that had brought him was to leave, ostensibly to take the treaty to Rome for ratification, and then to return to Belgrade with the ratified paper. In reality the Italians brought the instruments of ratification along with them. The idea behind these aerodramatics was Ciano's desire to make a "sensation—fly in, fly out and confuse the whole world." Subbotić to Stojadinović, March 11, 1937. (JBH)

[44] Politika (Belgrade), March 26, 1937. Beneš's memoirs relate that he was given a "bashful invitation" to visit Belgrade only after the pact was signed. Beneš, Memoirs, p. 31. The Yugoslav documents tell another story. Belgrade was making arrangements as early as November, 1936, for Beneš to arrive in Yugoslavia on April 5, 1937. It was the date of his visit that determined the date of Ciano's arrival, not the other way around.

Ciano found his Yugoslav counterpart to be "a Fascist. If he is not one by virtue of an open declaration of party loyalty," Ciano wrote later, "he is certainly one by virtue of his conception of authority, of the state and of life." Ciano found Stojadinović's position in his country "preeminent," for Prince Paul had declared "unlimited confidence in him." Stojadinović already had the "marks of a dictator," Ciano noted.[45]

Ciano may have correctly read the personality of the Yugoslav prime minister. But in 1937, Stojadinović was a realist acting on behalf of his country. Cynical and tough-minded, with an awesome faith in himself and his luck, Stojadinović had a personality peculiarly his own. Nonetheless, his policy was subject to Prince Paul's approval, and in carrying out that policy he acted as Prince Paul's representative in furthering the security of Yugoslavia.

The balance sheet of negotiations shows that Italy conceded a great deal to Yugoslavia. In the political pact Italy promised to respect the territorial integrity of Yugoslavia and not to tolerate on Italian territory any activity against the existing Yugoslav order. Their agreement to remain neutral in case one of them became the object of "unprovoked aggression by one or more powers" was canceled out by Italy's recognition of Yugoslavia's existing international obligations as a member of the Little Entente, the Balkan Pact, and the League of Nations.

In the economic pact, which elaborated Article V of the political accord, Italy made further concessions. Italy would not only import more Yugoslav products, but would also treat Yugoslavia as a most favored nation in all commercial relations.[46]

While the secret note on the Ustaše implemented the article on the terrorists, and the Slav minorities living in Italy received some privileges, the Italian note on Albania would prove of value only at some future date. To Italy, Yugoslavia's acceptance of the note implied tacit recognition of Italy's "acquired position" in Albania; for Yugoslavia, acceptance of the note opened the door to a "realistic revision of the already existing situation."

Why did Italy concede so much to Yugoslavia?

[45] Ciano, L'Europa, pp. 151-62.
[46] For the texts of the political accord and the supplementary economic accord, see Appendix A.

Ciano had indicated one reason: he feared the rising power of Germany and sought a way to balance that power. He explained to Heeren, who later repeated the conversation to the Yugoslavs, that Italy's policy toward Yugoslavia was "dictated by necessity." Within three years, Ciano forecast, Britain's rearmament program would be completed and its weight would be felt. He told Heeren he was not like Suvich [47] who, with the eyes of a Triestino, could look only East. Ciano felt he faced larger problems. [48]

In his talks with Prince Paul, Ciano returned to his original theme. The Adriatic Sea and the minorities ought, he held, to bind the two countries together, not to separate them.

Germany is a dangerous enemy but a disagreeable friend. The *Anschluss* is inevitable, the Italo-Yugoslav union a necessity in our future relations with Germany. As for the rest, our pact should attract other countries into our orbit. An understanding with Hungary is desirable. When Vienna becomes the second German capital, Budapest should be ours. [49]

The "inevitability" of the *Anschluss* and the necessity of building a barrier against the German drive toward southeast Europe probably became a factor in Italy's foreign policy calculations after the murder of Austrian Chancellor Engelbert Dollfuss on July 25, 1934, by Austrian Nazis. It is not inconceivable that Ciano saw in the *Anschluss* a threat to Trieste and the littoral since both were once Austrian territories. Italy, weakened by the war in Spain, imperatively needed Yugoslavia by its side to resist a German drive to the Adriatic. [50]

What of Yugoslavia's motivations?

President Beneš's interpretation of Yugoslavia's motives arose from his belief that his policy "rightly diagnosed what was the matter in

[47] Fulvio Suvich, under-secretary of state for foreign affairs.

[48] Minute of conversation between Prince Paul and Heeren, December 13, 1936. (JBH)

[49] Minute of conversation between Prince Paul and Ciano, March 25, 1937. Ciano added that he hoped to reestablish ties with Japan and to use Japanese battleships in the Spanish war. He also told Prince Paul that the Grand Rabbi of New York [sic] had told Mussolini: "Who eats Jews, dies!" The Duce was so certain of the truth of this that he decided not to attack Jews as such but as Free Masons, Communists, etc. (JBH)

[50] In November, 1940, Hitler told Soviet Foreign Minister Molotov that after the war the former Austrian territories were to fall within the German sphere of influence. *NSR*, p. 237.

Europe." He was convinced that Prince Paul "wanted to join the Berlin-Rome Axis against the axis of France, the Popular Front and the Soviet Union." Hence he went to Belgrade because, he said, "world peace was at stake." [51] Beneš had not applied this standard of international morality so rigorously to himself five months earlier (November 13-14) when he told the Germans that his policy was favorable to the Reich. He told them then he had made it clear to France that his country would not join in "any preventive war against Germany" and that he was ready to sign a "nonaggression" or even a "comprehensive" treaty with Hitler's Germany.[52]

If world peace was the reason for Beneš's visit to Belgrade, his conversation with Prince Paul did not reflect this thinking. He failed both to sound the tocsin of alarm, to warn his allies of the coming dangers, or to make demands of any kind. Rather, he displayed more optimism than foresight when he told the Yugoslav quite frankly that he did "not believe in the German danger, German strength or German designs on Czechoslovakia. Hitler does not want the Sudeten Deutschen, who were always the most radical element in the late Habsburg monarchy."

Beneš also told the Yugoslavs that:

As for Germany, internal conditions are terrible. There are several factions. Neurath is getting stronger daily. Hitler is a puppet in the hands of the army, who will get rid of him as soon as they no longer need him. England's one desire is to make friends with Italy and form an anti-German bloc with that power and France.[53]

As to the mutual assistance pact proposed by France earlier in the year, Beneš thought it had quite a few good aspects but also many bad ones. He did not want more from the Yugoslavs than they could

[51] Beneš, *Memoirs*, pp. 30-33.
[52] Weinberg, "Secret Hitler-Beneš Negotiations in 1936-1937," *Journal of Central European Affairs*, 28 (January, 1960), 366-74.
[53] Minute of conversation between Prince Paul and Beneš, April 6, 1937. (JBH) Apparently Beneš misread the signs, for Hitler dismissed Neurath as foreign minister ten months later. Beneš told the noted Yugoslav historian, Ćorović, that Germany's anti-Czech activity was more a bluff than a real expression of power and that he personally was very optimistic about the future. In case of trouble Czechoslovakia was ready, and should there be serious trouble he had two powerful allies: France and the Soviet Union. Ćorović to Yugoslav minister of education, March 23, 1937. (JBH) See also, *FRUS*, I (1936), 246-47 and 328-29.

give, but at the very minimum he desired a "clear situation."[54]

More susceptible of validation than Beneš's "conspiracy" theory is the hypothesis that the new Yugoslav policy of neutrality was an expression of national interest. The external policy of Yugoslavia by the mid-1930s was wavering between two poles. Politically, it showed an intellectual attachment to the west—to the traditions of France and England. Economically, however, its policy was geared to the attractions of Germany and Italy.

In all, Ciano saw the pact as opening new political opportunities for Italy. "Italy," he wrote, "will be able, to its advantage, to take France's place with Yugoslavia."

Ciano was pleased with Italy's new relationship with Yugoslavia and was glad to see that French influence had greatly diminished in the Balkans and especially in the Little Entente. The entente, he noted, was "no longer a unit, in fact it was broken." Germany had been of great help during the negotiations and Italy's "new status with Yugoslavia was in full accord with Germany's wishes," Ciano told the American ambassador to Italy.[55]

The French, taken by surprise, put on a good face at the announcement of the Belgrade Pact. Léger believed it entirely a matter of prestige for Italy; Mussolini could now appear before his people and the world with a diplomatic victory. Nonetheless, the Yugoslavs were still members of the League, and the French and Little Entente pacts were still in effect.[56] Although the French claimed surprise, the Yugoslavs had told them, a week before Ciano's arrival in Belgrade, that negotiations with the Italians had been going on for months. When the French suddenly learned that the Italians had acquiesced to Yugoslavia's stipulations, they drew two conclusions: either the pact was an effort to restore Italy's prestige after its

[54] Stojadinović to Prince Paul, April 5, 1937. (JBH) See also, FRUS, I (1937), 66-68.

[55] FRUS, I (1937), 71.

[56] The French should not have been surprised. Purić had told French Foreign Minister Delbos the previous November that there was a possibility of improving Yugoslavia's relationship with Italy. Delbos, however, said he thought there was no need for Yugoslavia to hurry its conversations with Italy. Purić to Minister of Court Antić, November 27, 1936. (JBH) FRUS, I (1937), 267.

defeats in Spain or it was a means of permitting further Italian action on a large scale in the adventure in Spain.[57]

During the last months of 1937, Stojadinović moved methodically through Europe's diplomatic labyrinth. In Paris he reaffirmed the Franco-Yugoslav Pact of 1927. In London he talked with Chamberlain and Eden. He finally arrived in Rome on December 6th. Ultimately he would go to Berlin.

The trip to Rome was a courtesy call, reciprocating Ciano's visit to Belgrade in March. Mussolini and Ciano, who planned elaborate hospitality for Stojadinović, paid him the special courtesy of meeting him at the railroad station, thus setting him off from the usual run of official visitors. Bearing in mind the well-founded rumor that their guest liked nothing better than the company of pretty women, the Italians arranged a series of balls and official receptions, to which they summoned the beauties of Roman society.

Ciano went to such pains only because he believed the Belgrade Pact fundamental to Italian policy. The new alliance allowed Italy to view with calm the possibility of an *Anschluss*. But, political motivations aside, Ciano genuinely liked Stojadinović. He found him "strong, sanguine, with a resounding laugh and a vigorous handshake. He is a man who inspires confidence," Ciano wrote.[58]

In their conversations Stojadinović told Mussolini that he was firmly determined to avoid an agreement with the French on the matter of a European bloc. He would not recognize the Soviet Union. He would not assume further obligations to aid Czechoslovakia. He would continue to seek an understanding with Hungary. He was not at all sympathetic to the *Anschluss*. He planned to organize the young people of his party on the Italian model, but for reasons of domestic policy it was dangerous to issue a public statement on that at that time.[59]

[57] *FRUS*, I (1937), 259-60. Not unexpectedly, the French press vigorously attacked Yugoslavia. Delbos explained to Prince Paul that the reaction was akin to that of a jealous woman. But the accord was "made at a moment when Mussolini needed the success of prestige over France." To Prince Paul's comment that he had to look after his country's interests, Delbos grudgingly conceded that the moment to negotiate was well chosen. "A week later, Mussolini would not have given you so much," he said. Minute of conversation between Prince Paul and Delbos, May 14, 1937. (JBH)

[58] Ciano, *Ciano's Diary, 1937-1938*, p. 41

[59] *DGFP*, D, V, Doc. 153.

To Ciano, he reiterated his intention of rejecting the French mutual assistance pact because "in practice it would be impossible to fulfill and would produce unbelievable absurdities and contradictions." He distrusted the French Popular Front. He believed the French army would one day "face a profound material and psychological crisis." He agreed with the Duce's decision to leave the League and would use that event to write a commentary on the subject "to the effect that with the departure of Italy from Geneva, the League of Nations ceases to have any function or power." [60]

Their conversations over, Ciano escorted Stojadinović around the showplaces of fascist Italy and watched Yugoslavia's prime minister take more and more of a liking to the ideas of a dictatorship. Stojadinović adopted the Roman salute and told Ciano he was going back to Belgrade to build up his party on "the basis of a dictatorship." He approved Mussolini's formula of force and consent. King Alexander had had only force, he observed; he would make his dictatorship popular as well. [61]

Stojadinović left Italy just in time to greet Delbos, arriving in Belgrade from Bucharest. The French foreign minister now understood the course of Yugoslav foreign policy. He referred to the mutual assistance pact by giving his impression that the Rumanians "were fundamentally prepared to conclude a pact but felt that they were prevented by the Yugoslav refusal; independent action on the part of Rumania would mean dissolution of the Little Entente." Stojadinović smilingly replied that this was typical of Victor Antonescu. Aside from this, Delbos treated the question of the pact as if they had settled it while Stojadinović was in Paris in November. He complained that Stojadinović's influence had encouraged Mussolini to withdraw from the League. The Yugoslav replied that this "opinion of his influence on the policy of a great power was very flattering to him" but not in accordance with the facts. On the whole, he was satisfied with their exchange of views. [62]

Stojadinović arrived in Berlin in mid-January, 1938. At the railroad station to greet him and his party were Göring, Neurath, and five ministers of state—all were there to welcome him in the name of the

[60] Ciano, L'Europa, pp. 229-34.
[61] Ciano, Ciano's Diary, 1937-1938, pp. 41-42.
[62] DGFP, D, I, Doc. 85. See also FRUS, I (1937), 66.

Führer. They had confected his reception of the best Teutonic pomp. Yugoslav flags flew from all state buildings, and Göring's own air force regiment provided the honor guard. They had arranged banquets and hunts, and visits to armament factories and military installations. Military demonstrations invariably followed these trips.[63]

Stojadinović saw Hitler on January 17th. The Yugoslav minister-president told the German chancellor that Yugoslavia's policy toward Germany could be summed up in one sentence: Yugoslavia would never, under any circumstances, enter into a pact or coalition against Germany. The Führer replied that he shared Stojadinović's hope that never again would the two countries be enemies. Hitler then elaborated his political aims and plans. He was a foe of the Habsburgs, he said. Never would he permit them to return to Vienna; "he would crush with lightning speed any attempt" to restore the monarchy. Then he turned to the matter of Yugoslavia itself. He was in favor, he assured Stojadinović, of a strong Yugoslavia. The murder of King Alexander had worried him, he recalled, but now he looked forward to seeing a Yugoslav-Hungarian *rapprochement*. Although the North and the Baltic seas were German political objectives, he went on, the Adriatic was not. "In the Balkans we want nothing more than an open door for our economy," he assured Stojadinović. The present Yugoslav border would remain as inviolate as the present border at the Brenner pass.

In reply to Hitler's rambling monologue, Stojadinović praised the virtues and heroism of the German soldiers during the First World War, particularly in their defense of the Serbian people "against the arbitrary action of others." Since then, he told Hitler, nothing had distorted Yugoslavia's vision of Germany so much as viewing it through "French eyeglasses," adding that Yugoslavia had now removed the spectacles. As to the Austrian question, that was to Yugoslavia's mind purely a German domestic matter. As far as the Habsburgs were concerned, he was in complete agreement with Hitler and the Yugoslavs were willing to march with the Germans to put down a restoration. The Hungarian question was at the core of the Little Entente, he asserted, and would have to be solved within that frame-

[63] Report to Vienna by Tauschitz, Austrian minister in Berlin, reproduced in *Der Hochverratsprozess gegen Dr. Guido Schmidt* (Vienna: Osterreichischen Staatsdruckerei, 1947), pp. 505-6.

work. He assured Hitler that Yugoslavia relied on the word of the Führer. He had learned much in Germany, he acknowledged, and was particularly eager to win over the youth of his country, just as Hitler had done. The youth of Yugoslavia, he said, must learn to think of themselves as Yugoslavs rather than as Serbs, Croats, or Slovenes.[64]

On these trips Stojadinović seems to have told those to whom he talked what they wanted to hear. In discussing Austria with the Italians, he adopted their view; in discussing Austria with the Germans, he shifted to their position. Certainly his true position of non-interference in Austrian-German relations differed very little from King Alexander's: "If I fight to defend Austria from the Germans I must do so with my whole army, but by the time I get my army to the Austrian frontier half of it will be destroyed by the Hungarians. And do you think I can go against the German army with only half of my army, and that demoralized?"[65]

The problem of the *Anschluss* would be met when it occured, but now (the end of 1937) Stojadinović could adorn his hat with the feather of the Italian pact. The Yugoslav prime minister seemed eminently successful in carrying out a policy that was in no instance a marked departure from that of the late king. Alexander's dream of

[64] *DGFP*, D, V, Doc. 163.

[65] *FRUS*, I (1937), 208. When he said this, King Alexander did not believe anyone could prevent the *Anschluss*. And since the *Anschluss* was inevitable, it would be provident, he thought, if the great powers would organize a European bloc and thereby prevent Austria from becoming part of an anti-French bloc. The larger group would include Germany (and later Austria), France, Poland, and the Little Entente states. The great powers would have to underwrite political guarantees for these states and make agreements on the common exchange of goods, communications, and tariffs and on the payment of reparations. Alexander to Spalajković, April 6, 1931. (JBH)

Three years later Jevtić told the British minister to Yugoslavia, Nevile Henderson, that as between Italy and Germany the latter was decidedly the lesser evil. Germany recognized Yugoslavia as an established factor in Europe, he said, and would be willing to work with Belgrade. In the event of Nazi action in Austria, Yugoslavia would "probably prefer to take no action at all," but as a member of the League of Nations "she would be guided by the decisions of France and Great Britain." If Czechoslovakia became involved, Yugoslavia would confine its action to the preventing of any move by Hungary. Henderson believed Alexander had a predilection for Germany and that he sought only time and opportunity to come to a close understanding with Berlin. If Yugoslavia "ends in Germany's arms," Henderson wrote, "it will be Italy who put her there." *DBFP*, II, 6, Doc. 331; and *DGFP*, C, I, Doc. 279.

a settlement with Italy was at last made real. Or so it seemed in 1937.

Stojadinović could look back over the four years that had passed since Yugoslavia lost confidence in France as the keystone of the eastern defense system, and reluctantly decided to abandon its role as a French partner. On December 7, 1934, Pierre Laval had pushed through his resolution before the League of Nations ending the debate on the question of the responsibility for the assassination of King Alexander. To prevent further embarrassment to Italy and Hungary, Laval had forced the Yugoslav delegation to accept his resolution. He "compelled the Belgrade government and the Queen herself to renounce—with a broken heart—their plan of prosecuting the King's assassins." [66]

The unavenged shots that killed the Yugoslav king and the French foreign minister in October, 1934, presaged further disaster for French policy and power in Europe.

Looking back, Léon Blum saw the beginning of the French defeat of 1940 in his country's reluctance to prevent Hitler's march into the Rhineland in 1936. That year Stojadinović had told him it was no longer possible for Yugoslavia to strengthen its accord with France. "We are compelled," Stojadinović had reproved Blum, "to reckon with the German danger which you have permitted to grow and flourish." According to Blum, Prince Paul had expressed the same point of view to the British. Even the Czechs, "the most faithful, the most certain and the most brotherly of our allies," had wondered as had the Rumanians "whether they should not seek some ground for understanding with the Germans."

The question was everywhere the same, said Blum: "Now that Germany occupies the Rhineland, would you come to our rescue if we are threatened?" Blum does not give us his reply to this appeal save to say that relations with those countries remained good, "but something was broken—a principle—a confidence." [67]

It was not only the negative aspects of French policy that forced the Yugoslav government to reconsider its international position. It was not only French unwillingness to fight that caused the Yugoslavs

[66] Henri Torrès, *Pierre Laval* (New York: Oxford University Press, 1941), pp. 195-96; see also J. Paul-Boncour, *Entre Deux Guerres* (Paris: Librairie Plon, 1946), III, 22-27.

[67] *Les Événements Survenus en France de 1933 à 1945*, I, 126-28.

to attempt to remain free of treaties which might entangle them in the struggles of the great power blocs.

Pressure for an understanding with Italy had come from a number of sources, some of them unexpected. British Minister Nevile Henderson, whom Halifax once rebuked for his habit of confusing his personal point of view with state policy, was one who had attempted to apply pressure. To Prince Paul he had suggested "with some diffidence" that "the psychological moment has come to make a step forward as regards Italy." He saw, he wrote, "peace in the air. England . . . taking a greater interest in European affairs." It was "his humble opinion that the moment has come for a Yugoslav initiative. I can see nothing but advantage to be gained and disadvantage if you do not take the initiative." [68]

The fact remained that by March, 1937, Yugoslav policy had crystallized to the point where Stojadinović was able to instruct the Yugoslav minister in Paris to tell the French: "We have and will remain true to all our existing alliances and obligations, something no government during the past eighteen years has been willing to do." If one bears in mind the general indecisiveness of French policy, Stojadinović reminded Purić, along with "lack of firmness in dealing with Germany on the question of the Rhineland as well as toward Italy in recent days and in connection with the events in Spain, then one can understand why we want to achieve a policy of equilibrium in relations with all the great powers. A relationship which will not blindly bind us to any one of them." [69]

Yugoslav policy was based on fear of war with Italy, war growing out of Italian "vengeance and fury," and on the realization that the

[68] Nevile Henderson to Prince Paul, February 6, 1935. Pressure came even from a former United States ambassador to Turkey, Charles Hitchcock Sherrill, who volunteered to mediate between Italy and Yugoslavia because he admired King Alexander and Mussolini. Purić to Stojadinović, May 18, 1936. (JBH)

[69] Stojadinović to Purić, March 15, 1937. (JBH) On January 24, 1937, Yugoslavia had concluded a pact of "eternal friendship and everlasting peace" with Bulgaria. As the outcast state of the Balkans, Bulgaria was susceptible to pressure from any anti-Yugoslav state. Necessarily, therefore, Yugoslavia "embraced" it. This gesture of friendship brought no congratulatory messages from Yugoslavia's Balkan allies. Rüstü Aras explained that his country, Turkey, had sent none because neither Rumania nor Greece had sent them. Subbotić to Stojadinović, January 28, 1937. (JBH) For a Greek reaction, see FRUS, I (1937), 180. For the text of the treaty, see Recueil (1937), pp. 1-3.

French and their alliance system could offer no protection against Italian aggression.

This marked departure from traditional policies and systems reflected the Yugoslav government's reading of the times: events between 1934 and 1936 had symbolized the great powers' frantic sacrifice of the small states of Europe on the altar of political expedience. For Yugoslavia, security became more important than loyalty to seemingly immutable systems of alliance. Could this security be achieved through a policy of accommodation and equilibrium?

Although the new policy of neutralism, of maneuver and evasion was hardly popular with the people of Yugoslavia, Europe's mounting economic and political pressures and the many weaknesses of Yugoslavia and its allies in the French security system made such a policy inevitable. Its objective was to buy time, to seek some means of coexistence with a powerful neighbor, to preserve the Yugoslav state. To that extent the Italo-Yugoslav pact served a positive and logical purpose.

Could Stojadinović say the same of his domestic policies? It is doubtful if he ever thought of applying to internal politics the principle of balance that he sought to apply to the international scene. In December, 1937, he stood supreme in his constitutional position in Yugoslavia. No existing political party or coalition of parties could successfully challenge him. Yet he had failed to conciliate the recalcitrant Croats and to rejuvenate and reconstitute the Radical Party so that it would represent a majority of the Serbs. Only the Slovenes and the Moslems of Bosnia and Hercegovina were with him—to safeguard their own interests—and a few opportunistic Serb politicians.

From Prince Paul's point of view, it was necessary both to unify the country and to develop a flexible foreign policy. In September, 1941, when young King Peter would come of age, the regents could then hand over to the monarch a consolidated country at peace with its neighbors. Stojadinović seemed to have forgotten this intention. Obviously impressed with his success as foreign minister, he seemed to want to minimize, even evade, the internal challenge, the Croat problem. Nevertheless, he began to fabricate the political weapons that he would need to keep the Croats from overwhelming him in the national arena. He had four years during which to complete his plans before the king came of age, four years during which to apply the Duce's formula of "force and consent," to build up his own dictatorship, to continue to rule in conjunction with Prince Paul.

Perhaps he reasoned that the Prince Regent would permit him the same free hand in domestic affairs that he had enjoyed in foreign relations. In any case, he failed to take into account Prince Paul's loyalty to the monarch and the dynasty.

Stojadinović's understanding and exposition of his power as minister-president and foreign minister plus his emerging interest in the techniques of the authoritarian state were slowly bringing new elements to the Yugoslav scene. Was his expressed desire to identify himself with Mussolini and Hitler another verbal sop to the fascist leaders, or a candid statement of personal ambition?

In December, 1937, it was too early to tell.

IV

THE ECONOMICS
OF NEUTRALITY

Yugoslavia, a country of peasants, felt the depression of the 1930s in every phase of its economic life. Like the industrial countries of western Europe it suffered a crisis in banking and a tight money market, a sharp drop in prices and in international trade, and consequent indebtedness at home and abroad.

Four out of five Yugoslavs depended on the land for a living. Agricultural overpopulation had for years been an problem of increasing proportions. Where 131 peasants had lived on 100 hectares of cultivated land in 1921, there were 144 by 1938.[1]

The nature and direction of Yugoslavia's export trade reflected the primacy of agriculture in its economic life. In the years after 1936 the nature of its foreign trade also helped to mold, in many important respects, the course of its external policy.

What commodities did Yugoslavia export? To what countries did these exports go? What was their monetary value to the Yugoslavs, and their political impact?

Table I indicates the nature of the exports. From 1926 to 1939, agricultural and livestock products led the list, and accounted for 48.94 percent of all Yugoslav exports from 1926 to 1930, 46.18 percent from 1931 to 1935, and 46.57 percent from 1936 to 1939. As the war drew near, the importance of Yugoslav minerals as an export item doubled. Table II lists the countries to which Yugoslavia exported its agricultural and livestock products and its rich store of timber and mineral resources. Table III completes the picture by listing the countries which supplied Yugoslavia with the industrial equipment,

[1] Tomasevich, *Peasants, Politics and Economic Change in Yugoslavia*, pp. 309 and 322.

THE ECONOMICS OF NEUTRALITY 95

the textiles, the coke, and the vehicles that the Yugoslavs were not
able to produce for themselves.

TABLE I

YUGOSLAV EXPORTS OF MAJOR COMMODITIES, 1926–1939

(annual averages in percentage of value of total exports)

Commodity	1926-30	1931-35	1936-39
Agricultural products	23.43	23.17	23.84
Livestock and livestock products	25.51	23.01	22.73
Timber and timber products	19.95	18.81	15.53
Minerals	7.50	11.25	14.97
Cement	1.96	2.13	0.96
Total	78.35	78.37	78.03

Source: Tomasevich, "Foreign Economic Relations, 1918-1941," in *Yugoslavia*,
ed. by Kerner, p. 173.

TABLE II

YUGOSLAV EXPORT TRADE WITH SELECTED EUROPEAN COUNTRIES, 1926–1939

(annual averages in percentage of value of trade)

Exports to:	1926-30	1931-35	1936-39[a]
France	3.4	2.4	2.8
Great Britain	1.3	3.3	8.4
Czechoslavakia	9.2	12.8	10.6
Rumania	0.5	0.6	0.9
Greece	7.7	4.2	3.4
Turkey	0.2	0.1	0.2
Austria	18.9	17.9	11.4[b]
Hungary	7.0	4.5	4.2
Italy	25.8	21.4	7.4
Germany	10.4	14.1	28.3
Total	84.4	81.3	77.6

Source: Tomasevich, "Foreign Economic Relations, 1918-1941," in *Yugoslavia*,
ed. by Kerner, pp. 172 and 209.
 [a] Includes the period during which sanctions were levied against Italy by the
League of Nations.
 [b] Average for the period 1936-38.

TABLE III

YUGOSLAV IMPORT TRADE WITH SELECTED EUROPEAN COUNTRIES, 1926–1939

(annual averages in percentage of value of trade)

Imports from:	1926-30	1931-35	1936-39[a]
France	4.3	4.5	2.3
Great Britain	6.0	8.6	7.5
Czechoslovakia	18.2	14.3	10.9
Rumania	3.3	2.2	2.1
Greece	1.3	1.3	1.5
Turkey	0.4	0.1	0.1
Austria	18.2	13.8	9.2[b]
Hungary	5.7	4.0	3.4
Italy	12.2	12.9	7.8
Germany	14.2	16.0	34.8
Total	83.8	77.7	79.6

Source: Tomasevich, "Foreign Economic Relations, 1918-1941," in *Yugoslavia,* ed. by Kerner, pp. 172 and 209.

[a] Includes the period during which sanctions were levied against Italy by the League of Nations.

[b] Average for the period 1936-38.

Two elements stand out sharply in this economic picture. First, all of Yugoslavia's exports to France and Great Britain, the two countries to which it was ideologically and politically oriented, were less than its exports to Italy, considered its adversary. Second, Germany's role as an importer of Yugoslav products and as a supplier of industrial and consumer goods to Yugoslavia was becoming increasingly significant, was overtaking and even superseding Italy's prime position in the Yugoslav economy.

Between the latter part of 1933 and the early months of 1934, two more elements entered the Yugoslav economic scene.

On September 29, 1933, Italy presented to the League of Nations a memorandum advocating changes in the structure and method of foreign trade in the Danubian area, changes which would obviously aid Austria and Hungary. Within six months, on March 17, 1934, Italy signed a regional economic agreement—called the Rome Protocols—with Austria and Hungary. The agreement was unique for at least one reason: it was created by a state outside the Danubian area and a leading world power at that.[2]

The protocols had two aims: to increase trade among the three signatory countries and specifically to overcome the difficulties that had befallen Hungary in marketing its grain. Aimed at the Little Entente and at Yugoslavia in particular, the short-lived protocols did not, as Italy had hoped, improve its political and economic position in the Danubian area. Although there was an increase in Italian exports to Austria and Hungary, both countries had difficulty in paying for them.[3]

The protocols lasted only three years, but they had a serious effect on Yugoslav trade, which declined markedly with the three protocol countries.

Yugoslav officials, analyzing the agreement's impact, came to the conclusion that it was Italy's countermove to the Little Entente. No longer were Italy and Austria the main consumers of Yugoslav cattle, pigs, lumber, and fruit. On the other hand, Rumania and Czechoslovakia, the other states of the Little Entente, could not, by themselves, absorb Yugoslavia's surpluses. Consequently, on the one hand Yugoslav trade was trying to contend with planned and autarchic economies like Italy's and on the other with politically inspired regional groupings that were organizing their economies at Yugoslavia's expense. Milivoje Pilja, then head of the department of foreign commerce, came to the following conclusion: Yugoslavia must either find an economic *modus vivendi* with the protocol countries or counteract this grouping with another. The new grouping of states would have to be more effective than the Little Entente in its present political structure or the Little Entente would have to broaden and strengthen itself along economic lines.[4]

Paralleling the economic move represented by the Rome Protocols, the Little Entente set up an economic council for the "progressive coordination of the economic interests" of Yugoslavia, Rumania, and

[2] For the text of the memorandum, see G. Fr. de Martens, *Nouveau Recueil Général de Traités* (Leipzig: Librairie Hans Buske, 1935), 30 (1935), 4-10.

[3] Basch, *Danube Basin and the German Economic Sphere*, p. 163.

[4] Milivoje Pilja to Juraj Demetrović, Yugoslav minister of commerce, November 12, 1934. (JBH)

Czechoslovakia. The council, in the making since February, 1933, met for the first time in Zagreb in January, 1934. It elaborated a program aimed at increasing the exchange of goods and services and of coordinating the communications and banking facilities of the three states. Technically, this planning for interstate cooperation was of a high order although its ultimate goal was not the organization of a customs union. The constant flaw in these economic arrangements lay in the fact that the economies of the Little Entente states were competitive rather than complementary. Even so, the council might eventually have surmounted the difficulty had not the imposition of sanctions against Italy by the League of Nations intervened so decisively in Yugoslav economic affairs. The end result was the increasing domination by Germany of all trade in the Danubian area.

In the years between 1926 and 1935, Italy was by far Yugoslavia's best customer, taking approximately 24 percent of its exports. But then came a sudden drop. On October 3, 1935, Mussolini notified the council of the League of Nations that his country had "taken the necessary means of defense" against a warlike and aggressive Ethiopia. Four days later, the League declared Italy the aggressor. On November 18th, the League's coordinating committee, which included Yugoslavia, invited the 48 member states to apply two measures: first, to prohibit the importation of all goods other than gold or silver bullion consigned from Italy or its possessions, and second, to prohibit the exportation to Italy or its possessions of a certain number of products necessary to Italy's war effort. Ironically, the committee exempted coal, iron, and oil from the list of affected commodities. It also recommended the means of compensating member states for the loss of their trade advantages deriving from the most-favored-nation clauses of their commercial treaties with Italy.

As Tables II and III indicate, the League's sanctions against Italy had a disastrous effect on the Yugoslav economy. In 1935, Yugoslavia sold 672 million dinars worth of its products to Italy.[5] The following year, with the sanctions in effect, it sold to Italy products valued at

[5] Ministarstvo Finansija, *Statistika Spoljne Trgovine Kraljevine Jugoslavije za 1936 god* (Ministry of Finance, Statistics on Foreign Trade of the Kingdom of Yugoslavia for 1936), p. 30.

only 137 million dinars.[6] Italy had always been an important market for Yugoslav timber, but its purchases fell from 390 million dinars in 1935[7] to 38.5 million dinars in 1936.[8]

In perspective, Yugoslavia's wholehearted participation in the sanctions against Italy indicates either a lack of economic foresight or a great deal of faith in the capacity of its allies for providing economic assistance. Clearly, political considerations determined Yugoslav policy in this instance. Should Italy succeed in its aggression against Ethiopia and go unreproved by the League, it was reasonable to assume that it might be tempted to repeat the action, this time against Yugoslavia.

The sanctions lasted less than a year—until July 13, 1936. In that short time, the League failed to make good its assurances of economic assistance to Yugoslavia. Although both France and Great Britain promised faithfully that they would help close the trade gap caused by the sanctions, Britain only made an effort to do so. It granted to Yugoslavia its only concession to a state requesting assistance arising from trade losses caused by the sanctions, and permitted certain quantities of Yugoslav eggs to enter the United Kingdom duty-free, reduced the duty on Yugoslav turkeys and chickens, and increased the quota of Yugoslav bacon. These concessions totaled 100 million dinars.[9]

Yugoslavia was able to accomplish very little in obtaining concessions from France. The Yugoslavs pleaded with the French to increase their imports of timber and thus pick up a share of the lost Italian market. The French refused to do so and continued to buy their timber from nonsanctionist Austria.[10] They did increase their import quota for Yugoslav horses by eleven head.[11]

In all, the compensatory purchases by the United Kingdom, France, and Czechoslovakia made up less than 25 percent of Yugoslavia's trade losses. If France had been more astute politically and had followed Britain's example, Yugoslavia would have suffered much less.

[6] *Ibid.*, for 1935, p. 28.
[7] *Ibid.*, for 1936, pp. 38-48.
[8] *Ibid.*, for 1935, pp. 35-44.
[9] *Ibid.*
[10] The New York *Times*, July 19, 1936.
[11] Jozo Tomašević, "Naša trgovinska politika na prekretnici" ('Our Trade Policy at the Crossroads'), *Privreda* (Zagreb), July, 1936, p. 116.

As a consequence of all this, Dr. Hjalmar Schacht, acting in his capacity as president of the Reichsbank, arrived in Belgrade on June 11, 1936, as a kind of *deus ex machina.* Speaking before a select audience of Yugoslav leaders, he stressed that it was not Germany's purpose to tie Yugoslavia down permanently to the level of an agrarian state. Acknowledging that the desire of agrarian states like Yugoslavia to develop along industrial lines was entirely natural and comprehensible, he observed that they would have to establish iron foundries and tinplate works before automobile and watch factories. The growth of these basic industries would benefit both Yugoslavia and Germany, he said. The higher industrial development raised the Yugoslav standard of living, the more its consumers would demand. He emphasized that this increased purchasing power arising from industrialization would in turn benefit all industrial countries.[12]

Schacht's speech aroused considerable enthusiasm in the audience, which included Prime Minister Stojadinović. But it would take more than Schacht's seductive language to bring Yugoslavia into Germany's arms. A far more telling influence on the situation was Yugoslavia's overwhelmingly agricultural economy, hard-hit by the depression and now by sanctions against Italy.[13]

During the three days Schacht was in Belgrade he emphasized Germany's willingness to collaborate in "exploiting the riches of the Yugoslav soil, particularly those of interest to the German market." But, he assured Stojadinović, Germany's development of Yugoslav resources would "completely take into account the legitimate interests of the Yugoslav state." Heeren, in reporting the conversations to Berlin, noted that Stojadinović paid "the liveliest of attention" to Schacht's ideas. The two men agreed that in the beginning German experts would come to Yugoslavia to examine the iron ore deposits of Ljubija. They touched only lightly on the question of whether

---

[12] Hjalmar Schacht, *My First Seventy-Six Years* (London: Wingate, 1955), p. 331.

[13] Germany's motives in approaching Yugoslavia were less than altruistic. Von Neurath, the German foreign minister, made it clear during a conference of high Nazi officials in 1933 that Germany should try to give economic aid to Yugoslavia in order to gain political influence and to preserve it as an important market for German exports. *USMT*, Doc. NG 2456. Milivoje Pilja, the assistant minister for foreign affairs of Yugoslavia (in charge of economic matters), realized the danger for his country of becoming an economic and later a political satellite of Germany. *FRUS*, I (1936), 502.

or not Germany's armament industry would supply Yugoslavia's military requirements. Stojadinović made very clear his intention of ignoring the strong anti-German feeling that had prevented Yugoslavia from buying German arms in the past.[14]

Stojadinović's conversations with Schacht went far beyond the economic questions reported by Heeren. His notes, shown here as he jotted them down, covered a good deal of territory in the relations between the two countries:

Political questions: Relations with England, France, Italy, the Soviets, Czechoslovakia, Hungary, Bulgaria, Greece and Turkey.
No participation in any pact or bloc against:
Plan Beneš. Plan France.
What kind of protection against Italy?

Military questions: We are ready militarily. From now on we will be ordering war materials from them: aircraft, heavy guns, midget submarines and long-range coastal artillery.

Economic questions: Exchange of goods; our raw materials for their industrial products.
Exploitation of Ljubija.
The question of gasoline.
The question of coke.
The question of ersatz gas.[15]

The commercial *rapprochement* between Yugoslavia and Germany had its beginnings late in 1931, when the French stopped making loans to Yugoslavia. In a trade agreement signed in 1933, Germany promised Yugoslavia to increase its purchases of wheat and corn and permitted a preferential tariff on plums.[16]

In 1934, a second trade agreement, introducing exchange clearing [17]

---

[14] Auswärtiges Amt, Doc. 21.
[15] Stojadinović MS (undated). (JBH)
[16] *The Economist* (London), April 27, 1933.
[17] *The Economist*, June 2, 1934. Exchange clearing was a means of conducting foreign trade without transferring foreign exchange. The mechanism was simple: the Yugoslav importer of German goods paid in dinars the reciprocal value of the reichsmarks he owed to the Yugoslav Central Bank. The German importer of Yugoslav goods paid in reichsmarks the reciprocal value of the dinars he owed to the German bank. As the separate funds accumulated, the Yugoslav bank used the dinars to pay Yugoslav exporters and the German bank paid the German

as a method of payment, took Yugoslavia still another step out of the French orbit. It helped Germany gain an economic foothold in Yugoslavia and other states of the Little Entente, and restricted Yugoslavia's freedom of action in international trade. Because the Germans could terminate the agreement at their convenience, they were in an excellent position to exert pressure on Yugoslavia to suit their political purposes.

The agreement called for increased German imports of Yugoslav corn, wheat, and plums and for preferential German tariffs on the majority of Yugoslav agricultural products. This was only superficially a boon to Yugoslavia. The peasantry welcomed it as a means of expanding the market for their goods. Indeed, the Germans did purchase goods in such increasing amounts that the Yugoslav price level rose at a faster rate than the international price level.[18] A large clearing debt resulted, however, from these German purchases, which amounted to about 21 million reichsmarks.[19] This debt forced the Yugoslav government, in June, 1936, to decree that Yugoslavs could import only certain commodities—amounting to about 35 percent of the total volume of exports—from non-clearing countries and only under a special license issued by the Central Bank.[20] The government's objective in issuing this decree was to cut imports from the hard-currency countries and simultaneously to increase imports from the clearing countries, particularly from Germany, the foremost Yugoslav clearing debtor. This decree "increased Yugoslavia's dependence on trade with Germany . . . under the existing conditions there was no other alternative."[21]

German-controlled investments in Yugoslav enterprises accumulated rapidly. In 1937, Germany had invested 55 million dinars in Yugoslavia. After the Nazis absorbed Austria, their Yugoslav investments rose to 820 million dinars, and when Czechoslovakia came under

---

exporters in reichsmarks. This system worked satisfactorily provided there were no large differences at either end of the account.

[18] P. Pejčinović, "Le Dinar a-t-il une parité?" in *Service Économique Yougoslave*, Serie II (January, 1939), No. 29, quoted in Elizabeth Wiskemann, *Prologue to War* (New York: Oxford University Press, 1940), p. 163.

[19] *Financial News* (London), June 4, 1936.

[20] Tomasevich, *Peasants, Politics and Economic Change in Yugoslavia*, p. 627.

[21] *Ibid.*, p. 628.

German control they rose to an estimated 1,270 million dinars.[22]

The Germans were energetic in their efforts to expand and reconstruct Yugoslav industry. In March, 1936, the Krupp works received the contract to convert the Zenica iron works in Bosnia into a modern iron and steel plant for the manufacture of armaments. In the months that followed, other German firms obtained contracts to rebuild the Kragujevac arsenal and to deliver German coal and cloth, electrical, bridge, and railroad equipment.

Nor were the Germans loath to mix politics with economics. They also intervened in the Yugoslav economy by negotiating directly with the peasants or with their cooperatives. The result was continuing pressure on Belgrade from the peasants themselves on behalf of the Germans. As an example of both economic and political penetration, in February, 1937, German representatives approached managers of Yugoslav agricultural cooperatives and offered to buy their entire output of plums. They were willing to pay 2.30 dinars per kilogram, far more than the current market price of 1.40 dinars. They remitted the difference between these two prices to Zbor, an ultranationalist, pro-German, pro-Orthodox, anti-Catholic organization headed by the fanatic Dimitrije Ljotić. As a result of these manipulations, Yugoslavia found itself subsidizing a subversive organization.[23]

Enriched by its conquest of Austria and Czechoslovakia, Germany was able to obtain control of what were once Viennese investments in Croatia and Czechoslovak investments in Yugoslavia's machinery, armament, sugar, and textile industries. The Germans bought out the French interest in an important Yugoslav antimony mine, thus in-

---

[22] Wiskemann, *Prologue to War*, p. 156; and Royal Institute of International Affairs, *South-Eastern Europe* (London: Royal Institute of International Affairs, 1940), p. 124.

[23] Mühlen, *Hitler's Magician: Schacht*, p. 132. There were results other than ideological of Germany's economic maneuvers in Yugoslavia. For example: In September, 1939, Germany stopped buying Yugoslav plums. With their plums a glut on the market, the Yugoslavs increased the production of slivovitz, the native plum brandy. As the price fell below 8 dinars (16 cents) a gallon and the supply of brandy outran the supply of bottles and barrels, the entire province of Bosnia seemed to join in the task of drinking up the excess. The result was a wave of mass drunkenness, 20 murders, and the mutiny of some army reservists. *The New York Times*, October 25, 1939. The hangover that followed had at least one economic consequence: the Bosniaks were able to absorb on a mass scale the aspirin dumped in Yugoslavia by the Germans through clearance agreements.

creasing to 25 million dinars the value of their antimony mine holdings in Yugoslavia.[24] They also bought from its French and American owners the Standard Electric Company, the firm that supplied the city of Novi Sad with its light and power. I. G. Farben purchased several leading Yugoslav drug firms and in 1939, with Krupp, established a company to exploit Yugoslavia's mineral wealth. The capital for this firm came from the profits of other German subsidiaries in Yugoslavia despite the fact that Germany owed money to Yugoslavia on its clearing operation.

In another ethical lapse, typical of many, a German firm violated the clearing agreement by first exporting machinery outside the clearing mechanism and then investing the proceeds in Yugoslavia, thus avoiding turning them over to the Yugoslav Central Bank.[25]

In January, 1938, Clodius, the deputy director of Germany's economic policy department, counseled his government to practice restraint in its relations with Yugoslavia. True, Germany had pushed Italy out of first place in Yugoslavia's foreign trade and this growing economic tie, he noted, was expediting and facilitating Yugoslavia's withdrawal from anti-German political groupings in the Danubian region. He regretted that it was not expedient to discuss with Stojadinović the obvious connection between economic interdependence and political relationships. To do so, he reasoned, would only intensify the fears held by many in Yugoslavia that their country was becoming too dependent on Germany. He therefore advised the foreign office to restrict all comments to thanking Stojadinović for his personal role in the development of good relations between Yugoslavia and Germany.[26]

But Dr. Walter Funk, the Reichsminister of economic affairs, was not ready to follow this suggestion. When he went to Belgrade in early October, 1938, during a tour of the Balkans, he felt he was in a far better position to bargain with the Yugoslavs than Dr. Schacht had been two years earlier. In the interval the Reich had expanded its frontiers to include Austria and the Sudetenland and all their attendant wealth. As an agrarian country Yugoslavia could not compete with the highly industrialized states of Europe, even though

---

[24] Wiskemann, *Prologue to War,* pp. 155-56.
[25] *The Economist,* February 25, 1939.
[26] *DGFP,* D, V, Doc. 159.

it was rich in such mineral resources as bauxite, magnesite, and copper.

What could Dr. Funk as a representative of the leading power in central Europe offer Yugoslavia? Nothing less than a contract in which Germany offered to take 50 percent of all Yugoslavia's exports, to provide technical assistance to increase the production of metal ores, and necessary capital to export the ores. All the Yugoslavs had to do was to buy more German products. After all, Dr. Funk told them, effective economic gestures should accompany their protestations of political friendship.[27] They met his offer with firm resistance. They heard his dictum uneasily, for they were aware of the measure and methods of Germany's bloodless economic invasion of their country.

Between late 1936 and 1939, the Yugoslav government tried, without effect, to extricate the country from the German net.

In 1936, Prince Paul successfully persuaded Eden to increase England's imports of Yugoslav products. Eden assured the Prince Regent that England had only the most friendly feelings toward Yugoslavia. Pointing out that he considered all economic questions from a political angle,[28] Eden promised every support to Yugoslavia because, he said, he was aware of the political consequences of Germany's dominance of Yugoslav trade. In the following months, Britain's trade position with Yugoslavia did improve considerably but not enough to overtake Germany's lead.

The next step taken by the Yugoslavs to offset German preeminence in their foreign trade was the negotiation of the pact with Italy. This pact,[29] signed in March, 1937, made it possible for Yugoslavia to re-enter the Italian market for the first time since the imposition of sanctions. It also gave Yugoslavia the most-favored-nation treatment hitherto accorded by Italy only to Austria and Hungary.

But Italy was never in a position to meet Yugoslavia's requirements for manufactured goods. As a matter of fact, Italy, despite brave words, seemed to be withdrawing from its position in central Europe

[27] *The Economist,* January 28, 1939.

[28] Minute of conversation between Prince Paul and Eden, November 17, 1936. (JBH)

[29] For the text of the economic accord, see *Recueil* (1937), pp. 418-22, and Appendix A, pp. 302-3.

and leaving the field completely to Germany. For that reason, the Yugoslavs refused in June, 1937, to conclude a similar trade agreement with Germany even though German Foreign Minister von Neurath urged it on them.[30]

In the latter part of 1938, Prince Paul again went to London to seek British aid. Again he pointed out that the German economic machine was strangling his country and again he asked the British to increase their trade with Yugoslavia.[31] The British board of trade responded that it would take every practical measure to do so.[32] But the British government was never in a position to surpass or even to emulate the Reich in the matter of bulk purchasing. This was so primarily because bulk purchases required governmental subsidies, and Britain's *laissez-faire* code in matters of international economics effectively inhibited subsidies.[33]

Even if the British had had the political sophistication to use preemptive buying as a political instrument there is considerable question whether they would have realized its timeliness. When, in the House of Commons, Chamberlain depreciated the political motivation of Dr. Funk's activities in the Balkans he displayed either a great deal of innocence about the interrelationship of economics and politics as the Germans understood it or he proved himself a master of dissimulation.[34]

Speaking in the same place less than a month later, R. S. Hudson, the secretary of Great Britain's department of overseas trade, acknowledged that Germany was getting a stranglehold on the Balkans by bartering, selling below cost, and arranging long-term credits and easy methods of payment. Hudson deplored the situation.[35] His solution, partially put into operation before the war came, was to organize British industries so that they could, in effect, say to their German counterparts: "Unless you are prepared to put an end to this

---

[30] *The Economist*, June 30, 1937.

[31] *SIA* (1938), p. 62.

[32] *The Economist*, November 5, 1938.

[33] Fisher, "The German Trade Drive in South-Eastern Europe," *International Affaire*, XVIII (1939), 143-70.

[34] *Hansard*, CCCXL (November 1, 1938), col. 80. Possibly, in his flush of victory after Munich, Chamberlain refused to doubt the purity of Hitler's motives.

[35] *Hansard*, CCCXLII (November 30, 1938), cols. 501-2.

way of doing business and agree to sell goods at a reasonable return, then we shall fight you and beat you at your own game."

The Germans undoubtedly recognized that the British definition of "a reasonable return" referred only to profits for the individual investor. It therefore differed markedly from their own expectations, which were clearly determined by the political and military needs of the Reich. Consequently, the Germans paid little heed to British strictures and proceeded along their own political path.

Unlike the British, the Yugoslavs did not consider foreign trade a game. Stojadinović clearly understood the dynamic relationship between foreign trade and foreign policy. "England should not abandon southeastern Europe to German economic penetration," he argued. He was looking forward to trade talks with Britain, for increased trade with Britain meant credits with which to buy fighter and bomber planes and anticraft guns. He hoped that the guns and planes could be delivered on credit and paid for in clearing. Yugoslavia heretofore had had to pay for its British purchases in pounds sterling, since the British clung to the principle of selling war material only for cash. The Germans and the Italians, in contrast, sold it on credit. It was little wonder, Stojadinović observed, that the British manufacturers could not compete with those of other nations.[36]

The Yugoslavs again presented their trade problem to the British in Geneva in May, 1939. Their representative, Dr. Ivan Subbotić, spoke earnestly and in private with Lord Halifax, then foreign secretary. Subbotić put the matter bluntly. Germany had succeeded in absorbing 50 percent of Yugoslavia's foreign trade at attractive prices. But Germany was mixing politics with economics. The products it obtained from Yugoslavia were going directly into its war industries. What Yugoslavia needed was not credit in pounds, which it would have to repay, but larger sales of goods to Britain.

To this appeal for economic cooperation, Halifax replied that it was the custom of his country to allow the businessman to buy wherever he wished. Subbotić did not question the principle of free trade—which, he wrote later, he knew was holy writ for the English— but said that in view of the political situation Britain ought to assure Yugoslavia of mass purchases over a long period of time. Certainly,

[36] Stojadinović to Minister of Court Antić, November 27, 1938. (JBH)

he told Halifax, the British government must give some consideration to the basic fact that Germany was gaining control of vital Yugoslav raw materials. The problem, he reminded Halifax, was not a commercial one but political and above all military.

Halifax answered that he understood the nature and importance of the problem. He assured Subbotić he would think it over and discuss it with the competent department heads in London.[37]

But that conversation took place on the eve of the war and the British gave very little thought to the matter of increased trade with Yugoslavia or to Germany's increased hold on the Balkans. By that time the German camel had entered the Yugoslav tent. Elsewhere, the prospects for the sale of Yugoslav products were dim. There was no one to whom to sell. Italy, at one time Yugoslavia's best customer, no longer had its former rank or role in Europe.[38] As the war drew near, old markets disappeared. Only one buyer remained—Germany. For internal political and economic reasons it was impossible for Yugoslavia to decrease the volume of its trade with Germany. The Germans, fully aware of the situation they had worked to create, knew that by simply ceasing to buy Yugoslavia's agricultural products they could bring disaster on the entire Yugoslav economy.

The slow but marked decline of markets for Yugoslav products was a process that began in 1931 with the cessation of the French loans. It speeded up in 1935-36 during the sanctions against Italy, creating a situation that enabled Germany to tap new markets in the Balkans. In 1936, Yugoslavia warmly welcomed Germany's entrance into the trade picture. But by 1939, the Nazis had outworn their welcome, and Yugoslavia now looked on the mechanism of commerce with Germany as an economic and political incubus of ugly proportions.

[37] Subbotić to Yugoslav ministry of foreign affairs, May 5, 1939. (JBH)

[38] By 1940, Germany had taken off the gloves. Wiehl, the director of the economic policy department, instructed the German legation in Belgrade to point out to the Yugoslavs that with Italy's entry into the war Belgrade must adopt a new trade policy. *DGFP*, D, IX, Doc. 442.

V

THE ANSCHLUSS
AND AFTER

"Poor Austria," despaired Nevile Henderson in a letter to Prince Paul.
"The most I hope for, or have ever hoped for," he wrote in March,
1938, "is that Austria keeps her *soi-disant* independence on the lines
of a prewar Bavaria. But if the bell rings at Berlin, Vienna will in
future have to answer it. That I fear is inevitable."[1]

Less than a week later the Wehrmacht marched into Austria—well
ahead of the schedule set up on November 5, 1937. At that time
Hitler had met with a small group of intimates to review his four-and-
a-half years as Führer and to announce his plans for the future.
Neither autarchy nor increased participation in world economic life,
he told his aides, would produce the space needed by the "German
racial community." Only the conquest of Austria and Czechoslovakia
would provide it—by 1945 according to the timetable he had decided
upon, by 1938 should the French suffer internal paralysis or should
the French and English turn on Italy.[2]

He had judged the situation well. The climate of international
politics indeed favored his first move in the process of recasting the
map of Europe. Under Ribbentrop, the German foreign office assidu-
ously furthered the Führer's policies and program. In so doing, it
received no little assistance from Neville Chamberlain, whose pen-
chant for personal diplomacy led him to dispense with the services
of Vansittart and Eden, both anti-German and pro-French.[3]

Chamberlain replaced Eden with Lord Halifax, who shared his

[1] Nevile Henderson to Prince Paul, March 8, 1938. (JBH)
[2] *DGFP*, D, I, Doc. 19.
[3] *DGFP*, D, I, Doc. 128. Henderson was not sorry to see Eden go. "I wish I
could say, see the last of Eden but I am afraid that the wheel will turn again. I hope
not too soon, for I am infinitely happier with Halifax as my chief .... The Germans
are bad enough but when one has to fight on two fronts it is bad business. I think

opinion that the Axis was "a pillar of European peace" and expressed
to Hitler the view that "the *status quo* in eastern Europe could not
be maintained unconditionally forever."[4] In Berlin, Henderson assured Hitler that he "had himself often advocated the *Anschluss*" and
denied that the anti-*Anschluss* sentiments of Selby, the British minister
in Vienna, represented the opinion of His Majesty's government.[5]

If Britain, once the *Anschluss* occurred, could take no other action
than to "register protest against use of coercion, backed by force,
against an independent state, in order to create a situation incompatible with its national independence,"[6] if France could do little more
than Britain, and if Italy, furious and resentful of Hitler's successes,
could do no more than dream about a new anti-German pact with
Belgrade or Rumania,[7] Yugoslavia could only accept the *Anschluss* as
inevitable.

Stojadinović's position was within the context of that taken by King
Alexander and his foreign ministers five years earlier. Then, Alexander had wanted, for two reasons, to prevent the *Anschluss*: because
it might prejudice the independence of Czechoslovakia and because
the existence of a greater Germany might restrict Yugoslavia's freedom of action, politically and economically. But once Italy became
prominent in Austrian affairs, as it had in the early 1930s, Germany
was less of an evil than Italy. Jevtić, Alexander's minister for foreign
affairs in 1934, told Henderson that "if it becomes a matter of choice
between Italy and Germany, there is no question at all as to which we
would prefer. Germany recognizes Yugoslavia and would be willing
to work with us." In reporting this conversation, Henderson predicted
that Yugoslavia would be noncommittal in the event of an *Anschluss*,
and would prefer to take no action at all or to be guided by the decisions taken by Great Britain and France. If Czechoslovakia became

N.C. will pull it off as far as Italy is concerned but Germany will be a much longer
and more difficult affair." Nevile Henderson to Prince Paul, March 8, 1938. (JBH)

[4] *DGFP*, D, I, Docs. 130 and 147. See also *DIA* (1937), pp. 70-71.
[5] *DGFP*, D, I, Doc. 138.
[6] *DBFP*, III, 1, Doc. 47.
[7] Ciano, *Ciano's Diary, 1937-1938*, pp. 76, 79, 88, 99. In January, 1937, Göring,
despite Hassell's recommendations to the contrary, told Mussolini that Germany
might annex Austria. Although Mussolini became upset at this news, Göring
believed the Duce would offer no resistance because of Italy's dependence on
Germany. *DGFP*, D, I, Docs. 199 and 207.

involved, Yugoslavia would confine itself to preventing any move by Hungary, Henderson wrote.[8]

When the French then urged Stojadinović to join them in protesting against the possible "forced assimilation of Austria and against a possible *Anschluss*," he turned a deaf ear. Indeed, he reminded Heeren, Yugoslavia came into existence as a result of the "right of peoples to self-determination." How then could his country logically take a position counter to this principle?[9] While his government would prefer a stable and independent Austria above all, it would accept a "German solution" as the only permanent guarantee against Habsburg and Italian intrigue in Austria.[10]

Stojadinović made this clear to the Germans, to the Italians, to the United States minister, and to Lothar Wimmer, Austria's minister in Belgrade. His assistant, Andrić, even went so far as to tell Wimmer that the Yugoslavs considered Germany and Austro-Hungary as one unit. Wimmer believed personalities as well as economics and politics helped German diplomacy in Yugoslavia. The French, "haughty and stubbornly peevish," behaved as if Yugoslavia were still prewar Serbia and complained of Yugoslavia's lack of gratitude for French help during the First World War, just as politicians of the Dual Monarchy had once reproached Serbia. The French did not know how to approach Stojadinović either politically or personally. They had no rapport with him. They would constantly badger him with what Stojadinović described as lectures on the righteousness of their position and the need for him to come out openly and support it.

The Germans *did* know how to approach Stojadinović. Besides supplying him with proof that the Czechs financed the Serbian opposition parties seeking his overthrow, they knew how to cater to his gourmand tastes and manners. In return, he knew how to please the German palate. This compatibility was colorfully described by Wimmer after a hunt given by Stojadinović for the gentlemen of the diplomatic corps and their wives. The accommodations reflected the prime minister's appreciation of the fleshly pleasures of old Austria,

---

[8] *DBFP*, II, 6, Doc. 331.

[9] *DGFP*, D, I, Doc. 321.

[10] *DGFP*, D, V, Doc. 174; and *FRUS*, I (1938), 414. Heeren reported that clerical influence caused a decisively anti-*Anschluss* attitude in Slovenia and Croatia.

Wimmer noted. There were sleighs, flourishes, and fanfares, and silver and linens bearing the coat of arms of the Archduke Frederick. On the day after the hunt, trumpets summoned the guests to a great tent and a banquet table heavy with wines and food. In high spirits generated by his native plum brandy, Stojadinović began to dance the *kolo* with the German minister's wife. As the dance gathered momentum he became more and more excited, and soon jumped on the food-heavy table. With a crash the table came down, and Stojadinović and Frau von Heeren rolled into the wines, tea, ham, salami, cheese, and fruit compote now carpeting the banquet tent. "I cannot say what people thought," Wimmer ended his report to Vienna. "One old footman crept towards me and kissed my hand." [11]

Amenities aside, the Germans made certain that Stojadinović understood their position. They would tolerate no opposition. Ribbentrop made it clear that Germany knew "how to defend herself with all her might" if foreign powers intervened in "this internal German affair." [12]

On March 11th, the day before the German army moved into Vienna, Stojadinović discussed the situation with United States Minister Arthur Bliss Lane, stressing that if Austria wished to join Germany in accordance with the Wilsonian principle of nationalities, Yugoslavia would not object. He pointed out that the core of the problem was the maintenance of European equilibrium. That, he insisted, depended on the great powers, not on Yugoslavia. In Stojadinović's opinion, France and Great Britain had brought on the entire mess. If Eden had recognized the Italian conquest of Ethiopia, thereby gaining the Italians as allies, Germany could not have considered *Anschluss*. The British habit "of talking like professors to other countries" had irritated everybody, he complained. "There will be no troop movements in Yugoslavia," he assured Lane. "Yugoslavia remains with her arms folded." [13]

The Yugoslav government relaxed this air of neutrality almost at once, however, to instruct its frontier guards to cooperate with the German officials now stationed along the old Austrian border. Having

---

[11] Wimmer, *Expériences et Tribulations d'un Diplomate Autrichien*, pp. 221-24, 236-42, and his report to Vienna, reproduced in *Der Hochverratsprozess gegen Dr. Guido Schmidt* (Vienna: Osterreichischen Staatsdruckerei, 1947), pp. 553-54.

[12] *DGFP*, D, V, Doc. 174.

[13] *FRUS*, I (1938), 431-32.

demonstrated its desire to cooperate, Belgrade then asked the Reich to guarantee the inviolability of the Yugoslav frontier.[14] Three weeks later, the *Anschluss* accomplished, Hitler responded to the Yugoslav appeal. He announced that Germany had no aims beyond Austria and that the Yugoslav frontier would in no case be affected. "We were lucky," he said, "in having here such frontiers that we were relieved of the trouble of defending them militarily."[15]

All Europe waited for Hitler's next move. It was no secret that his timetable listed Czechoslovakia. If the Germans alone invaded Czechoslovakia, Yugoslavia was not obligated to defend its Little Entente ally. But if Hungary, either alone or with Germany, attempted to regain territory lost to Czechoslovakia after the First World War, Yugoslavia would have to honor her pledge to Prague.

For Stojadinović, then, the key to the Czech-German question was Hungary. Any action Yugoslavia would take to resolve the problem depended on Hungary's action. During a private visit to Rome in June, 1938, Stojadinović implored Ciano to try to prevent Hungary from taking the initiative in attacking the Czechs. If Hungary would not attack, Yugoslavia would remain indifferent to the fate of Czechoslovakia, although it was obvious that Germany would annex the Sudetenland and that Poland and Hungary would in time get their share of Czech territory.[16]

But there were other considerations that determined the Yugoslav position.

The Prince Regent's "temperament," Whitehall was informed by Terence Shone, first secretary of the British legation in Belgrade, naturally inclined him to be more anxious and pessimistic than usual in a situation of this kind. Prince Paul's one reaction to the blossoming Czech crisis was pessimism. While he was willing to follow the lead of the British government, he did not see what his country could do if it were cut off from western aid by Italy and Germany, working together. Furthermore, the Yugoslav government was reluctant, Shone reported, to urge a plebiscite upon Prague as the answer to the

---

[14] *DGFP*, D, V, Doc. 184.
[15] *IMT*, Doc. 2719-PS.
[16] Ciano, *L'Europa*, pp. 328, 301-3; *DGFP*, D, II, Doc. 463; *USMT*, Doc. NG-2390.

Sudeten question. That method of settling an international dispute might be used against Yugoslavia at some later date, in Slovenia, in the Dalmatian littoral or in Croatia, where loyalties and allegiances to Belgrade were thin.[17]

The Yugoslav general staff, analyzing the international situation, deduced that Germany was now their major enemy. As Jevtić had foreseen, the *Anschluss* had raised the Sudeten question and at the same time had destroyed the Rome Protocol system. With the Germans in Austria, Hungary was no longer within the Italian sphere of influence. Therefore, the Yugoslav military believed, it was only with Yugoslav cooperation that Italy could maintain its interests in the Balkans. This was not to say that Italy would abandon the Rome-Berlin Axis and align itself with France and England. Rather, he predicted, Mussolini would make an effort to strengthen his position by depending less on Hitler and assuming the role of arbiter between Germany in the east and England and France in the west. The Yugoslavs foresaw that Italy had to protect itself from Germany and needed Yugoslavia as well as France and England at its side.

Germany also needed the friendship of Yugoslavia in its drive toward the Balkans and Turkey. In this move toward the southeast, for which it was well equipped administratively, politically, and militarily, Germany had the power to attract the German minorities. For this reason, the Yugoslav generals realized, Germany was dangerous, despite the common friendly relations and beneficial economic cooperation between the two countries.

Moreover, although Italian pressure on Yugoslavia's western borders had lessened as a result of diplomatic negotiations, the appearance of Germany on the northern border had made it possible for the Reich to increase economic, military, and political pressures on the Yugoslavs. This was particularly true of military pressures. Germany's Wehrmacht had power and Germany's geographically strategic position made military action possible through Hungary, which was clearly falling more and more under German influence.

From all these calculations, the Yugoslav general staff could draw only one conclusion: Hitler was the more significant and dangerous enemy and they must therefore give top priority to bolstering the

[17] *DBFP*, III, 2, Docs. 774 and 795.

border against Germany. Only after that would there be time for strengthening the frontier against Italy.[18]

There was undoubtedly a causal relationship between the conclusions reached by Yugoslavia's military leaders in that spring of 1938 and the course pursued by Yugoslavia's diplomats during the summer and early fall. First, they had to steer a middle course between the expansionist ambitions of Germany and the desire of England and France for peace at any cost. On the question of whether or not to help Czechoslovakia, Prince Paul was anxious and pessimistic over the turn of events. Although he wanted to adopt the British point of view, not yet clear, he questioned what Yugoslavia could possibly do to help the Czechs—with the German army controlling the land approach to Yugoslavia and with the Italian army and navy in a position to block Yugoslavia from the Strait of Otranto to the Ljubljana Gap. The Yugoslavs might mobilize, but they could not aid the Czechs unless they could count on military assistance from the British and French and on neutrality from the Italians.[19]

If the Czechs could get no assistance from the Yugoslav government save under the circumstances prescribed in the Little Entente pact, neither could the Germans and Hungarians obtain a promise of neutrality from Yugoslavia. The Hungarians were willing to pay for Yugoslav neutrality by making no claims on territory taken from Hungary after the First World War—territory now incorporated into Yugoslavia. They would accept the present Hungaro-Yugoslav frontier as definitive. Stojadinović was not willing to promise Yugoslav neutrality because he considered the boundary assured and realized furthermore that negotiations with Hungary on the frontier question would only bring him into conflict with Rumania and Czechoslovakia, the other Little Entente states.[20]

As the Czech crisis mounted, the aspirations of the Hungarian revisionists and of the Hungarian minority in Yugoslavia posed problems for Yugoslav diplomacy. Out of these problems rose the strong conviction that the pact of the Little Entente was hampering Yugo-

[18] Minutes of a conference held under the chairmanship of the Yugoslav minister of army and navy, May 13, 1938. (JBH)

[19] *DBFP*, III, 2, Docs. 774 and 795.

[20] *Documents Secrets du Ministère des Affaires Étrangères d'Allemagne*, II, Doc. 24; *DGFP*, D, V, Doc. 141.

slavia in its search for security. The next task was to find a formula
that would bring both Czechoslovakia and Hungary to terms with
each other within the framework of the Little Entente and thus
eliminate the possibility of trouble between them—trouble that was
certain to involve Yugoslavia.

This formula the Yugoslavs sought at the conference table. Stojadinović laid such a firm foundation for the negotiations that only two
days after the permanent council of the Little Entente convened in
Bled on August 21, 1938, he had found his formula: in return for the
right to maintain a larger army than that permitted by the Treaty of
Trianon, Hungary promised to abstain from using force against Yugoslavia, Rumania, and Czechoslovakia.[21]

On the question of minorities, Hungary on the one hand and
Rumania and Yugoslavia on the other agreed to a supplementary
protocol. The Czechs, however, balked when the Hungarians demanded that they recognize a Hungarian minority in Czechoslovakia
but refused in return to recognize the Czech minority in Hungary.[22]
The council urged the two states to continue negotiations and held up
publication of any part of the protocol until the two recalcitrants
could reach an agreement. This proved impossible.

Once upon a time this conflict between Hungary and the Little
Entente would have been a matter for consideration by the League of
Nations. Now it had to be settled without recourse to Geneva. For
the second time the Little Entente had concluded that the League
lacked any real influence.[23]

The results of the Bled meeting gave the Germans no satisfaction.
Clearly annoyed, Ribbentrop told de Kánya that Hungary's renunciation of force would not have its intended political effect of protecting
Hungary against Yugoslavia. The Hungarians replied, as always, that
they would have to be certain of Yugoslav neutrality before they
marched north or east.[24]

But for Yugoslavia the menace of Hungary remained. Although

[21] Stojadinović to Prince Paul, August 22, 1938. (JBH)
[22] *DBFP*, III, 2, Doc. 690. For the text of the Bled Agreement, see *DIA*, *I*
(1938), 274-84.
[23] Circular letter to Yugoslav missions abroad from the Yugoslav ministry of
foreign affairs, August 24, 1938. (JBH)
[24] *IMT*, Doc. 2796-PS (*DGFP*, D, II, Doc. 383); *DGFP*, D, V, Docs. 221, 223,
and 224.

German claims to the Sudetenland had not threatened Yugoslavia's national interests, Hungarian claims were another matter. So long as Hungary asked only for the cession of Magyar border regions within the framework of Germany's new holdings, Yugoslavia would raise no objection. But should Hungary extend its historic claims to the non-Magyar territories of Czechoslovakia, the Yugoslavs would feel "great uneasiness"—even if Hungary asked merely for a plebiscite.[25] Stojadinović knew that Yugoslav public opinion would not countenance the satisfaction of Hungarian claims to any non-Magyar territory because that would inevitably lead to claims on lands now part of Yugoslavia.

Because Stojadinović's calculations never excluded the possibility of a Czech-Hungarian conflict, he continued—even after Chamberlain's hurried visit to Berchtesgaden on September 15, 1938—to question the viability of the pact of the Little Entente. Soon he learned from Jan Lipa, the Czechoslovak minister in Belgrade, that Hungary was mobilizing. "What would Yugoslavia do?" the Czech asked. To gain time, Stojadinović requested Lipa to supply more precise information. Privately, he expressed to Minister of Court Antić the opinion that Yugoslavia should apply the principle of *rebus sic stantibus*. The situation had changed since the signing of the pact; the Czechs would lose two million citizens in an international dispute, invalidating the covenant. On the other hand, he felt it would not be a "popular act to deny our assistance and behave like the French." The situation was difficult and "something must be figured out," he said. The Czechs, he rationalized, would not go to war but they probably would want "a negative answer from us to justify themselves." And had not the Hungarians told him they considered the Bled Agreement a gentlemen's agreement definitively recognizing the Hungaro-Yugoslav border? Although Stojadinović hoped the Italians would restrain Hungary, he concurred in the suggestion of his minister of war that Yugoslavia partially mobilize.[26]

Two days after the Czechs warned that the Hungarians were mobilizing, Stojadinović traveled with Petrescu-Comnène, the Rumanian foreign minister, from Subotica on the Hungarian border to

[25] *DGFP*, D, IV, Doc. 9 and D, V, Doc. 229.
[26] Stojadinović to Prince Paul, September 22, 1938; Stojadinović to Antić, September 24, 1938. (JBH)

Veliki Kikinda on the Rumanian border. Comnène voiced the opinion that although no state wanted war Britain and France had made their last concessions to Germany. Any further yielding to Germany, he believed, would lead only to new humiliations. The Hungarian and Polish demands for joint borders were disturbing the Rumanians. If these demands were acceded to, five million Slovaks and Ruthenes would come under the control of Hungary and Poland, and Hungary would enormously increase both its territory and its prestige. Another danger was that Hungary might attack Czechoslovakia, putting Yugoslavia and Rumania in the undesirable position of either having to enter a war they did not want or of betraying their signatures on the pact of the Little Entente. This was a danger to avoid at all costs. Comnène recommended that he and Stojadinović take steps to stop Hungary's moves toward Slovakia and "Sub-Carpathian Russia." He also pressed Stojadinović to ask Göring to oppose the idea of a joint Hungarian-Polish border and armed intervention by Hungary in Czechoslovakia. On the spot, Stojadinović drafted a telegram to Yugoslav Minister Aleksander Cincar-Marković in Berlin for oral transmission to Göring.

Because the Hungarian government had declared the Bled Agreement in effect and because Germany would protect Yugoslavia's interests, Stojadinović then recommended to Comnène that Rumania and Yugoslavia step softly and protest only the possibility of Hungarian action against Czechoslovakia and the absorption of Sub-Carpathian Russia. Since only the great powers could resolve the differences between Germany and Czechoslovakia, Comnène agreed that it would serve no purpose for Rumania and Yugoslavia to expand their existing obligations to the Czechs. They should await decisions by Paris and London. Comnène believed that in case of war Rumania and Yugoslavia must remain neutral until they could see who was winning and who would be willing to support them militarily, financially, and industrially.[27]

Belgrade's fear of a conflict over Czechoslovakia proved groundless. In a four-power conference at Munich in late September, Britain, France, and Italy helped release the Sudets, the "solid Teuton minor-

---

[27] Stojadinović to Prince Paul, September 25, 1938. (JBH) For Comnène's version, see Comnène, *Preludi del Grande Dramma*, pp. 104-6, 115-17.

ity," from subjugation to a "Slav central government at Prague."[28]
To Heeren, Stojadinović expressed his "boundless admiration" for
Hitler's success in expanding the Reich. In the end, he had no reason
to fear that his country would have to fulfill its obligations to Czechoslovakia. On November 2, 1938, Germany made the first Vienna award
to Hungary of 12,000 square miles of land and about one million
inhabitants of southern Slovakia and Carpatho-Ukraine.

From his post in Paris Yugoslav Minister Purić disdainfully watched
the behavior of the French and the British in the Czech crisis. With
Munich ended a period of international history. No longer was there
respect for treaties, for fulfilling one's obligations, for the moral necessity of keeping one's word. He saw in Munich the downward
course of humanity and wrote to Stojadinović with irony and cynicism:

If Chamberlain keeps on as he is doing, we will reach an era when war will
not be waged at all because he intends to solve the question of colonies,
Spain and the Mediterranean by a policy of giving [to Hitler] so that he
does not take it by himself.

In Purić's opinion the Franco-Polish treaty existed only on paper and
showed little promise of continued existence. Poland's peace depended only on German good will, and Poland would, he felt, "inevitably suffer the fate of Czechoslovakia."

Purić drew lessons from the Czech crisis for his own country. More
valid than ever was old Pašić's policy of "free hands." The grand old
man of Serbian politics had cautioned against Yugoslavia's binding
itself to any power, great or small, save to neutralize it as an eventual
agent of an opposing power. The Yugoslav government, wrote Purić,
should expand its war industries and assimilate its potentially troublesome minorities without coercion.[29]

Yugoslavia's ministerial crisis of February, 1939, like so many other
of its political conflicts, came to a head as a result of forces operating
outside the country. It had its origins in the *Anschluss*. Although the
effects on the Yugoslav domestic scene of the German triumph in
Vienna were not immediately discernible, it seems clear that Musso-

[28] *DBFP*, III, 2, 623-24.
[29] Purić to Stojadinović, October 1, 1938. (JBH)

lini's desire to emulate Hitler actually led, within a year, to the downfall of Yugoslavia's premier.

With the *Anschluss* the Yugoslavs now had the Germans as neighbors. They would therefore, Ciano reasoned, have to seek a military alliance with Rome to redress the power balance. Belgrade could have its military alliance, he decided, if it acquiesced in Italy's absorption of Albania. Yugoslavia's nonopposition if not its participation, he wrote, was essential to the success of the project. He must tie Yugoslavia to Italy, militarily and politically, so that by the time Italian troops marched into Tirana the Yugoslavs would be "compelled to look sympathetically on the Italian game." As a further concession Ciano was willing to stop all irredentist movements directed toward the Albanian minority in Yugoslavia.[30] This was the way he saw the situation in May, 1938.

The following month, during a private visit to Rome, Stojadinović told Ciano he had rejected Albanian overtures for a pact of friendship because he recognized Italy's unique position in Albania. The meeting ended on this happy note. Stojadinović invited Ciano to visit Yugoslavia and Ciano accepted, provided the Duce approved.[31]

As his plans for annexing Albania matured, Mussolini began to hesitate. He was not concerned about British, French, or Greek reaction. He gave no thought to his commitments under the Belgrade Accord of 1937 to maintain the political integrity of Albania, nor even to the possibility of a military counterstroke by the Yugoslavs. What did concern him was the possibility that he would lose Yugoslavia's friendship, to the advantage of the Germans. With that in mind he felt it necessary for Ciano to talk to Stojadinović. Together they should study the question of compensation for Yugoslavia, "possibly at the expense of Greece, i.e., Salonika."[32] Now, for the first time, an Axis partner would hold out to Yugoslavia the bait of Salonika.

Unlike Mussolini, Ciano never had any doubts about Stojadinović. The September crisis had clearly revealed how unambiguous was Stojadinović's position vis-à-vis the axis. During those troubled weeks, Hristić, the Yugoslav minister in Rome, had come to Ciano every

---

[30] Ciano, *Ciano's Diary, 1937-1938*, pp. 94, 105, and 114 and *L'Europa*, pp. 313-14.

[31] Ciano, *L'Europa*, pp. 331-32.

[32] Ciano, *Ciano's Diary, 1937-1938*, p. 203.

evening to "receive his instructions." But the Italian had no assurance that Prince Paul shared Stojadinović's views. Although Ciano saw it was not possible, at that time, to bring Yugoslavia into camp, he never had reason to doubt Stojadinović's "solidarity with the Axis." [33]

Nor was Ciano the only one to heed the numerous signs of Stojadinović's fascist inclinations and his growing drive for personal power. Prince Paul had noted with dismay the prime minister's manipulation of the government party, the Yugoslav Radical Union (JRZ), as an instrument to advance his authoritarian ambitions. Stojadinović had politically repressive measures at his command, buried in regulations on the budget. This armory included electoral laws and regulations on the control of the press and on the right of political association and assembly. The prime minister could, with cabinet approval alone, enforce such existing laws and regulations as would suit his purpose, and could easily re-establish a dictatorship by decree. With such powers he was in a position to force Maček and the opposition to cooperate on his terms. If Maček refused, Stojadinović believed he could legally and easily crush the Croat Peasant Party.

For some time the Prince Regent had silently questioned Stojadinović's political probity and had become increasingly concerned about the growing fascist character of the political machine that the prime minister was fabricating. He knew, according to Ciano, that Stojadinović had indulged in "shady business speculations" and "had accumulated considerable money in banks abroad." [34] True or false, this was the kind of information that would impress the Italian.

By November, Prince Paul's doubts had reached the point where he decided to check into the rumors reaching him about Stojadinović's political maneuvers. He thereupon instructed the chief of the Belgrade police, Milan Aćimović,[35] to investigate the JRZ's use of the fascist salute and of the word *vodja* (leader) in referring to Stojadinović. It is questionable how sincerely the police chief wanted to carry out this order. Instead of making a thorough investigation, he went, with undetective-like directness, to Stojadinović, purportedly for an ex-

[33] *DGFP*, D, IV, Doc. 434; and Ciano, *Ciano's Diary, 1939-1943*, p. 13.

[34] Ciano, *Ciano's Diary, 1939-1943*, pp. 35-36.

[35] It is noteworthy that Aćimović later was minister of the interior from September, 1941, to November, 1942, during the German occupation of Serbia. He was more powerful than Nedić, the Pétain of Serbia, and overruled him on many occasions.

planation but apparently to warn him that Prince Paul harbored certain suspicions. Stojadinović denied that he and his party had fascist leanings. That accusation, he said, was a canard coined by the opposition. The word *vodja* simply referred to his position in the JRZ, he explained. He denied that it was his wish, or his party's, to make Yugoslavia over into a totalitarian state. The green shirts that his party members wore, the Roman salute they used, their cries of *Vodja! Vodja!* had an entirely different meaning, Stojadinović insisted. What their actual significance was he did not say. Ačimović returned to Prince Paul with assurance that the prime minister would do nothing not in harmony with the wishes of the Regent. The JRZ's questionable hand salute, for example, was really quite different from the Roman salute, he reported, particularly when seen "from the time of raising the arm until the time of lowering it." [36]

Prince Paul was not naïve nor was he susceptible to Stojadinović's charm and political influence. The regency was coming to an end and if Stojadinović obtained control of the state now he would likely retain control when young King Peter ascended the throne. In view of his predilections, now beyond doubt, it was necessary to remove him promptly, for the safety of the dynasty and the state. There were, however, other factors to consider. Because he held office by constitutional right it would be possible to remove him only by constitutional means. And although his dismissal seemed a matter of considerable urgency, a national election was at hand. Clearly this was not the proper time to set in motion the machinery that would remove him.

The election would come in December, three weeks after Ačimović submitted his report to Prince Paul. In the interval Stojadinović complained to Prince Paul that the minister of the interior, Father Anton Korošec,[37] was neither firm nor energetic in his handling of the political opposition. Korošec was "about to break the record [as]a liberal minister of internal affairs," he told Prince Paul. His actions, Stojadinović reported, displeased German Minister Heeren and Consul-General Neuhausen.[38]

Government leaders ordered the election for varied reasons, Stoja-

---

[36] Ačimović to Prince Paul, November 24, 1938. (JBH)
[37] Head of the Slovene Populist Party and a confidant of Prince Paul.
[38] Stojadinović to Prince Paul, November 24, 1938. (JBH)

dinović because he believed his popularity at its peak, Korošec because the parliament elected in 1935 had not included any Slovenes despite the fact that his party was a member of the government, Prince Paul because he wished to speed up the democratization of Yugoslav political life. The voting went badly for Stojadinović.[39] In Slovenia, the Slovenian Populist Party won a majority. In Croatia, the Croatian Peasant Party won. In the Serbian part of Yugoslavia, the JRZ won, but by a slim majority. Stojadinović's candidates in Croatia suffered severe defeat. The popular vote indicated the need for a settlement with the Croats, a need which Stojadinović refused to recognize.

Immediately after the election Stojadinović called together all the Serbs in the government (including Milan Aćimović, Korošec's subordinate) to work out an anti-Croat policy designed to negate Maček's significant strength at the polls. Stojadinović also set out to compel Korošec's dismissal. It was Korošec's fault that Stojadinović had lost so many votes, the prime minister complained; he had even gone so far as to let the government employees vote as they wished. Stojadinović wrote Prince Paul that he found Korošec's presence in the cabinet impossible. "Personally I like him very much," he explained, "but I must tell the truth to Your Royal Highness. I have always been an optimist but confronted by the present situation even my eternal optimism ceases to exist."[40]

Meanwhile Korošec, through his efficient intelligence system, learned of the meeting called by Stojadinović and of the impending demand for his resignation. To maintain the coalition, he asked Miha Krek, the only other Slovene in the cabinet, to remain in the government and to insist that additional cabinet posts be given to Slovenes.

[39] Voting was by list. Three parties comprised the government list: the Jugoslavenska Radikalna Zajednica, Stojadinović's coalition of dissident Radical Party members; the Slovenska Ljudska Stranka led by Korošec; and the Jugoslavenska Muslimanska Zajednica under Mehmed Spaho. Opposed to the government's list stood a group of parties headed by Maček, the leader of the Croats, under the banner of the United Opposition. This group included the Croatian Peasant Party, the National Radical Party and the Peasant-Democratic Coalition. The government list received approximately 59 percent of the votes cast and the United Opposition got the remaining 41 percent. The government, however, received 52,000 fewer votes and the opposition parties 250,000 more votes than they had received in the 1935 election. More than 650,000 Serb voters supported Maček.
[40] Stojadinović to Prince Paul, December 16, 1938. (JBH)

With Prince Paul's approval, Korošec resigned. In his place, Stojadinović appointed Milan Ačimović.

By the middle of January, 1939, Stojadinović realized that the JRZ
might fall apart if Korošec's party left the coalition or if Korošec
himself remained within the coalition only to work for its destruction.
To jettison Korošec was no easy matter; Stojadinović knew the Slovene
was a confidant of Prince Paul. Moreover, Korošec required neither
patronage nor support from Stojadinović to remain leader of Slovenia's
largest political party, the Populist Party. Because he had an independent position of power, he could wield considerable political
influence whenever he chose to do so.

Korošec's political power had to be neutralized; he had to be kept
in the government but in a position where he could not wreck the
JRZ. Accordingly, the premier recommended to Prince Paul that
Korošec be appointed president of the senate. Korošec, after consulting the Prince Regent, accepted on January 16th. He did so for
one reason: in times of domestic crisis the president of the senate
was the first man called on to advise the crown.

Stojadinović was not aware, perhaps, of the consequences of his
recommendation. Probably he did not realize that in moving Korošec
into this position he had taken the first administrative step in removing
himself from office.

For Stojadinović, time was running out. He had had his day.

About this time, Ciano arrived in Yugoslavia to assure Stojadinović's
cooperation, or nonintervention, in Ciano's Albanian project. Prior
to his departure for Belgrade Ciano told Mackensen, German ambassador in Italy, that a friendly relationship with Yugoslavia was the
keystone of Axis policy in the Danubian area. He insisted that Stojadinović was a man whose internal position was perfectly secure and
who was, above all, "miles ahead" of other Yugoslav politicians.

Stojadinović received Ciano in Belje and there unveiled his political
ambitions. On the domestic side, said the prime minister, he intended
to model his JRZ after the Fascists, and to underscore his sincerity
he paraded green-shirted party members before his gratified guest.
The parliamentary situation at that time, he told Ciano, gave him
full freedom to act as he saw fit. He intended to take full advantage
of that freedom. In foreign relations he intended to remain on good
terms with Germany and at the same time seek some means of

protection against Germany. Clearly, the only country that could protect Yugoslavia was Italy. Logic alone, he told Ciano, dictated that Yugoslavia strengthen its ties with Rome so as to "find a balanced situation and security within the framework of the Axis." Logic should have told Ciano that his Yugoslav counterpart was ambitious as well as authoritarian. His ambitions, authoritarian or not, fed on opportunism. Logic should also have told Ciano that if the balance of diplomatic and military power in Europe were being weighted in the direction of the democracies, Stojadinović would have spoken in liberal political accents.

Ciano replied that he would hold fast to the Belgrade Agreement and to the Axis. He would oppose any attempt to encircle or put up a barrier against Germany—unless Germany itself abandoned the Axis policy and turned southward. In that case, of course, Yugoslavia and Italy would find themselves together. But there was no fear of German expansion toward the Mediterranean, Ciano assured Stojadinović. He had the Führer's word on that.[41]

Ciano had not come to Belje merely to discuss Axis policy, however. He had come to promote his plans for Albania, and the conversation turned to King Zog. Both men had found him unreliable and inclined to try to play Yugoslavia against Italy, and both believed he would side with France in a moment of crisis. Stojadinović suggested that they either replace Zog or partition Albania between them. Ciano stressed the advantages to Yugoslavia of an Italian occupation of Albania: demilitarization of the Albanian frontier and

[41] Ciano, *L'Europa*, pp. 405-12; *DGFP*, D, V, Docs. 276, 434, and 430; and Stojadinović to Prince Paul, January 20, 1939. (JBH) To show the extent of Axis intelligence services and at the same time to dramatize Italy's trust in Stojadinović, Ciano presented his host with photostatic copies of two dispatches sent by British Minister Campbell to Lord Halifax. Stojadinović showed them to Prince Paul but would not give them up. Upset by the disclosure, the Prince Regent asked Campbell to take the first train home and tell Halifax that the security of the foreign office had been penetrated by the Axis. Then he himself wrote to Halifax, sending the letter by messenger. Months later, during a visit with King George VI in London, Prince Paul asked Chamberlain whether the spy had been uncovered. The prime minister said the whole story was completely unknown to him. Much later Campbell told Prince Paul that it took over a year to unmask the agent, who had worked in the archives section of the British foreign office and had had a Russian mistress. She had delivered the documents to the Russian embassy and Soviet Ambassador Maisky had turned them over to Italian Ambassador Grandi to make political mischief as he saw fit.

corrections in the northern sector, a military alliance with Italy and the promise of Salonika whenever Yugoslavia wanted it.

Stojadinović never was able to get from Ciano a clear idea of which parts of Albania would be occupied by Yugoslavia and which by Italy. Whenever he spoke of partition, Ciano spoke of the correction of frontiers. The Yugoslav prime minister, Ciano wrote later, seemed to favor the thought of providing his country with an increase in territory. He urged Ciano to bring up the question of Albania in his conversations with Prince Paul. The premier's relations with the Prince Regent, Ciano noted, did not seem good.[42] But if he believed Stojadinović wanted part of Albania as a peace offering to the regent or as a show of political strength, Ciano made no mention of it.[43]

In his report to Prince Paul, Stojadinović indicated neither the extent nor the depth of his talks with Ciano. Clearly, he failed to mention any plans for dividing up Albania. Later, when Ciano raised with the Prince Regent the Albanian question and the possibility of territorial changes, he found Prince Paul somewhat "less interested" in Albanian real estate than was Stojadinović. "We already have so many Albanians inside our frontiers, and they give us so much trouble," Prince Paul complained, "that I have no wish to increase their number." Ciano considered this a favorable sign for Italian ambitions.[44]

But the conversation proved less of a boon to Stojadinović. To Prince Paul, it was only the latest in a series of events that illuminated the authoritarian character and ambition of the prime minister. Stojadinović was too egotistical a man to remember the circumstances under which he came to power. He should have recalled his motivations when he entered the Jevtić government in December, 1934, as minister of finance. As a Radical Party member he served Jevtić, a member of the Nationalist Party, for only one major purpose: to

---

[42] Ciano, *L'Europa*, p. 411; and *Ciano's Diary, 1939-1943*, p. 14.

[43] Both Stojadinović's and Ciano's accounts of their meeting agree in all respects save the most important—Albania. Eight months earlier, Ciano considered a partition plan which would give Yugoslavia control of the whole Lake of Scutari, a declaration of renunciation of the rights to Kosovo and a promise to demilitarize Albania. Ciano, *L'Europa*, p. 313.

[44] Ciano, *L'Europa*, p. 313. The Duce was happy to hear of Yugoslavia's policy toward Germany and was "delighted so far as Albania is concerned." *Ciano's Diary, 1939-1943*, p. 14. See also, *DGFP*, D, IV, Doc. 440, and D, V, Doc. 276.

wait for the proper time to obtain the premiership for himself. Within a short time, he was able to organize a large enough group of politicians and to make certain that even the deputies elected on the Jevtić slate would follow him at the critical moment. Stojadinović's chance had come after the May, 1935, general elections.

Despite the government's repressive measures and gerrymandering, the political parties united against Jevtić rolled up an impressive vote in the 1935 election. When the deputies elected by the opposition parties refused to take their seats in the parliament, the more extreme nationalistic members of the Jevtić government intemperately attacked the boycotters. This was the moment Stojadinović hoped for. He and four members of the cabinet resigned, bringing down the Jevtić government on June 20th. Two days earlier, Stojadinović, not one to leave his future to time and chance, had submitted a memorandum to Prince Paul on the formation of a new political party, one with the support of the Slovene and Moslem parties and of Aca Stanojević, octogenarian leader of the once strong Radical Party. The purpose of the new party was to seek Maček's cooperation, lessen internal tensions, call new elections, and organize a government which, unlike Jevtić's, would "represent the opinion and wishes of the great majority of people."[45] These Jevtić had failed to do. And his failure had given Stojadinović his chance. Now Stojadinović himself had failed, and it was the cream of the jest that he failed for the very same reasons. The political drama of June, 1935, was about to be repeated in 1939 with some variations. But the theme would be the same: failure to conciliate the Croats.

Now Ciano's allusions to an agreement on the division of Albania incensed Prince Paul. The failure of the prime minister to consult the cabinet or the regents before making an agreement of this kind—an agreement that would place Yugoslavia firmly, even without a pact, in the Axis camp—indicated to Prince Paul that the time had come to dismiss Stojadinović. He would have to go.

It was never a question of whether or not Stojadinović should be forced out of office. It was even less a question of how the deed was to be done, for it would be done in proper form. It was only a question of choosing the precise time. The replacement was ready. The per-

---

[45] Stojadinović memorandum on the formation of the JRZ, June 18, 1935. (JBH)

sonnel were ready. Prince Paul stood opposed to the dictatorial measures introduced by the prime minister in dealing with domestic matters, as well as to his foreign policies. Korošec and Spaho, who had played their part four years earlier in bringing Stojadinović to power, were ready to see him go. In addition, there were a number of deputies led by Dragiša Cvetković, minister of social policy, who were dissatisfied with the premier's Croat policy and were ready to desert him.

The stage was set, then, for Stojadinović's dismissal. Not all the actors knew what roles they would play, and only Prince Paul and Korošec seemed to know the plot. But all stood ready in the wings.

The precise moment for action came on February 3, 1939, when Bogoljub Kujundžić, the Yugoslav minister of forests and mines, spoke out in the parliament on the superiority of the Serbs over the Croats and the Slovenes.

The Serbs who fought at Kajmakčalan,[46] he shouted, had made so many sacrifices for Yugoslavia that the Serb voices "would always be listened to and Serb policies would always be the policies of this house and this government." He was particularly caustic in referring to the Croats, especially those who had refused to cooperate with the Stojadinović government. Kujundžić's pan-Serb and anti-Croat sympathies were obvious to everyone in the room. Greatly concerned, Spaho, the head of the Moslem party, urged Stojadinović to counter the speech with remarks calculated to eradicate the bad impression left by Kujundžić. But to the consternation of his non-Serb colleagues the prime minister remained silent.

Late that night, with the speed and quiet of a long-planned maneuver, Korošec, president of the senate, adviser to the crown, the man whom Stojadinović most feared, called to his apartment five members of the government: Minister of Transport Spaho, Minister of Social Policy Cvetković, Minister of Construction Krek, Kulenović and Snoj, both ministers without portfolio. There, presumably on instructions from Prince Paul, Korošec asked them to resign their posts. They hurriedly composed and signed a joint resignation. In it they protested Kujundžić's outrageous views. They said they pre-

[46] Kajmakčalan was a major battle on the south Serbian front during the First World War. There the Bulgarian army was destroyed by the Serbs. Kajmakčalan thus became a national symbol for Serb patriots.

sumed from this speech that there existed "a variety of opinions
within the government concerning the question of an agreement with
the Croats." It was imperative, they wrote Stojadinović, that the
government keep its promises, made before and during the election,
and come to complete agreement with the Croats. The five cabinet
ministers held that "the government, in its present composition, hinders
the solution of this important question." In the light of this conclusion,
there was nothing the five men could do but resign.[47] The joint
resignation was sent to the prime minister. In the normal course of
events he would simply have accepted it and selected replacements
for Prince Paul's approval. But this, it soon became clear, was no
ordinary situation. For the Prince Regent refused to let Stojadinović
organize a new cabinet and within a few hours the prime minister
himself was out of the government.[48]

The new prime minister was Dragiša Cvetković, a former mayor
of Niš and minister of social policy and public health in the Stojadinović government. He had two qualifications for the premiership:
he had sought and would earnestly continue to seek an agreement
with the Croats and he was acceptable to Maček, the Croat leader.
For some time Cvetković had been discussing a possible agreement
with Maček, who looked on him as the one Serb politician who was
ready to meet the demands of the Croats. Each looked to the other
for help in realizing his ambitions, Cvetković who wanted to retain
the premiership, Maček who wanted a greater degree of self-rule
for Croatia.

Maček's first contact with Prince Paul came shortly after the death
of King Alexander. At best, it was an indirect contact, for the Croat
Peasant Party leader was interned. In a moment of candor, he spoke
his mind to his physician, Dr. Lujo Shaller, who, without telling
Maček, sent a summary of Maček's views to Regent Stanković.
Maček was firm, Shaller wrote, in his belief that Croatia could exist
only as a part of Yugoslavia. If it were not part of the kingdom, the

[47] Letter of resignation, signed by Spaho, Cvetković, Krek, Kulenović, and Snoj,
to Milan Stojadinović, president of the council of ministers, February 3, 1939. (JBH)
[48] Grigore Gafencu, the Rumanian foreign minister, who had heard the rumors
of crisis and plot, later wrote that Stojadinović was laughing and confident the
day before his dismissal. Gafencu left for home that evening and even before he
reached Bucharest learned that "the powerful Stojadinović had vanished as if
through a trap door." Gafencu, *Last Days of Europe*, p. 142.

Croats would "be only servants of servants," Maček had said. He would like to take part in general elections. Personally, he had admitted, he favored King Alexander's policy of the morning of January 6, 1929 (the date of the establishment of the dictatorship), but he disliked the policies of the men who entered the government that afternoon! [49]

Maček was released from internment in December, 1934. In June, 1935, at the time of the Jevtić cabinet crisis, he, as head of the opposition, was called in for consultation with Prince Paul. In this formal conversation, Maček suggested that the constitution be set aside and that new elections for a constitutional assembly be held. Prince Paul rejected these suggestions and empowered Stojadinović to form a new government. More than a year later, in November, 1936, through the efforts of Dr. Milorad Stražnicki, a former Yugoslav minister to The Hague and one of Maček's school friends, Maček was invited to Castle Brdo, Prince Paul's summer retreat in Slovenia, for private conversations. Maček's position of June, 1935, had not changed. Neither had that of the Prince Regent. The only practical result of this conversation was that Dr. Stražnicki, a Croat, was appointed to the post of minister to Sweden. The role of intermediary between Maček and Prince Paul then passed to Dr. Ivan Šubašić, who later became *ban* (governor) of Croatia.

Meetings between Maček and Prince Paul continued regularly throughout 1937 and 1938. Each man stood firm in his beliefs and no positive results were reached. In the course of these informal talks, the Prince Regent urged Maček to talk to Stojadinović and try to bring about a partial settlement of the Croatian problem. Stojadinović and Maček met in Brežice, near Zagreb, in January, 1937. Stojadinović was not willing to make any concessions until Maček joined his government. This Maček refused to do. In spite of their failure to come to any agreement, Prince Paul continued to meet with Maček in the hope of persuading him, eventually, to come into the government.

The new prime minister, Cvetković, had begun to make his political connections with the Croats back in 1928. Then, as a delegate of the Radical Party deputies, he took part in negotiations to form a coalition

---

[49] Dr. Lujo Shaller to Regent Stanković, October 21, 1934. (JBH)

government. This venture never reached the stage of minimum agreement. Radić, the Croatian Party leader, was directing an intransigent campaign against the Serbian Radical and Democratic parties, accusing them of seeking to impose Serb hegemony on Yugoslavia. Nevertheless, Cvetković's relations with the Croats never became unfriendly. A decade later, in November, 1938, Stojadinović permitted him, in the name of the government, to "sound out the terrain" for an agreement with the Croats. Stojadinović gave his permission grudgingly and only because the mission had Prince Paul's support.[50] In reality, Cvetković had been acting privately on this matter for over a year. By late summer of 1937, Cvetković reported that he had been able to establish contact with two of Maček's lieutenants, Ivan Pernar (one of the men wounded at the time of the shooting of Radić in parliament in 1928) and August Košutić, and had convinced them that it was time for Maček to work energetically for an agreement. All believed concessions should be made by both sides to facilitate understanding and make agreement possible. In this way, they could deal "a deadly blow to all those elements of destruction that try to take advantage of every opportunity to overthrow the régime."[51]

Whatever his aides may have thought, Maček had his own ideas on the way to get his program accepted by Belgrade. He seems to have pressured the regents from two sides. At the end of January, 1938, about three months after Maček and the three opposition parties agreed to work together toward a new constitution for Yugoslavia, Cvetković heard from Pernar and Košutić again. They told him Maček believed that the agreement with the opposition had failed and that only he and Prince Paul could settle the Croat problem. To this end, he visited Belgrade in August, 1938, as the guest of the opposition. An estimated 100,000 greeted him. According to Pernar, the visit was Maček's own idea. The trip was made over the protests of his associates, who believed it would redound to the benefit of the opposition rather than to Maček's. Again Cvetković impressed upon Pernar the necessity of drafting and signing a protocol assuring the Croats that through new elections, even under the present constitution, their demands would be met through cooperation in the new

[50] Cvetković to author.
[51] Cvetković to Prince Paul, August 7, 1937. (JBH)

parliament. Time was running out, Cvetković insisted, and failure to act would be disastrous.[52]

A week after the December, 1938, elections, Cvetković learned from his informants within the Croat Peasant Party that Maček was deeply disappointed by the limited success of the opposition. Moreover, Maček's aides were "acting in a conciliatory way to improve the atmosphere for conversations."[53] This, then, was the time to start conversations with him. Cvetković left shortly thereafter for Zagreb, at Prince Paul's request, to see what could be done in that direction. The day he was to see Maček, December 22d, Stojadinović ordered him to return to Belgrade. The following day Cvetković, curious to know what motivated this sudden change of program, called Belgrade. He learned that Stojadinović had relieved Korošec of his post as minister of the interior and had replaced him with a devoted friend, Milan Aćimović. The new minister was none other than the former police chief of Belgrade who had denied to Prince Paul that Stojadinović had authoritarian ambitions.[54] The political climate was becoming foggy and it seemed to Cvetković that it would be wiser for him to be in Belgrade.

The following month, Prince Paul sent a strong message to Maček, again emphasizing the necessity of concluding an agreement. Maček did not seem to have the same negative reaction that he had always shown in the past. On February 2d, Cvetković again learned from his informants that Maček approved the organization of a committee to study a Serb-Croat agreement. He was also willing to enter the government with younger men of his party, to participate in a coalition cabinet, to work with the new parliament elected in December, and to postpone general elections until the fall of 1939. The informant told Cvetković that Maček depended on the word of Prince Paul, "of whom he speaks only in the highest terms and in whom he has a great deal of faith."[55]

There matters stood on the eve of Stojadinović's dismissal.

Now it was Cvetković who held the trump card, the card that would bring him the premiership: conciliation of the Croats.

[52] Cvetković to Prince Paul, January 30 and August 6, 1938. (JBH)
[53] Cvetković to Prince Paul, December 15, 1938. (JBH)
[54] Cvetković to author.
[55] Cvetković to Prince Paul, February 2, 1939. (JBH)

The new prime minister now had to assure the Germans and the Italians that the change of Yugoslavia's first minister did not mean a change in Yugoslavia's foreign policy. Accordingly, Cvetković reaffirmed to Heeren his country's friendship for Germany, said he would work, as he had in the past, for better German-Yugoslav relations, and announced that the new foreign minister would be Aleksander Cincar-Marković, the former minister to Berlin.

Heeren had some reservations about all this. He deplored the fall of Stojadinović. To him it meant the end of authoritarian government in Yugoslavia, the end of a type of politician who merited German confidence and approval. Now what would happen? Heeren foresaw the rise of a democratic government in which the Croats would have considerable influence along with "Serbian leftists." It would be to Germany's advantage to cultivate the Croats, he decided, for they had close cultural ties with Germany and feared the Italian advance into Yugoslav affairs.[56]

But Yugoslavia was no longer a positive factor to Italy now that Stojadinović was gone. What mattered to Mussolini was not Belgrade's relations with Rome, which would not officially change, but the future of the Albania project on which the two countries had almost reached agreement. Now an unknown factor headed the Yugoslav government. The Duce and his foreign minister agreed that if the Stojadinović policy still held they would go ahead with the plan of partitioning Albania between Yugoslavia and Italy. If Cvetković would not go along with this idea, then Italy would occupy Albania without, and if necessary in spite of, Yugoslavia. Moving fast so as to prevent the new Yugoslav government from strengthening its contacts with the democracies, Mussolini and Ciano scheduled the invasion for Easter Week, 1939.[57]

What was to become of Stojadinović, so recently a power in southeast Europe? Would he accept his enforced resignation with restraint and restrict himself to being a member of the opposition? Such behavior would not be in character. The ex-minister-president was far

---

[56] *DGFP,* D, V, Docs. 291, 310, 311, and 385.

[57] Ciano, *Ciano's Diary, 1939-1943,* pp. 23-24. Ciano believed that the Germans had something to do with the fall of Stojadinović and that it was an anti-Italian maneuver to halt the spread of Italian influence among the Croats. *DGFP,* D, VI, 1110.

too uncompromising for that, and much too ambitious to sit by. Within a week after Cvetković had replaced him, Stojadinović told Indelli, the Italian minister in Belgrade, that the "Prince Regent was at the bottom of the plot against him." He said he had no intention of remaining silent and would return to power, for he knew the people supported him. Then he would take his "revenge." But Ciano, reading Indelli's report, was skeptical of Stojadinović's chances of recouping his political fortunes.[58]

With Prince Paul, the ex-prime minister took quite another line. Protesting his innocence of any desire for personal power, decrying the "incredible intrigues and untruths" surrounding his departure from the government, he asked Prince Paul to receive him so that he might disprove the lies being told about him. "I feel the need to tell all that is in my heart," he wrote.[59]

His plea went unheeded. Yugoslavia had new leaders, though its problems had not changed.

In the year that had just passed a great deal had happened. Yugoslavia had watched the disintegration of the League of Nations, the death of the Little Entente, and the reintroduction, after more than 150 years, of the principle of partition of small states by the great powers of Europe. Fascism's triumph in Spain, Germany's successes in Austria and at Munich, these had destroyed the fabric of the old order. A new pattern for the reshaping of Europe was in the making. A fundamental tenet of international law—the principle that sovereignty over territory derived not from conquest but from voluntary assignment by the preceding ruler—had fallen.

The ultimate destruction of the Czechoslovak state was apparent to almost all. Poland would obviously follow as the next object of German aggression. Neutrality—a policy of friendship with all and commitments to none—was common to all the small states. For Yugoslavia, the maintenance of a good-neighbor policy required more and more prudence, restraint, and political agility. The role of neutral took a great deal of effort and no one in Yugoslavia liked it—

---

[58] Ciano, *Ciano's Diary, 1939-1943*, pp. 24, 33-34. Heeren and Ciano were both wrong in their reasoning as to what lay behind the fall of Stojadinović. In reality, his dismissal was a pro-Yugoslav act. Indeed, since he was a favorite of the Axis governments, his dismissal can also be described as an act of courage.

[59] Stojadinović to Prince Paul, April 27, 1939. (JBH)

neither the government nor the people. Instead of uniting the country, the doctrine of peace with all aggravated deep-seated domestic conflicts that continually tempted two giants to intervene in Yugoslavia's internal affairs. But the policy of neutrality was necessary. It was the only policy that held any hope for a small nation caught between giants.

The government could find no other way.

VI

ON THE TIGHTROPE

Many in Yugoslavia heard with sympathy and understanding the continuing clamor of the Ruthenian and Slovak separatists in truncated Czechoslovakia. The cry for autonomy in Slovakia echoed across Croatia. Nor was the Croatian dream of independence only for those ultranationalists, the Ustaše. At a meeting in Zagreb on January 15, 1939, all newly elected Croatian deputies to the Yugoslav parliament urged in a resolution that the great powers intervene in Yugoslavia to assure the Croats "liberty of choice and destiny." As they saw it, events from 1918 on had proved the impossibility of the Yugoslav idea, of a state common to both Serbia and Croatia. Claiming to speak for the Croatian people, they denounced as null and void all acts of the Belgrade government, particularly the treaties concluded between Yugoslavia and foreign powers.[1]

In the psychological war between Zagreb and Belgrade this declaration was more than mere words. And Belgrade realized it was more than mere words. When Maček's first lieutenant, August Košutić, went to Prague in mid-March for "personal reasons," Belgrade officials believed his real purpose was to learn the technique by which a state could become a German protectorate. About the same time, a number of Maček's followers attempted to see Göring in Berlin. He refused to receive them on the ground that their political discussions with any government other than their own should take place with Italy, not with Germany. In short, Göring told both Maček's men and Ciano, Yugoslavia belonged completely in Italy's sphere of influence.[2]

[1] Auswärtiges Amt, Doc. 13; *FRUS*, I (1939), 82.
[2] *DGFP*, D, VI, Doc. 205.

But despite his assurances to Ciano, the Nazis stepped up their efforts to cultivate the Croats. As they increased their political activity in both Croatia and Slovenia, the Yugoslav government grew apprehensive and the Italians grew frantic, jealous, and fearful. Mussolini, sullen over Germany's successes in Austria and Czechoslovakia, came to the conclusion that he must postpone his project in Albania. An invasion might destroy Yugoslav unity and in doing that bring on German protection of Croatia, or cause Maček to proclaim an independent Croatia under German protection. The Duce would not tolerate the swastika's flying over the Adriatic. For Italy, there was but one thing to do: that was to make strong representations directly to the Germans.

Ciano therefore called in Mackensen, the German ambassador, and bluntly told him of his anxiety over the developments in Croatia—the resolution, the visits to Prague and Berlin, the general political unrest. He strongly implied that Germany was back of it all. The Croats were undoubtedly spurred on by the events in Bohemia and Slovakia, Ciano recognized, but in the interests of the Axis Italy could not adopt the same attitude toward events in Croatia as it had toward the situation in Czechoslavakia. Italy, he added, considered the *status quo* in Yugoslavia a fundamental factor in maintaining the peace in eastern Europe. Mackensen protested Ciano's implication. Reiterating that his government had no desire to intervene in Croatia, he said he would nonetheless convey Ciano's protest to the Führer. There was no doubt that the Führer would substantiate all his denials, he told Ciano.[3]

Mussolini and Ciano were not content merely with protesting to Berlin. They felt they had to erect a wall to keep the Germans out of Yugoslavia in the future. In a telegram to Prince Paul they claimed they had put a halt to German activity and urged him to hasten the negotiations with Zagreb, for "any loss of time would be fatal." Prince Paul reacted cynically to this piece of gratuitous advice. He doubted that Germany would take Croatia. He wondered at the spectacle of an Italy "which had always fomented trouble in Croatia" now endeavoring to bring Serbs and Croats together.[4]

[3] Ciano, *L'Europa*, pp. 418-19; and *Ciano's Diary*, 1939-1943, pp. 46-51.
[4] *FRUS*, I (1939), 82.

Mackensen's prediction of his Führer's reaction was entirely correct. In a long personal letter to Ciano, Ribbentrop assured his Italian colleague that Germany had no desire to poach on Italian preserves. He reinforced everything Mackensen had already told Ciano. He was eager, he wrote, to assure Ciano clearly and unequivocally that Germany had no interest in the Croatian question and would in the future "take action in that direction only in the closest harmony with Italian wishes."[5]

Ever present in Ciano's mind was the realization that Croatia might erupt into civil war. At times he relished the prospect and at other times he thought of it with dismay. If Yugoslavia disintegrated once the civil war began, Italy had to be ready to get its share of the booty. Ciano began to cast about for suitable instruments to advance his policy of preparedness; and thereby cleared a trail for plots and counterplots, spies, counterspies, and *agents provocateurs*.

The first new character to step onto the stage (Pavelić, the Ustaše leader, had long occupied the spotlight) was a Croatian landowner, the Marquis de Bombelles. Ciano had met him some time before during a hunting party organized by Prince Paul. Bombelles, now presenting himself to Ciano as a spokesman for the Ustaše, described what he called the harsh treatment suffered by the Croats at the hands of the Serbs. He spoke of the Croats' desire for revenge and envisioned the day when Croatia would be an autonomous kingdom ruled by an Italian prince. At this time he asked for no financial assistance from Italy for the Croatian separatist movement; he was content to warn Ciano of Serb treachery. Ciano listened carefully and promised his visitor that he would keep in touch with him. Later he arranged for Bombelles to talk to Pavelić, the man to whom Italy looked as its most effective propagandist among the Croats.

At best, Italy's plans for subverting Yugoslavia were slipshod. They ranged from stimulating an irredentist movement among Yugo-

[5] Ciano, *L'Europa*, pp. 419-22; and *DGFP*, D, VI, Docs. 15, 45, 55, 94, and 144. Ciano told Mackensen that although Italy favored the existence of Yugoslavia, if the Croatian separatist movement grew Italy would expect Germany to maintain complete disinterest in that area. Five days after this interview, the German foreign ministry notified its missions that the Reich would unquestioningly support Italy's plans in the Mediterranean countries. In the future, continued the instructions, German missions should have no contact with Croat organizations.

slavia's Albanian minority and permitting Slovenes in Italy to print
a Slovene-language newspaper (thereby demonstrating Italy's sympathetic attitude toward minorities) to subsidizing Maček and his
separatist movement.[6] Bombelles continually urged the Italians to
forestall German intervention in Croatia by intervening themselves,
and Ciano actually contemplated sending his troops. In all this he had
the considered advice of the marquis, whom he considered his "man
of confidence" and his avenue to Maček. But Ciano's high hopes for
action through Bombelles tumbled with the news, relayed by Pavelić,
that the German intelligence service, penetrating "Serbian" military
headquarters, had discovered Bombelles was Belgrade's spy.[7]

As Bombelles played out his role, another Croat, one Carnelutti,
waited in the wings for an audience with Ciano. In great secrecy
he presented himself as Maček's special envoy. Warning Ciano that
the Croats, although anti-German, would ask Germany's help if Italy
rejected their appeal, he begged the Italian foreign minister to insist
that Belgrade permit the Croats a larger measure of self-rule. If this
failed, the Croats would revolt against Belgrade and appeal to Italy
for help. Then they would establish a Croatian republic allied to
Italy by a customs and monetary union. Ultimately they would unite
with Italy, said Carnelutti. When Mussolini heard about this, he told
Ciano to support the Croats in carrying out these plans.[8]

Maček tells a different version of these negotiations. He says that
after Ciano's visit to Belje and Belgrade in January, Zagreb buzzed
with rumors to the effect that he and Stojadinović had made an
agreement detrimental to Croatia's interests. Sometime after Ciano
left Belgrade, Carnelutti came to see Maček. Although of Italian
descent (he had a brother in the Italian diplomatic service), Carnelutti
considered himself a Croat. He was a member of the Croatian Peasant
Party and a reporter for *Hrvatski Dnevnik* (Croatian Journal), the
official newspaper. On his way to Trieste to see a relative, Italian
Propaganda Minister Alfieri, Carnelutti stopped by to ask Maček if
he could do something to help the Croat cause. Maček said he could.

    [6] Ciano, *Ciano's Diary, 1939-1943*, pp. 41, 58, 64, 74, 81, 105-6, and 117.
    [7] Ciano, *Ciano's Diary, 1939-1943*, p. 247; and Hagen, *Die Geheime Front,*
pp. 209-10. When Pavelić came to power in Zagreb in 1941, he sent Bombelles
to his death in the Jasenovac concentration camp.
    [8] Ciano, *Ciano's Diary, 1939-1943*, p. 51.

He could try to find out what had occurred between Stojadinović and Ciano. Carnelutti accepted the assignment and asked for a letter of authorization. The letter Maček provided said that the bearer was a member of the Croatian Peasant Party, and nothing more. This meeting occurred in March, 1939, and Maček did not see Carnelutti again until May.[9]

In the interval, negotiations between Maček and Prime Minister Cvetković over the settlement of the Croatian problem broke down. Thereupon Carnelutti reported to Ciano that Maček would continue his separatist movement, since he could not come to an agreement with Belgrade. According to Ciano, Carnelutti asked for a loan of 20 million dinars ($400,000) with which to finance an uprising in the fall.[10] Carnelutti and Ciano met again later and drew up a memorandum to the effect that Italy would finance Maček's revolt. It specified both the amount of the subsidy and the time of the uprising. Once the revolution got under way, Maček was to call in Italian troops to restore peace and order. Croatia would proclaim itself an independent state in confederation with Italy, with common ministries of foreign affairs and national defense. The Italians could keep an army in Croatia and install an Italian governor. The Croats would decide later when to unite with Italy. According to Ciano, all this was in the memorandum, which Mussolini approved subject to countersignature. In the meantime, payments to finance the insurrection began.[11]

Carnelutti returned to Yugoslavia to get Maček, then vacationing in Slovenia, to sign the memorandum. Maček's version of this document differs markedly from Ciano's. Maček says it was typewritten in the Croatian language and bore no signature of any kind. He says there was no mention of an Italian subsidy for his movement and no statement obligating him to start a rebellion. Instead, the agreement specified that in case of an Italo-Yugoslav war, the Croats would call in the Italian army to assist them against Belgrade. They would then proclaim Croatia an independent state tied to Italy through a personal union and through common ministers of defense and foreign affairs. According to Maček, Carnelutti told him he could change

[9] Maček to author.
[10] Ciano, *Ciano's Diary, 1939-1943*, p. 89.
[11] Ciano, *Ciano's Diary, 1939-1943*, p. 93.

the document on any point except one, the matter of personal union with Italy.

Maček's reaction to all this was swift. He told Carnelutti he had sent him to Italy to get information, not to enter into negotiations of any kind. With this, he folded the draft, put it in his pocket and left the room.[12]

To Ciano, Carnelutti justified his failure to obtain Maček's signature with the explanation that the Peasant Party leader had resumed his negotiations with Belgrade and still wished to clarify some points with Ciano. On the other hand, Bombelles, who had not yet been found out, told Ciano that Maček might have refused more categorically because of other commitments or because he was a democrat and wanted to avoid any understanding with fascism.[13]

Maček does not know by what means Bombelles learned of his refusal to deal with the Italians, for he spoke with no one about the episode. Nevertheless, on Maček's return from his vacation, the pro-fascist elements of Zagreb were already whispering about his lost opportunity to liberate Croatia.[14]

In the light of Maček's recurring public threats to seek foreign assistance in Croatia's fight for home rule, it may be that Carnelutti's mission to Rome was as he described it.[15] Certainly Maček's supreme desire was to obtain autonomy for his people. He preferred, of course, to obtain that autonomy within the Yugoslav state. But he was not averse to using other means to protect his beloved Croatians.

The Italians were certain that they could easily cut up and annex Croatia as a kingdom. It was apparent that Yugoslavia's viability and effectiveness as a state would face a major test during and immediately after the absorption of Albania into the Italian empire.

From an informant in Italy the British foreign office learned early in March, 1939, that the Italians planned to invade Yugoslavia for the purpose of establishing order among the Serbs, Croats, and

---

[12] Maček to author.
[13] Ciano, *Ciano's Diary, 1939-1943*, pp. 96-97.
[14] Maček to author.
[15] Carnelutti returned to Zagreb and during the Second World War was of invaluable assistance to those who opposed the Ustaše terrorist regime. He disappeared after May, 1945.

Slovenes. The invasion, accompanied by a landing in Albania, would take place about April 1st. On March 12th, Foreign Minister Halifax sent the information, in strictest confidence, to Prince Paul.[16]

Prince Paul received it gratefully but believed it out-of-date, for he had just had a telegram from Mussolini urging him to make a settlement with the Croats. Trying to analyze the motives of the Italians, Prince Paul decided they were looking for a pretext for occupying Slovenia so as to forestall a German push to the Adriatic. Maček, Prince Paul believed, was still loyal to the dynasty but he was making impossible any agreement between the Croats and the government despite Belgrade's best efforts to come to reasonable terms with him.[17]

But the information Halifax had sent was correct in many respects. Ciano told Hristić, the Yugoslav minister in Rome, that Italy had only pacific intentions toward Croatia, but he expressed no such intentions regarding Albania. The Italians were soon to make their strike in Albania, although only after they had assured themselves that Belgrade would not interfere. Hristić presented no objections except to say that Italy should not use Albania as a base for an attack on Yugoslavia.[18]

Outwardly, those in the Yugoslav foreign office attached no importance to the rumors of an imminent Italian landing on the Albanian coast. The Italian minister assured them that they should feel no anxiety whatsoever and categorically promised that Italy would respect the *status quo* in the Mediterranean.[19]

Although Ciano lulled all the western powers with his talk of Italy's good intentions toward Albania, he had a hard time convincing Hristić of his good intentions toward Yugoslavia. Hristić was skeptical enough to ask him to take no action without first informing Belgrade and, above all, to preserve the existence of the Albanian state as a matter of form. As if mollifying a child, Ciano told Hristić all the steps the Italians had taken in Albania and their plans for the future. The Yugoslav "took it all with remarkable resignation,"

[16] *DBFP*, III, 4, Doc. 378.
[17] *DBFP*, III, 4, Doc. 379.
[18] Ciano, *Ciano's Diary, 1939-1943*, pp. 54 and 58.
[19] *Greek White Book* (Washington: American Council on Public Affairs, 1943), Docs. 3-5 and 7.

remarking as he left the interview that Zog was coming to the same end as Beneš.[20]

The Italian forces landed on the Albanian coast on Good Friday, April 7, 1939. At eleven o'clock that night Hristić called on Ciano, who feared he had come to announce a change in Yugoslav policy. This was an eventuality for which he had prepared by arranging for the Hungarians to have six divisions mobilized and ready to go to the Yugoslav border to "exert pressure on the Serbs." But his fears were unjustified. Hristić had come only to ask the extent of the occupation and its aims. Ciano would not commit himself as to what would be Albania's frontiers; after all, he reminded Hristić, the Italians had landed only to reestablish peace and order. Nor would Ciano discuss just what the Italian government's attitude would be if the Yugoslavs decided to occupy certain points on the Yugoslav-Albania frontier. But he said he would be glad to discuss the entire matter with the new Yugoslav foreign minister, Aleksander Cincar-Marković.[21]

The Yugoslav government undoubtedly hoped the Italians would agree to rectify the border in favor of Yugoslavia. Other than that, there was little the Yugoslavs could do except reinsure themselves with Germany against Italy. Now Italy was by far the greater enemy.[22] The best Yugoslavia could hope for now was that the Italians would occupy Albania only temporarily, that they would not establish a protectorate, that their action had not nullified the Italo-Yugoslav Agreement of 1937, and that they would be generous enough to "take account of Yugoslav desiderata."[23]

Cincar-Marković took gracefully the events of Good Friday, 1939. He told the Germans that his country's attitude during the invasion of Albania demonstrated its undeviating loyalty to the long-established policy of friendship with both Rome and Berlin. He asked from Germany the same assurance his predecessor had requested at the time of the *Anschluss*: release to the public of an authoritative statement stressing Germany's interest in a strong and united Yugoslavia.

[20] Ciano, *Ciano's Diary, 1939-1943*, pp. 61-63.

[21] *Ibid.*, p. 64; and Ciano, *L'Europa*, pp. 423-25. According to Cvetković, the Yugoslav government informed the British of Italy's intentions in Albania. The Cvetković government was ready to act if assured of British support. But the British reaction was not favorable. Cvetković to author.

[22] *DBFP*, III, 6, Doc. 8, and *DDI*, VIII, 12, Doc. 738.

[23] *DBFP*, III, 5, Doc. 92.

In return, Yugoslavia would guarantee never to become involved in any combination hostile to the Axis.[24] Next, he told Ciano of Yugoslavia's desire to cooperate more closely with the Axis. As a matter of fact, he said, only adverse public opinion prevented his country from joining the Axis. His countrymen accepted the invasion of Albania as an accomplished fact and appreciated Italy's decision not to send large numbers of troops north of Durazzo-Tirana. In response, Ciano assured Cincar-Marković he was not interested in Kosovo, the part of Yugoslavia largely inhabited by Albanians. Not to be outdone, Cincar-Marković asserted that the Yugoslavs would adhere to a policy of unarmed neutrality, that they had refused any kind of British guarantee, and that they would continue to seek the economic support of Italy and Germany and work within the Axis system. As to the League of Nations, Cincar-Marković promised that Belgrade would become more and more indifferent to the League's demands and responsibilities.[25]

While the Axis powers accepted Yugoslavia's neutrality as homage and a tribute to their power, the British minister in Yugoslavia accepted it as the only reasonable policy open to a country in Yugoslavia's exposed and delicate position. It was in line with Anglo-French interests. If war broke out, fresh Yugoslav forces could, at the proper moment, give the Allies "real and efficient assistance." This help would be possible only if Germany and Italy did not impose on Yugoslavia conditions that would force it to adopt a pro-Axis policy.[26]

The British reacted to Hitler's aggression in Czechoslovakia with two moves designed to preserve the peace through collective security. First, they proposed that they, the French, the Russians, and the

[24] *DGFP*, D, VI, Doc. 192.
[25] Ciano, *Ciano's Diary, 1939-1943*, pp. 75-76. For Ciano's report to the Germans about this meeting, see *DGFP*, D, VI, Doc. 256; and for the British report from Belgrade, see *DBFP*, III, 5, Doc. 544. When Ciano reported to Ribbentrop on his conversations with Cincar-Marković they agreed that it was necessary to preserve the *status quo* in Yugoslavia. If the kingdom fell apart, however, Italy would take charge. Ciano, *L'Europa*, p. 431.
[26] Cincar-Marković to Prince Paul, April 11, 1939. (JBH) Sir Ronald Campbell, British minister in Belgrade, reminded his government that Yugoslavia's geographical position would oblige it to preserve neutrality as long as possible, "which under the stress of economic conditions might even tend to favor Germany and Italy." *DBFP*, III, 4, Doc. 100.

Poles organize to protect "international society from further violation
of fundamental laws on which it rests." Next, Britain asked France,
Poland, Turkey, Greece, and Yugoslavia what they intended to do
if Germany invaded Rumania.[27]

When Sir Ronald Campbell put this question to Prince Paul,
the Prince Regent seemed annoyed and asked what Britain itself
was prepared to do in that situation. It was a pertinent and fair
question, and Sir Ronald said as much. He asked Prince Paul to put
himself in Halifax's position. The time was coming, he said, when Germany's "smaller neighbors would have to decide whether they would
become her vassals or defend their independence." The Prince Regent
replied that he would have to consult his cabinet, his military advisers,
and his country's allies.[28] He spoke at length of Yugoslavia's difficult
position. It was not only a matter of geography but of obtaining war
materials. Where could his country buy replacements for an already
low stock of armaments? Sir Ronald agreed that Yugoslavia was
indeed in a "parlous situation." He reported to the foreign office
that he did not believe Yugoslavia would commit itself in advance
to war against Germany. It would remain neutral, Campbell predicted, until the last possible moment. With its neutrality under
continuous pressure from the Axis, it would cooperate grudgingly
with Germany and Italy. He thought the Serbs (he said he could
not speak for the Croats) would defend themselves, would never
"cave in as the Czechs had done" and in the "later stages of a war
if things were going well ... might play a useful part if supplies
could be gotten through to them." At the moment, he reported,
Prince Paul thought it would be a mistake for the small powers
within Germany's reach to join in any declaration of a common front.
It might precipitate the very aggression it tried to avert. A firm
declaration by the great powers, however, would encourage the
smaller states.[29]

[27] *DBFP*, III, 4, Docs. 446 and 390.
[28] *DBFP*, III, 4, Doc. 420.
[29] *DBFP*, III, 4, Docs. 426, 511, and 542. Shortly after this conversation, Halifax
asked Milanović, the Yugoslav chargé d'affaires in London, whether Yugoslavia
would defend itself if attacked. Milanović replied that he would need instructions
from Belgrade to answer this question. "What would Britain do if Yugoslavia
were attacked?" he asked. Halifax replied that if Poland and France were ready
to act, Britain would also be ready.

The Yugoslav government's determination to avoid joining any common front and to maintain its neutrality against all pressure— German, Italian or British—is well illustrated by its reaction to the Anglo-Turkish Declaration of May 12, 1939. This declaration, a countermove to Italy's annexation of Albania, pledged Turkey and Great Britain to cooperate in the event of war in the Mediterranean area.[30] The Turkish minister in Belgrade, explaining his government's abandonment of neutrality, told Cincar-Marković the Turks hoped their decision would influence Yugoslavia and Rumania and change their attitude on remaining neutral.[31]

Cincar-Marković believed this development would have serious consequences. The declaration violated the pact of the Balkan Entente, which pledged each of its signatories to join no combination without the consent of the others. The declaration might cause the Axis to make painful inquiries in Belgrade and Bucharest as to whether Yugoslavia and Rumania intended to remain in the Balkan Entente, particularly after it had abandoned its independence and tied itself to the anti-Axis powers.[32] Cincar-Marković thought the problem of safeguarding the peace in the Balkans concerned the Balkan states alone. He opposed any interference by the great powers.[33]

Yugoslavia's refusal to look on the declaration with equanimity, Sir Ronald Campbell believed, grew out of its insistence on maintaining a position of independence. For him, neutrality was too ambiguous a word to use in referring to Yugoslavia's policy. Belgrade did not want to commit itself to any power or combination of powers. This was a point Sir Ronald stressed time after time in his dispatches to London. Yugoslavia would remain aloof until someone threatened

---

[30] For the text of the declaration, see *Hansard*, CCCXLVII, cols. 952-53.

[31] Memorandum of conversation between Cincar-Marković and the Turkish minister, May 8, 1939. (JBH)

[32] *DBFP*, III, 5, Docs. 440, 555, 626, 633, and 686.

[33] *DGFP*, D, V, Doc. 428, and Ciano, *Ciano's Diary, 1939-1943*, pp. 53 and 85. Yugoslavia's anxiety stemmed from Clause 6 of the declaration: "The two Governments recognize that it is also necessary to insure the establishment of security in the Balkans and they are consulting together with the object of achieving this purpose as speedily as possible," *Hansard*, CCCXLVII, cols. 952-53. See also, *DBFP*, III, 6, Doc. 21, for a discussion of this clause.

its interests. Only then would it take sides. Only a war on its doorstep would bring Yugoslavia's position into the open.[34]

War was inevitable. That was Prince Paul's conclusion on his return to Yugoslavia after a state visit to Berlin in June, 1939. There the Germans had demonstrated Teutonic hospitality of massive proportions. They had budgeted over 30 million marks for decorations, had mobilized thirty thousand storm troopers for security services, had displayed thousands upon thousands of portraits of Hitler and Prince Paul, had published in the newspapers and in special editions of magazines long and laudatory articles on the "wonderland of Yugoslavia." The German propaganda machine had outdone itself. For four days the German people were "bewitched by a Yugoslav spell." There were banquets and receptions and bestowing of medals. And there were the usual parades of German armed power—men, tanks, and planes.

During the conversations between Hitler and Prince Paul, the Führer made every effort to bring Yugoslavia into his camp. He strongly recommended that Prince Paul and Cincar-Marković make some gesture unmistakably demonstrating Yugoslavia's friendship for the Axis. Ribbentrop suggested, as an example of the sort of gesture desired, that Yugoslavia withdraw, within the month, from the League of Nations. Cincar-Marković indicated great reluctance. Although Yugoslavia had largely dissociated itself from the League, he pointed out, it would be difficult to withdraw entirely before September. He would reflect on this question, he decided.

Ribbentrop then requested closer consultation between the Yugoslav and German foreign ministers on developments among the states of the Balkan Pact. He followed that with the suggestion that Yugoslavia join the anti-Comintern Pact. This was impossible, said Cincar-Marković. To the Yugoslavs, the pact was an unpopular instrument directed against Russia, with whom they had sentimental Slav ties. Hitler reiterated that it was important for Yugoslavia to define its policy toward the Axis. For the Yugoslavs, clarification of their position would have two advantages. First, it would simplify their

[34] *DBFP*, III, 6, Docs. 52, 88, and 149. See also *DBFP*, III, 5, Doc. 705. For the reports of the Yugoslav talks with the Italians, see *DDI*, VIII, 12, Docs. 270, 425, 542, and 733.

domestic problems. Once the Croat and Slovene separatists realized that the Axis powers supported the *status quo* in Yugoslavia and therefore would not aid them, they would cease their subversive efforts. Second, an open statement of friendship for the Axis would eliminate Italy's hostility toward Yugoslavia. The Duce, notoriously inclined to act on impulse, needed to know whether Yugoslavia was his friend or his foe.[35]

The conversations were a great disappointment to Hitler. Colonel Vladimir Vauhnik, the Yugoslav military attaché, waiting in the anteroom, saw the Führer as he left, making no attempt to hide his chagrin. For the Germans, Prince Paul's visit had failed.

For the Yugoslavs, it had some educational values. They saw the power of the Wehrmacht and Vauhnik was able to give Prince Paul an estimate of its fighting strength. They also began to foresee what the Germans might demand of them. As he left, Prince Paul told Vauhnik to "try to keep up the friendship with Germany. I shall take care of the other powers myself."[36]

Prince Paul came to several conclusions as a result of his visit to Berlin. War was inevitable because Hitler would not go back on his publicized promise to claim Danzig as a part of Germany, and neither Great Britain nor France would back down on their refusal to permit Danzig's incorporation into the Reich. War was inevitable because Danzig had now become a matter of prestige. Hitler, on the other side, did not believe war was inevitable. He did not believe Britain would fight to prevent his taking Danzig. Prince Paul's suspicion that Hitler was negotiating with Russia grew out of the fact that Hitler and Göring would tell him nothing when he asked them what they knew about Russia's intentions. As a matter of fact, he became so uneasy that when he spoke to Neville Chamberlain in

[35] *DGFP*, D, VI, Docs. 262 and 474. Earlier conversations between Ribbentrop and Cincar-Marković along these lines had taken place in April. See also Ciano, *Ciano's Diary, 1939-1943*, p. 90.

[36] Col. Vladimir Vauhnik, Auf der Lauer nach Hitlers Kriegsplänen (MS). (JBH) The late Colonel Vauhnik served the Allied intelligence services. In his manuscript he recalls the period of his service in Berlin. Of his reports Walter Schellenberg, chief of the intelligence service for the German high command, writes, "His knowledge of the political and military plans of the German leadership was amazingly comprehensive and correct." Walter Schellenberg, *Labyrinth* (New York: Harper, 1956), p. 175.

July, he warned the prime minister that if England did not come to an agreement with the Russians, Germany would.[37]

Concerned over the proximity of war, the Prince Regent sent General Petar Pešić to Paris and London in July for consultation with the French and the British military leaders. He chose General Pešić for this mission because he was the man the late King Alexander had chosen to lead the Yugoslav army if a war should break out.

Gamelin told Pešić that Yugoslavia would find it impossible to remain neutral. The Axis, he predicted, would make all kinds of demands and force Yugoslavia to enter the war on the side of the Allies. If that were not enough of a reason, when war broke out the British and French forces would take Salonika to prevent it from falling into the hands of the Italians. Once Salonika was occupied by the Allies, Yugoslavia would have no reason for staying out of the war.

The French general staff, Pešić reported, did not believe the quality of the German army was as good as it had been in July, 1914. It lacked sufficient trained reserves and good officers. The morale of the army was low, according to the French, and if war broke out there might even be a revolution in Germany.[38]

After discussing the Pešić report, Cvetković and the Yugoslav cabinet decided to speed up their armament and fortification program and to try to bring the Croats into the government. They realized they would have to take other measures also to complete the defense of Yugoslavia. The internal political structure needed repairs, if not a complete overhaul. Belgrade and Zagreb had to come to terms, completely and quickly.

The elections of November, 1938, reflecting growing strength among pro-Croat and anti-Stojadinović elements, had given Stojadinović's followers only a weak majority in the parliament and played a large part in his dismissal. His successor, Dragiša Cvetković, told parliament on March 10, 1939, that the settlement of the Croatian

[37] FRUS, I (1939), 198-200, 287-88. Chamberlain did not believe there was any danger of an agreement between the Germans and the Russians. Hitler was highly intelligent, said Chamberlain, and therefore would not run the risk of having to wage a world war.

[38] Dokumenti o Jugoslaviji, Paris (March, 1956), No. 7.

problem was the most urgent task facing the country. The central government had to reckon with the fact that the Croats, because of geography and culture, had developed a national individuality. The country must, he said, find a solution that would guarantee "a normal common life" for all the people of Yugoslavia.[39]

As a matter of fact, negotiations between Cvetković and Maček had been going on since December, 1938, despite attempts by Stojadinović to discourage them. Cvetković, acting as a "mandatory of the Crown," picked up the thread of negotiations in March. Their legal basis stemmed from those powers allocated to the crown in Article 116 of the constitution.[40]

The two men were able to agree on many points: on fusing the provinces of Croatia and Dalmatia and parts of Bosnia into one administrative unit; on dissolving the parliament and holding new elections for a constituent assembly; on placing control of the armed forces and foreign affairs within the jurisdiction of the central government; on reserving to the constitutional assembly the responsibility of deciding which ministries would remain centralized and which would come under the jurisdiction of the new province, and of completing a definitive reorganization of the state.[41]

After agreeing on these principles Maček and Cvetković sent Košutić to Belgrade with an invitation to the Serbian parties which were members of the United Opposition to participate in the signing of the formal agreement. There Košutić met with representatives of the United Opposition in the home of Dr. Momčilo Ninčić, a leader of the Serbian Radical Party and a former foreign minister. There were sixteen in the group, among them three Serbian politicians: Miša Trifunović of the Radical Party, Milan Grol of the Democratic Party, and Milan Gavrilović of the Agrarian Party. Košutić told them he had come to Belgrade with messages for Prince Paul and Prime Minister Cvetković. Then he disclosed the reason for calling them

---

[39] Dragiša Cvetković, "Srpsko-Hrvatski Sporazum, 1939" ('Serb-Croatian Agreement, 1939'), *Dokumenti o Jugoslaviji,* Paris (1952), pp. 18-26.

[40] Article 116 of the Yugoslav constitution of 1931 permitted the crown, in situations threatening the "public peace, safety of the state" or "public interest" to issue necessary temporary decrees for all or part of the kingdom. These decrees ultimately had to have the approval of the parliament.

[41] Maček to author.

together. It would take time, he said, for the government to meet the demands made by the United Opposition in its Declaration of 1937, which Maček had signed. Meanwhile, through the Maček-Cvetković agreement they could realize some of their hopes for the Croats. He explained the main lines of the agreement and assured them that the Croatian Peasant Party would sign the document with Cvetković. He asked them to assent to the agreement and to authorize Maček to sign on their behalf.

This they refused to do. Gavrilović advanced a number of arguments. He said that by signing this document with Cvetković, Maček would separate the Croat people from the Serbs at a time when unity, especially in foreign affairs, was essential. An agreement with Cvetković meant, for example, supporting the government's policy toward Italy. Now, with the Italians landing in the Balkans, with the certainty that a war in Europe was coming, it was necessary that the Croats and Serbs stand together in the face of danger.

To this argument Košutić gave a particularistic reply: He said he wanted to see an autonomous Croatia, even if it existed only four days before being overrun by an invading army.[42]

Then came another hitch in the proceedings. The Prince Regent refused to approve the draft agreement. According to Maček, Prince Paul was probably under pressure from the Serbian politicians, who saw a threat to their positions in a reorganized state, as well as from Spaho, who feared Bosnia and Hercegovina might be subdivided. Prince Paul approved only the amalgamation of the provinces of Croatia and Dalmatia and the town and county of Dubrovnik.

As soon as he heard that the Prince Regent had disapproved the draft agreement, Maček issued a statement blaming the regent for the failure, called a meeting of the Croat National Assembly, which gave him full authority to represent the Croat nation,[43] and left for a vacation in Slovenia.

Shortly afterward, Ivan Šubašić, one of Maček's advisers, received

---

[42] Milan Gavrilović to author.

[43] *The Times* (London), May 9, 1939. According to Count Csáky, Hungarian foreign minister, Maček was indirectly requesting Germany, Italy, and Hungary to support his movement with propaganda. Both Hungary and Germany agreed not to interfere in Yugoslavia's internal affairs. It was in their interest that tempers in Yugoslavia quiet down. *DGFP*, D, VI, Doc. 295.

an urgent invitation to visit Prince Paul. Their conversation resulted in the resumption of negotiations at meetings on the Šubašić farm. There Cvetković and Maček decided to conclude an agreement on the noncontroversial issues and to postpone discussion of the issues on which they disagreed. Maček gave up insisting on a personal union and asked only for decentralization of the state administration.[44]

Each named three experts to elaborate their various stipulations and draft them into the appropriate legal form. The six experts worked through the hot months of June and July. All went smoothly until they came to the matter of the *gendarmerie*, at that time under the joint jurisdiction of the ministries of interior and war. The Croats had long regarded this police force as a primary instrument of Serbian hegemony. As a consequence, they wanted to place it under the control of the *ban* (governor) of Croatia. The experts representing the central government refused to yield on this point, and the negotiations broke down once more.

Maček's reaction was to threaten secession. If Belgrade could not bring order to the country, he told the foreign press, Germany could. He saw an analogy between the situation of the Croats and that of the Czechs.[45]

Maček spoke with great authority in Croatia. His Croatian Peasant Party was more than a political party within a state. It was almost a state within a state. Like Stojadinović, Maček was acclaimed *vodja* (leader) by his followers. While the youth of Stojadinović's JRZ paraded in green shirts, Maček's Peasant Guards drilled in black and white homespun, their *vodja* astride his white horse at the head of the column. Maček's sphere of influence was smaller than Stojadinović's but the political and economic power he commanded was in many respects greater.

This display of Croatian nationalism was a matter of pride of accomplishment and was not, as many observers believed, completely chauvinistic or separatist. Maček's strength flowed from the achievements of the peasants themselves through their wide-ranging economic cooperative (Gospodarska Sloga) and their cultural societies (Seljačka Sloga), both organized by the Croatian Peasant Party.

The economic cooperative, with 11,000 branches and approximately

---

[44] Regent Perović to Prince Paul, July 30, 1939. (JBH)
[45] *New York Times*, August 2, 1939.

1,500,000 members, had much to its credit. Among other things, it had organized a more efficient system of distributing agricultural products, negotiated minimum wage agreements for agricultural workers, and carried on educational health programs.[46] The cultural cooperative's objective was to wipe out illiteracy among the peasants by 1942. In 1937 alone the cooperative taught fifty thousand men and women the rudiments of reading and writing.

Because many able and devoted people served in these cooperatives to raise the Croatian peasant's standard of living, Croatian nationalism had a program far more substantial than mere slogans calling for resistance to alien rule. Moreover, the system of cooperatives, well-organized and well-manned, had an important political side effect: it provided an effective network for maintaining the solidarity of the Peasant Party machine. This link, in turn, enabled Maček to speak for the majority of the Croatian people in negotiations with Cvetković.

It was not Maček's threats that brought the two parties together again. Instead, it was increasing pressure of events outside Yugoslavia that brought both parties back to the conference table. The Pact of Steel between Germany and Italy, signed on May 22, 1939, and the rumors that the Nazis and the Russians would conclude a non-aggression pact kept the men at the work of negotiation. Public opinion in Yugoslavia was demanding an agreement as a means of strengthening the state. The people quickly grasped the significance of Mussolini's warlike and anti-Yugoslav speech in Rijeka, of Crown Prince Umberto's inspection of Snežnik, a mountain on the Italo-Yugoslav border, and of Marshal Badoglio's June tour of inspection in Albania, particularly around Korče and the shores of Lake Ohrid.[47]

As if these events were not enough, Maček required the reports received early in August from Dr. Juraj Krnjević, a leader of the Croatian Peasant Party self-exiled in Geneva, to convince him that war was inevitable and that it would break out at any moment. Maček concluded that it would be inadvisable for him and his party to contribute to the disunity of the country by remaining in opposition to the government when Hitler's armies marched. Reopening negotiations, Maček and Cvetković intervened only when the experts

[46] Tomasevich, *Peasants, Politics and Economic Change in Yugoslavia,* pp. 614-20.
[47] Perović to Prince Paul, July 30, 1939. (JBH)

were unable to work out a compromise on a specific issue. They temporarily solved the question of the *gendarmerie* by leaving its training to the ministry of war and giving the control of its day-to-day duties to the governor of Croatia. By August 20th, the experts had completed their work and Cvetković took the finished draft to Prince Paul for his approval. On August 23d they signed the *Sporazum* (agreement) and on August 26th formed a new government with Maček as vice-premier.[48]

The *Sporazum* brought together into one administrative unit the provinces of Croatia and Dalmatia and seven adjoining districts where Croats predominated. The central government retained control of foreign affairs, national defense, foreign trade, commerce, transport, public security, religion, mining, weights and measures, insurance, and education policy. Croatia was to have its own legislature in Zagreb, and a separate budget. Its governor would serve at the pleasure of the crown. Crown and legislature would share in making the laws.

In 1939, Maček accepted the proposals offered by Cvetković— although he had rejected these same proposals when they were offered by Stojadinović two years before. That he accepted them now is a commentary on his patriotism and his faith in Prince Paul's word that the agreement would be carried out in full. He recognized the imminence of war, and he did not want his Croats to be branded as subversives, as they would be if they continued to boycott the government in the face of danger to the state.

A Cvetković-Maček government now had to be formed. It was clear that Maček was in a better political position than Cvetković, but if he recognized his superior position, he never flaunted it. He was undoubtedly aware of the possibility that Cvetković's successor, while in favor of the Serbo-Croat agreement in principle, might prove to be more difficult to work with than Cvetković. A number of other elements worked in favor of the Maček-Cvetković collaboration. Maček was exclusively interested in domestic affairs, particularly in transferring, as quickly as possible, jurisdiction over all the rights written into the *Sporazum* from the central government to the new Croatian administrative unit. Cvetković's interests were much broader

---

[48] Maček to author.

and included foreign affairs. A number of Serb political leaders were appalled when they learned that Cvetković was appointed premier. They objected to him as "unserious," variable in opinion, and unqualified by experience to hold the highest position in the government. They thought he had gone too far in giving concessions to the Croats. Moreover, by his obstinacy and "hunger for power" he had, they claimed, prevented a coalition of democratic forces and thereby imperiled the unity of the state on the eve of war. Maček saw Cvetković as a naturally intelligent political partner, shrewd, generous, and loyal to his friends, who would carry out the conditions and spirit of the *Sporazum*.

These, then, were the two men who were to form a new government five days before the Second World War broke upon them. In addition to Cvetković, the new national leadership included Maček as vice-premier, four members of the Radical Party, four members of the Croatian Peasant Party, one member each of the Serbian Agrarian and Independent Democratic Parties, the Slovenian Populist Party, and the Yugoslav Moslem Organization, along with nonparty individuals who held the key portfolios of foreign affairs and defense. Šubašić became governor of Croatia. Premier Cvetković dissolved the national parliament elected in 1938 and the crown empowered the new government to promulgate a new electoral law.

No one in the government was sure the *Sporazum* would pacify Yugoslavia's internal discontents. For example, Maček very soon learned that Cvetković did not consider the boundaries of the new Croatia as definitive because the central government had not yet decided on the new frontiers for Serbia and Slovenia. Maček immediately called together all the members of the parliament who belonged to the Croatian Peasant Party and the Independent Demotric Party. He told them he would not object if the government decided to combine Hercegovina and the remainder of Bosnia and to give the new unit the status of a province. But should the Serbs attempt to incorporate Bosnia and Hercegovina into Serbian territory, the Croats would demand an additional share.[49]

The Yugoslav government still faced three other problems: how

[49] Maček to author.

to prepare the country, economically and financially, for defense; how to strengthen the army; and how to use the Balkan Entente to reinforce the neutrality of the Balkan states.

On May 20, 1939, the Yugoslav destroyer *Beograd* steamed into Portsmouth Harbor. Awaiting it on the quay were General Radović, the Yugoslav attaché in London, the vice-governor of the Yugoslav National Bank, nine trucks, and numerous armed guards of the Bank of England. Instead of passengers, the *Beograd* carried 7,344 gold ingots, a large part of Yugoslavia's gold reserve.[50]

The German foreign office got wind of the transfer in July and urgently requested Heeren to make inquiries in Belgrade. If true, the transfer of gold would imply that anti-Axis propaganda was succeeding in Yugoslavia. Berlin also instructed Minister Heeren to report on another worrisome matter, Prince Paul's visit to London that month. Hristić, the Yugoslav minister in Rome, was not as pro-Axis as he used to be,[51] the foreign office told Heeren, citing this as further evidence of the decline of Axis prestige in Yugoslavia. Although at first Heeren could get no confirmation of any gold shipments, he finally learned from a "reliable source" that as result of the Czech crisis the Yugoslavs had indeed shipped gold to Britain. As to their attitude toward the Axis, he reported that Germany had nothing to fear. Belgrade would avoid being drawn into a conflict between the great powers. If war should come, Yugoslavia would become a war profiteer by selling its products in the same markets it supplied in peacetime, and it would avoid any open breach of neutrality.[52]

Yugoslavia's transfer of its gold reserves to the safer shores of Great Britain and the United States symbolized its hopes for the future and belied its pronouncements of neutrality. About the same time, the Yugoslav government issued in rapid succession a series of decrees that deeply affected the nation's economic and social life. In August, 1939, it authorized the National Bank of Yugoslavia to discount 600 million dinars in national defense bonds. In September, it permitted the armed forces to make "exceptional purchases" without regard to existing regulations and authorized the army to purchase

[50] The Royal Yugoslav government later deposited gold to the value of $47,000,000 in the Federal Reserve Bank in New York.

[51] *DGFP*, D, VI, Doc. 680.

[52] *DGFP*, D, VI, Doc. 691.

up to 300 million dinars worth of cattle and vehicles. In October, it established a system of subsidies to families whose heads were called up as reservists, and ordered the postponement of rents if they were called for a term of fifteen days or more; it also decreed a moratorium on debts and rents for certain other classes of reservists. In early December, the government promulgated a rigorous law under which the state could requisition all goods, private or public, movable or immovable. In principle, it was to pay for these goods in cash or in government bonds.[53] In mid-December it took another important step in financing the war effort by establishing a national defense fund. It ruled that the state could pay for war material in war bonds if the government purchasing agencies lacked cash and authorized the National Bank to raise the legal debt limit and to discount the bonds without limitation.[54]

These, then, were some of the steps toward economic mobilization taken by the Yugoslav government during the first months of the war. These strenuous measures had only one major purpose: to enable Yugoslavia to buy arms. How did the Yugoslav political and military leaders see their defense requirements? What was the nature and condition of the Yugoslav army?

Back in December, 1938, Stojadinović, then premier, had raised the question of defense requirements in a conference with Minister of War Nedić. In that last winter of peace optimism pervaded the conference. The minister of war was certain that Yugoslavia could obtain 100 twenty-millimeter antiaircraft guns from Italy by August, 1939, and 500 fifteen-millimeter guns from Czechoslovakia not later than 1940. The construction of a factory for the manufacture of gas masks was to start at once and would be completed by 1941. The German firm of Krupp would construct a new mill at Zenica for the manufacture of steel for artillery shells and guns. The awarding of the contract to Krupp was particularly advantageous for Yugoslavia since there were several million reichsmarks to Yugoslavia's credit in

[53] Banque National du Royaume de Yugoslavie, Service des Études Économiques, *L'Activité Économique en Yougoslavie en 1939,* Supplement au No. 12 de 1939 (Belgrade, n.d.).

[54] *Službene Novine,* December 2, 1939. The National Bank discounted 558 million dinars of national defense bonds in December, 1939, By February, 1941, the bank had discounted over 7 billion dinars in national defense bonds.

the German clearing account. Nedić believed that the 750,000 artillery shells still on hand from the First World War, together with 180,000 new shells, would be ample for a time. All they needed were the proper fuses, and these they could obtain from Czechoslovakia.

As to aircraft, available to the Yugoslav air force at the beginning of 1939 were 50 reconnaissance planes, 50 fighters, and 50 bombers. Air Force General Dušan Simović recommended that the government buy 150 more aircraft, including 50 Hawker Hind reconnaissance planes, 50 Messerschmidt fighters, and 50 Dornier bombers. Stojadinović was satisfied. With 300 planes Yugoslavia would have by far the strongest air force in the Balkans.[55]

The government advanced $2\frac{1}{2}$ billion dinars ($50 million) to the air force, artillery, and miscellaneous services. Of this, it expected to borrow 600 million dinars from Germany and Italy.

These were the plans; their fulfillment proved difficult. First Krupp demanded from Germany a 100 percent guarantee on the Yugoslav order, which amounted to 100 million reichsmarks. Then Stojadinović had to overcome the opposition of the Yugoslav military, who had always opposed buying equipment from Germany, preferring Czechoslovakia as a source for arms; only after removing two generals from their posts did Stojadinović get his way. Finally, although Göring's agent on the spot, Consul-General Neuhausen, strongly favored closing the deal, at the time of Stojadinović's dismissal he advised postponing the final decision.

But there were further obstacles ahead for Yugoslavia, including a continuing conflict between Germany's ministry of economics and its foreign ministry. Ribbentrop insisted that Göring provide no military or economic assistance without his approval. Yugoslavia became a test case in the struggle between the two ministries. Ribbentrop, seeking to recover all the prerogatives lost by the foreign office to Göring, demanded a "tight, unified conduct of foreign policy" with foreign trade under his control.

Yugoslavia's request for credit and armaments thus became a football for ambitious German bureaucrats as well as an instrument

[55] Report on conference between Prime Minister Stojadinović and Minister of War Nedić, December 23, 1938; Stojadinović to Prince Paul, January 26, 1939. (JBH)

of German foreign policy. The slowness of the procedure caused the Yugoslav minister in Berlin, Ivo Andrić, to complain to the German foreign office that if his government did not get arms from Germany it would have to place orders elsewhere, with Sweden, for example. This, he pointed out, would give the world a strange impression of Germany's relations with Yugoslavia.[56]

It was not until June, 1939, four months after negotiations first began, that an agreement was in sight. Yugoslavia would receive an unspecified amount of credit, always subject to later decisions. Rumors that the French had offered assistance to Yugoslavia may have hastened the signing of the protocol, which finally took place in July. But there was a big drawback. Because the protocol did not specify the amount of credit Yugoslavia was to receive it became a useful lever by which to exert political pressure on Yugoslavia.[57]

For a time the Führer aggravated the situation by delaying deliveries of antiaircraft guns and planes. Finally, however, he dispatched a number of Heinkels and Messerschmidts to appease the uneasy Yugoslavs. Later, needing raw materials for Germany's war industries, the Germans decided to strike a one-sided bargain with Belgrade. In return for Yugoslavia's entire output of copper, plus substantial shipments of lead, zinc, tin, and hemp, they promised to turn over 100 Messerschmidt planes, 120 Skoda antiaircraft guns and 250 (later reduced to 100) Skoda antitank guns.

In this way they forced the Yugoslavs to seize and send to Germany the output of the French-owned Bor copper mine and the British-owned lead and zinc mines. This act served only to inflate German self-esteem since most of the output of these mines, even while they were under French and British management, had always been sold to the German market. But the gesture of confiscation was enough to satisfy Berlin. To the German government, it indicated that Yugoslavia was practicing "benevolent neutrality."[58]

Germany now controlled all the avenues of supply open to Yugoslavia. American armament manufacturers, having already committed their output to the British and the French, were unable either to

[56] *DGFP*, D, V, Docs. 288, 300, 307, 409, and 683.
[57] *DGFP*, D, VI, Docs. 573, 615, 620, 686, 210, 279, 687, 703, and 758.
[58] *DGFP*, D, VIII, Docs. 53 and 117; and *DGFP*, D, VII, Doc. 532.

accept orders or to make deliveries earlier than eighteen months after receipt of the order.[59]

Before signing the contract with Germany which turned over the total output of its copper, lead, and zinc, the Yugoslav government turned to the Unted States, offering bauxite and cement for American cotton. They also wanted to buy antitank and antiaircraft guns and heavy cannon. Prince Paul pointed out that he could obtain these items from Germany on terms that would place Yugoslavia in economic bondage. He emphasized that although there were excellent fortifications on Yugoslavia's frontiers with Germany and Italy, there was not a single heavy cannon to place on those fortifications.[60] But the concept of bulk purchasing as a means of assuring a state's neutrality had not yet entered the calculations of the United States Department of State or of the Munitions Board. The idea of economic warfare was a thing of the future.

Almost the only resource Yugoslavia did not have to ship to Germany was its army. The Yugoslav infantryman was a hardy soldier and the Serb soldier particularly had earned a well-deserved reputation during the First World War for his courage, stamina, and tenacity. The Yugoslav army in January, 1939, totaled 1,457,760 men,[61] including reserves. When fully mobilized the army would consist of thirty infantry divisions, one guards division, and three cavalry divisions.

While the training of the men was excellent, the discipline was extremely severe, reducing personal initiative to a minimum. The reason for this lay as much in the nature of the officer corps as in the military system per se. A high percentage of the generals were Serbs[62] who considered the army an exclusive Serb institution and looked on it as a means of expressing and expanding Serb hegemony. By becoming a political instrument the army opened still wider the gulf between the various national groups. As Slovene and Croatian

---

[59] Fotitch, *War We Lost,* pp. 22-24. See also *FRUS,* I (1939), 448.

[60] *FRUS,* II (1939), 888-90.

[61] Yugoslav Ministry of War, *Statistical Survey of the Yugoslav Army, January 1, 1939* (MS). (JBH)

[62] Of the 165 generals in active service in 1938, 161 were Serbs, 2 were Croats, and 2 Slovenes. Tomasevich, *Peasants, Politics and Economic Change in Yugoslavia,* p. 242. On the other hand, most high-ranking naval officers were Dalmatians and Slovenes.

opposition leaders began to show increasing hostility to the central government, many Serb officers went so far as to look on the troops from Slovenia and Croatia as potential subversives, reasoning that those who followed anti-Serb leaders were necessarily antistate.[63]

Despite the older officers' resistance to technical information and their inability to recognize the need for change, the younger Serb officers received satisfactory military training. Those in the higher ranks, those who served during the First World War, lived in the glory of the past and thought in terms of the past—of trench warfare, for example, rather than of air strikes and blitz tactics. Confronted with the need for change, they resisted, justifying their position with repeated references to such Serb victories as that at Kajmakčalan. The situation was no better in the general staff. It was composed mainly of Serbs, who relied on Croatian and Slovene officers to solve the important and difficult problems of training and supply.

The events of 1938-39 shook the confidence of the Serb generals. They began to look on the Croats as possible German agents and to fear them, and for this and other reasons they began to organize a special military force—the četnik odredi (chetnik detachments). One of their tasks was to check on, report, and if possible control the activities of Croatian civilians and soldiers. A consequence was a rapid deterioration in the discipline of the army. The fissures that had already existed among the national groups of Yugoslavia grew wider and wider.[64]

Yugoslav diplomacy turned next to the Balkan Entente as a hopeful means of keeping the country at peace and of keeping war out of the entire area. During the February, 1939, meeting of the Balkan

[63] Vauhnik to author. In 1939, General (then Colonel) Dragoljub (Draža) Mihailović urged Minister of War Milan Nedić to organize purely Serb units because, he said, "we cannot count on the Croats and the national minorities in case of war." Branko Lazitch, *Tito et la Révolution Yougoslave, 1937-1956* (Paris: Fasquelle Éditeurs, 1957), p. 53.

[64] Vauhnik to author. Vauhnik believed that if in 1941 the Yugoslav army had carried out its plans for a guerrilla war, it would have fulfilled its task with success and honor. The army was Yugoslav-minded. But the responsible generals and officers had grown weak from inactivity and twenty years of soft living. The generals lacked the courage to sacrifice themselves. For an intimate picture and concrete examples of Vauhnik's conclusions, see King Peter II, *King's Heritage*, pp. 49-54.

Entente in Bucharest, Gafencu, speaking for other members of the Entente as well as for Rumania, assured the German minister, Fabricius, that the Little Entente was dead and that the Balkan Entente would never become an anti-German instrument. The four countries concurred in the view that "Germany's drive toward the east was a natural phenomenon which would increase in strength." They admitted that the Balkans would have to realize this fact of life and cooperate closely with Germany, particularly in the economic sphere.[65] Gafencu said nothing to Fabricius about Bulgaria, the missing part of the Balkan political jigsaw puzzle.

Heretofore, the inability of the entente to rebuff the recurring interventions of the Axis in the political life of the Balkan peninsula was in large part a result of Bulgaria's lack of participation in the defense of the area. In this situation Bulgaria's territorial demands had become an instrument of great-power politics; Bulgaria would participate in a common Balkan defense effort only to the degree that Greece, Rumania, and Yugoslavia satisfied its territorial claims. From Rumania, Bulgaria claimed the southern Dobrudja, lost by the Treaty of Bucharest of 1913 after the second Balkan war, and from Greece parts of western Thrace, lost after the First World War. From Yugoslavia and Greece, Bulgaria demanded Macedonia, lost by the Treaty of Bucharest and confirmed by the Treaty of Neuilly of 1919.

Yugoslavia took the first step toward a *détente* with Bulgaria by signing a treaty of friendship on January 24, 1937. On July 31, 1938, at Salonika, the states of the Balkan Entente, together with Bulgaria, signed an agreement in which all parties renounced force in their mutual relations, permitted Bulgaria to increase the size of its army, and opened a way for further discussion of proposed revision of the Thracian frontier.[66]

These gestures did not satisfy the Bulgars. They would not enter the Balkan Entente without specific frontier revisions. For them, the Dobrudja question was urgent, so urgent that they told the Germans they were ready to cooperate economically and politically with them if Germany would only back their territorial demands.[67]

[65] *DGFP*, D, V, Doc. 304.
[66] *DIA*, I (1938), 287-88.
[67] *DGFP*, D, VI, Doc. 67.

By April, 1939, the British began to increase their efforts to rally the Balkan states into some form of collective union to limit the ever-widening spread of German influence. The British minister in Ankara, Knatchbull-Hugessen, urged the Turks to try to bring Bulgaria into the Balkan Entente. They could do it, he thought, by getting Rumania to promise to reconsider the Dobrudja question. Although for a while his appeal held some hope, Rumanian Foreign Minister Gafencu would agree only to take up the matter with Belgrade. If Yugoslavia refused to give up territory to Bulgaria, he pointed out, there would be little value in Rumania's doing so alone.[68]

Although in June, Germany told the Yugoslavs to dissociate themselves from the Balkan Entente,[69] they continued to make every effort to bring Bulgaria into a Balkan bloc. On July 4th, Cincar-Marković and Bulgarian Minister-President Kiosseivanov met in Bled to discuss relations between their two countries in view of the continued existence of the Balkan Pact and in the event it ceased to exist. They also discussed the advisability of joint neutrality in case of pressure from either the Axis or the western democracies, or both of these power blocs, and the length of time Bulgaria and Yugoslavia would be able to remain neutral. Both expressed the hope that the two countries, together and simultaneously, would join the same side if the time came when they had to abandon their neutrality. Bulgaria, according to Kiosseivanov, would enter the war on the side chosen by Yugoslavia and with Yugoslavia would also join all blocs permitted by its commitments. They also discussed the possibilities for political, economic, and military cooperation even to the point of a military alliance. They found they were in full agreement on all points.[70] In the words of the communiqué, "the two states agreed on a policy of economic collaboration [and agreed] that a policy of independence and neutrality served both the interests of the two countries and peace in the Balkans and that it was necessary that both governments continue a policy of good and friendly relations toward all their neighbors."[71]

The satisfaction expressed by Kiosseivanov on July, 10, in Bled

[68] *DBFP*, III, 5, Docs. 62, 63, 73, 162, 279, 285, and 297.
[69] *DGFP*, D, VI, Doc. 884.
[70] *Dokumenti o Jugoslavije*, Paris (July, 1956), No. 8.
[71] *Politika*, Belgrade, July 11, 1939.

became dissatisfaction ten days later in Sofia. Yugoslavia had refused to denounce the Balkan Pact on the ground that it was better to remain a part of the pact and direct its development. Kiosseivanov told the Germans he could not get an answer from Cincar-Marković on what position Yugoslavia would take if Turkey attacked Bulgaria, nor did he believe Prince Paul's visit to London would result in any good for Bulgaria.[72]

In London Prince Paul told Halifax that he would like to see the Dobrudja issue settled. But he was opposed, he said, to Bulgaria's obtaining a port on the Aegean sea. That, he feared, would give the Italians one more door by which to enter the Balkan house.[73]

Soon after Hitler's invasion of Poland, Cincar-Marković and Gafencu met to discuss ways of reinforcing the entente and to work out a solution to the Bulgarian problem, a solution agreeable to all members of the Entente. On three conditions, they decided, certain territorial claims of the Bulgars would receive consideration:

1. Bulgaria must become part of the Balkan Entente and assume all the commitments and responsibilities of a member state.

2. Each member state of the entente must contribute territory to the Balkan community with which to satisfy Bulgaria's demands.

3. The Bulgarian government must put down all agitators who would increase tensions among the states of the entente.[74]

Their declaration contained no specific reference to territorial

---

[72] *DGFP*, D, VI, Doc. 689. See also *DDI*, VIII, 12, Docs. 628, 629, 217, 441, 473, 490, 510, 533, 548, 551, 559, 596, and 612; *DDI*, VIII, 13, Doc. 190.

[73] *DBFP*, III, 6, Docs. 393 and 534.

[74] Gafencu, *Prelude to the Russian Campaign*, pp. 124 and 260; and *FRUS*, I (1939), 476-77. The word "Dobrudja" was a symbol. It inflamed the Rumanians, the Bulgars, and the Turks. The Rumanians would not part with a stick or a stone from that area. The Bulgars wanted much more of it. When they were not complaining of their irredenta, they complained that the Rumanians permitted a large number of Bulgars in the Dobrudja to flee to Bulgaria to avoid serving in the Rumanian army. This proved to Bulgaria that Rumania was not denationalizing the Dobrudja, as it had promised to do. Alexander Avakumović, counselor of the Yugoslav legation in Bucharest, to Cincar-Marković, April 18, 1939. (JBH) Yet the Turks could not even mention Dobrudja to the Rumanians without running the risk of halting any negotiations. In calmer moments the Rumanians considered exchanging populations as the only possible solution to this vexing problem. *DBFP*, III, 5, Docs. 329, 414, and 534.

changes. The four states did not get down to specific points until February, 1940, when the council of the Balkan Entente met in Belgrade. There they decided to support a policy of peace, to remain on good terms with their neighbors, to conclude agreements with all the Balkan countries, particularly commercial agreements, and to extend the life of the pact for seven more years.[75] The communiqué on the meeting did not mention their decisions to limit the military commitments of the Balkan allies to those stated in the pact and to draw up plans for a common defense against aggression.[76]

Although the Bulgars knew about these decisions and about the Balkan Entente's move to grant territorial concessions, they did not join the organized Balkan community, because in mid-February, 1940, the moderate Kiosseivanov government fell and was succeeded by a government much more sensitive to the opinions of Germany and the Soviet Union. Russia, which at one time had counseled the Balkan states to take a firm stand against Bulgarian territorial demands, now supported Bulgarian revisionism. Bulgaria undoubtedly felt it safer to endure the wrath of the Balkan Entente than to risk the anger of two great powers. Southern Dobrudja, the Bulgars told the Germans, was now a minimum national aspiration. They would continue to resist "the wooing of the Balkan Entente and again decline any offers of economic cooperation." Bulgaria could realize its national aspirations, they said, only when it stood side by side with Germany.[77]

By opening the dam of Bulgarian revisionism, Germany and the Soviet Union had washed away all plans for unified Balkan resistance to aggression.

The Führer was annoyed with the Yugoslavs in the days just before the outbreak of the war. Stojadinović's dismissal, Prince Paul's close

---

[75] *Politika,* Belgrade, February 5, 1940.

[76] Papagos, *Battle of Greece, 1940-41,* pp. 73-75 and 152-216. Although the member states did not then realize it, this was the last meeting of the Balkan Entente.

[77] *DGFP,* D, IX, Doc. 198. The "minimum national aspiration" was realized only after a chain of events that began on June 28, 1940. Then the Soviet Union wrested Bessarabia and northern Bukovina from Rumania. On August 30th, the Axis powers sliced northern Transylvania from Rumania for Hungary and a week later amputated southern Dobrudja for Bulgaria from a now truncated Rumania.

ties with the British, their failure, perhaps even refusal, to leave the League of Nations, their refusal to permit Germany to control the destiny of the Balkan Entente, Prince Paul's rejection of Germany's recommendation that he make an unequivocal statement on behalf of the Axis—all these caused Hitler to regard Yugoslavia as "an uncertain neutral."[78] To him, all this added up to one clear-cut policy: Yugoslavia would remain neutral only until the Allies were winning the war, and then Yugoslavia would come out openly on the side of the democracies. In this period of neutrality, he pointed out to Ciano, Yugoslavia was in a favorable position to influence the course of events to the disadvantage of the Axis. Consequently, he stressed, Italy should liquidate Yugoslavia. An act of this kind could only strengthen the Axis.[79] Earlier Ribbentrop had told Ciano that Yugoslavia was faithless and that he hoped the Italians would take advantage of the turmoil that would be caused by the German invasion of Poland to settle matters in Croatia and Dalmatia.

Disgusted, Ciano returned to Rome. He rejected the idea of Italy's being dragged into war. The Germans, he told Mussolini, were liars and betrayers. The Duce first agreed with him, but then the prospect of empire became too much for him. It smothered his sense of Italy's weakness as a war-making machine. He rationalized his desire for loot with a staunch belief that honor compelled him to go to war. He told himself that with the booty he would take out of Croatia and Dalmatia he could build a shrine to his honor.[80] He lost no time ordering his chief of general staff, Badoglio, to prepare for an attack on Greece and Yugoslavia.

Like Ciano, Badoglio was not enthusiastic about throwing his forces into Yugoslavia. What help could they expect from the Hungarians and Bulgarians? Could he use the Drava Valley? That is, could he swing his troops along the Hungarian border? In reply, Mussolini wrote that Hungary and Bulgaria would not oppose the Italian forces and would later come in on their side. For the time being, Badoglio should not use the Drava valley but wait for an opportune moment. Presumably, the Duce did not wish to offend

[78] *IMT*, Doc. TC 77. See also *USMT*, Doc. 3422.
[79] Ciano, *L'Europa*, p. 451.
[80] Ciano, *Ciano's Diary, 1939-1943*, p. 125.

Nazi sensibilities by sending Italian troops too close to a German sphere of influence.[81]

The very day he sent these instructions to Badoglio, Germany and the Soviet Union signed their nonaggression pact. This put a new light on the international situation. Ciano decided that Italy must wait, must make no hasty decision, must prepare "to gain something" for itself in Croatia and Dalmatia. It could do this by organizing a special army to strike in Croatia at the proper moment, and by establishing contact with anti-Yugoslav Croats in Italy and Yugoslavia.

Now the Duce became convinced of the importance of remaining neutral.[82] A more effective deterrent than Hitler's letter rejecting his assistance in the invasion of Poland was his sudden realization that Italy was not prepared for a long military campaign and that he was dependent militarily and economically on Germany.[83] The position of playing a neutral part in a Europe that was getting ready to fight humiliated the Duce, Ciano wrote. "But I can't see a way out," he added. "Our absolute military unpreparedness, our lack of adequate supplies, and our economic dependence will force us to remain in our present position for a long time, which doesn't displease me in the least. The day will come when everybody will see the great advantages that nonbelligerency has given Italy."

Mussolini had the desire for war in that August of 1939, but not the sinews of war, and thus the Kingdom of Yugoslavia was spared temporarily.

To the Yugoslavs, a neutral Italy meant a neutral Yugoslavia. They had declared their neutrality in the German-Polish war. But the Yugoslavs would fight if attacked, Prince Paul assured Halifax, although they knew it would mean their country would be overrun by Axis forces. Much depended, then, on what Great Britain could do to interrupt Italian communications with Albania and knock Italy out of the war as quickly as possible. The possibility should not be overlooked, Prince Paul told Halifax, that the Germans might send large air force reinforcements to assist the Italians in North Africa.

The Prince Regent read with suspicion and distrust Italy's declara-

[81] *DDI*, VIII, 13, Docs. 162 and 186.
[82] Ciano, *Ciano's Diary, 1939-1943*, pp. 131, 143 and 183. Italy became a non-belligerent, then a new term in international relations.
[83] Badoglio, *Italy in the Second World War*, pp. 6 and 8.

tion of neutrality at the outbreak of the German-Polish war. He assured Sir Ronald Campbell that if Great Britain permitted Italy to assume a position of neutrality, with the prospect of coming into the war later on the German side, then the consequences would prove incalculable. If Italy entered the war at a time when it could operate from Albania—under cover of German forces released from the Polish front—then the British would be responsible for starting a process of rot throughout the Balkans. Yugoslavia, Greece, Rumania, and perhaps even Turkey, Prince Paul predicted, would be driven sooner or later to make such terms as they could with Germany. The British considered the Prince Regent's outburst something akin to hysteria. Italy, they believed, would not prove to be a difficult enemy.[84]

The Germans too were kept informed by the Yugoslavs of their attitude toward Italy. If Italy entered the war and advanced on Salonika, the Yugoslavs would defend their neutrality. The road to Salonika led through their country.[85] After defeating Poland, the Axis might threaten, if not attack, them. To defend themselves, the Yugoslavs mobilized to a strength of 500,000 men and put two armies along the entire northern frontier, from the Adriatic to Rumania. Although Germany was furnishing planes and other war material to Bulgaria and giving nothing to Yugoslavia,[86] the mobilization went on.

In September, 1939, the Yugoslav government had little more in the way of equipment than unlimited determination to resist a forced entry into the war on either side or an invasion by the Axis. To maintain their independence, the Yugoslav government and people would have to have much more than determination. On September 1st, they had only to look at a map to realize their geographical predicament. They were almost completely ringed by a belligerent power, a so-called "nonbelligerent" and smaller states of dubious neutrality. To avoid being swallowed up, they would have to exercise more than determined will to survive as an independent nation. They would have to grant grudging benevolencies to the Axis for the time being so that at the proper moment they could come out on the side

---

[84] *DBFP*, III, 6, Doc. 393; and *DBFP*, III, 7, Docs. 554-56.

[85] *DGFP*, D, VII, Doc. 112.

[86] *FRUS*, I (1939), 420-21. King Boris of Bulgaria complained to the Germans that the Yugoslavs interfered with German arms shipments to his country. He said continued interference would compel him to obtain his supplies from Russia instead. *DGFP*, D, VIII, Doc. 229.

of the Allies. They would have to perfect the art of procrastination and bargaining.[87] They would have to have armed strength, high national morale and, above all, Allied understanding of their policy and Allied willingness to abet it.

Yugoslavia's diplomats, adept though they tried to be, and its policy, supple as they tried to make it, were limited by certain almost immutable facts. The country's defenses in pivotal areas—those where the face of the enemy came closest—were not buttressed by strong natural frontiers. The government knew that industrial power and military power went hand in hand. Lacking one, Yugoslavia perforce lacked the other. The economic structure of the country was shaky and ill-prepared for the introduction of a war economy. A breach in the Yugoslav political and social structure was newly and superficially healed. The therapeutic process had not been completely accepted or approved by all Serbian political parties. In parliament the followers of former Premier Stojadinović tried in vain to split the party he had fathered, by using Cvetković's Croat policy as a lever. Although not willing to recognize the validity of the *Sporazum,* some Serbian politicians of the Agrarian and Radical parties were willing to participate in the Cvetković government. Other Radical and National party members bitterly opposed the *Sporazum.* They still carried within themselves the fantasy of a Great Serbia populated and governed by valorous, hence superior, men who had routed the Turks from Serbian soil. Disintegration of the united front of political parties opposed first to the policy of King Alexander and then to that of Prince Paul accelerated with every politician who opposed government policy on one occasion and served it on the next. Cvetković's reliance for support on Serb politicians who did not represent the majority of their parties was the chink in his political armor.

Could the new Cvetković-Maček government, a jerry-built coalition of divergent historical, geographical and cultural interests, continue its program of internal pacification and at the same time develop a consensus enabling it to hold fast to its policy of neighborliness and neutrality? Each depended on the other. In the end, their relationship would determine whether Yugoslavia would remain neutral, or become a belligerent, or face an Axis invasion.

[87] *DBFP,* III, 4, Docs. 100 and 426.

VII

THE END OF
NEUTRALITY

Prince Paul spoke freely and frankly to Brugère, the French minister in Belgrade, in September, 1939. The Prince Regent seemed free of the worries that the Croatian question had caused him, and during most of the conversation they talked of Italy. Hristrić, the Yugoslav minister in Rome, had reported on an important conversation with Ciano. Italy would remain neutral, Ciano had said, only so long as the interests of the Axis required it and would enter the war whenever it saw fit to do so.

Although the conflict was less than a week old and the democracies were still mobilizing, in his talk with Brugère Prince Paul urged that the French land in Salonika as quickly as possible, with or without Italy's consent,[1] to prevent the Axis from bringing the war to the Balkans and to assure Yugoslavia an exit to the sea, a bridgehead to the west. A Salonika open to Yugoslav traffic would mean the continuance of Yugoslav neutrality, a neutrality that would one day transform itself into belligerency on the side of the Allies. Before that happened, however, the Allies would have to gain control of the Mediterranean and the Adriatic.[2]

But the French could not comply with Prince Paul's request, although the importance of Salonika was as apparent to them as to the Yugoslavs. General Weygand sent word to Prince Paul that it would take three months to put the first elements of the French expeditionary forces into the line in Greece.[3]

[1] Brugère, *Veni, Vidi Vichy,* pp. 165-66.
[2] *FRUS,* I (1939), 238. Purić, Yugoslav minister to France, told United States Ambassador Bullitt that Yugoslavia would be fighting with the Allies within sixty days after the British and the French wiped out the Italian fleet and won control of the Mediterranean. See also Auswärtiges Amt, Doc. 38.
[3] Brugère, *Veni, Vidi Vichy,* p. 4.

Plans for an Allied landing in the Balkans evolved slowly during the early months of the war. General Weygand was willing to send a corps from the Levant into Salonika, but only if Greece approved the landing and neutral Italy raised no objection to it.[4] The British generals, on the other hand, said sending troops into the Balkans was out of the question. In their opinion, Salonika was not a suitable base for operations.[5] They were horrified, in fact, at the thought of trying to work with the Balkan military because of the difficulty in maintaining strict security.

Weygand believed there were two fundamental reasons behind this opposition by the British. First, they wanted to give Italy no excuse for abandoning its policy of neutrality. Second, they thought it a sheer impossibility to supply war materials to the Balkans out of the Allies' meager reserves. But eventually the British and the French were able to get together on plans for a Balkan theater of operations, with the long-range objective of maintaining and occupying bridgeheads from Salonika to the Dardanelles, and making it possible for the French to come to the aid of the Yugoslavs.[6]

The Yugoslavs participated wholeheartedly in the planning of the operation. In November, Prince Paul suggested closer collaboration with the French and asked permission to send a military mission to Paris. On his part, Weygand wished to send an air force officer to Belgrade to maintain discreet contacts with the Yugoslav, Rumanian, and Greek high commands without involving the British.[7]

In the months between September, 1939, and May, 1940, Belgrade's policy of neutrality disintegrated together with the French military counterweight to the Axis. Prince Paul actively encouraged Franco-Yugoslav military collaboration despite the ubiquity of German spies in Belgrade. In mid-April, at his suggestion, Minister of War Nedić and French Minister Brugère exchanged views on the best means of reinforcing contacts between the Yugoslav and the French general staffs. They agreed, for example, that Nedić would permit one of

[4] Weygand, *Mémoires*, III, 41; Gamelin, *Servir*, III, 213.

[5] For a statement of the position of the British military, see Playfair *et al.*, *War in the Mediterranean and the Middle East*, I, 50-51.

[6] Weygand, *Mémoires*, pp. 48-50. The Greeks did not completely agree with Weygand's proposal. Papagos, *Battle of Greece, 1940-1941*, pp. 58-79, and Auswärtiges Amt, Doc. 131.

[7] Weygand, *Mémoires*, p. 64; Auswärtiges Amt, Docs. 50, 51, and 128.

General Weygand's associates to enter Yugoslavia in civilian clothes to visit, in the greatest secrecy, Yugoslavia's military installations. But a month later all such ideas went into limbo. With the British retreat from Norway General Weygand for the moment shelved his plans for a landing at Salonika, and a few weeks later had to abandon them permanently.[8]

But the fall of France in June, 1940, did not bury the issue. Like the phoenix, Salonika became a symbol that rose again and again before the year was over. The menace of Italy, its policy of dubious neutrality, hung like a cloud over the Balkans. Bluntly Prince Paul told Heeren he found no semblance of truth or sincerity in Italy's policy and had nothing but distrust for Germany's friends, the Italians.[9]

The Yugoslavs had good reason to suspect Italy's intentions. They had only to watch the railroad stations to determine Italy's attitude toward Yugoslavia at any given moment. Whenever Italian troops were moving north, they could conclude that relations were worsening. In addition, there was always talk in Rome of "seizing Greece or Yugoslavia in the same offhand way that one would decide to order a cup of coffee."[10] Ciano wrote that the Duce's hands fairly itched to grab onto Croatia, Dalmatia, and the islands of the Adriatic. Mussolini, Ciano reported, believed that neither the French nor the British would retaliate if Italy attacked Yugoslavia.[11]

During the early months of 1940 two seemingly disparate elements saved Yugoslavia from Italian aggression. In March the Germans flatly told Mussolini to keep his hands off the Balkans.[12] The Duce yielded—for a time. That was the first element. The second was Italy's state of military unpreparedness; Mussolini simply did not have the material with which to start real trouble.

[8] Auswärtiges Amt, Docs. 58 en 64.

[9] *DGFP*, D, IX, Docs. 100 and 191.

[10] Raymond de Belot, *Struggle for the Mediterranean, 1939-1945* (Princeton: Princeton University Press, 1951), p. 74. Admiral de Belot quotes the Italian admiral, Armellini.

[11] Ciano, *Ciano's Diary, 1939-1943*, pp. 234 and 331-32. He was correct. Churchill opposed going to war with Italy if it attacked Yugoslavia. He preferred to wait and see if it was an attack on Yugoslavia's integrity or merely a grab for naval bases in the Adriatic. Churchill, *Their Finest Hour*, pp. 128-29.

[12] *DGFP*, D, VIII, Doc. 669. See also Halder, *Diary*, entries for March 28, April 24, and May 8, 19, and 23, 1940 (mimeographed).

Toward the end of April the Yugoslav fever shook him again. He must force Yugoslavia to its knees, he told General Graziani. Only Yugoslavia could supply the raw materials—copper, lead, zinc, bauxite —that Italy so desperately needed. He would move offensively against Yugoslavia, defensively against France. But Graziani dashed his hopes, stressing the inadequacies of the army, showing that it might be bottled up as it neared the Sava river.[13] Even Ciano came to the conclusion that Yugoslavia must remain untouched for a long time.

But the Duce was not one to consider restraint a virtue, particularly when Yugoslavia was involved. As Hitler's armies won one victory after another in the Low Countries, both Mussolini and Ciano began to think of Pavelić, the Croat nationalist leader, and of putting him at the head of a Croat army. Behind their hasty plans lay the jealous fear that the Croats might line up with Germany before Italy brought them into camp.[14]

Through its Vatican contacts as well as its own intelligence sources in Italy, the Yugoslav government learned of the possibility of a Pavelić-led insurrection in Croatia and of the military preparations directed against Yugoslavia.

There was only one way, short of war, to discourage Mussolini's dream of dismembering Yugoslavia. That was with a diplomatic stroke of some kind. What was it to be? It was out of the question for Yugoslavia to reinsure itself with Germany by allying itself politically or militarily with the Nazis. Tradition and public opinion prohibited such a move. France and Britain would not be able to agree on a Balkan operation of any kind so long as Britain considered Italy's neutrality sacrosanct. Turkey's position was not at all clear. The reservations written into the pact of the Balkan Entente by the Greeks eliminated them as allies in an Italo-Yugoslav war. There was only one great power on the continent of Europe strong enough to stop Italy and Germany long enough for second thoughts—the Soviet Union. But for Yugoslavia to negotiate even the simplest of agreements

[13] Rodolfo Graziani, *Ho Difeso La Patria* (Milan: Garzanti, 1951), pp. 191-93.
[14] Ciano, *Ciano's Diary, 1939-1943*, pp. 243-44 and 246-49. In May, despite the promise of the Italians that they would not go into the Balkans, the commander-in-chief of the German army, Von Brauchitsch, told Ribbentrop that he personally should prevent Italy from creating chaos there. *DGFP*, D, IX, Docs. 245, 323, and 328.

with the Russians would mean the reversal of a policy of twenty-three years' standing.

Like Paris, Belgrade in the early twenties became a center for those who fled revolutionary Russia. Yugoslavia welcomed as victims of a regicide government the men of Denikin's and Wrangel's armies, and its government bureaus absorbed as many as possible. For their sons it established a military school, and for their daughters a replica of Smolny Institute, both administered in the best czarist tradition. The Yugoslavs, and particularly the Serbs, had both historical and dynastic reasons for welcoming the *émigrés* with such warmth. Many kept fresh the memory of Russia's friendship for Serbia in its struggle for independence and in the first hard years of the First World War. They shared the Orthodox Church, and there were, in addition, ties of kinship between the Houses of Karageorgević and Romanov. Furthermore, the Russian *émigrés* contributed a great deal that was of value to the material and cultural life of Yugoslavia. These refugees from the October Revolution, men and women of many diverse talents and professions, added to their new country's supply of doctors, farm and forestry experts, professors, musicans, ballet dancers, military and navy experts. Thus were Belgrade's doors opened to the Russian monarchists.

Until late 1939, a Mr. Strandtman, the former counselor of the imperial Russian embassy, represented czarist Russia in Belgrade. His name appeared in the *Liste du Corps Diplomatique* and the imperial double eagle hung over the entrance to the embassy across the street from the royal palace of the Karageorgevićs. Although by 1934 Yugoslavia had agreed, under pressure from the Czechs, not to oppose admission of the Soviet Union to the League of Nations, it had continued to refuse to recognize the U.S.S.R. for more than two decades after the war. After 1935, the Yugoslavs saw that they would ultimately have to recognize the Soviet Union, but they would do so only under certain conditions. It was necessary, Prince Paul advised the government, "to procrastinate as long as possible." [15]

Recognize the Soviet Union only if absolutely necessary and only when conditions in the country become completely quiet and orderly. Keep in

[15] Undated memorandum by Prince Paul. (JBH)

mind that the future Soviet minister will become the nucleus for all the dissatisfied elements [including] even the opposition. He would probably attract even the broader masses of the people by his Orthodoxy and Slavism.

Recalling that Hartvig, the Russian minister during the years before the First World War, had used Serbia to advance Russia's interests, Prince Paul proposed that they take a leaf from Hartvig's book.

We should make use of Russia, even a nationalist Russia, for our purposes. But we must never surrender ourselves to it, for since we are relatives it is that much more dangerous for us. At all costs prevent Russia from entering the Balkans, i.e., Constantinople.[16]

Nonetheless, by the fall of 1939, it seemed desirable for Yugoslavia to approach the Soviet Union. Internal conditions were propitious; the *Sporazum* had eased the Croatian problem. During the last week of September, observers noted that Prince Paul conferred with Mr. Strandtman. Not long after their meeting, Mr. Strandtman let it be known he was no longer functioning as a diplomat for a government that no longer existed. But there seemed no urgency in Prince Paul's decision to recognize the Soviet Union. Because of the Russian invasion of Finland, the Yugoslavs considered it advisable to defer negotiations so as to avoid irritating the French and the English, and it was not until the end of March, 1940—after the rumors from Italy —that the government actually began to lay the groundwork. Then Cincar-Marković instructed the Yugoslav minister in Ankara, Ilya Šumenković, to approach his Soviet counterpart, Terentiev, with the proposal that the two countries establish economic relations. At the same time, Šumenković was told to impress Moscow, through the Soviet Union's minister in Ankara, with Italy's expansionist tendencies, and to express the conviction that the Soviet Union ought not tolerate this policy. Moscow formally replied that it opposed Italy's aspirations in the Balkans, and came out energetically for the maintenance of the *status quo*. Underscoring this point, the Soviet Union said it was ready to begin economic discussions with Yugoslavia.[17]

---

[16] Undated memorandum by Prince Paul. (JBH) He told Heeren that he feared a strengthening of Soviet influence in southeast Europe, which might operate in Yugoslavia under the guise of pan-Slavism. *DGFP*, D, VIII, Doc. 155. See also *FRUS*, I (1939), 447.

[17] Sumenković to author.

On April 15th each government appointed its delegation to pursue the economic talks. On a diplomatic level, the Soviet Union appointed Lavrentiev, its minister in Sofia, to negotiate directly with the Yugoslav government. On April 21st the Yugoslav commercial delegation headed by Djordjević, former finance minister, left for Moscow. It represented all the national groups of Yugoslavia and included Obradović, the deputy minister of commerce, Mikić, vice-governor of the National Bank, Bičanić, a Croat and head of the Export Institute, and Avsenek, a Slovene industrialist.

Three weeks later, on May 11th, Djordjević and Obradović for Yugoslavia and the People's Commissar for Foreign Trade, Anastas Mikoyan, for the Soviet Union signed three documents: a treaty of commerce and navigation, a protocol covering methods of payments for goods, and an agreement establishing commercial delegations in Belgrade and Moscow. The Russians were particularly interested in metals, specifically copper, the Yugoslavs in gas and oil.

The People's Commissar for Foreign Affairs, V. M. Molotov, made certain that his government's attitude on developments in the Balkans would be clear to the Yugoslavs even if stated indirectly. Three times he told Djordjević of Moscow's position. He never said flatly that his government would oppose an Italian or German advance into the Danubian region. On the other hand, he "did not exclude the possibility." The Yugoslav delegation apparently translated this to mean that the Soviet Union would, more probably than not, openly oppose Axis incursions into the Balkans. This augured well for their country's defense.[18]

In this way Yugoslavia took the first step toward a *rapprochement* with the Soviet Union. Negotiations leading to formal recognition began at the end of May. At that time Šumenković received instructions to sound out Terentiev on the idea of establishing diplomatic relations. Speaking only for himself, Terentiev said he thought his government would look favorably on a proposal from Belgrade. In response to this question, Šumenković assured him the proposal was official.

On June 10, 1940, Moscow expressed its approval of negotiations leading toward recognition, and there followed two weeks of dis-

[18] Brugère, *Veni, Vidi Vichy*, pp. 167-68.

cussions about such minor questions as housing. The czarist embassy in Belgrade included on its non-extraterritorial grounds a Maison des Refugiés Russes and a chapel. These, for obvious reasons, the Yugoslav government could not turn over to the Soviet Union. The Russian negotiators proved amenable and accepted another property.

On June 24th in Ankara, Terentiev and Šumenković signed an agreement establishing diplomatic relations between the Soviet Union and the Kingdom of Yugoslavia, thus temporarily opening new avenues to Yugoslav diplomacy in its search for peace in the Balkans.

For its effect on domestic politics the Yugoslav government sent as its minister to Moscow a leader in the Serbian Agrarian Party and in the United Opposition, Milan Gavrilović. His mission was to arouse the Soviet leaders to the dangers surrounding Yugoslavia and the Balkans, to obtain armaments, and in case of Axis aggression against Yugoslavia, to obtain the help of the Red army. Unfortunately, the time was not right and Gavrilović was never able to complete his mission.

The Germans did not look with tolerance or understanding on the recognition of the Soviet Union or on Gavrilović's appointment. Like the Italians, they were convinced that his mission to Moscow was to conclude a military alliance. They found all the proof they thought they needed in Belgrade's appointment of a military attaché to the legation staff.

Before Gavrilović went to Moscow he had a lengthy talk with Heeren. The German minister minced no words. Berlin, he said flatly, opposed Gavrilović's appointment, mainly because of his reputation as a pro-French, pro-British liberal and democrat. His true mission, in the opinion of the Germans, was to injure German-Russian relations. In that case, said Heeren, they would oppose his efforts with all their means. Gavrilović agreed he was a liberal and a democrat. He was pro-French because he was a Serb; the lessons of the First World War had taught him that allegiance. As to his spoiling German-Russian relations, that was the greatest compliment ever paid him. How could a representative of a small country do such a thing? On the contrary, he was going to Russia to place Yugoslavia's interests "within the framework of present agreements." His countrymen liked Russia despite the régime and because of the past. Old Russia, he pointed out, had done a great deal for the Serbs.

The people knew this. They liked the Russian people. This was reason enough, he asserted, to prevent him from spoiling German-Russian relations: How could he spoil something that the Russian people had accepted?

Heeren listened carefully and attentively. He was courteous as he accompanied Gavrilović to the door but did not wish him success in his work.[19]

Prince Paul was firm in his belief that if Germany and Italy were victorious in the west they would then go on to attack the Soviet Union. He was apprehensive about Soviet aims in the Balkans, just as the Soviet Union was apprehensive about Axis aims there. First the Soviet Union marked its displeasure over the German advance into the area by establishing diplomatic relations with Yugoslavia on June 24th. The significance of this act was not lost on Hitler. If he had any doubts about its meaning, they evaporated with the Soviet Union's ultimatum of June 26th to Rumania, which demanded the return of Bessarabia and the northern part of Bukovina. On June 28th the Soviet Union absorbed the two provinces by force. To make certain that the Germans clearly understood Russia's interest in the Balkans, on July 13th Molotov repeated to Schulenberg, the German ambassador, a conversation Stalin had had a short time before with Sir Stafford Cripps, the British ambassador. Stalin ascribed to Cripps the statement that Britain believed it was rightfully the Soviet Union's task to unify and maintain the *status quo* in the Balkans.

Stalin's reply undoubtedly impressed the Wilhelmstrasse. No power, he said, had the right to an exclusive role in the consolidation and leadership of the Balkan countries. Nor did the Soviet Union desire such a mission, although it was interested in Balkan affairs.[20]

The arrow hit the target. On August 29th, Ciano, after a talk with Hitler and Ribbentrop, wired Mussolini that he sensed marked distrust of the Soviet Union among the Germans. The Russian policy, according to his German hosts, was to "exploit to the maximum the eventual complications. The Soviet Union would thrust forward, with the complicity of Bulgaria and Yugoslavia, as far as the Straits,

<hr>

[19] Undated memorandum from Gavrilović to the Yugoslav ministry of foreign affairs. (JBH)
[20] *NSR*, pp. 165-68.

the Aegean and even the Adriatic." [21] The last was undoubtedly added by Hitler to stir up the Italians.

Hitler was not one to accept the Russian seizure of Rumanian territory without a countermove of some dimension. Accordingly, on September 1st, Molotov officially received the news that the Axis had awarded a segment of Rumanian territory to Hungary and was encouraging Rumania to settle Bulgaria's territorial claims. He reacted with restrained emotion, methodically spelling out his complaints. The Soviet Union had not been consulted on this matter as required by the 1939 Treaty of Non-Aggression. Germany's action was not entirely loyal. Surely Berlin knew of the Soviet Union's interest in Rumania and Hungary.

To make matters worse, in Molotov's opinion, the world press assumed that Germany had consulted the Soviet Union before making the award.[22]

On November 12th, Molotov went to Berlin to clarify the Russian position with Hitler and Ribbentrop. Their final discussions took place during the last hours of November 13th in the air raid shelter of the Reich's foreign ministry. (The Royal Air Force was busy that evening contradicting Hitler's repeated claim that the British had lost the war.) The German plan was to direct the attention of the Soviet Union from the Balkans to the Persian Gulf and to obtain Molotov's signature on the Tripartite Pact.[23] After the pact was signed, the four powers could then proceed to assign spheres of control and influence.

Schulenberg later reported that the Soviet government had no objection, in principle, to signing such a pact if it met certain requirements—among other things, that the Soviet Union would have a base within the area of the Straits and that Bulgaria would sign a mutual assistance pact. Russia would not be diverted from discussing the Balkans. In fact, Molotov told Hitler that the Soviet government "would be pleased" to learn what the Axis contemplated doing about the future of Poland and about Rumania, Greece, Yugoslavia, and

[21] Ciano, *L'Europa*, pp. 582-83.
[22] *NSR*, pp. 178-80, 187, 190.
[23] The Tripartite Pact was an agreement signed by Germany, Italy, and Japan on September 27, 1940. The signatories agreed to cooperate with one another in establishing "a new order in Europe and East Asia."

Bulgaria. The last, he said, was a matter of primary interest to the Soviet Union.

The German government never replied to the questions raised by Molotov. Within a month Hitler had drafted his plans for war against the Soviet Union. The Russians, meanwhile, covertly prepared to resist the growing German advance in the Balkans by offering arms to the Yugoslavs.[24]

Prince Paul's desire to establish a power balance in the Balkans (and thus insure Yugoslav security) by recognizing the Soviet Union was logical and correct—at the time. When Yugoslavia and Russia began their negotiations there was, they assumed, a balance of military force on the western front. But on June 10, 1940, the very day they signed the final agreement, the western front disappeared with the German victories in France and the balance shifted in favor of the Axis.

For the Russians the allied defeat in the west and the concomitant release of German armies for use elsewhere on the continent meant the return to a defensive role in the Balkans. For the Yugoslavs the allied defeat meant they could not use the Russians to counterpoise the Axis. The military situation that had served as the basis for a political decision no longer existed.

According to Ciano, Hristić was "terrified" when he learned of Italy's impending entry into the war. "Would Yugoslavia be invaded?" he demanded. Ciano could only partially reassure him, saying that Italy would enter the war "by the front door, not by the back door."[25] Italy would take no action against Yugoslavia or Greece, Mussolini had assured Hitler, for the Balkans were the source of supplies no longer obtainable beyond Gibraltar.[26]

On June 10th from his balcony on the Piazza Venezia the Duce announced to his Blackshirts that he had entered Italy in the war on the side of his Axis partner. Italy, he insisted, did not intend to drag other nations into the conflict, specifically those with whom it shared land or sea frontiers. He urged the Yugoslavs to note his words. Yugoslavia alone could cause him to retract them, he shouted.

[24] *NSR*, pp. 255-59, 252-53, and 260-64.
[25] *DGFP*, D, IX, Doc. 341; and Ciano, *Ciano's Diary, 1939-1943*, p. 256.
[26] *DGFP*, D, IX, Docs. 356, 360, and 373.

Despite his public promise in June to practice forbearance toward
Yugoslavia, the Duce changed his mind in July and told Ciano to
tell Hitler that he planned to take the Ionian islands and to split up
that anti-Italian, Versailles-created country of Yugoslavia. The reason
for this decision is not clear. Perhaps he was reacting to the stimulus
of the recently conducted Soviet-Yugoslav negotiations. In any case,
Hitler did not try to dampen Mussolini's military ardor; he sought
only to channel it. He was in favor of liquidating Yugoslavia in a
manner favorable to Italy, but only at a time favorable to the Axis.
If the Duce acted unpropitiously, Hitler pointed out, he would set
the Balkans ablaze, provoke the Russians to intervene, and possibly
even create common concerns for Russia and Britain. Italy should
move in Yugoslavia, Hitler advised, only if an outbreak occurred
elsewhere in the Balkans. They agreed to exclude Yugoslavia from
citizenship in the new Europe the two of them were creating.[27]

All through August Mussolini felt strong German resistance to his
plan of attacking Yugoslavia in September.[28] Ciano wrote Jacomini,
the Italian lieutenant-general in Albania, that he must slow down
the subversive activity against Yugoslavia and Greece that he was
directing from Albania, although not to a point where the project
would die. Rather he should do nothing that would produce a crisis.[29]

The Italians dropped their plans for Yugoslavia—temporarily.

The worst Ciano could tell Hristić was that Italy wanted Stojadinović returned to power. Berlin also lacked confidence in the
Prince Regent, he said, because Yugoslav policy had changed essentially after he dismissed Stojadinović. When Hristić tried to counter
this assertion, Ciano interrupted him with a reference to the Gamelin

[27] Ciano, *Ciano's Diary, 1939-1943*, p. 275, and *L'Europa*, p. 569. One of the
reasons for Hitler's anger at Yugoslavia was the discovery of the Gamelin papers
(see Auswärtiges Amt). In them, he told Alfieri, the Italian minister to the Holy
See, he had found evidence of Yugoslavia's hostility toward Italy. Alfieri, *Due
Dittatori di Fronte*, p. 67. Ribbentrop agreed with this view. Even Himmler
raised his voice to say that the Yugoslavs were corrupt and perfidious. Simoni,
Berlin Ambassade d'Italie, pp. 183, 185, and 191.
[28] Ciano, *Ciano's Diary, 1939-1943*, pp. 281, 284, and 295, and Simoni, *Berlin
Ambassade d'Italie*, pp. 192-96.
[29] Ciano, *L'Europa*, pp. 580-88. In September Ribbentrop held it more important to direct the Axis effort against Britain than to disperse it along the periphery of the Balkans. Acknowledging that Greece and Yugoslavia were in the
Italian sphere he nonetheless implored the Italians not to do anything that would
bring the Russians to the Bosporus. *IMT*, Doc. 1842-PS.

papers found by the Germans. It was clear from this cache of documents that Yugoslavia's present policy differed from that adhered to in the days of Stojadinović. Italy's policy-makers would bear that fact in mind, he told Hristić.[30]

The Cvetković government, which had permitted Stojadinović to remain in Belgrade, now changed its mind. Since his presence in the capital attracted German and Italian agents as well as Yugoslavs whose political outlook mirrored his own, he represented not only a threat to the orderly course of Yugoslav domestic politics but an instrument of possible foreign intervention. In May, 1940, the government decided to arrest him and intern him in Bosnia.[31]

From his exile in Bosnia Stojadinović begged Prince Paul to believe in his everlasting devotion to the regency and expressed his gratitude for the decent housing and medical care he was receiving through the Prince Regent's personal intervention. Again he raised the question of his past activities. It was possible, he thought, that someone had given Prince Paul an incorrect account of his political maneuvers. He was certain many of the actions attributed to him "were but loathsome inventions malevolently described."[32]

Despite his continued promises to the Führer, the Duce did not give up his plan of attacking Greece. He felt the need to do something spectacular that the Germans could not prevent. His envy of

[30] Hristić to Cincar-Marković, October 10, 1940. (JBH)

[31] In June, 1940, Ciano and the Germans jointly warned Prince Paul that any attempt on the life of the former premier would displease Rome and Berlin. In a gentle rejoinder to this ill-considered attempt at intimidation, Prince Paul told Heeren he was no murderer "such as one sees nowadays in other countries." Von Hassell, *Diaries, 1938-1944*, p. 143.

[32] Stojadinović to Prince Paul, September 25, 1940. (JBH) It is possible to say that in the end the former premier owed his life to the Prince Regent. During the latter part of 1940, when Stojadinović applied for a passport to go to Switzerland, Cvetković denied the request but offered a passport if Stojadinović would go to Greece instead. Stojadinović refused. On March 15, 1941, Cvetković informed the British government that he was going to expel Stojadinović and asked if the British would admit him to some British territory and keep him there. They agreed to do so. *Hansard*, CCCLXX (April 2, 1941), col. 971. When he crossed the Greek border under Yugoslav escort on March 20th, Stojadinović was arrested by the British and interned at Mauritius. Cvetković probably expelled him on the grounds that the Germans might force the regency to reinstate him as the one man they could trust. In any event, his fate would have been uncertain if he had remained on his native soil after March 27, 1941. See also *DGFP*, D, IX, Doc. 517.

Hitler's successes probably reached its climax in October with the German control of Rumania, because he set October 28th as the date for his invasion of Greece.

Ciano disagreed with the general staff, which opposed this adventure. He believed the political moment was right. Greece was isolated. Yugoslavia, like Turkey, "would not make a move." The Bulgars would enter the war, if at all, on the side of Italy.

Ciano was wrong. Yugoslavia had to move if for only one reason— Salonika.[33] Salonika was still Yugoslavia's major outlet to the sea and the West.

With the news on October 28th that the Italians had crossed the Greek frontier members of the Yugoslav crown council gathered for an emergency session. They included Prince Paul, Prime Minister Cvetković, Foreign Minister Cincar-Marković, Minister of War General Nedić, Chief of Staff General Kosić, and Milan Antić, the minister of court, who took the minutes. They could not agree, although they all insisted that Italy must not get Salonika. Prince Paul urged mobilization near the southern frontier. Cvetković agreed with Prince Paul but opposed any hasty decision to mobilize. Yugoslavia could not fight both Germany and Italy. Nedić argued that they should wait and see what Germany intended to do. Mobilization would only thrust Yugoslavia into the conflict. Prince Paul expressed the opinion that Greece would be better off if Salonika were in Yugoslavia's hands rather than in Italy's.

The following day Minister of Court Antić instructed Cincar-Marković and Nedić to telegraph Colonel Vauhnik, the Yugoslav military attaché in Berlin, to query German military leaders on their probable reaction to a Yugoslav march on the Greek port. In the meantime, Yugoslavia would send troops to the south for concentration on the Greek border.[34]

To Colonel Vauhnik the telegram he received on November 1 seemed more than a little odd. For one thing, it was unusually long and discursive. It emphasized Salonika's importance to Yugoslavia

---

[33] Ciano, *Ciano's Diary, 1939-1943*, pp. 297-98. Salonika was important to the Italians as well. See the minutes of the general staff meeting of October 15, 1940 in *Hitler e Mussolini, Lettere e Documenti*, pp. 65-66.

[34] Antić minutes of the crown council meetings, October 28th, 31st and November 1, 1940. (JBH)

from a military and economic point of view. Gravely it pointed out that the port might fall into the hands of the Italians or the Bulgarians. The telegram was strange for several other reasons. It had come from Minister of War Nedić and not from the chief of the general staff, the official who usually communicated with Vauhnik. The chief of staff ordinarily sent messages of an administrative character; this telegram had an unmilitary political tone and violated all coding rules. As time passed, the document became still more suspect because no subsequent telegrams from the general staff ever referred to it.[35]

One more element in this puzzle also caused Colonel Vauhnik considerable concern. Before the telegram had ever arrived, contacts in the political section of the German secret police (Gestapo) had told him that members of the Serbian Cultural Club, an organization in Belgrade, had asked Germany's tacit approval of a plan for Yugoslavia to take Salonika when King Peter came of age in 1941. So far, the Germans had shown little interest in acting on their request.

Then the peculiar telegram came. Vauhnik felt he had to be certain in his own mind as to its real meaning. Why should the minister of war bypass established procedure by sending instructions to the military attaché, who was responsible only to the general staff? Since this was a political message, why had not Nedić sent it to the Yugoslav minister in Berlin, Ivo Andrić? When Vauhnik went to Andrić on the question of taking Salonika, the minister exploded with anger. The proposal, he argued, was an act of treason against Greece, Yugoslavia's ally.

In a last attempt to make certain about the telegram, Vauhnik telephoned Belgrade and asked the assistant secretary to the minister of foreign affairs if he had any information about the future of Salonika should the Greeks lose the war. The man in Belgrade could give him no help.

All these factors convinced him that the questionable message had reached him without the knowledge of the general staff.

At this point he decided on the steps to take. If he could, by using the Germans, prevent Salonika from falling into Italian hands, the credit would go to the Yugoslav government and not to General Nedić. Accordingly, he asked for an appointment with the political repre-

[35] Vauhnik to author. See also *DGFP*, D, XI, Docs. 110, 231, 320, 334, and 417.

sentative of the German high command. Received by the chief of political intelligence, General Quentzsch, and by Colonel Von Mellenthin, the liaison officer with foreign military attachés, Vauhnik opened with a reference to the Italo-Greek war. Yugoslavia, he said, was interested in Salonika and he feared an Italo-Yugoslav conflict if Italy attempted to occupy the port. It would therefore be in the interests of peace if Germany would explain the situation to the Italians and counsel moderation. Acknowledging that an insignificant group of Belgrade politicians had already raised the Salonika question with Berlin, he suggested that the Germans expend no time nor effort on this group's schemes. What was really important was the fact that Yugoslavia as a whole was interested in Salonika and was prepared to intervene if Italy attempted to occupy the city.

Expressing surprise, General Quentzsch said he had not sufficiently thought through the repercussions of the Italo-Greek war. So far as he knew, the high command itself knew nothing of any plans concerning Salonika. The only thing he could do was to raise the entire question with the ministry of foreign affairs, which would then advise the high command of all the political implications.

It was clear to Vauhnik that Quentzsch would report their conversation to the foreign ministry, which would relay a summary to the Italian government through its ambassador and its military attaché, General Marras. This was just what he wanted.

Vauhnik then informed Belgrade that it would have to wait, since the individuals competent to discuss this question were out of town. Besides, the German military were far less interested in what happened to Salonika than were the Italians. Despite his counseling them to exercise patience, officials in Belgrade insisted that he press the Germans for a reply to his query and that he hurry home with his report.

This was a blow to Vauhnik. For a moment he feared his whole plan would fail. Fortunately for him, the Greeks began their offensive. Telephoning Mellenthin, he asked if in the light of the new developments on the Greek front they should not drop the matter of Salonika. Mellenthin replied that Salonika was now a matter for the Italian government to decide and that the German ministry of foreign affairs had not yet advised the high command on its disposition. He suggested that Vauhnik be patient.

Vauhnik then persuaded the Greek military attaché, Colonel Leggeris, to tell General Marras that he had heard from Ankara that Yugoslavia was thinking of intervening if Italy did not withdraw its troops from Greek territory. One consequence of this conversation was that General Marras went out of his way to be friendly to Vauhnik. He organized two dinners and receptions in Vauhnik's honor. He told Vauhnik that he was anti-Fascist at heart and that he and his colleagues did not like the Germans. The real aim of Italy's war in Greece, he revealed, was to prevent Germany from establishing itself in the Mediterranean. His advice to the Belgrade hotheads was to keep their hands off the Salonika powder keg.

Once again the telegrams flew in all directions. Vauhnik was pleased with his work. All was perfect until Belgrade wired him to get whatever information he could and take the first plane home. There was nothing to do but comply, although not until he had kept a previously arranged appointment with Mellenthin. They discussed the Salonika question only incidentally with Vauhnik pointing out that Salonika no longer had any real pertinence since the Greeks were chasing the Italians out of their country. Mellenthin looked uncomfortable, Vauhnik noted.

He was preparing to leave Berlin when Minister Andrić notified him that Prince Paul had dismissed Nedić, one of the fathers of the plan to take Salonika. Thereupon he canceled his plane reservation. His conversation with the German had, it seemed clear, set off a chain reaction. As if responding to his maneuvers, Italian planes had on November 5th and 6th bombed Bitolj (Monastir), a town in Yugoslavia very near the border with Greece. When Prince Paul asked General Nedić why he did not send planes to prevent further bombing of Yugoslav soil and why he had not taken proper defense measures, Nedić replied that Yugoslavia had reached a point in the war where it would have to state its position. The government, he asserted, must no longer shilly-shally. If Yugoslavia ceded a small part of its territory to Germany, he told Prince Paul, the Axis would spare the rest.

That was preposterous, the Prince Regent replied. Germany had never asked for Yugoslav territory and Yugoslavia would not give up any territory.

With astonishing candor, Nedić voiced the opinion that if Yugoslavia had a clever diplomatic policy it would have no need for an army. With that, Prince Paul asked for his resignation.

The Nedić-Antić attempt at backdoor diplomacy had ended dismally. But that did not deter Antić from further ventures as an amateur diplomat. Nor did he exclude Rome as a field of operations. Although in his view Yugoslavia would ultimately have to clarify its relations with Germany, he believed it could in the interim use Italy to lessen or even avoid pressure from Germany. In contrast, Cincar-Marković saw Germany as the major power in Europe. Yugoslavia had to come to a total agreement with Germany, he argued, because Germany was the only power that could guarantee Yugoslavia's neutrality. It would never, he insisted, ask Yugoslavia, as it had asked Hungary, Rumania, and Slovakia, to sign the Tripartite Pact.

Acting entirely on his own, Antić sent a Belgrade lawyer with many Italian connections, V. Stakić, to see Ciano. He could not use Hristić in this exploratory effort for by this time almost all personal contact between Hristić and Ciano had ceased. Stakić's was truly a secret mission, secret not only from Cvetković and from the Allies but also from Berlin. The Germans were too anxious to prevent Italy and Yugoslavia from coming to any agreement that anyone could interpret as anti-German. As a consequence five days after the bombing of Bitolj, Ciano received Stakić, whose specific task was to find out whether or not Italy still considered viable the Belgrade Agreement of 1937. Did the agreement still form the basis of Italy's policy toward Yugoslavia?

Ciano strongly reaffirmed his loyalty to the accord. It represented his policy, he asserted. He believed a strong and independent Yugoslavia was necessary for Italy's own sake. Yugoslavia should be spared from war, he assured Stakić, adding that Italy respected and demanded the maintenance of Yugoslavia's territorial integrity. Then Ciano said he would like, however, to go beyond the 1937 document and to see an alliance with Yugoslavia in the broadest sense of the word. He stressed that the Yugoslavs had nothing to fear from Italy, whose ambitions lay south of Albania. The war against Greece was only Italy's way of safeguarding the Adriatic and Ionian seas, he said. Italy did not want to occupy Salonika either temporarily or permanently.

Ciano then proposed a new Italo-Yugoslav agreement. Yugoslavia could prove its friendship by demilitarizing the Adriatic coast. When Stakić asked against what power they would direct such an alliance,

Ciano replied, "I know the Prince's outlook and I therefore do not ask for an alliance against Great Britain. However, would it not be useful against the Soviet Union?"

"And perhaps one day against the Germans too?" Stakić interjected.

"Perhaps," replied Ciano with a smile.[36]

Belgrade rejected the suggestion out of hand. An alliance would rob Yugoslavia of its sovereignty, said Prince Paul, and Yugoslavia would receive nothing in exchange.[37]

On November 18th, a week after Stakić's trip to Rome, a worried Ciano went off to Fuschl to talk to Hitler. He had to ask the Germans for assistance in Greece.[38] The war there was not going well. He found that for Hitler the key to the entire Balkan situation was Yugoslavia. Everything depended on Belgrade, the Führer asserted. Italo-Yugoslav relations were already bad, he observed, and if it was Mussolini's intention to make them worse the future was indeed black. When Ciano told him that confidential negotiations were in process between Rome and Belgrade, Hitler brightened and saw a rosy future. Was Mussolini prepared, he asked, to make a pact with Yugoslavia that guaranteed its frontiers and ceded Salonika in exchange for demilitarization of the Adriatic coast? Ciano said he believed such a pact was possible. If the Axis powers gave Belgrade an interest in the operation against Greece, Hitler responded, they would drive the British out of the Mediterranean.[39]

To make certain Ciano would not misinterpret his views on the war, the Führer warned Mussolini in a letter that

The Yugoslavs would have to abandon their interest in the Greek situation. It would be even better if they would cooperate with us. In any event, without being sure of the Yugoslavs we cannot risk a war in the Balkans.

[36] *Naša Stvarnost*, Johannesburg (June, 1953), No. 3.

[37] *Ibid.* Ciano indicates in his diary (p. 305) that the idea of an alliance, including the demilitarization of the Adriatic, came from Stakić. Ciano and Mussolini wholeheartedly approved it, for they believed an attack on Yugoslavia would be difficult. An alliance with Belgrade was better, Ciano wrote, than an understanding with the "uneasy and untrustworthy Croats."

[38] Halder, *Diary*, entry for November 18, 1940.

[39] Ciano, *L'Europa*, pp. 614-15, and *Ciano's Diary, 1939-1943*, pp. 307-8.

A war anywhere in the Balkans was impossible before March. A threatening move against Yugoslavia now would be valueless, Hitler stressed, because Italy could not follow through before early spring. This was "well known to the Serbian [sic] General Staff. Therefore, Yugoslavia must be won, if at all possible, by other ways and means."

The Duce hastened to reply. He agreed with the Führer that Yugoslavia was indeed a trump card in the war against Greece. He was ready to guarantee Yugoslavia's present borders, he wrote, and under specific conditions to recognize Salonika as belonging to Yugoslavia. The Yugoslavs must adhere to the Tripartite Pact, demilitarize the Adriatic coast, and put troops into the war only after the Italian forces had given Greece a "shock."[40]

Hitler was eager to consummate the new plans for Yugoslavia as soon as possible. On November 20, 1940, at the ceremony of Hungary's adherence to the Tripartite Pact he told Ciano he planned to call Prince Paul to Berlin and propose "the alliance."[41]

But Prince Paul did not go to Hitler. Instead, Yugoslav Foreign Minister Cincar-Marković made the trip to Fuschl in late November, 1940.

Hitler's aim was to emphasize to the Yugoslavs that a major opportunity lay at hand if they joined the Axis. Yugoslavia and Germany must establish a close, friendly relationship, he told Cincar-Marković. This was the only way, he said, that the Yugoslavs could satisfy their ambitions—for Salonika, for peace between the Serbs and Croats, and for protection from Italy—ambitions that the Yugoslavs had not been able to satisfy heretofore even in their dreams.

Yugoslavia was important to Germany for economic reasons, the Führer told Cincar-Marković. He insisted that he had no territorial aspirations in the Balkans and wanted a strong Yugoslavia. If Yugoslavia joined the German combination, he promised, it would get a guaranty for its existence, plus Salonika. In return, it would have to do only one thing—demilitarize Dalmatia. Recent events permitted him to bring influence to bear on the Italians, he explained. "Three months from now," he added, "the situation might be less favorable for Yugoslavia." He stressed that the Yugoslavs need not take part

---

[40] *Hitler e Mussolini, Lettere e Documenti*, Docs. 33 and 34.
[41] *Ciano's Diary, 1939-1943*, p. 308.

in any military action. Naturally, however, Germany would use its discretion, he said, in distributing what it conquered.[42]

The Yugoslavs resisted Hitler's blandishments. Even the bait of Salonika had no effect. A month after the Führer saw Cincar-Marković he wrote Mussolini that the Yugoslavs were being cautious and perhaps evasive toward his proposition. Under certain circumstances, he wrote, he saw the possibility of concluding a nonaggression pact between Italy and Germany on the one hand and Yugoslavia on the other. In no case, however, he acknowledged, would the Yugoslavs adhere to the Tripartite Pact at that time. That should come, he concluded with a derogatory reference to Italian military talents, only when military successes improved the psychological situation.[43]

The Italo-Greek war became a nightmare for the Yugoslavs. Heretofore they had been important to Germany for political and economic reasons. Now they were beginning to be important militarily, for with every Greek victory the Germans grew more certain they would have to intervene to rescue the Italians. Germany's political relationship with Yugoslavia was beginning to have a military component.

By alerting the Germans to the importance of keeping the Italians out of Salonika, Yugoslavia opened a big box of troubles for itself. Seeing an advantage, the Germans set out to use Salonika as a decoy to bring Yugoslavia into their camp. For the Yugoslavs, the military threat from Italy remained. But the diplomatic pressure that once had come only from Rome now came almost entirely from Berlin.

Bound to Greece with ties of history, treaty, and marriage, Yugoslavia found it difficult to remain truly neutral when an ally was

---

[42] Halder, *Diary*, entry for December 3, 1940; and *Hitler e Mussolini, Lettere e Documenti*, Doc. 36. Hitler told the Duce that he had not spoken of a German-Italian guarantee but had indicated the possibility of a nonaggression pact. He was unable to define precisely what he meant by "the demilitarization of the Adriatic." This was no longer important because the Italians had withdrawn that demand. Hitler hoped, he said, to be successful in "winning Yugoslavia for us, for their benevolent neutrality is very important" (*ibid.*). While these negotiations were under way, the German army went ahead with its plans to compel Yugoslavia, in the spring of 1941, to adopt a definite pro-Axis position. This was necessary to prevent a Russian attack on Germany from the rear. *IMT*, Proceedings, VII, 331.

[43] Simoni, *Berlin Ambassade d'Italie*, p. 220; *Hitler e Mussolini, Lettere e Documenti*, Doc. 37; and Von Hassell, *Diaries, 1938-1944*, p. 148.

under attack by a common enemy. Although outwardly indifferent, Prince Paul felt he had to find a way of aiding the Greeks.

Shortly after the Italians invaded Greece, Nikola Stanković, owner of the Vistad armament works in Yugoslavia, received a visitor. He was Milorad Djordjević, the former minister of finance, and he had come to complain of the Maček-Cvetković government's apparent refusal to send munitions to Greece. Even the Prince Regent's personal pleas, he told Stanković, had failed to move the government from its position of strict neutrality. Stanković, himself sympathetic to the Greek cause, proposed that Djordjević ask Prince Paul to authorize him to manufacture and ship war materials to Greece at his own risk. The Prince Regent heard the idea with enthusiasm and put Djordjević in contact with the Greek representatives, who accepted Stanković's proposal and worked out a shipping procedure.

Stanković sent all shipments to the Greek army through the Turkish minister in Belgrade, addressing them to a Turkish businessman in Istanbul. He sent them at his own risk, falsely declared as ordinary merchandise, through Salonika. Once the railway cars bearing the "merchandise" crossed the Yugoslav-Greek border, the Greek authorities took charge. Within two weeks after receiving an order for 200,000 hand grenades, Stanković delivered them to the Greek army.[44]

Stanković and Djordjevič were wrong in thinking that the Cvetković government refused to assist Greece. During the last week of November, 1940, Greek Prime Minister General Jean Metaxas asked Prince Paul for permission to organize a supply depot on Yugoslav territory. The Prince Regent readily agreed and issued confidential instructions to that effect to Cvetković, to Minister of War General Pešić, and to the ministers of finance and of commerce and industry. Rosettis, who at that time was Greek minister in Belgrade, later wrote that the Yugoslavs continued their "wholehearted assistance" up to the last day of the Albanian campaign. Hundreds of tons of materials left Yugoslavia for the Greek lines. Rosettis wrote that he was particularly grateful to the firm of Vistad for furnishing "hundreds of thousands of hand grenades, artillery fuses" and other war materials otherwise procurable only in Hungary and Germany. In addition, the Greek cavalry bought from Yugoslavia all the horses it needed.

[44] N. Stanković to author.

It was an "incontestable fact," Rosettis wrote, that Prince Paul's generous and friendly help had made it possible for the Greeks to defeat the Italians in Albania.[45]

Just as Yugoslavia's unofficial policy aided the Greeks by supplying them with material, its official policy of apparent neutrality also worked for them by preventing the flow of German supplies to the Italians over Yugoslav roads and railways. About the middle of November the Italians asked permission for a convoy to cross Yugoslavia from Fiume to Albania. Then on November 24th Heeren asked Cincar-Marković for permission to send 1,000 German trucks across Yugoslavia to an unknown destination. Heeren reported to Berlin that he believed the size of the shipment had made quite an impression on Cincar-Marković, who heard the request with utmost gravity and asked if it had anything to do with the Italians' request a few days before. Heeren denied any relationship between the two and emphasized that his government was counting on cooperation. Concluding his report to Berlin, Heeren said the Yugoslavs showed great reluctance to comply with the request.

On December 7th he reported that Cincar-Marković was continuing to resist all his pressures on the matter of the 1,000 trucks. Cincar-Marković reminded him that he had turned down earlier a similar request from the Italians. He could not believe, Marković went on, that Germany would really persist in such a demand. After all, he said, Germany could find other routes to Albania that did not lead through neutral Yugoslavia.

At this point the Germans decided to rouse the Yugoslavs to the facts of political life in contemporary Europe. At the suggestion of the economic division of the foreign ministry, and in view of Yugoslavia's attitude on the question of the truck convoys to Albania, Ribbentrop acceded to Italy's request that he cut off German deliveries of aviation materials to Yugoslavia.[46]

It became obvious that the Yugoslavs could no longer look to Germany for arms. They would have to seek new ways of relieving pressure from the Axis. France and Czechoslovakia were gone from the map of Europe as effective states. The British, dreading a possible German invasion, were defending their islands from the Luftwaffe's

---

[45] Rosettis to Prince Paul, June, 1952. (JBH)
[46] *USMT,* Doc. NG-3404.

nightly visits of destruction; they were barely able to hold their own in North Africa. The Greeks were causing the Italians much anguish. The Turks, remote and uneasy about possible Russian and German plans to drive toward the Black Sea and the Straits, were designing their own version of neutrality and survival. King Carol of Rumania, after abdicating in favor of his son Michael, turned over plenary power to General Ion Antonescu; with this transfer of power, Rumania renounced all treaties that were local in nature, specifically the Balkan Pact. The Bulgars remained adamant in their demands for territorial revision.

That left Hungary. Whether it could be of any help to Yugoslavia was still to be proved. The Hungarians had approached the Yugoslavs in March, 1938, shortly after the *Anschluss*, to negotiate a pact of friendship[47]—and incidentally to drive a wedge between Yugoslavia and Czechoslovakia. Stojadinović undoubtedly believed that to sign such a treaty would not be politic. It certainly would not be well-received either at home or abroad and very little would be gained. What Prince Paul sought in 1939 were two bilateral arrangements to improve relations: a pact between Hungary and Yugoslavia and another between Hungary and Rumania. Hungary's response was disappointing to the Yugoslavs, and Prince Paul asked Lord Halifax if the British would encourage the Hungarians to reconsider their answer and proceed along the lines suggested by Yugoslavia.[48]

After the French defeat in May, 1940, Prince Paul sent private emissaries to the regent of Hungary, Admiral Horthy, to hasten negotiations on a pact of friendship. Both Yugoslavia and Hungary wanted nothing more than to be left in peace, Horthy later testified.[49] Certain-

[47] Baron G. Bakách-Bessenyey (former Hungarian minister to Yugoslavia) to author.
[48] *DBFP*, III, 6, Doc. 393. In reporting this conversation with Prince Paul, Halifax stated that the prince regent told him of Ciano's offer to partition Albania. Prince Paul said he had refused it and believed he was right in doing so. The Prince Regent also told Halifax he still distrusted Russia, but hoped Britain would succeed in reaching a settlement with it. See also *DGFP*, D, IV, Doc. 441 and D, V, Docs. 272, 273, 277, and 292.
[49] Horthy interrogation by the Department of State Special Interrogation Mission headed by Dewitt C. Poole. See also Antal Ullein-Reviczky, *Guerre Allemande Paix Russe* (Paris: La Presse Française et Étrangère, 1947), pp. 74-78; and John F. Montgomery (United States minister to Hungary), *Hungary, The Unwilling Satellite* (New York: Devin-Adair, 1947), p. 124.

ly, he and Prince Paul believed, the Germans could not take exception to such a desire.

If the regents of these two states looked on the treaty only as a vehicle for expressing "eternal friendship," their foreign ministers had other thoughts. For some time the Hungarian foreign minister, Count Csáky, unaware of the private negotiations between Horthy and Prince Paul, had been pondering the usefulness of a pact with Yugoslavia. He had at least two reasons for believing it necessary. It might be the first step toward territorial changes favoring Hungary and it would undoubtedly be looked on with approval by the Germans. As a matter of fact, he himself would have to make sure that they did not see it as a hostile act but as the best way of bringing Yugoslavia into Hitler's east European system. This was the interpretation he told Bakách-Bessenyey, his minister in Belgrade, to take to Cincar-Marković.

The Yugoslav foreign minister did not hesitate for a moment. He sought and obtained Prince Paul's approval to begin negotiations with Hungary.

Whether Csáky himself completely believed in the policy he had laid down is questionable. It was his principle in dealing with the Germans to gain their confidence at any price. Once this was obtained, they would accept at face value everything put before them. On the other hand, if they believed he was negotiating behind their back with one of their enemies, nothing he could do or say would satisfy them. Therefore, to make certain that they would not look on the pact with hostility, he sent the draft to Berlin for suggestions.

Ribbentrop replied that the agreement said everything that such a paper could say.[50] Later State Secretary Weizsäcker of the German foreign office cautioned the Rumanians against attaching any real importance to the treaty and said there was no reason for them to jump to the conclusion that Hungary, by signing this document, had put itself in the position of mediator between Yugoslavia and the Reich.

Csáky also had another reason for sending the draft to Berlin. Sooner or later, he realized, German intelligence agents would supply

---

[50] *USMT*, Docs. NG-2712 and NG-2658. For the text of the treaty, see Royal Institute of International Affairs, *Bulletin of International News* (London: Royal Institute of International Affairs, December 31, 1940), p. 1746.

Ribbentrop with reports on negotiations between Bakách-Bessenyey and Cincar-Marković.[51] His suspicions were confirmed almost immediately. On December 10th, just before he left for Belgrade to sign the pact, Otto von Erdmannsdorff, the German minister in Budapest, relayed to Csáky, word for word, United States Minister Lane's coded report to Washington on a conversation with Prince Paul on December 9th. Prince Paul had told Lane that he looked on the pact as a barrier against further German encroachment and therefore considered it pro-Allied in intent.

On his arrival in Belgrade, Csáky hastened to warn Prince Paul that his exchange with Lane was known to the Germans, who now had additional proof of his anti-Nazi views. Moreover, the American code was now in German hands. That meant Prince Paul could not talk frankly to Lane and could tell him little or nothing of Yugoslavia's plans.[52]

As their discussion proceeded, Csáky said nothing to Prince Paul about territorial changes or about the meaning the pact might have for the Germans. Instead, he said it opened "a window to the west for Hungary." The danger from Germany was greater than that from Russia, in his opinion. He said he believed that a German-Russian war was inevitable and that Hitler was capable of plunging his country into bolshevism. He made it clear that the Hungarians would not give up the Danube without a war, nor would the Russians give up Transylvania.

Speaking rapidly, and with unaccustomed candor, Csáky expressed his contempt for the leaders of the Axis. He said Hitler disliked both Prince Paul and King Boris, but looked on Mussolini as a wayward younger brother and spoke of him with mawkish sentimentality. When he talked of the Duce's defeats in Greece, tears came to his eyes, Csáky reported disdainfully. Hitler had revealed to Csáky that he had had no advance notice of Mussolini's intention of invading Greece. He himself wanted peace in the Balkans, he said; indeed, the attack had been launched on the eve of his visit to Italy, a trip undertaken for the sole purpose of urging the Duce to patch up his differences with the Greeks.

But the wayward "brother" would have none of this, Csáky told

[51] Bakách-Bessenyey to author.
[52] Bakách-Bessenyey to author.

Prince Paul, turning to Mussolini's side of the story. The Germans had promised him nothing, the Duce had complained. They had even refused to give him Nice. "I have nothing in my hands," he had told Csáky petulantly.

Csáky warned Prince Paul of Mussolini's imperialistic intentions toward Salonika and of Ciano's mercurial opinions on war and peace with Yugoslavia. One day he would tell Csáky that there would be no war with the Yugoslavs. The next day he would ask Csáky whether Hungary could supply troops if there were such a war. Again he would declare, "I who have great influence, I shall not attack Yugoslavia because Germany has asked me not to. Therefore you should not go to war with Rumania either."

Ciano had suggested that Csáky mediate the friction between the Bulgars and the Serbs so as not to alarm the Russians. If the Italians tried to do so, alarm bells would ring in the Kremlin.

Ambivalence was typical of the Italian leaders, Csáky observed to Prince Paul. They followed no set policy. "There is no policy in their politics," Csáky phrased it. They veered between two extremes: action and apathy. This, Csáky said, was why their campaign in Greece was proving a fiasco. It was the result of bad diplomacy plus poor planning by an inefficient general staff.

Concluding his discursive monologue, which had covered all the effective states of Europe, Csáky forecast a major offensive in March, but he would not say against whom it would be launched.[53]

The Yugoslavs looked on the treaty with Hungary as a device which reinforced their position in negotiations with the Germans. It neutralized, for a time at least, one avenue of invasion.

This view was not shared by Washington and London. Both the state department and the foreign office doubted Belgrade's assurances that the pact was an anti-Nazi measure, defensive in its intent. Hungary, for all practical purposes, was under German control, and Csáky would not have negotiated the pact without Berlin's prior approval. The pact therefore put Yugoslavia one step closer to the Axis orbit.[54] This was Washington's reasoning—Csáky's arguments played back, not by Germany but by the United States and Britain.

[53] Minute of conversation between Prince Paul and Count Csáky, December, 1940; and Bakách-Bessenyey to author.
[54] Fotitch, War We Lost, pp. 38-39.

Moscow's reaction, immediate and drastic, was to rescind its offer of arms to the Yugoslavs. That offer, extended early in November, had probably been stimulated by Hitler's support of Hungarian and Bulgarian demands for territorial revision, support that the Führer had reiterated November 13th in his last conversation with Molotov. At the invitation of Assistant Commissar for Foreign Affairs Andrei Vishinsky, Gavrilović had submitted a basic list of war materials needed by Yugoslavia. The response of Shaposhnikov, chief of the Soviet general staff, had been even more than the Yugoslavs had hoped for. He had said that all the items asked for would be forthcoming, and immediately at that. Furthermore, he had said that they would be provided in greater quantities than the Yugoslavs had specified. What's more, he had said that the Yugoslavs could fix the prices and the rates of exchange. The Russians had asked only that the transaction be held in confidence; Germany, Bulgaria, and Rumania must not learn that the Soviet Union was aiding the Yugoslavs.

For security purposes, therefore, the Russians had insisted that all negotiations be carried on through military channels. On November 22d, they had urged the Yugoslavs to submit a detailed report on the types and number of weapons needed. "Any delay will be dangerous," Shaposhnikov had warned Popović, the Yugoslav military attaché in Moscow, who hastened to supply him with the enlarged list on the following day.

That day, November 23, 1940, had been the last the Yugoslavs had heard of the whole matter. The chill of Russian reserve had replaced the warmth of Slavic brotherhood. At first, the Russians had given technical reasons for the delay. Then they had raised political objections. Finally, after weeks of trying to cut through to the truth of the matter, Popović had been able to get a straight answer from the Soviet ministry of war. On February 4, 1941, he was told that negotiations had come to a halt "as a result of the conclusion of our treaty with Hungary and our trade pact with Germany (October 20, 1940). These treaties are interpreted as an estrangement from Russia. This, just like their insistence that the price did not make any difference, shows they are trying to exploit our request as a political game." [55]

[55] *USMT*, Veesenmayer defense document No. 110; *NSR*, pp. 258-59.

Popović was right. The Hungarian-Yugoslav treaty was a convenient peg on which the Kremlin could hang its denial of military assistance. To have helped the Yugoslavs would only have exacerbated Nazi-Soviet relations, already tense. On November 26th, Molotov told Schulenberg that the Soviet Union was prepared to transform the Tripartite Pact into a four-power pact. Only a few protocols would have to be added to satisfy Soviet security requirements. It seems clear that the Soviet Union believed a four-power pact with firm guarantees, and no war, was better than risking war and the future by shipping arms to Yugoslavia.

This was not the only frustrating development during the year. There were also the domestic crises that grew out of the *Sporazum* of August, 1939. Maček had publicly asserted that if a *banovina* were created out of those parts of Bosnia and Hercegovina which had not been given to Croatia under the 1939 agreement, he would make no "territorial demands." On the other hand, if the Serbs tried to incorporate any of this territory into Serbia, he would demand an equal amount for Croatia. To the best of his knowledge, no one ever objected, officially or unofficially, to this ultimatum.[56]

Apparently Cvetković believed it the better part of political astuteness to say nothing in the face of Maček's warning. He responded with less equanimity, however, to trouble from another quarter. This was the mounting indifference shown by Džaferbeg Kulenović, who had become the new leader of the Moslem Party on Spaho's death the year before. When Cvetković noted that Kulenović was boycotting meetings of the government party's inner council, he assigned Korošec to find out why and to make sure that Cvetković could count on the Moslem Party's continued support.

Korošec found Kulenović sullen and angry. First he complained about rumors that the name of the government party, the Yugoslav Radical Union, would be changed to Yugoslav Radical Party, a name which stood for Serb hegemony all over Yugoslavia. If this were done, he told Korosec, the Moslems could no longer cooperate with Cvetković. Then he became more specific, and complained about the treatment he, his party and his coreligionists seemed to be getting. He said they were getting only the crumbs of political patronage instead of

[56] Maček to author.

fair slices of the cake. He was annoyed at Maček's success in enlarging Croatia so that it now included parts of Bosnia and Hercegovina, with their large Moslem populations. He was annoyed by the talk that Cvetković and Korošec were going to establish separate *banovinas* for the Serbs and Slovenes, with the same rights of home rule that had been given to Maček and his Croats. He wanted his share: a fourth *banovina,* made up of the remaining parts of Bosnia and Hercegovina and including the large Moslem population of the historic Sandžak region.[57]

There were some grounds for the first complaint. It was true that Cvetković had discussed resuscitation of the Serbian Radical Party with the ninety-year-old Aca Stanojević, a founder of the Yugoslav Radical Union and the personification of the pre-world-war Serbian Radical Party. Despite his years, Stanojević seems to have possessed a sharp political sense. He had contended all along that Maček, in his negotiations with Cvetković, had an edge as the head of a strong and united political party. Cvetković on the other hand, as the head of the jerry-built JRZ coalition, lacked the reliable backing that a monolithic Serb party—the Radical Party, of course—could provide.[58] As the first step toward reviving the party, Cvetkovič and Stanojević agreed to the calling of a countrywide congress of their fellow Radicals who were now members of the JRZ and the Yugoslav Nationalist Party.

It seems clear that Cvetković was trying to build up a political apparatus of his own in Serbia and to expand the coalition government into a government of national union. The project was doomed from the start because of the egocentric and vindictive nature of the political leaders with whom he had to deal. In January, 1940, after twenty years of agitating for an accord with the Croats, the Serbian Democratic Party reversed itself, attacked the accord and accused Cvetković of oppressing the Serbs who lived in Croatia. When the Democrats opposed the holding of general elections until the 1931 constitution was replaced by one more democratic, Maček tried to pacify them by promising that he would work for a new electoral law and then hold elections. The fact that Maček came to the defense of Cvetković enraged them all the more.

---

[57] Korošec to Prince Paul, January 28, 1940. (JBH)
[58] Mita Dimitrijević to Minister of Court Antić, February 15, 1940. (JBH)

In this atmosphere of recrimination and counterrecrimination it became increasingly difficult to organize a government of national union. The old-line Radicals under Miloš Trifunović and the Democrats led by Milan Grol refused to enter the Cvetković government. Both these leaders were highly ambitious and both were eager for high office: Trifunović wanted to be premier, Grol foreign minister.[59]

It is difficult to believe that Trifunović and Grol really expected Cvetković to resign on their behalf or to relieve Cincar-Marković for a man whose knowledge and experience in conducting foreign affairs was nonexistent. In rejecting Trifunović as a candidate for a cabinet post, Cvetković was aware that he would lose followers. He was also aware that Prince Paul had his objections to both Trifunović and Grol. He disliked them for personal and security reasons. Both were known in the coffee houses as gossips. Both, Prince Paul believed, would not be above sabotaging the Serb-Croat agreement once they were in the cabinet. In his opinion, their participation in the government was not worth endangering the solution of a national problem.

Maček looked on all this as a purely Serbian affair. After all, the Croats were already concentrated in his person and his party. He, like Prince Paul, was skeptical of Trifunović's and Grol's attitude of support for the *Sporazum,* and he was suspicious of their motives. These two were not unknown factors to him; he had worked with them for years in opposing Belgrade. He therefore supported Cvetković against Trifunović. If Trifunović entered the government, in any capacity, Maček predicted the life of that government would be short.

After that, Cvetković did his best to enlarge the government with Democrats and old-line Radicals and without appealing for support from Trifunović and Grol, but he only failed in his efforts.

To keep Yugoslavia from shattering under the confluence of internal and external pressures was a task without mercy and without rest. By January, 1941, barely a year after the outbreak of the war, the

---

[59] Their ambitions were later satisfied by the Yugoslav government-in-exile in London. Their tenure was short, however, lasting only from June through August, 1943, when the cabinet fell because the Serbs refused to stand by the *Sporazum.* To his sorrow, Grol later entered the interim government formed in 1944 by representatives of the London government and Tito's partisan forces.

Yugoslav foreign policy of prudence and neutrality in the face of ubiquitous belligerents required national cohesion and a willingness to compromise for the national welfare. Neither of these was forthcoming in measurable amount or quality.

Prince Paul, conscious of his shortcomings, convinced that he should remain as regent only so long as he could usefully serve the country, considered resigning in late 1940. The difficult years following the death of King Alexander had weighed heavy. The Prince Regent rejected the suggestion of Maček and other politicians that he remain as regent until 1944, although a constitutional amendment for this purpose had already been prepared.[60]

His letter of resignation was drafted. His principal goal, he wrote, had been to ameliorate the internal quarrels and preserve peace on the borders. He had always tried to preserve the dignity of Yugoslavia before the world and to act in its best interests, so that it might prove to be a solid, healthy, and independent state. Nevertheless, he wrote, he believed he should remain as regent only so long as he could be of use to his country. Now he was convinced that his presence no longer served Yugoslavia's best interests. He had not succeeded. The failure was his alone. He had not been able to infuse confidence in his intentions in those who should have been his closest collaborators and whose support would naturally be expected. The future of Yugoslavia, he stressed, lay in the brotherhood and understanding of the Serbs, Croats, and Slovenes, working in harmony and accord around their king.

This sentiment, idealistic as it may sound, was an appeal to the original idea that had founded Yugoslavia twenty-two years before. It reflected a sense of common political origins that very few in Yugoslavia shared with the Prince Regent.

When the news that Prince Paul had drafted his resignation reached his counselors, they spent hours urging him to change his mind. Eventually they succeeded.[60] Greater than his desire to bow out was his reluctance to abandon young King Peter and leave him to cope with a situation that had tried and thrust aside men of years, experience, and more wisdom than a boy of seventeen could command.

[60] Maček to author.

VIII

THE ROAD TO VIENNA

The Yugoslav foreign minister was nervous. German troops were moving into Rumania that first week of January, 1941, sending the emotional temperature of Belgrade to an alarming point. During his conversation with the German minister, Cincar-Marković was tense, and listened with skepticism to Heeren's assurances that the Germans intended only to establish peace and order in the Balkans. He said he understood their need to prepare for all possibilities but doubted that the British would try to open a new front in southeast Europe. More of a possibility, in his opinion, was the danger of communist expansion in the Balkans. Indicating his uneasiness over the progressive military encirclement of his country by Germany, he also stressed his concern over the domestic situation in Bulgaria. Should trouble arise there, Heeren assured him, Germany would deal with Bulgaria just as it had dealt with Rumania. The Yugoslavs could count on the Germans to dissipate any troubles the Bulgarians might cause.

Heeren was under instructions to avoid any discussion with Yugoslavia on the movement of German troops in case of war in the Balkans. The German foreign minister feared the Yugoslavs might pass information along to Germany's enemies.[1]

On leaving Cincar-Marković, Heeren reported to Berlin that the Yugoslavs were not considering an offensive against Bulgaria even to prevent military encirclement of their country.[2]

For the Yugoslavs, all this dissembling did not obscure the fact

[1] *USMT,* NG-2978.

[2] *USMT,* Doc. NG-3245. State Secretary Weizsäcker replied to Heeren's report by instructing him to tell the Yugoslavs that the movement of German troops into Rumania was a political and not a military move, and that they should assume this measure was not directed against Yugoslavia. *USMT,* Doc. NG-3376.

that the German troops streaming into Rumania would ultimately push
through Bulgaria to bail out their Italian friends in Greece.[3] What
were Yugoslavia's security prospects if a German army invaded Bulgaria or if Bulgaria unconditionally joined the Axis?

For the answer we look to the geography of the Balkans. The road
from Bulgaria to Greece runs through the Struma Valley, paralleling
Yugoslavia's eastern frontier only a few miles away. To protect this
lifeline the Germans had to make certain of Yugoslavia's neutrality.
This alone accounts for much of Hitler's amiable attitude toward the
Yugoslav government.[4] True, better roads to Greece lay through the
Monastir and Vardar gaps. But this was Yugoslav territory and only
an invasion would give him the right of way. He was unwilling to
risk a secondary war, with its attendant problem of holding down
a rebellious Serbian population, for the sake of an alternative route
to Greece. Once German troops marched into Bulgaria, however, and
then into Greece, Yugoslavia faced complete encirclement. When
the German and Italian armies linked, Yugoslavia would no longer
be able to take advantage of German-Italian differences. Yugoslavia
would then have to make a choice; either to go along with Germany
or to go against it.[5]

All during January the Germans were without success in enlisting
Yugoslavia's support for their Greek venture. Weizsäcker told the
Italian ambassador in Berlin that the talks with Yugoslavia were
"just dragging along." But he was optimistic, he said, and certain
that the Yugoslav government would fall into line as soon as the
general trends in the Balkans became more obvious. Meanwhile,

[3] *USMT*, Doc. NG-3155. In 1940, Marshal Antonescu of Rumania agreed to
cooperate with Germany. All that remained for the Germans to do was to talk
with King Boris of Bulgaria about the building of bridges, barracks, and supply
depots in his country for the use of the German army. German troop strength in
Rumania exceeded 500,000. *USMT*, Doc. NG-3765.

[4] Hitler's recollections of impressions he received during the First World War,
when the Serbian army became famous for its tenacity and bravery in the field,
may have conditioned much of his thinking about the Yugoslavs.

[5] The Germans wanted to delay the announcement of their military aims in
Bulgaria as long as possible. General Jodl proposed playing a game with Bulgaria.
At the invitation of the Bulgarian government, the Germans would send training
units into Bulgaria; and to safeguard the operation against Greece that would
begin in April, Bulgaria, Turkey, and Germany would sign a nonaggression pact,
as would Bulgaria and Yugoslavia, according to General Jodl's plans. *USMT*,
Docs. NG-3097 and 3167.

because the Yugoslavs were so slow to cooperate, Weizsäcker ordered his colleagues to give them no special economic consideration.[6]

Like Cincar-Marković, Metaxas also understood the meaning of the German troop movements into Rumania. Writing in January of his fears that the Germans might eventually violate Yugoslav territory, he urged Prince Paul to reject all Nazi requests to use Yugoslavia as a base from which to attack Greece. He wrote that he firmly believed Yugoslavia would resist such a German demand—with arms if necessary. In so doing, he asserted, it would remain loyal to its heroic traditions, defend its threatened independence, contribute to the easy annihilation of the Italian army in Albania, and probably even bring Russia into the struggle.

Prince Paul responded that he would not permit German troops to march through Yugoslavia. Acknowledging this message, Metaxas expressed gratitude and said he was deeply touched by the Prince Regent's assurance that Yugoslavia would never fail in its regard for "the laws of honor and its glorious tradition" and by Prince Paul's "appreciation" for the unequal struggle fought by Greece.[7]

The Italo-Greek war marked the beginning of the struggle between Germany and Great Britain for Yugoslavia. The Germans used the facts of power: economic, military, geopolitical. The British used such appeals as the desirability of cooperation with Turkey, the emotional pull of Prince Paul's personal and family ties with England, and the promise of future aid from the armory of the United States.[8]

At the suggestion of the British,[9] the Turkish minister in Belgrade submitted a proposal to the Yugoslav foreign office on January 19th. Noting that the German army, now in Rumania, could move against the Soviet Union, against Greece, or against another Balkan country,

---

[6] USMT, Docs. NG-3373 and 3374.

[7] Metaxas to Prince Paul, January 6 and 17, 1941. (JBH)

[8] The idea that they could use the Yugoslavs to oppose the Italians became apparent to the British almost a year after Prince Paul had recommended that the Allies establish a front in the Balkans. On June 6, 1940, in the first of a series of moves involving Yugoslavia, Winston Churchill instructed the foreign office to encourage Yugoslav mobilization as a counter to the threat from Italy. Churchill, Their Finest Hour, p. 162. See also the letters from King George VI to Prince Paul in John W. Wheeler-Bennett, King George VI (New York: St. Martin's Press, 1958), pp. 491-93.

[9] Knatchbull-Hugessen, Diplomat in Peace and War, p. 159.

he suggested that Ankara and Belgrade lay out a plan for common action.[10] The Yugoslavs rejected the suggestion, however, because they believed that the Turkish government lacked concrete plans in case of an emergency and that the Turkish army was not prepared militarily. The Turks had already refused to enter the war, along with Yugoslavia, on the side of Greece.[11]

A few days later Colonel William Donovan arrived in Belgrade, an emissary from President Roosevelt and an agent to advance the British aim of establishing a Balkan front. He remained in Belgrade from January 23d to the 25th, meeting with Prince Paul, cabinet ministers, and military leaders. The Prince Regent told him that the Bulgars would yield to Nazi pressure and that Yugoslavia, a divided country, might fight if the Germans occupied Bulgaria, although he was doubtful. To this, Donovan responded with a veiled ultimatum: if the Yugoslav government let German troops cross the boundary, the United States would not intercede for Yugoslavia at the peace table. Cvetković assured him that attempts by the Germans to enter Yugoslav territory by force would mean war. Yugoslavia would not permit German war materials or troops to cross its frontiers.[12]

Although Donovan's mission failed—for the Yugoslavs did not agree to enter the war—it had a psychological side-effect. It led many in Belgrade to believe that he brought from President Roosevelt a moral commitment to supply them with arms and planes as soon as they attacked the Italians.

[10] Sumenković to author.

[11] Cvetković to author. See also King Peter II, *King's Heritage*, p. 59; and Knatchbull-Hugessen, *Diplomat in Peace and War*, pp. 160 and 166. The Turks state that they never received an answer to their proposal and that it met with ironical laughter. Cevat Acikalan, "Turkey's International Relations," *International Affairs*, London (October, 1947), p. 483. Metaxas was convinced that the Turks would remain neutral under all circumstances. Papagos, *Battle of Greece, 1940-1941*, pp. 310-11. According to General Wavell, the Turks would make no move to provoke the Germans. William L. Langer and S. Everett Gleason, *Undeclared War, 1940-1941* (New York: Harper, 1953), p. 396; and Sir John Kennedy, *Business of War* (London: Hutchinson, 1957), pp. 41-44.

[12] Langer and Gleason, *Undeclared War, 1940-1941*, pp. 396-98; Hull, *Memoirs*, II, 928; and Cvetković to author. Donovan's reports contradict Churchill's comments that "fear reigned" in Belgrade and that "ministers and the leading politicians did not dare to speak their minds" (Churchill, *Grand Alliance*, p. 158). See also report by Joseph Alsop and Robert Kintner in the New York *Herald Tribune*, April 2, 1941, and *FRUS*, II (1941), 938-39 and 947-48.

During this period the Germans did not appear concerned about the possibility of political or military action by the Yugoslavs. Ribbentrop realized that Yugoslav public opinion was anti-Axis. Nevertheless, he believed that nothing would transmute the mass feeling into action by the Belgrade government.[13] Still, as the day drew closer for the move into Bulgaria and then into Greece, Berlin had to make certain Yugoslavia would remain quiescent.

For the Yugoslavs the day was drawing near when their government would be forced to make a choice. Belgrade tried to temporize. Perhaps, said Cincar-Marković, the Russians can help us. On February 3d he asked Gavrilović to determine Moscow's attitude toward German policy in the Balkans. Did the Soviet Union consider the presence of German troops in Rumania and their possible entry into Bulgaria a danger to Soviet and Yugoslav interests?[14]

Vishinsky's answer led Gavrilović to the opinion that, above all, the Russians did not want war. It was clear that they were interested in Balkan affairs and were paying special attention to developments in Bulgaria and in the Straits neighborhood. Vishinsky expressed willingness to offer *sub rosa* assistance to all Balkan countries provided that it did not lead to war with Germany. (Here he may have been thinking of the decision in November to halt discussions on arms shipments to Yugoslavia.) He made it plain that if the British opened a Balkan front, the Soviet Union would enter the war against Germany. Soviet troops would move directly toward Bulgaria and the Straits. On the other hand, if the Soviet Union did not enter the war and if the Germans were defeated by the western powers, the Red army would move into Rumania and Hungary.[15]

If the Germans entered Bulgaria, Gavrilović theorized after his talks with the Russians, the Soviet Union would not interfere. The German move would actually help them, he believed, for when Germany lost the war and German troops withdrew the Bulgarians would be ideologically ready to welcome the Red army.

Simultaneously, Cvetković urged Plotnikov, the Soviet minister in

---

[13] Ciano, *L'Europa*, p. 627.

[14] Cincar-Marković to Gavrilović, February 3, 1941. (JBH)

[15] Gavrilović to Yugoslav ministry of foreign affairs, February 8 and 13, 1941. (JBH)

Belgrade, to persuade his government to assist Yugoslavia. Making no effort to conceal the weakness of the Yugoslav army, Cvetković enumerated its shortcomings in armored units, motorized units, and equipment of all types. Plotnikov promised help with everything, and when he left for Moscow in March he took with him a complete list of Yugoslav military requirements. He and the list disappeared across the frontier, and Belgrade never heard of either of them again.[16]

About this time the Germans were drawing up their timetable for combined diplomatic and military operations designed to outflank a Soviet diplomatic offensive in the Balkans. The first step would be to urge the Bulgars to renew their nonaggression pact with Turkey. Then they would unquestionably sign the Tripartite Pact. It would be more difficult to persuade the Yugoslavs to sign, but when that had been done the Germans would have completed the process of excluding Russia from the Balkans.[17]

The Bulgars and Turks renewed their pact on February 17th, discomfiting Prince Paul and bringing new fears to the Kremlin. Gavrilović reported that although the Russians denied they wanted war in the Balkans, privately they admitted they would make no effort to prevent it. War in the Balkans meant a breakdown of the capitalist system, a disaster for others but a boon for the Russians. In the chaos of war they could take over, weakening Germany at the same time.

Gavrilović believed that if the Russians intervened at all they would do so only after the Turks attacked the Germans in Thrace and Bulgaria. The Germans would easily defeat the Turks, and the Yugoslavs too for that matter. At that juncture, the Russians would move in and take the Straits.

In any case, it was clear that the Russians did not want Yugoslavia to remain neutral. Gavrilović therefore advised his government to work closely with Greece, Turkey, and Britain to prevent Soviet aggrandizement. He was not sure what the British could do nor how far they were prepared to go in defense of the Balkans, but he was certain that when the last battle was fought, the victors would be Britain and the United States.[18]

[16] Cvetković to author.
[17] *USMT*, NG-3097.
[18] Gavrilović to Cincar-Marković, February 24, 1941. (JBH)

By early March, Gavrilović raised in cable after cable the possibility that the Russians would enter the war against Germany only when Hitler's defeat seemed imminent. Indirectly, Soviet military chiefs spoke to Popović about the value of a military pact between their country and Yugoslavia. In Germany the two countries had a common enemy, they pointed out. They specified that Yugoslavia should initiate negotiations, and through normal diplomatic channels rather than through the military.

Gavrilović urged Cincar-Marković to take certain Soviet assumptions into consideration as he made decisions on foreign policy; they might be made to work to Yugoslavia's advantage. One was that the war would go on for some time now that Germany seemed to have given up the idea of invading the British Isles. Another was that Germany would now drive toward the east. And the third was that sooner or later the Soviet Union would have to enter the war to protect its own interests at the peace table.[19]

Meanwhile, the Yugoslav government conjectured, perhaps a settlement with Italy would lighten the pressure from Germany. Minister of Court Antić, briefing Stakić for another trip to Rome, instructed him to say that the Yugoslavs had not accepted Italy's earlier proposal for a new treaty, because doing so would have looked as if they were bowing to diplomatic blackmail. Even now, Yugoslavia was not yet ready to negotiate a new agreement with Italy. Instead, Stakić was to ask Ciano if Italy would first get Berlin's approval of a proposed new Italo-Yugoslav agreement as a substitute for Yugoslavia's signature on the Tripartite Pact. In brief, since Yugoslavia would not join the Axis, would a new pact of friendship between Italy and Yugoslavia satisfy Germany?

When Stakić talked to Mussolini on February 4 the Duce said he was willing for Yugoslavia to have Salonika in return for a pact with Italy, and offered to exchange the Yugoslav minority for the Albanian minority in Kosovo. He agreed to take up these questions with Hitler, although in his opinion they were strictly Italo-Yugoslav matters.[20]

On February 9th Stakić reported to Prince Paul on his conversations

---

[19] Gavrilović to Yugoslav ministry of foreign affairs, March 8 and 14, 1941. (JBH)

[20] *Naša Stvarnost*, 1953, No. 3. From the Italian point of view, an agreement with Yugoslavia would hasten the destruction of Greece and obviate an excuse for German intervention, which would severely wound Italian pride.

in Rome. While he was happy to hear that the Axis countries would not ask Yugoslavia for territorial concessions nor request transit rights for their troops, Prince Paul would not accept the offer of Salonika. The seaport was the property of a people fighting for their freedom and for the freedom of the Balkans. He could make no alliance with Italy while Italy warred on Greece, he asserted. Nor did he favor transferring whole populations. Slovenes and Croats had lived in Istria for more than a thousand years. Yugoslavia would neither move them nor abandon Istria to the Italians.[21]

The Germans did not like the idea of a new Italo-Yugoslav pact. Weizsäcker told the Italians to wait, and they obeyed.[22]

The Führer's next step was to invite the Yugoslav prime minister and foreign minister to Salzburg for talks on February 14th.[23] First he treated them to his analysis of the Balkan situation. According to his sources of information, British troops were ready to debark in Greece. He for one would never permit a British soldier to set foot on the continent. Since Italy had not been able to end its war with Greece successfully he would have to go to the aid of his ally. This was all the more necessary since the British were aiding the Greeks and intended to form a front in the Balkans. Hitler then bluntly asked the Yugoslavs their intentions.

Replying, Cvetković said his country did not wish to see the war extended to the Balkans. He was certain others shared this view, specifically the Bulgars and the Turks. He was equally certain that Germany wished to see the Italo-Greek war localized. Therefore, said Cvetković, Yugoslavia was ready to come to an understanding with Bulgaria and Italy so that the three of them could oppose any aggression—regardless of its source—that would extend the war.

Hitler's response lacked enthusiasm. The best way to keep peace in the Balkans, he said flatly, was for the Yugoslavs to join the Tripartite Pact.

Cvetković and Cincar-Marković tried to sidestep at once, explaining

---

[21] *Naša Stvarnost,* 1953, No. 3.

[22] Simoni, *Berlin Ambassade d'Italie,* p. 247.

[23] On February 8th Prince Paul told United States Minister Lane that Yugoslavia's situation was desperate. Cvetković and Cincar-Marković would have to go to Germany. Lane believed the regent disposed to avoid war at all costs. Hull, *Memoirs,* II, 928.

that Yugoslavia could not accept the pact because it required the signatories to collaborate politically and militarily. Hitler dismissed the objection. He would not ask military collaboration of any kind from the Yugoslavs, he assured them. He would not ask for the right of passage for his troops, nor for the use of Yugoslavia's railways, nor for bases, nor for anything else that would force Yugoslavia from its neutral position. The Axis powers would guarantee Yugoslavia's territorial and political integrity. They would do nothing that would humiliate Yugoslavia's national pride. After all, Hitler reminded his guests, Yugoslavia's neighbors had accepted the pact with no reservations. It was now Yugoslavia's turn to sign, for it was necessary to regularize German-Yugoslav relations.

The conversation lasted four hours. Cvetković's last word was that they could not accept the pact. As they left the conference room, Hitler asked Cvetković to give his best wishes to Prince Paul. Then he put the question: Would the Prince Regent come to see him in Berchtesgaden? Cvetković agreed to relay the message but asked that Hitler, in accord with diplomatic custom, transmit the invitation through Heeren. This the Führer agreed to do.[24]

During these talks, according to the German foreign office, Cvetković and Cincar-Marković left all decisions to Prince Paul. They left the impression that the Yugoslavs were not at all interested in Salonika but were willing to act as mediators in the Italo-Greek conflict. Hitler believed Mussolini might accept their services of conciliation and referred their offer to Rome.[25]

When Cvetković and Cincar-Marković returned from Salzburg, Prince Paul faced the necessity of deciding whether to reject the pact and risk war with Germany or to sign it and possibly open the door to the Germans. His first step in arriving at his decision was to question Ronald Campbell,[26] the British minister in Belgrade, regarding the probable extent of British aid to Yugoslavia in case Germany attacked. Expressing the fear that Germany could crush

[24] Cvetković to author. The German army high command, knowing the talks were going on, made a point of asking Ribbentrop if, as a result of the talks, the Yugoslavs had agreed to allow German troops through their territory. *USMT*, Doc. NG-3244.

[25] Halder, *Diary*, entry for February 17, 1941.

[26] Mr. Ronald Ian Campbell became British minister in Yugoslavia on December 13, 1939, succeeding Sir Ronald Campbell.

and destroy the Balkan states, the Prince Regent asked if British troops then on their way to Greece would be able to remain in Greece for as long as they were needed. He got no reply. Campbell responded only that Britain, unlike Yugoslavia, believed the Balkan states could successfully resist the Germans if Yugoslavia, Greece, and Turkey would only stand together. Proposing that they form a bloc against the German advance in the Balkans, he promised that Britain would support their efforts to the full extent of its wealth and war material. He reminded Prince Paul that Britain had already given Greece and Turkey considerable military aid and was prepared to supplement this with supplies from the United States.[27]

This was begging the question, and Prince Paul found it disheartening. His problem was immediate. He had asked if Britain would come to his aid if he alienated the Nazis by refusing to associate Yugoslavia with the Axis. He had received no help in solving the problem at hand, only long-range promises.

On February 18th Heeren called on Cincar-Marković and learned that Prince Paul had not yet reached a decision on Hitler's proposal. Heeren reported to Berlin that although the date of the Prince Regent's visit to Berchtesgaden was still open, he believed that the regent was prepared in principle to make the journey.[28]

Again the Yugoslavs turned to Italy in an effort to avoid the German pincers. Again Stakić went to Rome, and again Antić told him to tell Mussolini that Yugoslavia could not accept the Tripartite Pact and to request of him some gesture that would ease the tensions building up among the Yugoslavs—tensions that grew out of their fear of Italy.

Stakić saw Mussolini on February 24th. The Duce was annoyed with the Yugoslavs for holding conversations with the Germans and for showing too little interest in an agreement with Italy. Stakić explained the extent of Berlin's demands on Belgrade. Was it possible, he asked, for Yugoslavia to avoid adherence to the pact? Could Italy

[27] *Stajerski Gospodar* (Styrian Economist), Ljubljana, September 27, 1942. The entire Commonwealth Expeditionary Force that arrived in Greece in March, 1941, amounted to one British armored brigade, one New Zealand division, one Australian division, and seven RAF squadrons. Various specialist units were already there. Churchill, *Grand Alliance,* pp. 94-98.

[28] *USMT,* Doc. NG-3372; see also *Peace and War, United States Foreign Policy, 1931-1941,* p. 619.

and Yugoslavia maintain their relationship on the basis of the Belgrade Accord of 1937 without making a new agreement?

Mussolini went to the point. Since Germany had brought up the question of the Tripartite Pact, Italy and Yugoslavia could no longer exclude it from consideration and future negotiations. Their 1937 agreement was no longer sufficient because of the marked change in major aspects of the international situation. Only by negotiating a new accord could Italy persuade the Germans to take the pressure off Yugoslavia. In a short time the Bulgars would sign the Tripartite Pact. Yugoslavia's turn would come next unless it made a new agreement with Italy. In that case, Mussolini pointed out, Yugoslavia would not have to sign the pact.[29]

To Prince Paul's way of thinking, a new Italo-Yugoslav agreement would only make the conquest of Greece that much easier for Mussolini, and he rejected the idea.

Now Yugoslavia no longer faced simple alternatives: of making a new agreement with Italy or of signing the Tripartite Pact. Now it was clear that a new treaty with Italy would be only a curtain-raiser to the pact itself. No longer was there much chance that Yugoslavia could maintain its preferred position of neutrality, nor even much chance of an agreement with the lesser giant except under such odious conditions as an exchange of populations or a promise of Salonika after the Italian conquest of Greece.

No longer was it possible to play Rome against Berlin. Hitler now held all the winning cards. A week after Stakić returned home, Mussolini ordered his minister in Belgrade to halt negotiations with the Yugoslavs, and relinquished the field to the Germans.[30]

None of the great powers wanted a neutral Yugoslavia; Yugoslav neutrality was just as distasteful to Churchill and Roosevelt as to Hitler and Mussolini. As Churchill saw it, British aid, both direct and indirect, to Greece would bring Yugoslavia to the side of the Allies. As a direct measure he wanted to help the Greeks with arms and men. At the same time, he wanted to create a Balkan front by welding Yugoslavia, Greece, and Turkey together.[31]

[29] Naša Stvarnost, 1953, No. 3.
[30] Simoni, Berlin Ambassade d'Italie, p. 249.
[31] Churchill, Grand Alliance, pp. 10 and 95.

With that in mind, Foreign Secretary Anthony Eden left London on February 12th for talks in Cairo with Greek and Turkish representatives. There he proposed, among other things, that they find out whether or not the Yugoslavs intended to enter the war, on which side, and under what conditions. They decided to call Prince Paul's attention to the danger facing Salonika and to ask his views on the question of keeping the port out of the hands of the Italians. This was only a day or two after Prince Paul had put a related question to Campbell and had received a discouraging reply. As a consequence, his response to the questions raised by Eden from the conference in Cairo was almost as uncommunicative as Campbell's reply. Yugoslavia, he said, would defend itself from aggression and would not permit German troops to cross its territory. He added that it was not then possible to say what reaction Yugoslavia would have if the Germans moved into Bulgaria.[32]

Eden met Campbell in Athens on March 2d to discuss Yugoslavia's attitude toward the German drive into Greece and to review the steps Britain could take that would encourage Yugoslavia to come out openly on the Allied side. One by one Campbell spelled out Belgrade's difficulties in maintaining national unity. The Serbs were pro-Allies, he pointed out, but the Croats, who lived near the border with the Reich, were pro-German. The government was under pressure from the Nazis to sign the Tripartite Pact. Campbell said he believed that if they told Prince Paul the extent of British help to the Greeks they might be able to convince the Yugoslavs to join the Allies. Eden accepted the suggestion and sent Campbell back to Belgrade with a personal letter to the Prince Regent. He told the minister not only to deliver the letter but also to give Prince Paul an outline of Anglo-Greek progress and plans, to emphasize that Salonika was Yugoslavia's one point of contact with the free world, and to reiterate that Salonika's defense depended solely on the Yugoslavs. If they failed to act, the consequence was obvious, Eden noted, adding that he would welcome Yugoslav staff officers in Athens where they and the British military could lay plans for the common defense.[33]

[32] Playfair et al., War in the Mediterranean and the Middle East, I, 374, 379, and 382.
[33] Playfair et al., War in the Mediterranean and the Middle East, II, 70-71.

The voice of the United States, still at peace, now joined the others —Great Britain, Germany, Italy, and the Soviet Union—in clamoring for the attention of the Yugoslav government. Like Yugoslavia, the United States had declared its neutrality at the outset of the war. Like the Prince Regent of Yugoslavia, the President of the United States trusted that his country would remain neutral in policy. Each recognized, however, that not every citizen could or would remain neutral in thought. The Prince Regent could easily agree with the President in his contention that the most dangerous enemies of peace were those who "without well-rounded information on the whole broad subject of the past, the present and the future undertake to speak with authority... to give to the Nation assurances or prophecies which are of little present or future value." [34]

As the representative of a great power that was outwardly neutral, United States Minister Lane expressed his personal conviction that countries which did not resist aggression were not worthy of independence. Nor, in his opinion, could they count on the support of the United States when geographical readjustments were made at the end of the war. He never defined the meaning of the term aggression; he simply made it plain that aggression should be resisted.

Lane found it difficult to obtain information from the Yugoslav foreign office. Officials would talk to him only with reluctance. All was shrouded in "great secrecy," he complained in his reports to Washington. After days of delay he finally saw Prince Paul on February 18th and again on the 23d. After the United States minister

---

Britain began mobilizing Yugoslav public opinion in early February when the British Council persuaded a number of prominent Yugoslavs—all known to be anti-Nazis or anti-Fascists or members of opposition parties—to leave the country under British auspices. Yugoslavia was in danger and so were they, the English told them, urging them to come out of the country to carry on the struggle against Hitler. As soon as those who accepted the British offer received their passports, the British imposed security precautions. The British provided those who agreed to leave with false papers—*laissez-passer* dated back to 1939 and bearing the seal of the British consulate in Bratislava. Each Yugoslav was given a Czech alias and was told to think of himself as a Czech and to memorize the personal data in the *laissez-passer*. They left by train, in small groups, and went first to Salonika and then on to Istanbul. There they received funds and waited for transportation to Jaffa. The ship that carried them to Palestine also carried Bulgars, Czechs, Rumanians and other refugees from east and central Europe.

[34] S. Shepard Jones and Denys P. Myers, *Documents on American Foreign Relations, July 1939-June 1940* (Boston: World Peace Foundation, 1940), II, 4-5.

had delivered his admonitions and advice on how to conduct Yugoslav foreign relations, Prince Paul assured him that Yugoslavia, without question, would fight if the Germans invaded.

In answer to Lane's query as to what action he would take if German troops entered Bulgaria, Prince Paul replied that Yugoslavia would do nothing at all. To do otherwise, he said, would put Yugoslavia in the wrong before the world. Nonetheless, Yugoslavia's military position would become impossible if German troops moved into Bulgaria. From there, they could attack Yugoslavia, cut the northern Yugoslav armies off from Serbia, and crush the country in two weeks. If he removed troops from the Croatian and Slovene frontiers and used them to protect Serbia he would be faced with civil war; the Croats and Slovenes would claim they were being sacrificed for Belgrade and the Serbs.

"What do you expect me to do?" he demanded of Lane. The British could give his country no help, he reminded Lane. And as for the United States—Yugoslavia would be destroyed long before help arrived from there. His voice became bitter and he lashed out at the Germans. They had made their plans with fiendish cunning, he said, and their assurances that Yugoslavia was in no danger of attack meant nothing.

As they talked, Prince Paul became increasingly pessimistic. Twice he told Lane he wished he were dead. "We have always kept our flag flying," he said with unmistakable pride. Despite his deep pessimism, Lane reported to Secretary of State Hull, the Prince Regent believed in ultimate victory for Britain.[35]

Yugoslavia's dilemma was not new. It had faced the regency since the days when Mussolini warred on Ethiopia. It was always the same: Could Yugoslavia maintain a policy of normal relations with its Axis neighbors and at the same time keep its friendship with Great Britain and France? After the fall of France in 1940, the dilemma sharpened. How could Yugoslavia continue to refuse commitments to Germany and Italy which placed it in opposition to its old friends, Great

[35] *FRUS*, II (1941), 943-48 and 957. The term aggression was used loosely by Lane and the department of state. Both used it in a variety of ways: in the sense of military attack or "attack military and diplomatic." A United States memorandum to the British embassy on February 19, 1934, defined aggression as the invasion of the territory by armed force by another state in violation of treaty rights. Nothing is said of diplomatic aggression. *FRUS*, I (1934), 22-23.

Britain and the United States? Was it possible for Yugoslavia to find a position which could not offend either the Axis on the one hand or the Allies on the other?

At the end of February, Hitler told the Japanese ambassador in Berlin that he believed the Yugoslavs were willing to live in peace with the Axis. Calmly he awaited developments. Sooner or later Yugoslavia would have to come into the Axis camp, either by signing the Tripartite Pact or by some other arrangement. Although Prince Paul seemed to hesitate, Hitler said he was convinced that the Prince Regent would have to bow to the national interest.[36]

The developments that Hitler awaited with so much assurance occurred on March 1st. With hardly a murmur of protest, the Bulgars unconditionally signed the Tripartite Pact. Thereupon Germany notified Yugoslavia that the Wehrmacht would move into Bulgaria. At six o'clock the morning of March 2d the German 12th Army streamed toward Sofia. Yugoslavia made no comment, a reaction that greatly perturbed the Germans. Only when they were sure of no opposition from the Yugoslavs would they feel safe in moving to the Greek frontier.[37]

Yugoslavia now had its back to the wall. Fully aware that Bulgaria had become a base for the German army, Cvetković and Konstanti-nović, the Yugoslav minister of justice, drew up a series of solutions to the problem facing their government. Beginning with the proposition that all of Germany's proposals would advance its military and political aims in southeastern Europe, they listed the various demands that they could expect from Berlin: [38]

1. Passage of German troops through Yugoslav territory. To accept this, they agreed, would be to commit immediate suicide. When the Germans made this demand, the Yugoslavs would tell them at once that it was unacceptable.

2. Signing of the Tripartite Pact. Because the pact called for

[36] *IMT*, Doc. 1834-PS.

[37] Halder, *Diary*, entries for February 28 and March 2-3, 1941.

[38] Cvetković to author. According to Paul Schmidt, Hitler's interpreter, the Führer wanted to deal with Yugoslavia in the same manner he had used with Bulgaria: peaceful penetration and control. It was safer for him and more in accord with Germany's interests. Report of the Poole interrogation mission. See also Halder, *Diary*, entry for March 5, 1941.

military collaboration and the transit of German troops through Yugoslav territory, and because it was incompatible with Yugoslavia's obligations to Greece and Turkey, they would refuse to sign. Cvetković and Konstantinović believed that Yugoslavia might sign the pact if not required to give passage to German troops. But, they asked themselves, what guarantee would Yugoslavia have against Germany's demanding passage as soon as the Nazis found it convenient? Another major drawback was that adherence to the pact might bring Yugoslavia into conflict with England and America.

3. A tripartite pact of nonaggression. The Yugoslavs viewed this as a dangerous proposal because it would place the remaining Balkan states in the hands of the Germans and the Italians. They agreed to reject this type of pact on the grounds that they had concluded enough accords with Italy and saw no necessity for another.

4. A pact of friendship and nonaggression with Germany. They saw in such a paper the same dangers as those in the Tripartite Pact. If forced to sign it, they would ask the Germans to guarantee their independence and integrity.

5. A fifth possibility was that Yugoslavia offer to serve as an intermediary in liquidating the Italo-Greek war, preliminary to the negotiation of an understanding with Germany in which the Balkan states would guarantee that they would not permit the use of their territory for military operations by any foreign power. Cvetković did not believe the Germans would accept this since they already occupied a special position in Bulgaria. They might, however, ask the right of control and supervision, which would convert the Balkans into a kind of semiprotectorate. On the other hand, he believed that with this kind of understanding Yugoslavia would avoid imminent danger.

But he had to admit he had no real, clear-cut answer to his country's dilemma.

Although he did not know Berlin's intentions, one thing was clear:

the German penetration towards the south through Bulgaria means a deadly danger for us. The shortest and best route between Germany and the Aegean coast leads through our country. We therefore cannot agree to any proposal that might give Salonika to the Germans, for after obtaining Salonika we would slowly be strangled. It is better for us to be directly attacked than to be slowly tormented. Although our end would be the same in both cases, the means of attaining this end would not be the same. If we are attacked and we resist, our honor will be served, and this will mean something at the time when this war is over.

Cvetković and Konstantinović sent the entire document to Prince Paul, who agreed with their ideas. This document became the basis of the cabinet's discussions in the fretful days that followed. Fast-moving events during the next three weeks would help them to come to a decision on what Yugoslavia would do. Meanwhile, Cvetković and Cincar-Marković decided that Prince Paul should see Hitler. He went to Berchtesgaden on March 4.

From the outset of their five-hour talk Hitler tried to convince the Prince Regent that the Yugoslavs should take an active part in the new order that he was establishing in the Balkans. He was not interested in a pact of eternal friendship. For egotistical and economic reasons he needed a strong Yugoslavia, he said, but he could not protect it from Italy unless the Yugoslavs signed the Tripartite Pact. Prince Paul responded that he would not remain a regent for a week if his government allied itself with Germany and Italy. His countrymen would never approve a military alliance with a country whose leader was responsible for the death of their king. Furthermore, why was it necessary for Germany to invade Greece? Hitler replied, as he had to Cvetković in February, that he would not let the British land on the European continent. Immediately he returned to the subject of Yugoslavia and the pact. Prince Paul commented that the Yugoslavs would never accept the clauses that would permit the Axis to use their territory for military purposes. Again Hitler dismissed this criticism as a minor matter. He would eliminate the military clauses; Germany would not request the passage of its troops through Yugoslav territory. To this Prince Paul responded that he would have to counsel with his advisers and with the cabinet. The pact was too serious a matter for him to make a decision on the spot.

On March 5th, Prince Paul returned to Belgrade, depressed and uncertain. Would Hitler demand that Yugoslavia capitulate? Would he declare war? Or would he continue to allow normal diplomatic relations? The last seemed too much to hope for. At the very least, the cabinet would have to prepare itself for the possibility that Germany would insist on Yugoslavia's joining the Tripartite Pact.

Anticipating that Hitler would push the issue relentlessly, Prince Paul called a crown council meeting on March 6th. The council, an advisory body to the throne, acted as the executive committee of the cabinet.

They met in the White Palace in Dedinje, at the edge of Belgrade. There were nine at the conference table: Prince Paul and the other two regents, Stanković and Perović, Prime Minister Cvetković, Foreign Minister Cincar-Marković, Minister of War Pešić, Minister of Court Antić, Vice-Premiers Maček, the Croat, and Kulovec, the Slovene.[39]

Prince Paul reviewed his conversation with Hitler and told the council of the Führer's insistence that Yugoslavia sign the pact. After stressing the gravity of their situation, he called on Cincar-Marković for a complete analysis of the problem confronting their country. The foreign minister dwelt on the possibility of an invasion by the Italians and presented a plan for Yugoslavia's adherence to the Tripartite Pact. He said he was certain that the Germans would have no territorial designs on Yugoslavia so long as they were not winning the war. Furthermore, he argued, the Yugoslavs could check Italy's ambitions only by signing the pact, since in exchange for their signature Hitler was ready to guarantee the integrity of their territory against all powers, including Italy. Cincar-Marković was confident that Hitler would give the Yugoslavs certain assurances: that no Axis soldiers would enter their territory; that no war materials or even wounded soldiers would pass through Yugoslavia; that they did not have to enter the war on the side of the Axis; and that when the war was over Hitler would do his best to obtain for them the city and the port of Salonika.

When he finished, Cincar-Marković had to answer a good many anxious questions. Was the situation so precarious that they had no alternative but to sign the pact? This, he replied, was exactly the case. Kulovec, the Slovene, was the first to accept Cincar-Marković's proposal. In case of war, he said, Slovenia would be the first Yugoslav territory to be invaded. Stressing that he had no choice, Kulovec added, "Qui habet tempus habet vitam."

Cvetković then spoke up. He declared that above all Salonika must not be occupied by Axis forces. If Salonika were occupied, Yugoslavia

[39] Maček to author.

would be encircled. Germany would then be in a strategic position to demand more and more, both militarily and politically, of the Yugoslavs. If the Yugoslavs signed the Tripartite Pact, they would be part of the German political system and in no position to prevent the occupation of Salonika. Therefore, Cvetković said, he opposed the pact, although he would not object, perhaps, to a treaty of friendship with Germany. In almost the identical words that Chief of the General Staff Simović had used in his talk with the German military attaché in 1939, Cvetković repeated that Salonika would have to be defended and that if Yugoslavia were faced with the prospect of war, then the Yugoslavs would fight.

Regent Stanković too opposed signing the pact. Such an act would rupture Yugoslavia's relations with the western Allies. Bringing on war would be bad, he cried, but signing with the Nazis would be worse. Maček then asked the big question: Would Cincar-Marković frankly tell the council whether refusal to sign would really mean war with the Axis? The foreign minister said it would. Maček then turned to General Pešić for an estimate of their prospects in case of war.

Once war broke out, the general calmly replied, it was obvious that the Germans would soon be in possession of the entire northern part of Yugoslavia, including the plains of the Danube and the Sava and the three main cities, Ljubljana, Zagreb, and Belgrade. The army would have to withdraw to the mountains of Bosnia and Hercegovina, where it could resist for about six weeks. After that, it would have no ammunition and no food. Nor was there, he added, much chance of help from the outside; the British had said they were not in a position to grant the Yugoslavs any substantial military help, especially munitions. For over two years, Pešić observed, the Germans had had control of Czechoslovakia's Skoda Works, once Yugoslavia's source of arms. Without munitions, the army could do nothing but capitulate to the Germans, he concluded.

An argument began at once. Acknowledging the odds, Regent Stanković asserted that Yugoslavia must enter the war if only symbolically. "I'm an old soldier," retorted Pešić, "but I have never heard of a symbolic war. What is it?" he demanded. Stanković said he meant that Yugoslavia should find a De Gaulle, that the king and the government, with 100,000 soldiers, should force their way to Greece. There they would be able to join with the British forces, stay with them when they left Greece, and be in a position to come back after the war.

"This selfish view," Cvetković interrupted, "would mean saving our own skins and leaving the rest of the people to the mercies of the German and Italian invaders."

Stanković stood alone in his opinion. Picking up the discussion, Cvetković summarized the arguments. The majority seemed to be in favor of signing the pact but a vote had to be taken. All those present voted except Prince Paul, and all voted to recommend acceptance of the pact by the cabinet provided Germany made the guarantees listed by Cincar-Marković. Cvetković observed that if Yugoslavia signed the pact Germany's assurances would have to be published because the Yugoslav people had to know what was going on. Maček did not comment on the Salonika matter, probably because Cincar-Marković argued that refusal of the Germans' offer of Salonika would cause them to doubt Yugoslavia's sincerity.[40] Before adjourning, after almost three hours of talk, the members of the council agreed to keep secret both their discussion and their decision.

At noon the following day, March 7th, Cincar-Marković called Heeren to his office and told him that the question of signing the pact was regarded by the Yugoslav crown council as a serious problem. In view of Yugoslav public opinion, which was strongly anti-Axis, the members of the council realized they faced a terrible decision. They were also concerned over Bulgaria's revisionist demands and over the hostility toward Yugoslavia expressed in the Bulgarian press. After hours of discussion, they had come to the conclusion that before they could make a final decision they would have to get Germany's answer on one major question: If Yugoslavia signed the pact, would Germany and Italy guarantee, in writing, to respect its independence and integrity, to demand no military assistance and no transit of troops through Yugoslavia during the war, and to consider favorably Yugoslavia's request for free access to the Aegean, via Salonika, "in the new order of Europe"?

Cincar-Marković told Heeren that both he and Cvetković had received the impression that Germany was ready to accede to these

[40] Maček to author.

demands. In fact, Prince Paul had reported to the crown council that
Ribbentrop had offered a written guarantee on these three points.
Nonetheless, the Yugoslavs wanted Heeren to get a precise answer
to these questions "in order to fully clarify the situation." If in the
affirmative, the answer "would make it much easier for the government to agree to the desired policy."

Heeren was firmly convinced that if Germany and Italy guaranteed
the points in question the Yugoslavs would sign the Tripartite Pact.
Otherwise, a new talk would be necessary. In his opinion, Belgrade's
military and political circles expected some kind of an agreement
with Germany. Only public opinion resisted it. He believed the
Yugoslav government could indulge public opinion by gradually
"proclaiming" an agreement with Germany, and in that way avoid
joining the pact.[41]

Ribbentrop believed Prince Paul would waver in his negative
attitude toward the pact. If another meeting could be arranged, he
wrote Heeren on March 7th, they could induce the Prince to agree
to Yugoslavia's signing. Relying on his sometime acquaintance with
the Prince Regent, Ribbentrop considered suggesting that the two
of them meet in Bled a week hence. He cautioned Heeren, however,
against raising the question with the Yugoslavs for the time being.[42]

In a long and frank conversation on March 7th, Prince Paul told
Lane he was "wavering" in making a decision. Yugoslavia was imperiled by German encirclement. What could he do in the face of
such a threat?

The conversation between Lane and the Prince Regent had something of the atmosphere of an interrogation of a criminal or of one
suspected by the Holy Office of heresy. The American minister,
even more than his British counterpart, questioned, insisted, be-
seeched. Both used every means at their disposal to coerce Prince Paul
and others in the Yugoslav government into bringing their policies
into line with the dogma of strategy enunciated in London and
Washington.

As his talks with Lane progressed, Prince Paul described the two
courses then open to him. The Yugoslavs could resist. It would cost
them two or three hundred thousand lives, the enslavement of other

[41] *USMT*, Doc. NG-3542.
[42] *USMT*, Doc. NG-3542.

thousands, as in Poland, the devastation of the country and its partition among Hungary, Germany, Italy, and Bulgaria. Or they could keep quiet and permit the country to be occupied, with some conditions of slavery but without loss of life. He said he knew all the arguments in favor of the first course, of preserving the national honor; he himself was an honorable man. But in this situation he had to act not on the basis of what was best for an individual but for an entire nation. And the people of Yugoslavia were not of one mind as to what their government should do, he reminded Lane. While many Serb voices cried for war against the Axis, the deep silence of Croats and Slovenes marked their reluctance to take any step that would bring the armies of Germany and Italy into their land. Would it be better to hand over to King Peter a country intact or one in ruins? Lane argued that he should turn over to the king a country of which the king would not be ashamed, one which had fought to preserve its freedom.

Apparently overlooked was the fact that the government had for some time been standing off a determined German diplomatic offensive. Prince Paul made it clear that the Yugoslavs would likewise resist military aggression. "We will not capitulate," he assured Lane. "We will never be on our knees."

But that was not the immediate problem; the Germans had not yet attacked Yugoslavia militarily. When they got to Salonika, however, Yugoslavia would be completely surrounded, and then attack would be fatal. Meanwhile, Prince Paul did not think Greece would permit the Yugoslavs to occupy Salonika. The only other action still open —a suicidal one—was to take the offensive and attack Germany. At hand, however, and each day more pressing, was the question of the pact.[43]

In his discussions with Yugoslav government officials, Lane discerned three schools of thought on the Salonika question: there were the appeasers; there were those who wanted to occupy the port before Yugoslavia was surrounded; and there were those who favored a compromise between the two. Lane believed the last represented the majority of the people. But in all his talks he was never able to get specific official information on the course of negotiations

[43] *FRUS*, II (1941), 949-50.

between Yugoslavia and Germany. The best he could report was that some observers believed a compromise document insuring Yugoslavia's neutrality might be signed.

It was a matter of regret to Lane that he and the British minister could not maintain steady pressure on Prince Paul, for he was convinced that any action taken by Yugoslavia which fell short of the outright rejection of German demands would be dangerous to the Allied cause. This included the signing of a nonaggression pact. Secretary of State Hull's view, expressed in a message to President Roosevelt, was more temperate. He believed "that the only further step which can be of real help in these developments would be the promise on the part of the British government to lend material military aid with air force and ground forces to the Yugoslav and Turkish governments in the event they find it necessary to resist the entrance or passage of German troops." [44]

At this point the Yugoslavs resorted to another delaying tactic by dispatching Major Milislav Perišić, a Yugoslav general staff officer, to Athens for talks with British and Greek military representatives. Arriving on March 8th as "Mr. Hope," he told the Anglo-Greek mission he had come on behalf of the Yugoslav minister of war to explain the situation in which the Yugoslav government found itself, and the choices it faced, and to gain such information as would help in making the final decision.

The Yugoslavs needed assurance, he said, that the Anglo-Greek forces would create a southern front if it became necessary for the Yugoslav army to withdraw toward the Aegean, would designate Salonika as a base for the Yugoslav southern army and cover it from attack as long as needed, and would provide both the northern and southern forces with naval assistance and war materials if they became cut off from their own depots. The Yugoslav particularly wanted to know how soon the Anglo-Greek forces could establish a front running from the Gulf of Orphanos to Lake Dojran.

The British and the Greeks could reply only in general terms. There was much to gain, they told Major Perišić, from a Yugoslav attack on the Italian rear in Albania; such a move would give the

[44] *FRUS*, II (1941), 951-53.

Allies abandoned Italian equipment and would release Greek troops from that sector to oppose the Germans elsewhere. If the Yugoslavs entered the war they would share war materials from a common store as well as from the arsenals of Britain and the United States. As to a front to cover a Yugoslav withdrawal, Anglo-Greek forces would provide the necessary protection.[45]

Although the meeting was inconclusive, it gave the British some hope that the Yugoslavs would enter the war. But the British needed more than hope in the spring of 1941. Eden strongly believed that Yugoslavia would not fall into Axis hands if he could only convince Turkey of the necessity of a determined position in the event of German aggression in the Balkans.[46] On March 18th, he met with Turkish Foreign Minister Sarajoglu in Cyprus to urge that Ankara openly notify Belgrade that it would regard a German attack on Salonika as a *casus belli* if the Yugoslavs would do the same. Sarajoglu would not go that far. He would say only that the Turks would resist any German aggression against their own country.[47] In Belgrade, meanwhile, Campbell queried the Yugoslavs. Cvetković replied with a concrete question: Would the Turks consider a German attack on Greece a *casus belli* and, along with the Yugoslavs, defend Greek territory? The Turks answered him in exactly the same terms they had used in answering the British: if the Germans attack us, we shall defend ourselves.[48]

Early in his conversation with Campbell on March 15th Cvetković indicated that the Yugoslavs would sign a non-aggression pact with Germany similar to the Bulgar-Turkish pact. He said Yugoslavia had definitely refused to let the Germans move troops through Yugoslavia, had refused to let them use the Yugoslav communications system, and had refused to sign the Tripartite Pact with a military

[45] *FRUS*, II (1941), 951-53. See also Churchill, *Grand Alliance*, p. 110.
[46] Playfair *et al.*, *War in the Mediterranean and the Middle East*, II, 72.
[47] Playfair *et al.*, *War in the Mediterranean and the Middle East*, II, 72.
[48] Cvetković to author. Knatchbull-Hugessen argues that by March, 1941, the Balkan Pact had disintegrated, with Rumania most to blame. If Rumania had made some accommodation with Bulgaria, he thinks the situation might have ended differently. Knatchbull-Hugessen, *Diplomat in Peace and War*, p. 163. The Balkan countries could have organized their forces as late as February 17th, the day the Bulgars and Turks signed a nonaggression pact, giving Germany the opportunity of sending troops into Bulgaria without fear of a Turkish reaction. After that, it was impossible to organize the Balkans for effective action.

clause. The British minister's suggestion that the Yugoslavs take "a positive stand" provoked Cvetković. "Do you want us to attack Germany?" he demanded. Lane does not record Campbell's reply.

Later on, at the close of the conversation, Campbell asked whether the Yugoslavs had actually made a decision. Cvetković shrugged. "Decision, no," he said.

The inconsistency of his replies, puzzling to Campbell and Lane, came naturally to Cvetković. He was a Serb through and through, and he had a high tolerance for ambiguity. To those raised in the Anglo-Saxon tradition, valuing straightforward behavior, his attitude was incomprehensible. But the influence of Byzantium, cultivated during centuries of Turkish occupation, had taught his Balkan forebears the art of evasion and the practice of delay. Many a Serb learned early to acquiesce to unacceptable demands—and to procrastinate in carrying them out. Faced by an enemy of overwhelming power, he resorted to delaying tactics while the odds were against him. To delay any decision which might commit him to an objectionable course of action, to postpone a face-to-face encounter until strong enough to resist, was to survive one day more.

The Yugoslavs made no attempt to hide their dire predicament from the British, nor to understate the extent of the pressure from Germany.[49] Dismay at the thought that the Yugoslavs might, after all, sign the Tripartite Pact impelled Eden to appeal once again to Prince Paul, this time through Terence Shone, the British minister in Egypt. Shone, formerly British first secretary in Belgrade, had known Prince Paul for many years. Perhaps, Eden reasoned, Shone could reinforce his letter, which urged the Yugoslavs not to sign the pact and reiterated much that Major Perišić had heard in Athens ten days before. Although the message proposed that representatives of the British and Yugoslav general staffs confer, it carried no promise of the massive military aid or manpower needed by the Yugoslavs to backstop their own limited military strength.[50]

On March 19th, Shone had a long talk with Cvetković, who described at length all the military and political difficulties in which Yugoslavia found itself. It was too late, even for such seemingly harmless gestures as conferences between generals. The Yugoslavs

[49] Hull, *Memoirs,* II, 932.
[50] Playfair *et al., War in the Mediterranean and the Middle East,* II, 78.

THE ROAD TO VIENNA

were determined to do nothing at all that could give Germany the frailest excuse to increase its already nerve-wracking pressures on the Yugoslav cabinet. It was clear to Shone that the Yugoslavs had come to the end of their rope. There was nothing to do but to try to understand their position. Carefully he phrased his response: he felt he now completely understood the extent of Yugoslavia's problems, he told Cvetković. He would be a faithful witness, he said, to the government's expressed intentions of sparing its people from a catastrophic war and at a later and more favorable moment of entering the war on the side of the Allies.[51]

Eden had counted a great deal on the expectation that Prince Paul's essentially pro-British attitude would in the end determine the position taken by the Yugoslav government. What he overlooked was that the Cvetković cabinet as a whole, and not one man alone, made Yugoslavia's decisions. Furthermore, Prince Paul himself had always acted primarily to advance the interest of Yugoslavia as a whole, rather than to satisfy his own prejudices, within the limits set by the conflicting interests of the Serbs, Croats, and Slovenes. As a consequence, Eden's appeal had no chance of succeeding.

The Germans, meanwhile, were not so certain as the British that the Yugoslavs would sign the Tripartite Pact. On March 11th Heeren had called Berlin to report that they insisted on having a categorical statement that the Germans would not ask them for military assistance. Cincar-Marković believed such a statement would facilitate negotiations. As a matter of fact, he said, "everything would be made easier" if the sentence obliging signatory states to assist each other militarily were eliminated. Ribbentrop told Heeren it couldn't be done.[52]

But at 6:05 that evening the German government had acceded to this demand. In another telephone conversation, Ribbentrop told Heeren to notify Cincar-Marković at once that the Führer had agreed to the following formulation:

---

[51] Cvetković to author. See also *DGFP,* D, VII, Doc. 43.
[52] Telephonic intercepts by Yugoslavia's Central Press Bureau, March 11, 1941. (JBH) Cvetković believed the Yugoslavs should take their time in the negotiations; he was convinced that the Germans would accept all Yugoslavia's conditions.

Considering the military situation of the Yugoslav government, Germany and Italy promise that they will not request military assistance from it. If the Yugoslav government changes its mind at any time, ... and should it desire to participate in military operations in accordance with the Tripartite Pact, it will be left to the Yugoslav government to undertake and obtain the necessary military agreement with the powers of the Tripartite Pact.

Impatient to hear the Yugoslav reaction, Ribbentrop had again called Heeren at 10:10 that night, only to learn that there were no new developments.

The next day the Yugoslavs had new demands. Now they asked that the Germans permit the publication of notes in which the Axis would guarantee to respect their country's political and territorial integrity, to demand no military assistance and no transit of troops through Yugoslavia during the war, and to consider favorably Yugoslavia's interest in Salonika. And now they asked for the guarantee of a territorial link with Salonika, not simply for free access to the port. The Yugoslav crown council would meet, Heeren told his chief, as soon as there was a reply on these points.

Cincar-Marković exceeded his instructions when on March 12th he raised the Yugoslav demand from "free access" to "a territorial link" with Salonika. To Allies and Axis alike, Cvetković and Prince Paul had displayed a restrained interest in the Greek port. Both had repeatedly told Lane and Campbell that the German occupation of Salonika would not be a cause for war. Bulgarian and Italian occupation of the port was another matter. Germany's drive to the east might be less of a threat to Yugoslav interests than action by the two German satellites, who could use control of Salonika to pay off old scores against Yugoslavia.

It was Minister of Court Antić who introduced the subject of "a territorial link" with Salonika at the meeting of the crown council on the 12th. He would like to see such a link, Antić told the council, for the duration of the war. Cvetković's reaction was pointed. The government, he reminded Antić, was interested in keeping the existing arrangements alive. It was interested only in making certain that Yugoslavia's rights in the free zone of Salonika would not be denied if the port should fall to the Germans.

Giving Cincar-Marković this general instruction, Cvetković authorized him to continue to negotiate this issue with the Germans. The

Yugoslav foreign minister did not agree with Cvetković. He felt he had to take into account a number of alternatives. His first duty, he believed, was to prevent Italy or Bulgaria from blocking Yugoslavia's route to the sea. In the long run, Germany would lose the war. In that case, Salonika would be given back to Greece and Yugoslavia would have its original privileges there. But if the war reached a stalemate or ended in "peace without victory," Salonika should be in Yugoslav hands. Then it could be returned to the Greeks when Europe was once more tranquil.

Cincar-Marković had undoubtedly consulted Antić on the problem, for the minister of the court had an emotional investment in Salonika. In 1926, he had negotiated a treaty of friendship and alliance between Yugoslavia and Greece, then ruled by the dictator Pangalos. The treaty included articles extremely favorable to Yugoslavia. As its architect, Antić took immense pride in his work. Unfortunately for him, Pangalos was ousted in a *coup d'état* and the newly elected Greek National Assembly refused to ratify the treaty on the grounds that it derogated Greek sovereignty. Instead of renegotiating a treaty with the Yugoslavs, the new prime minister, Venizelos, signed a treaty of friendship with Mussolini, Yugoslavia's outspoken enemy. Simultaneously he denied Yugoslavia the right to share in the control of Salonika's railroad facilities and to transport arms and other war materials through the port.

Antić, his self-esteem still bruised from these events of fifteen years before, thus considered the Salonika problem as his special preserve. He could no longer take his revenge against Venizelos, who had acted against Yugoslavia's interests out of consideration for Italy, but he could try to talk Ribbentrop into making a commitment that would militate against Italian interests in the Balkans.

Hitler's insistence on the clause permitting Yugoslavia to change its mind and enter the war on the side of the Axis was interpreted by the council as meaning that he might try to engineer shifts in the unsympathetic Yugoslav cabinet. They specifically feared he would try to bring Stojadinović back to power and thus make Yugoslavia safe for the Axis. As a consequence, they decided at this March 12th meeting to ask the British to take the former premier into custody. The British agreed, and Stojadinović was turned over to them at the Greek border on March 20th.

On March 14th an exasperated Ribbentrop dispatched a long telegram to Heeren. The German government, he pointed out, had already acceded to Yugoslavia's demands to such a degree that it had expected no new requests from Belgrade. Now there were more. Instructing Heeren to define Germany's views once again, he said the Yugoslavs could publish the German-Italian promise to respect Yugoslavia's sovereignty and territorial integrity the day they signed the pact. They could also make it clear in their newspapers that joining the pact did not obligate them to intervene in the Greek conflict. But, Ribbentrop told Heeren, he did object to a public declaration of the promise that during the war the Axis powers would not demand that Yugoslavia permit troops and convoys to pass through its territory. He objected, he said, because the Axis had not given other signatories this assurance and because it might create an undesirable precedent. Nonetheless, because he realized this promise had special significance for the Yugoslavs, Ribbentrop would let them publish a special note on this point. But under no circumstances could he agree to the publishing of Germany's assurance that it would not demand military aid from them. Instead, when they signed the pact he would put this assurance, as well as the promise of free access to the Aegean Sea via Salonika, in a secret note to them.

Ribbentrop instructed Heeren to present his arguments to Cincar-Marković in a friendly but firm way. He should make it clear that it was up to the Yugoslavs themselves to decide whether or not to join the Tripartite Pact. The Germans had complied with Cincar-Marković's wishes insofar as possible. Heeren was to make clear to him that this was Yugoslavia's opportunity "in view of the possibilities offered to it to firmly establish its sovereignty and integrity in the future and to see fulfilled its ancient desire for access to the Aegean Sea without having to make any sacrifices on its part." [53]

Between March 14th and 19th Ribbentrop consulted with Mussolini, who accepted all of Yugoslavia's stipulations.

After relaying this information to Heeren at 6:43 on the 19th, Ribbentrop said:

Tell those gentlemen in Belgrade that this is a unique opportunity that must not be allowed to pass. If they do not agree immediately, various

[53] USMT, Doc. NG-3542.

technical difficulties will arise and the whole matter will be more difficult.

I have accepted their proposals and the matter cannot be postponed. The Japanese are coming on the 25th. They will remain here for five days . . . this business with the Yugoslavs must be finished now.

The signing must take place on the 23rd or possibly on the 24th.

Two hours later Heeren reported that the Yugoslav cabinet would meet the next day. Although Cincar-Marković would commit himself to nothing significant, Heeren told Ribbentrop, he had promised to pass on to the cabinet all that the Germans had told him. Heeren said it looked to him as if the Yugoslavs were trying to postpone having to vote for or against the signing of the Tripartite Pact.[54]

Heeren was right. The Yugoslavs were stalling, and with good reason: they had learned some weeks before that Germany planned to attack Russia. If they delayed long enough, the Germans, preoccupied with a war in the east, might pay less and less attention to the Balkans.

The first hints that Germany would attack the Soviet Union reached Vauhnik from two sources. Toward the end of 1940, he learned from Reichsmarshal Göring that by spring Germany would have at its command more than 200 air divisions. Where was he going to use all this airpower? Against Britain he would need 50 air divisions, at most, in Africa no more than 6. Where did he think he would need 200? Vauhnik remembered hearing that Molotov had infuriated the Nazis during his visit to Berlin in November, 1940. Perhaps Hitler was planning to attack Russia. A few weeks later, early in 1941, Vauhnik learned from the Slovak military attaché, Major Tatarko, that Germany, in preparation for an attack on Russia, had asked Slovakia for 2 infantry divisions. From a network of his fellow Slovenes who worked on German roads and railroads and in German factories Colonel Vauhnik picked up other bits and pieces of information about preparations for the march to the east.

Other sources were Count Sigismund Bernstorff and his cousin Albert. They often spoke of the possibility of war between Germany and the Soviet Union. One day Count Albert, in a communicative

[54] Telephonic intercepts by Yugoslavia's Central Press Bureau, March 19, 1941. (JBH)

mood, forgot himself so much as to tell Vauhnik that a "German attack against Soviet Russia was no longer a mere possibility but a fact. The decision has already been made."[55]

Still another source was Vauhnik's friend Willy Pabst. Once a major on the German general staff, he had abandoned his military career for business. Whenever his former colleagues, now high-ranking officers, came to Berlin they liked to visit Willy, a delightful host. He in turn often dined at Vauhnik's home, and thus the information brought by Pabst's friends found its way to Vauhnik's table. Some time during the second week of March, Pabst became very explicit. Preparations for the attack against Russia were in full swing, he said. Materials were on their way, airfields ready. He sighed as he passed the information to Vauhnik. "My friend," he said, his chin on his chest, his whole body slumped in his chair, "my friend, this means the end of Germany."

The next day Vauhnik learned through a German informant that operations would start during the second half of May and that 200 German divisions would engage the Russians.[56]

At this point Vauhnik, convinced he had something more than well-verified rumors, passed his information on to Belgrade, to both the Yugoslav general staff and to Prince Paul's first aide-de-camp. Although his coded messages contained data on German troop movements, with names and registered numbers of German divisions, the general staff never acknowledged their receipt and never referred to the information either in replies to Vauhnik or in special bulletins. When he realized he was getting no reaction from the general staff, Vauhnik asked Andrić, the Yugoslav minister in Berlin, to relay the information to Cincar-Marković, in the hope that he would find it useful in his negotiations with the Germans. Perhaps, he reasoned, if the government could convince the Germans they had nothing to

---

[55] Vauhnik to author.

[56] Vauhnik to author. Through the Swedish military attaché in Berlin, Colonel Vauhnik notified the British of Germany's preparations. The British in turn notified the Russians, who received the information without comment. Gavrilović, Yugoslav minister in Moscow, was of the opinion that the Russians, who did not trust the British, believed this an attempt to draw them into a war against Germany, a war they did not want. Gavrilović to Yugoslav ministry of foreign affairs, March 23, 1941. Vauhnik himself also notified Major-General Tupikov, the Russian military attaché, who already had the information but refused to believe it.

fear from Yugoslavia, there would be less chance of a German attack.[57]

By March 19th, Cincar-Marković was an uneasy man, and far less devious than Heeren believed him. The Germans had agreed to all Yugoslavia's demands; notes embodying the Yugoslav proposals had been approved by Ribbentrop. There would have to be another crown council meeting, and then a cabinet meeting, and now Cincar-Marković and the others could no longer raise new issues nor contrive new delays.

The council convened late the morning of the 20th. The point of decision came when Cincar-Marković reported he had found a way of publishing the protocols: Yugoslavia would release them to the press, not as part of the pact but separately, and the Germans would neither confirm nor deny their authenticity. Now members of the council had to make a decision. There was no way of avoiding it or delaying. Far from happy over the news that the Germans had agreed to their demands,[58] they now saw no way out, no way to avoid keeping a humiliating rendezvous in Vienna. They were quiet, seeming to accept the inevitable, seeming at the same time to hope that something would happen to defer final action, wondering what position Britain, the United States, and the Soviet Union might take if Yugoslavia signed the pact.

Britain's policy was clear. The decision to aid Greece sprang from purely political motives. It contradicted all military advice given to Churchill, for it meant he had to take men and material from Britain's thin defenses in the Near East. Yugoslavia's function was to underpin his *beau geste,* to supply men and arms as a barrier, no matter how

[57] Vauhnik to author. Vauhnik believed that the reason the British never published the information was fear that it might frighten the smaller European countries, make them even more pliant to German demands, or cause them to join with the Germans in a crusade against bolshevism. After the *putsch* in Belgrade, Vauhnik told the United States military attaché, Colonel Bernard Peyton, and his assistant, Captain John Lovell, all he knew of the German plans.

[58] Von Hassell, *Diaries, 1938-1944,* p. 161. Both the British and Greek governments gave Campbell, the British minister in Belgrade, permission to propose that the Yugoslavs, if they signed a nonaggression pact with Germany, require recognition by Germany of Yugoslavia's vital interest in Salonika. A Lane report to Washington indicates that the Yugoslavs had put forward proposals that they were certain Germany would refuse. Now they were chagrined because Germany had accepted their terms. The British argued that German acceptance of the "absurd terms" was proof of Nazi weakness and should encourage the Yugoslavs not to sign. *FRUS,* II (1941), 957-59.

temporary, against the Germans as they came to the aid of the faltering Italians.

If Churchill pondered the political consequences for the Yugoslavs should they go down to defeat, he gave no evidence. They, the last of the Balkan neutrals, were expendable. He saw a magical shift in the balance of military power—if only the Yugoslavs would fall on the Italian rear in Albania. "No country," he wrote President Roosevelt on March 10th, "ever had such a military chance." There "is no measuring what might happen in a few weeks."[59] Churchill urged the President to instruct his ministers in Turkey, the Soviet Union and, above all, in Yugoslavia to bring concerted influence on those states. Unfortunately, the Turks were unwilling and unable to fight for Greece, especially since the renewal of their nonaggression pact with Bulgaria, and the Russians were willing to enter the war only if it proved strategically gainful and then only if they were sure the Germans were losing. In this context, known to both Churchill's and Roosevelt's ministers in 1941, it was possible even then to measure "what might happen in a few weeks." If the Yugoslavs threw themselves on the Italian rear in Albania, the Germans and the Italians would fall on the Yugoslav rear. The maneuver promised certain foreseeable consequences: for the Axis, a quick and easy triumph; for the Yugoslavs, a land devastated and a people broken; for the British, a few weeks of respite before they too would have to withdraw from Greece in the face of relentless power.

Churchill's attitude toward neutrals and the methods to be used in dealing with them were crystallized in 1939. Great Britain, he wrote then, had the duty and the right to abrogate for a time some of the conventions the democracies were seeking to reaffirm. Small nations, like Yugoslavia, must not tie the hands of the great powers who were fighting for the rights and freedom of small powers. The letter of the law should not obstruct those entrusted with that task. A technical infringement of international law, unaccompanied by acts of inhumanity, would not deprive Britain of the good wishes of the neutral countries. The United States, the greatest of neutrals, would handle matters "in the way most calculated to help us," Churchill declared. "And they are very resourceful."[60]

[59] *FRUS*, II (1941), 951-52.
[60] Churchill, *Gathering Storm*, p. 547.

The United States, officially committed to a policy of neutrality, indeed proved resourceful. On behalf of the British cause, Acting Secretary of State Sumner Welles warned the Yugoslavs on March 21st that if they entered into any agreement with Germany that diminished either the sovereignty or the autonomy of Yugoslavia; if they facilitated a German attack on Greece or on the British forces in the Mediterranean; if, in any way, they assisted the Axis powers in a military or naval sense, the United States government would immediately freeze all Yugoslav funds. It would further refuse to consider any request for help under the Lend-Lease Act that Yugoslavia might subsequently make. It might conceivably understand and even palliate a nonaggression agreement—but nothing more— between Yugoslavia and Germany. An agreement of any other kind "which in any sense permitted Germany military facilities would place Yugoslavia outside the pale of the sympathies" of his government, Welles warned.[61]

Lane had no trouble conforming to this view. He had already told Cvetković this was the position of the United States. He had even drawn the obvious conclusions: Yugoslavia's status as a sovereign and autonomous state would be defined not by Cvetković or even by Hitler but by the United States government.

Prince Paul and Princess Olga were under no illusions about the United States position when they dined privately with Lane on March 20th. They were told by their host that although they admitted the democracies would eventually win the war they, unlike President Roosevelt, would not look to the future. The Prince's advisers, he said, were men who looked only to the present and to their own material interests. Then he touched on a nerve. Signing the pact, he reminded the Prince Regent, meant striking a blow against an ally, Greece, Princess Olga's homeland. Why not, then, refuse to sign?

The Prince Regent seemed self-possessed. He agreed that the pact would be no guarantee against a future German attack; past events had proved that German guarantees were useless and that the pact would only tie Yugoslavia's hands for future diplomatic or military action. But if he refused the German guarantees, and war came, he was certain that the Croats and Slovenes would not fight. He had

[61] *FRUS*, II (1941), 959-66.

been urged to sign the pact by the Croats and Slovenes, the other two regents, and the opposition Yugoslav Nationalist Party. If, after giving Yugoslavia specific guarantees, the Germans attacked, only then, in Prince Paul's opinion, would the country unite against the aggressor.

Lane argued that public opinion was opposed to the signing of the pact. He thought of the fierce anti-German and antifascist talk so often heard in the streets, restaurants, and coffee houses of Belgrade; many Serbs showed open disdain for the "blonde ones."

Prince Paul again disagreed. What was true in Belgrade was not necessarily true in Zagreb. There was not one public opinion; there was, indeed, a nation deeply and tragically disunited. He had only a few more months of service as a trustee for King Peter. During those months he was going to do everything he could to avoid taking the step that would lead inevitably to bloodshed.

When the appeal to public opinion failed, Lane then raised a geopolitical argument. He assured the Prince Regent that Yugoslavia was in a geographically strategic position. Because of its common frontiers with Germany and Italy neither country wished to see the other in control of Yugoslav territory. Therefore, he concluded, attack from abroad was unlikely. The fact that the Germans accepted every Yugoslav proposal was proof of this theory.

Again Prince Paul disagreed. If Germany invaded Yugoslavia, Hungary, Italy, and Bulgaria would join in partitioning the country.

Since the Prince Regent seemed convinced that a German invasion was inevitable, why not preserve Yugoslav neutrality, Lane asked. Signing the pact would destroy that neutrality. Refusal to sign would keep Yugoslavia's integrity intact and maintain its reputation abroad.

Prince Paul's voice was sad and tired. "You big nations are hard," he replied. "You talk of our honor but you are far away."

There was truth as well as irony in his answer. The British had already informed him, through a private channel, that Yugoslavia should not count on British military support in case of war. The navy, he was bluntly told, could not get through the Strait of Otranto. Prince Paul should expect the worst, regardless of the position he took on an agreement with the Germans.

The precarious foothold of the tiny British army in Greece conditioned the vigorous and unrelenting response of the United States government to the news from Yugoslavia. For the same reason, the British stimulated an unwilling Soviet Union to take a stand.

On March 23d, the day Lane last spoke to Prince Paul, Sir Stafford Cripps suggested to Vishinsky that Russia try to restrain Yugoslavia from joining the Tripartite Pact powers. Vishinsky refused to do so. His government, he told Cripps, could find no basis for discussing with the British government any subject extraneous to the relations between their two states.

Distrustful of British motives, Vishinsky at once called Gavrilović. The Yugoslav minister had two questions: What was the Soviet government's view on the signing of the pact? If Yugoslavia did not sign, what could the Soviet government do for Yugoslavia if it needed assistance against the Axis? Vishinsky said he did not know the answers but would discuss them with Stalin and Molotov. He called Gavrilović back about midnight with their reply. It now looked, he said, as if Yugoslavia would sign the pact. It was therefore too late for the Soviet Union to do anything. If it developed that Yugoslavia did not sign, then the Soviet Union would consider the matter again and decide what action it would take. That action, Gavrilović sourly reported, would at best be only diplomatic, not military.[62]

As the discussions with Germany had reached their final stages, Prince Paul assigned to Cincar-Marković the task of informing each Serb opposition leader of the nature of the pact. He was told to stress that the signing of the pact, with its qualifying notes, would not modify Yugoslavia's policy of neutrality. Cincar-Marković did not divulge, except to Miloš Trifunović of the Radical Party, the nature of the notes to be annexed to the pact. To Trifunović, he fully disclosed the contents of the notes. At the same time Prince Paul saw to it that the military leaders were informed; he himself gave Dušan Simović, commander-in-chief of the Yugoslav air force, full details.[63]

---

[62] FRUS, I (1941), 298, and Gavrilović to Cincar-Marković, March 23, 1941. (JBH)

[63] About the same time Cvetković, learning that Bora Mirković, an ambitious brigadier general of the Yugoslav air force, was openly criticizing the regency's foreign policy, invited him to his office for a talk. There the general denied that he had spread rebellious talk around the city. After all, he insisted, he was an officer and a disciplined one. Moreover, he felt he could talk familiarly to Cvetković

As the political crisis had mounted, Prince Paul's deep-rooted personal struggle had mounted with it. The leaders of the Serbian opposition parties and Patriarch Gavrilo of the Serbian Orthodox Church had given no quarter. Without exception, they would not admit to the necessity of signing the pact. Without exception they opposed Yugoslavia's having anything to do with it. Trifunović had gone so far as to say to the troubled Prince Regent: "If you accept the pact we shall accuse you of being pro-German. If you go to war we shall accuse you of dragging us into the war because of your [Greek] wife." [64]

It was obvious, Maček wrote later, where the Prince Regent's sympathies lay. He had gone to school in England, the friends of his Oxford years were now important figures in British politics, his sister-in-law was a member of the British Royal House, his wife a Greek princess. It was clear which side his feelings put him on. "But," he told Maček, "I have a conscience too, and a sense of tremendous responsibility toward our people. I cannot lead them to slaughter, and that is what we must expect if we precipitate a war with Germany."

When the full cabinet convened late the night of March 20th, Cincar-Marković again reported on the country's international position and asked for permission to sign the pact as recommended by the crown council. Of the seventeen ministers, only three declared themselves against it: Minister of Social Welfare Srdjan Budisavljević and Minister of Agriculture Branko Čubrilović resigned immediately. After the meeting, the third, Minister of Justice Mihailo Konstantinović, offered Cvetković his verbal resignation but withdrew it the following morning. [65]

When Heeren telephoned Berlin at 6:55 the evening of the 20th he was certain the cabinet would approve Cincar-Marković's motion. When he called Berlin again at 1:20 the morning of the 21st he could

---

because he was the best friend of the prime minister's late brother who had been killed in the Balkan wars, and therefore he was Cvetković's friend. The general had only one complaint. Why could not the prime minister find the means of appointing him commanding general of the air force? Cvetković and C. Nikitović to author.

[64] Maček to author.
[65] Maček to author.

report only that there had been a crisis and that the cabinet would meet again the next day, probably to reach a favorable decision.[66]

This news stirred the German foreign office to direct action. With the Japanese foreign minister and his entourage arriving in only a few days, time was short, German self-esteem at stake. The Yugoslavs *must* sign. On the 22d Ribbentrop told Heeren to deliver to the Yugoslav foreign office a note to the effect that the Yugoslavs must tell Berlin by midnight March 23d whether or not they would sign the pact and whether or not March 25th was acceptable as the date for the ceremony. If they refused to sign or delayed the signing, Germany would not accept the responsibility for their having missed a "unique opportunity."[67]

In the meantime, Cvetković was busy seeking suitable replacements for the two ministers who had resigned. Successful by the evening of the 23d, he went to the White Palace to ask Prince Paul's approval of his nominations: Dragomir Ikonić as minister of social welfare, and Časlav Nikitović as minister of agriculture. While Finance Minister Šutej and Maček waited in Cvetković's office for his return, Minister of Justice Konstantinović burst into the room. "Everything has gone wrong!" he cried, near hysteria. "Something terrible is going to happen!" At that moment, the telephone rang. It was Cvetković, calling all three to the palace at once.

There they joined Minister of Court Antić, Cvetković, and Prince Paul, who had news for them. That afternoon, Prince Paul related, he had had a caller, the commander of the air force. General Simović had gone straight to the point with a warning he had expressed

[66] Telephonic intercept by Yugoslavia's Central Press Bureau, March 22, 1941. (JBH)

[67] Von Hassell, *Diaries, 1938-1944*, p. 163. Schmidt told the Poole interrogation mission that the Yugoslavs seemed to have no special interest in Salonika, with which Germany had baited the hook. Until the moment of signing, they continued to plead for time to prepare public opinion for Yugoslavia's adherence to the pact. Although Heeren urged Berlin not to force the hand of the Yugoslav officials, Ribbentrop was in a hurry and willing to use pressure but not outright threats. Schmidt believed it possible that the Yugoslavs confused Nazi methods of pressure with actual threats. See also Paul Schmidt, *Statist auf Diplomatischer Buehne* (Bonn: Athenaeum Verlag, 1951), p. 529. On March 23d Prince Paul told United States Minister Lane that the Yugoslavs had until midnight to decide whether they would sign the pact. *FRUS*, II (1941), 965.

several times before: if the cabinet approved the signing of the Tripartite Pact, he could not guarantee that his officers would not mutiny and overthrow the regency. Prince Paul asked their views on this new development. No one wanted to venture an opinion until they heard what General Pešić had to say. The aged general had already gone to bed and more than an hour passed before he arrived. Told the reason for his summons, he said he knew Simović too well to take his threat seriously. In the morning he would call Simović, reprimand him and thus settle the whole affair.[68] Pešić was not the only one to dismiss the threat; Maček wrote later that he too did not take Simović's warning to heart because he had never heard of a *coup d'état* announced in advance and then actually carried out.

At midnight of March 23d Cincar-Marković informed Heeren that the Yugoslav government would sign the Tripartite Pact. Less than an hour later Heeren telephoned the German foreign office that a seven-member Yugoslav delegation would leave for Vienna on the 24th.[69]

At 3:30, afternoon of March 25th, in heavily guarded Belvedere Palace in Vienna, Cvetković and Cincar-Marković put their signatures to the protocol of adherence to the Tripartite Pact. Then they received three notes in German and Italian signed by Ribbentrop and Ciano.

The first note obliged the Axis powers to respect the territorial integrity and sovereignty of Yugoslavia. In the second note the Axis powers promised not to ask Yugoslavia for any military assistance and left it to the Yugoslavs to make their own military arrangements within the framework of the Axis; Germany and Italy asked in this note that its provisions not be made public. In the third note they promised not to ask Yugoslavia for permission to move military forces across its territory during the war.[70]

A fourth note, which seems never to have been delivered to the Yugoslavs, was to remain secret and unpublished unless Germany and Italy approved its publication later on. In it the Axis powers

[68] Maček to author.
[69] Telephonic intercept by Yugoslavia's Central Press Bureau. (JBH) The Yugoslav foreign office did not notify its missions abroad of the decision to sign the pact until six o'clock the morning of the 24th.
[70] Auswärtiges Amt, Docs. 68-71. See also Appendix B.

promised that "when new adjustments in Balkan frontiers are made, consideration will be given to Yugoslavia's interest in a territorial link with the Aegean Sea with the extension of Yugoslavia's sovereignty over the city and port of Salonika."[71]

Because of its confidential character, this fourth note presumably was to have been delivered by Heeren to Cincar-Marković at a later date. Although Cvetković did not sign a receipt for it, the existence of the note itself in the Italian and German archives, along with the record of Hitler's conversations with Cvetković and Cincar-Marković after the formal ceremonies in Belvedere Palace, leaves little doubt that Yugoslavia was promised an access to the Aegean Sea.

The pact signed, the Yugoslavs returned to Belgrade with the Axis guarantees.[72] The contents of the first and third notes were not kept secret from the Yugoslav people. They were broadcast on the 25th by the radio stations and published the following day by the newspapers.

About the time of the German "ultimatum" Churchill wrote to Cvetković in stirring phrases. If Yugoslavia signed the pact, wrote England's champion, it would commit "the crime of Bulgaria" and stoop to the role of "accomplice in an attempted assassination of Greece." It would face ruin. Together the Yugoslavs, Turks, and Greeks should strike. Together they would stay the Germans' hand and win the final victory.

On March 26th he sent frank instructions to Campbell, the British minister in Belgrade: Campbell was to "pester, nag and bite" Prince Paul and his ministers. Campbell was not to admit defeat. If these methods failed, Churchill wrote, then Campbell was not to "neglect any alternative to which we may have to resort if we find present Government have gone beyond recall."[73]

One alternative, the important one, was revolution and intervention into the Yugoslav domestic scene. On March 26th Leopold Amery, British secretary of state for India, appealed to Yugoslavia in a radio

[71] Auswärtiges Amt, p. 23.
[72] Hitler expressed his satisfaction over the event to Ciano. With Yugoslavia's position defined, Germany's military action against Greece was no longer an "extremely foolhardy venture." *IMT*, Doc. 2765-PS.
[73] Churchill, *Grand Alliance*, p. 160-61.

message over the BBC. Actually he addressed his remarks not so much to all Yugoslavs as to the Serbs alone. Recalling their valor in the First World War, he asked why the Serbs should now leave all the glory to the Greeks and class themselves with the Bulgars and the Rumanians. The Allies would win the war, he assured the Serbs; Hitler could not prevail against England and America together. Then he appealed more specifically to clergymen and students. Through the centuries they, he said, had kept alive the flame of the national spirit. He reminded them of the tradition of Kosovo and the heroic King Lazar, who preferred a heavenly kingdom to one on earth. Reaching the climax of his inflammatory broadcast, Amery asserted that the Yugoslav government could not "claim the right to sign away the honor and independence of sixteen million people. If the people clearly show that accession to the Axis pact is regarded by them as a betrayal of honor and independence, then surely it is the duty of the government to consult the people before the pact is ratified. No, it is not too late for that. The whole future of Yugoslavia is on the razor's edge." [74]

Campbell knew what the alternative was to be. The present government of Yugoslavia was beyond redemption and the one remaining course was to supplant it with one more receptive to Churchill's exhortations.

Plans for fostering a revolt had been made a year before when Churchill invited Hugh Dalton, Labour Party leader and minister of economic warfare, to administer a new organization, the Special Operations Executive. The SOE, British equivalent of the United States Office of Strategic Services, had two assignments: subversion and sabotage. Military personnel in mufti and civilians worked together in what Dalton fondly described as his "Ministry of Ungentlemanly Warfare." They used covert means to weaken the enemy's will to fight and to strengthen his opponents'. They encouraged and trained guerrilla fighters and resistance movements, used clandestine propaganda, bribery, mayhem, and murder. Dalton, the social reformer, responded with boyish enthusiasm to Churchill's signal to "set Europe ablaze." [75]

[74] British Broadcasting Corporation, News Release, March 26, 1941, No. 21.
[75] Hugh Dalton, *Fateful Years, Memoirs: 1931-1945* (London: Muller, 1957), pp. 366-67.

By the summer of 1940, Dalton's men were beginning to operate in Yugoslavia.[76] One was Tom S. Masterson, whose considerable experience as a representative of British oil interests in Rumania gave him a wide knowledge of Balkan affairs. In November, 1940, he was appointed a temporary secretary at the British legation in Belgrade with responsibility for economic warfare. One of his jobs was to cultivate antiregency elements and to organize them into a tangible political force for use at a later time. Now that time had come.

When SOE headquarters learned that the Yugoslavs would sign the Tripartite Pact, Dalton signaled his agents in Belgrade "to use all means to raise a revolution." He was confident of success, for as he reported "all was well prepared beforehand."[77] Masterson and his associates had operated very quietly among the opposition politicians; so quietly, in fact, that General Bora Mirković, the man who led the revolt, learned only later, as a refugee, that the British intelligence service had distributed funds with the aim of supporting a national uprising.[78] Moreover, they had worked within a situation already ripe for violent change. They had concentrated on a few individuals who would shape the policies of a new government born of revolution. Their assurances of success and promises of power had carried more weight in political warfare than had simple bribery. Their efforts, however, were not altogether necessary. Ancient hatreds between Slav and Teuton were at work, and neither Serb nor Nazi needed any encouragement from an Englishman.

[76] Fitzroy Maclean, "Tito: A Study," Foreign Affairs, 28 (January, 1950), 235.
[77] Dalton, Fateful Years, Memoirs 1931-1945, pp. 373-75; and Randolph Churchill, in the Daily Telegraph and Morning Post (London), February 9, 1953.
[78] Daily Telegraph and Morning Post, March 3, 1953.

IX

INTERMEZZO

One evening during the last week of March, 1941, Svetozar Rašić,
the Yugoslav minister at Budapest, received instructions to meet a
special train bearing distinguished compatriots, the Yugoslav premier,
Dragiša Cvetković, and the Yugoslav minister for foreign affairs,
Aleksander Cincar-Marković. On their way from Vienna to Belgrade,
they would stop briefly in Budapest, not at the main railway station
but, for security reasons, at a freight stop on the outskirts of the city.

With Legation Counselor Milovanović and Secretaries Mijusković
and Luković, Rašić arrived at the freight station about ten o'clock.
As they entered they passed a cart bearing a coffin. "This is no good.
It's an evil omen," Milovanović muttered with a nervous shudder.

"What evil omen?" Rašić demanded, plainly annoyed. "What
makes you think the sins of this dead man would be visited on our
ministers?"

Milovanović explained. "A dead man isn't out of place in a freight
station. But our ministers . . . if they had stopped at the main station,
they would have met the living, not the dead. Bad men and good,
but living."

On the platform they found the German, Japanese, and Italian
ministers. They too had come to pay their respects to the Yugoslav
premier and foreign minister and to another passenger, the German
minister to Yugoslavia, Viktor von Heeren. As they exchanged greet-
ings they heard the whistle of the train now nearing the station.
Rašić paced the slow-moving cars, located the Yugoslav section, and
prepared to enter and greet his chiefs. The moment the train stopped,
however, a door flew open and Cvetković rushed out. Seeing Rašić,
the premier clutched his arm and pulled him off to one side.

Rašić was appalled. "Mr. President," he murmured. "Mr. President, you must greet the ministers."

"Never mind," the president replied sharply, without a glance at the waiting diplomats. After a moment they disappeared into the car to greet Cincar-Marković.

Rašić remained on the platform with the premier. Before he could say a word, Cvetković spoke again. "What could I do?" he asked in a distracted tone. Together they went into the car, Rašić hoping to find Cincar-Marković.

He found him depressed, apathetic, resigned. Rašić had known his chief many years, and knew his moods and mannerisms. Never had he seemed so downcast. It showed in his entire bearing. As they talked, Rašić saw fear in the faces and gestures of Cvetković and Cincar-Marković, fear of the storm that they knew would shortly break over their heads.

The time came for the train to leave. The three Axis ministers, now back on the platform, stood patiently, correctly, near the prime minister's car where Cincar-Marković slumped at a table, silent, immobile. As Rašić said good-bye, he pleaded, "Please, at least when the train starts, look out the window and wave your hand."

But Cincar-Marković was indifferent. "Eh, my dear Rašić, I would as lief wave my foot at them as my hand."

The train pulled out of the station and sped on through the rain-swept Pannonian plain toward Belgrade. There, as before, it did not stop at the main passenger station but went on to the suburban Topčider. It was ten o'clock the morning of March 26th.[1]

Vice-Premier Maček met the train at Topčider. With some pride he described to Cvetković how he had broken up a protest meeting against the signing of the pact.

When Cvetković and Cincar-Marković left for Vienna, Maček had remained in Belgrade at the head of the government. On the morning of the 26th, he had learned from Drinčić, Belgrade's chief of police, that the opposition parties had announced an outdoor meeting to protest the signing of the pact. In fact, Drinčić had reported, between 4,000 and 5,000 people had already assembled near the Serbian town of Kragujevac. The police feared the meeting might lead to rioting

---

[1] Rašić to author.

and property damage. Although a battalion of field police were ready to break up the gathering, Drinčić thought they would need reinforcements and asked Maček for permission to send in more gendarmes. Maček refused. Instead, he told Drinčić to load two trucks with copies of the Official Gazette containing the text of the pact and the so-called secret notes, send them to the meeting place, and have police agents distribute them. Maček reported to Cvetković that when the people discovered Yugoslavia did not have to enter the war on the side of the Axis they calmed down and dispersed, leaving a relatively small group of 300 to 400, including a few Serbian Orthodox priests. The meeting had lost its political significance, he proudly concluded his report.[2]

After this account of how he had prevented a "revolution," Maček returned to Zagreb.

That afternoon Cvetković reported to Prince Paul. Tired and worn, the Prince Regent was on the point of entraining for Brdo, his home in Slovenia, where he wanted to rest for a while. He invited the premier to join him for part of the trip. The two left Belgrade at nine o'clock from the station at Topčider. Cvetković rode as far as Stara Pazova, about thirty miles from Belgrade, and then returned to the city by car.

Prince Paul continued on his way north. At four o'clock the morning of March 27th, at a small railway station, his aide-de-camp received a telephone call from Belgrade. There was trouble in the capital, he was told. Then the line went dead. He roused Prince Paul to report what he had heard. The train and its passengers continued to Zagreb, arriving about seven o'clock that morning.

---

[2] Maček to author.

X

YUGOSLAVIA ENTERS
THE WAR

Regicides and palace revolutions are common landmarks in Serbian history, and cited as precedents for the events of March 27, 1941. These acts supposedly worked within a tradition of long standing. When a Serbian king persisted in performing acts or promulgating policies considered unpatriotic by the community, the army stepped into the picture, either forcing the king to abdicate or killing him. After installing or permitting the assembly to install a new king, the army withdrew from the scene until the monarch again became "unpatriotic" or authoritarian. Then the players reenacted their roles usually to the cheers of the people. So runs the myth.[1]

How valid is this stereotype of military intervention in Serbian political affairs? In the turbulent years between 1804 and 1941 the Serbs had nine rulers. Of these, two died on the throne, one abdicated, one went into exile, and one was denied his throne by a communist revolution. Four kings were murdered: two by political rivals, one by international conspirators, and one by army officers. Only this last regicide—the assassination of Alexander Obrenović and his wife in 1903—involved the military as a political force.

The story of this murder began in 1889 when King Milan Obrenović abdicated, leaving a regency to govern until his thirteen-year-old son, Alexander, came of age. By the time he was seventeen, the strong-minded Alexander contrived his own *coup d'état*, arrested the regents and installed himself as king. In the next ten years, Alexander's personal life as well as his domestic and foreign policies so alienated many people that they decided to resolve matters by force. On

---

[1] Temperley, *History of Serbia*, pp. 52, 195, 263, 280.

June 10, 1903, a plot two years in the making came to a head when Serbian army officers, with the tacit approval of leading politicians and the country as a whole, murdered Alexander, his morganatic wife, Draga, and a score or more of the members of their greatly despised court.

This marked the downfall of the Obrenovićs, the resurgence of the House of Karageorgević under Peter I. Using cajolery and force, Alexander Karageorgević, who came to the throne as regent in 1914, was able to bring the army under control. A dramatic theatrical court-martial in Salonika in 1917 decreed death for the leaders of the *coup* of fourteen years before.

Colonel Dragutin Dimitrijević, better known by his pseudonym "Apis," was the best known of the defendants. He was intimately connected with the murder of Alexander Obrenović and his wife and with the Sarajevo murders of 1914. A general staff officer, he was for a time chief of the intelligence service. He and the other defendants were members of a revolutionary organization *Ujedinjeje ili Smrt* (Union or Death), sometimes referred as to the Black Hand. The word Union stood for the union of all Serbs regardless of religion or place of birth. The driving force behind the organization was the officer corps of the Serbian army. Most of them were disdainful of the slow process of rule by law, disdainful of party systems and civil government, and chauvinistic in their appraisal of the position Serbia should take in a union of South Slavs. These men had used their position in the army and their control of the Black Hand for their own political purposes. They had believed themselves to be the guardians of the Serbian gate; it would be they who, after the war, would check the credentials of those returning to Serbia, they who would filter out the unworthy from the true patriots. This was the philosophy of the men charged by the military prosecutor with plotting mutiny and revolution in Serbia, with attempting to murder Prince Regent Alexander and to overthrow the dynasty before concluding a separate peace with "a foreign power." But these charges were only a veneer to cover the real issues at stake, for the Salonika trial was the final episode in the struggle that would decide who was to control the Serbian army and dictate the foreign policy of the state after the war: the sovereign and his ministers or the Black Hand.

After that, the army became a docile instrument of the crown.

Nevertheless, memories of the army's role in the palace revolution of 1903 remained fresh in the minds of the strongly individualistic Serbs, civilian and military alike. Here they had a precedent for direct action if the head of the state violated their heroic code or their national honor.

In January, 1929, when King Alexander established his dictatorship he went far to revive the revered tradition that it was the army's duty to act for the community and to step into the leadership of the nation in moments of crisis. To General Petar Živković, himself a veteran of the military conspiracy of 1903, the king gave the premiership. Between them, the army and the centrally controlled police administered the Alexandrine dictatorship.

In the years following King Alexander's death new forces and new faces gave a new direction to the course of Yugoslavia's domestic policy, and to some extent of its foreign policy. The regency slowly eliminated the remnants of the Živković camarilla from the government and released imprisoned leaders of the political opposition. Forced into reluctant political retirement were Serbian army officers who would quietly, if unwillingly, have accepted exclusion from the councils of government if King Alexander had ordered it; he was a soldier and one of them. Prince Paul was another matter. Since he had never taken part in government or politics he was almost a stranger and, what was even worse, a civilian; his policies were anathema in their eyes.

In the main, not all Serbian politicians of the opposition were able to adjust to the changes that occurred after 1934. Cast in 1929 into political obscurity, they no longer knew how to work for a policy, only against it. Their isolation had bred in them a psychology of continual opposition for the sake of opposition. Many, offered an opportunity to share in the government, declined to do so, preferring to play out the role of recalcitrant, determinedly opposing the foreign as well as the domestic policies of their state.

If this Serbian opposition, a composite of stubbornness, negativism, and democratic ideals, had chosen to transform itself into a loyal opposition it would have had to recommend new approaches to foreign affairs. It would also have had to assume responsibility for carrying out those recommendations. Seemingly, it was prepared to do neither.

The conclusion of the Cvetković-Maček agreement in August of 1939, although a triumph for the prime minister, had no ameliorating political effect on many Serbs. As the Croats and the Slovenes increased their influence in the government, the position of the Serbs, once dominant, sharply diminished. It was natural, then, that the Serb politicians who had remained out of power so many years would become increasingly frustrated and therefore increasingly hostile to the regency. With the United Opposition no longer functioning, with their own ranks split, Serb leaders hostile to the regime could do only one thing: decry the honesty and integrity of Prince Paul's motives and policies. They went far beyond criticizing the regent's policies; their propaganda extended into his personal life and his relations with young King Peter and with the Dowager Queen Marie as well.[2]

By 1941 the precedent of military intervention in national affairs; the regency's downgrading of some of the old-line Serb military officers from their positions of influence; the regency's refusal to bring back on their own terms the politicians, either pan-Serb or United Opposition, who could not see the need for flexibility; the regency's agreement with the Croats that so offended the centralist-minded Serbs, whose entire outlook was grounded in a living history of struggle, first against the Turks and then against the Austrians; Prince Paul's insistence on acting as a Yugoslav rather than as a Serb; the regency's neutral rather than openly pro-Allied policy—these were the confluents of the torrent that on March 27th would sweep away the regency.

Like those who planned and carried out the *coup* of 1903, the Yugoslav army officer who fathered the *coup* of 1941 thought of it as a strictly military operation to be carried out for the public good. He was Brigadier-General Bora Mirković of the Yugoslav air force. Deeply imbued with the spirit of Serb nationalism, more shrewd than

[2] For an excellent example of the use of malicious gossip, see the pamphlet, *Prince Paul of Yugoslavia,* anonymously written and privately published during the war by a number of Serbian members of the Yugoslav government-in-exile then in London. Privately they acknowledged that their aim in publishing the pamphlet was to influence public opinion among upper-class Englishmen who looked on Prince Paul as a friend and not as the pro-Nazi enemy pictured by these Serbs. He was, after all, a member of the Order of the Garter, Britain's oldest order of knighthood.

intelligent, discontented, temperamental, unknown except to a few, he took pride in the military heritage of his family and country. For Mirković, the execution of Apis was only yesterday. Like Apis he was energetic and secretive, and would speak his mind only to those he considered trustworthy. Like Apis, he had no "conception of civil and political life and its requirements," and could not distinguish the possible from the impossible. His political ideas, like those of many other Serbs of his generation, were fuzzy and romantic, colored by the heroic Serbian past. Like Apis he had many fixed ideas and was incapable of compromise on those he considered matters of principle. He was "convinced that his ideas were the right ones on all matters... his opinions and activities enjoyed the monopoly of patriotism." Anyone who did not agree with him might be either a subversive or a fool. Like Apis and most other Serbian army officers, he believed that conspiracy required "him to plan, organize and command, others to obey and carry out his orders without questioning."[3]

Mirković was old enough to remember the exciting days of 1914 when Serbian Premier Pašić and the Black Hand were in conflict over many questions of foreign policy. The Serbian newspaper *Piemont* had ominously recalled the assassination of Alexander Obrenović and his wife. Those were days of struggle between the government and the Black Hand so pronounced that a violent clash between the two seemed probable at any time. Mirković may have remembered when *Piemont* described the royal family as lacking in prestige and King Peter I as all but nonexistent. In these days the Austrian minister in Belgrade reported to Vienna that the army was the determining factor in Serbia and that there was a possibility of "violent eruptions, even of an overthrow of the Government or a *coup d'état*" unless the government capitulated to the military party.[4]

To Mirković, the army was the custodian of the national honor and the defender of the state. Had it not met and defeated the Turks and Bulgars? Had it not, after the bitter retreat to Corfu, returned to Serbia to destroy the Austrians? Had it not rescued the Croats and Slovenes from the grip of Rome and Vienna, and made the union of

---

[3] Stanoje Stanojević, "Die Ermordung des Erzherzogs Franz Ferdinand," in Luigi Albertini, *Origins of the War of 1914* (London: Oxford University Press, 1953), II, 28-29.

[4] *Ibid.*, p. 34.

South Slavs a reality? Memories of this kind colored the political outlook of a man like Mirković.

Mirković probably began to give form to his plans for a *coup* around the time of the signing of the Italo-Yugoslav pact of 1937. Deeply imbued with his sense of historic but parochial patriotism, he convinced himself that the time had come for the army to resume its ancient role and for its officers to behave like true Serbs and stop the drift to disaster. Once again the army must become a force to be reckoned with and must act for the national welfare, just as it had a little over three decades before when Dimitrijević plotted against Alexander Obrenović.[5]

After extensive observation, Mirković decided that no one supported the government policy. No segment of Yugoslav opinion and society—the armed forces, the civil service, the politicians, peasants, and ordinary citizens—approved the regency's policies. That something had to be done, and done quickly, became for Mirković a matter of personal duty and honor. By 1938 he had decided he must find the man who could provide the military and political leadership needed to bring the nation back to the path of greatness and rectitude.

First he turned to General Milan Nedić, then minister of war, who in the past had been friendly toward him. Mirković tried to draw him out and direct conversation to the point where his own intentions would become apparent. But he had no success. Nedić would say only that all was lost no matter what was done.

Then Mirković approached General Stanković, commander of the Royal Guards. Stanković listened very politely but would not commit himself. He was in a most delicate position, he explained, and could not get involved in such a venture. Besides, he said, he was not capable of giving political leadership to the people. Certainly he would never send the Royal Guards against the people, he assured Mirković. Above all, he would never betray Mirković's conversation with him.

Mirković then went to General Bogoljub Ilić, who would one day become minister of war. Ilić fully agreed with Mirković but he too felt unworthy of providing the moral and political leadership the country needed.

[5] Speech by General Bora Mirković, March 27, 1951, published verbatim in *Seljačka Jugoslavija* (Peasant Yugoslavia), London (April 8, 1951), No. 110.

Four years went by as Mirković evaluated the suitability of his candidates for high office. Finally he spoke to General Dušan Simović, commander of the Yugoslav air force, a man well-known both in military and civilian circles. Simović heard the proposal without blanching, accepted the responsibility of leading the country in the emergency, and assured Mirković that if the *coup* succeeded he would continue the twin tasks of military and political leadership. Mirković was a very happy man that day. His already high opinion of Simović soared still higher. Simović was the greatest man in the country.

Simović, reputed for his ambitions and his ability at army politics, had a checkered record. His ambitions once had caused the authorities to transfer him from the air force to an army corps in Bosnia. Later he was removed as a deputy to the chief of the Yugoslav general staff and ordered to the infantry and artillery school in Sarajevo. In the autumn of 1939, having risen again to a lofty post as chief of the general staff, he had his heart set on becoming minister of war. Instead, he was appointed commanding general of the air force. Demoted, he always managed to come again to the top.

Mirković reserved for himself alone the decision as to the time and technique of the *coup d'état*. He wanted to be the one who would open the door for democracy. He confided in no one and committed to memory his entire plan for the deployment of troops. To prevent betrayal or detection by Cvetković's agents, he put nothing on paper. "No one in the whole world" knew of his plans, he later claimed. In actual fact, it was common gossip in Belgrade that a plot was brewing.

He had not yet decided the specific day the plan was to go into action. But he did know it would be the day that Cvetković returned from Vienna after signing the Tripartite Pact. In the signing of the pact, therefore, he found not an inspiration but a moral dictate for carrying out an idea he had fostered for years. According to Vauhnik, it never entered Mirković's head that the Germans might retaliate if his *coup* succeeded. Göring was a fellow professional, an airman even as Mirković himself; the marshal's autographed photograph commanded the place of honor in his quarters.

The organizational structure of the *coup* was on three separate but interrelated levels. The over-all direction, of course, was provided by Mirković, who alone knew when and where action would take place. The troops could be deployed without attracting undue attention because part of the armed forces, especially Simović's air force, was already on a stand-by basis. Some units had actually been alerted and equipped with live ammunition.

Very few of Mirković's lieutenants had been assigned specific tasks, and even fewer were aware of the plan for a *coup*. Most of them were junior grade air force officers, some in active service, and a very substantial percentage were reserve officers on active duty as part of their annual training. Few if any of them were unaware of persistent rumors that "something would be done" to terminate the pact and "save the nation's honor."[6]

The second level could be found among the members of the Reserve Officers Club in Belgrade. In 1940 and 1941 the majority of the active members of this club were air force reserve officers. In them, the British military attaché, Lt. Col. C. S. Clarke, and the air attaché, Wing Commander A. H. H. MacDonald, found a receptive audience.

The third level was bifurcated. First, there were the career officers, mainly belonging to the military elite of the general staff school and centering around Major Živan Knežević, then a commander of a Guards infantry battalion. They expressed the strong feelings about national honor and the Tripartite Pact held by the junior Guards officers—feelings illustrated by the flight on March 26th of Lt. Vučković and Lt. Smiljanić to Greece in protest against the pact. Although they were young officers, the impact of their action on public opinion was considerable, as one was the stepson of a general and the other the nephew of the under-secretary for foreign affairs. Their denunciatory letter, left at the point where they crossed the Yugoslav-Greek border and addressed to Prince Paul, was mimeographed and widely circulated in Belgrade.

Also operating at this level were those who served as liaison between the general staff and the opposition. One was Major Knežević's brother, Professor Radoje L. Knežević, who had been King

[6] Through a report from Heeren, Berlin knew on March 26th that a *coup* was in the making with Simović as the leader. Heeren reported that Simović and the British air attaché were consulting with each other on the exact details of British assistance to the Yugoslavs in case of war against the Axis which, Simović realized, would be inevitable if he successfully pulled off the *coup*. Heeren told Berlin he believed the Cvetković government knew what was going on and would be able to put down the *coup*. Auswärtiges Amt, Doc. 75.

Peter's tutor in French and secretary of the Democratic Party's executive committee. Through the Serbian Cultural Club, he maintained contact with the intellectual élite of the University of Belgrade who clustered around the well-known historian, Professor Slobodan Jovanović.

The Serbian Cultural Club, then a relatively new organization, included many of the upper-middle-class professionals and intellectuals. There were a great many professors of the University of Belgrade, and some diplomats. On the periphery was Ivo Andrić, the Yugoslav minister in Berlin, whose novels have recently appeared on United States best-seller lists. The older members, with personal knowledge of the price they had paid during the Balkan wars and the First World War to see their country grow, were deeply committed to the Yugoslav idea. Others wanted to establish the primacy of Serbia in the Yugoslav culture and eventually to organize a new nationalist party.

Among the active members of the political opposition, young Professor Knežević stood out. Although his ideas were more libertarian than revolutionary, they had proved too radical for the Stojadinović government and the minister of court, who had dismissed him from his post as the king's tutor of French. Mr. Knežević, it seems, taught politics along with irregular verbs. Hurt by the court's rejection, his sense of justice already inflamed, he had cast his lot with the opposition and through his brother, Major Knežević, had taken it upon himself to bring together the dissidents of the Serbian Cultural Club and of the Yugoslav air force.[7]

Mirković had not set out to enlist the cooperation of civilians, but in the sympathetic minds of the Serbian Cultural Club he found eager accessories.

The complete success of the *coup* was due to the coalescing of a number of different elements. With the exception of a few individuals, the Serbs—especially the "old generals," the intelligentsia and leftist students, the opposition, the army, the air force, and the Orthodox Church—and some Croats and Slovenes believed the signing of the pact betrayed old alliances and doomed Yugoslavia to dishonor and penalty after the inevitable Allied victory over Germany. More-

[7] Vauhnik to author.

over, they were convinced it would encourage Croat separatism and Italian territorial claims, and thus bring an end to the Yugoslav state.

Cvetković himself contributed in no small measure to the success of the *putsch* by failing to maintain an effective internal security and intelligence system that would act in the government's interests.

The top conspirators built their network of personal contacts in almost every garrison in the country. In every instance, the key people were Serbian officers; the conspirators took into their confidence none of rank who had ever been attached to the army of the Dual Monarchy and very few from Croatia and Slovenia.

After the *coup* became an accomplished fact, they found additional allies in General Petar Živković, the man who was prime minister during the dictatorship, and his brother, General Dimitrije Živković. These two followed other discontented generals, such as General Bogoljub Ilić, commander of the Second Army at Sarajevo, who participated in the *coup* and was later rewarded with an appointment as minister of war. Each of these elderly generals had a concept of patriotism; each also had a reason for despising the regency. For some it was an early retirement or reserve status "at the disposal of the minister of war" with a salary but no position, for others a posting to an obscure station to keep them out of politics. Each sought revenge for the personal injury done him as well as for what he considered Prince Paul's unpatriotic insistence on Yugoslavia's remaining neutral.

By the 26th of March, the conspirators were ready to move. They had only to wait for the signal from Mirković. They had a division of the Royal Guards, including an infantry regiment, two cavalry regiments, and an artillery regiment. They had a battalion of tanks, a company of engineers, a motorized infantry company, and other miscellaneous groups. They had the headquarters of the air force at Zemun Airport. They had an inspector of posts, telegraph and telephone, who would cut off communications between Belgrade and the rest of the country as soon as operations began. They even had the blessing of the hierarchy of the Serbian Orthodox Church.

Late in the afternoon of the 26th, Mirković learned that Cvetković and Cincar-Marković had returned from Vienna. This was the moment of decision; he decided the *coup* would take place within twenty-four hours. He went to Simović's office and there set up his headquarters.

Among his first telephone calls was one to General Simović. Mrs. Simović answered the phone. The general was asleep, she said, but she would be happy to waken him if General Mirković were calling on an urgent matter. Mirković demurred; the excitement of coming events could not be detected in his voice. No, he had nothing urgent to say, but when the general wakened would she ask him to drop by his office?

Simović came about five o'clock that evening. Although rested by his sleep, he was not prepared for the news which greeted him. "I have decided," announced Mirković, "to remove the traitors tonight." Simović was aghast. He became excited and nervous. His answer to Mirković's proposal, given so casually once upon a time, now made him an accessory to treason. He pleaded with Mirković to postpone the operation for just a little while.

Mirković was stern. He may have felt that Simović's patriotism was melting under pressure. This was no time to retreat. Growling that he would permit no deviation from the course he had set, Mirković said his decision was final; he neither wanted to wait a moment later nor did he have any reason to wait. With this reprimand to the commanding general of the air force, Mirković dismissed him and ordered him back to his home to wait for further instruction.

Simović did not go home immediately. It was midnight before he got there and in that interval he was undoubtedly a very unhappy man. He must have feared the consequences of the *coup*, whether it failed or succeeded. He may have gone to his co-conspirators for comfort in that time. There is no record of what he did in that span of five or six hours, but it is almost certain that any show of confident optimism he may have put up was a façade for grave misgivings.

Mirković, cool and efficient in his work of patriotism, remained in Simović's office and began to issue orders for mobilization of the *coup*, as a military exercise. The air force was his one trusted weapon. The infantry, artillery, and tank forces were only auxiliaries. He would give the first order at 11:30 that night, the last at 1:00 A.M. By 2:20 the *coup* would be completed. He left no margin for error or betrayal; three hours was too short a time for anyone to take action against him.

When the time came, his orders were carried out with silent swiftness. Quietly troops moved toward the center of Belgrade. There they surrounded the government offices and cut off the avenues leading out of the sleeping city. The officer commanding each sector reported by telephone as he completed his assigned task. The police, gendarmerie, and army were "spiritually united" to the people through Mirković and the other conspirators. By three o'clock members of the cabinet were out of their beds and on their way to general staff headquarters in the custody of air force officers.

Mirković knew that he, in his own words, "had fulfilled the wishes of my people." It was 3:30 and he had only one more task to carry out. Routing General Simović out of bed, he ordered him to general staff headquarters and there transferred to him his temporary command. Then he returned to his regular post of duty at Zemun Airport. He was satisfied that he had acted as a true son of Serbia. His night of work meant that "from that time on the nation would be led by responsible democratic leaders." He had only one regret: a *coup* that would otherwise have been bloodless was marred by the death of a policeman in an accident. It was, however, no accident; the policeman died because he refused to hand over the radio station to the rebels, who shot him at his post.

As Mirković left the offices of the general staff it was past dawn. The army was in complete control.

By ten o'clock the morning of the 27th Yugoslav, British, French, and United States flags fluttered from almost every building. By noon crowds filled the streets and squares, marching, singing, shouting against the pact.[8]

In their hatred for the Germans, in their belief that their government had made a military alliance with Germany, in their love for fallen France and their respect for Britain—in this complex of emotions and ideas many Serbs, particularly those in Belgrade, welcomed the *coup* with a deep sense of moral and national fulfillment. The slogans they shouted that morning reflected their strong pro-Allied feelings. Concocted though they were, such slogans as *Bolje rat nego pakt* ('Better war than a pact'), *Bolje grob nego rob* ('Better a grave than a slave'), and *Nema rata bez Srba* ('No war without

[8] Mirković speech, March 27, 1951; also *Daily Telegraph and Morning Post*, March 3, 1953. For details on the military mechanics of the *coup*, see Un Temoin, "Le Coup d'Etat de Simović," *La France Intérieure*, September and October, 1945; also King Peter II, *King's Heritage*, pp. 66-70.

Serbs') were the very quintessence of Serb history and Serb psychology.[9]

The conspirators did not act in ignorance. They had full knowledge of the reservations accompanying the Tripartite Pact, reservations which vitiated it as a military, economic, and political instrument. Nonetheless, they used the signing of the pact as an excuse for their *coup*, for what General Mirković and some of his co-conspirators wanted above all else was to put Yugoslavia on the side of Great Britain. Like the crowds that supported them, the *putschists* passionately hated the Germans, they wanted to help England, cherished the unwarranted belief that they could do so, and evaluated with utter lack of realism the possible military and political consequences of their act.

Maček reached Zagreb at ten o'clock the evening of March 26th. At six the next morning his telephone rang. From his fellow Croat, Finance Minister Šutej, he learned that a group of army officers headed by General Mirković had seized control of the government and were in the midst of forming a new cabinet with General Simović as premier, that they had forcibly detained the four Croat ministers in the deposed Cvetković government—Šutej himself, Smoljan, Andres and Torbar—and that Simović insisted on their joining his government. This they had refused to do without Maček's approval. Maček temporized, telling Šutej to call back in two hours for his answer. He felt he had to speak first with the vice-president of the Croatian Peasant Party, Košutić, and with its general-secretary, Krnjević. Maček called the two men and asked them to come to his house, and then went back to his bedroom to dress. When he returned to the living room ten minutes later Vikert, the chief of the Zagreb police, was there with a message from Prince Paul. The Prince Regent, Vikert reported, was on the royal train now standing in the Zagreb station.

---

[9] These slogans dominated the air by 10:30 the morning of the 27th. The Communists entered the scene after 10:30. The first slogan they launched was *Pakt sa Rusijom* ('Pact with Russia'). About noon they issued others, *Bratski Sovjetski Savez* ('Brotherly Soviet Union'), *Beograd-Moskva-Savez sa Rusijom* ('Belgrade-Moscow-Union with Russia') and one used during the Czech crisis, *Branićemo zemlju* ('We will defend the land'). Other than a brief appearance on Slavija Square, the Yugoslav Communists played no part in the *coup*.

He wanted Maček to drive to Brežice (twenty-five miles from Zagreb in the direction of Ljubljana) to meet him.[10] Since the train was still in the station, Maček said he preferred to go there at once.

At the train he found General Nedeljković, the commander of the Fourth Army Corps, which had its headquarters in Zagreb. The general had asked to see Prince Paul and had been told he was still asleep. Ignoring this, Maček entered the train. In the car an aide invited him to the regent's sleeping compartment where Prince Paul, awake and half-dressed, demanded, "Tell me what happened!"

Maček reported what he had heard from Šutej. In the pause that followed Prince Paul sighed deeply. "What's to be done?" he asked. The practical Maček suggested he finish dressing. Then, seeing through the window that Šubašić, Košutić, and Krnjević had arrived in the station, he proposed that they all drive to the governor's palace and there decide what they could do. Leaving Prince Paul's compartment he went to the drawing room of the train to meet the others. In a few minutes the Prince Regent joined them. Saluting, Nedeljković reported, in the standard phraseology of the military, "The situation is normal" (*stanje redovno*).

As they were leaving the station, Maček drew Chief of Police Vikert to one side. "How many men do you have?" he asked. "And do you have the courage to arrest Nedeljković?"

"You give the order and I'll carry it out," snapped Vikert.

"Good," Maček whispered. "Follow us to the palace and be ready."

At the palace, all except Vikert and Nedeljković went into the governor's private office where Prince Paul again asked, "What can we do?" Again Maček spoke up. They should not regard the *coup* as an accomplished fact, he pointed out. The first thing to do was to arrest General Nedeljković, a man in whom he placed little confidence. Then, he said, Prince Paul should entrust the command of the Fourth Army, made up almost entirely of Croats, to Nedeljković's deputy, General Marić, also a Croat. With this army, all its units safely loyal, behind him, the Prince Regent would be in a position to negotiate with the rebels in Belgrade. Maček said he thought an immediate appeal from Prince Paul, backed by the Croat troops, would influence a great number of the army officers in Belgrade since most of them

---

[10] Maček to author.

were not part of the conspiracy They could break up the whole rebellion, Maček asserted.

Prince Paul did not welcome the suggestion. The king had assumed control, he pointed out. To call on the army now to support the regency would itself be an act of rebellion against the king. Maček disagreed. They would not be rebelling, he insisted, but trying to protect the king from a group of irresponsible officers. Prince Paul would have none of it. Besides, he reminded Maček, his wife and children were at the mercy of the rebels. Unable to reply to this kind of argument, Maček said he had no further suggestions; Prince Paul should do what he thought best. With the finality of a man worn out by an intolerable burden, Prince Paul ended the discussion. In a strained voice he said he was sick and tired of trying to solve the problems of government and wanted nothing so much as to leave the country. He hoped the new leaders would allow him and his family to go quietly.

Having decided to return to Belgrade, Prince Paul sent for General Nedeljković. There in the governor's office, in the name of the king and the new government, the general formally requested Prince Paul to return to Belgrade at once. Prince Paul agreed to do so and asked that his train be ready at noon. Before leaving Zagreb he asked the British government, through its consul-general there, for permission to take refuge in a British colony.[11]

In the midst of this conference, Simović called Maček. Repeating everything Šutej had reported earlier, he pleaded with Maček to let the four Croat ministers join the new government. He assured Maček that his group not only accepted the 1939 Serb-Croat agreement in every detail but also were prepared to go further and grant complete autonomy to the Croats.

Then he spoke to Prince Paul, begging him to persuade Maček to cooperate. Prince Paul went further than that: he pressed Maček himself to join the government, in the hope that the move might delay an almost certain attack by Germany and in the knowledge that the Croat leader's participation would strengthen the authority of the Simović government and help maintain national unity in the critical days ahead.

[11] Cvetković to author.

Although Maček said he was not ready to make a decision, Simović persisted. Maček was making things extremely difficult for him, he said. He had already announced the list of new ministers, with himself as prime minister and Maček as vice-premier, in the Official Gazette. Maček was annoyed at this presumption but in view of Prince Paul's attitude saw that further reluctance on his part would be unwise. Šutej, Smoljan, Andres, and Torbar would join the government, he told Simović, but for the moment he himself would not. Simović continued to press for Maček's personal participation but Maček was adamant. This was his decision for the time being, he said flatly, and ended the conversation.[12]

At noon of the 27th Prince Paul left Zagreb to return to Belgrade.[13] At Prince Paul's request, Šubašić went with him, to evaluate the situation in Belgrade and to negotiate the conditions under which the Croatian ministers would serve in the new cabinet.

The conspirators' first problem was to establish their legitimacy as a government. Under the constitution of 1931, they could do that only by obtaining the king's written approval.

In the early morning of March 27th, as their gray-green tanks moved in to block the thoroughfares of Belgrade, they drew up a proclamation declaring King Peter's accession to the throne and appointing General Simović as his prime minister. To make the document legal they had to get the king's signature. That was no easy matter the morning of March 27th, for many stood in the way of the young officer entrusted with the document. To shoot his way into the palace might endanger the life of the king himself. Failing in his search for a safe route to the monarch, the messenger returned to the ministry of war. There, since speed was imperative, the conspirators decided to act as if King Peter had signed the document.[14] Consequently, when Peter turned on his radio about nine o'clock that morning he heard a voice much like his own proclaiming that he had taken the royal power into his own hands, that the regents had

[12] Maček to author. See also *FRUS*, II (1941), 969.
[13] Maček to author. Maček escorted Prince Paul to his train. This, he told me, is the last time he saw the prince.
[14] R. Knežević to author.

resigned, and that he had charged General Simović with the formation of a new government.[15]

Assuming that the king would approve their action and legitimatize their new government, the conspirators still had to decide what form that government should take. The argument raged during the early morning hours of March 27th at a meeting in the ministry of war. General Mirković, who had fathered the revolt, by now a military success, had definite views that were patently at odds with his earlier idea of clearing the way for democracy. Envisioning an authoritarian régime along the lines of that set up by his Rumanian counterpart, General Antonescu, he argued for a cabinet of generals with a general, presumably himself, as prime minister. Radoje Knežević energetically fought this proposal. Pointing out that the cabinets since 1929 had not represented the nation, he urged that the new government seek its legitimacy from the people themselves.[16] Knežević reasoned that in establishing the dictatorship in 1929 King Alexander had destroyed the 1921 constitution and broken his contract with the Yugoslav people. From that day on, to Knežević's way of thinking, Yugoslavia had had no legitimate government—only *de facto* governments, all of them stained with the "sin of perjury," controlled by the royal court and therefore oppressive. "A tyrant—and a perjurer at that—cannot demand loyalty from his victims," Knežević wrote. "Between him and them the relationship is one of force only." He saw the *coup d'état* as putting an end to the dictatorship and giving the power back to the nation.[17] As he phrased it, the *coup* "put a halt to moral anarchy by restoring the political and moral order trampled upon twelve years earlier."

Presumably Knežević meant the Serb nation for he believed the Serbs had never had proper representation in the previous governments. On the other hand, since the Croat and Slovene representatives in the deposed Cvetković government were true spokesmen for their people, he believed they ought to continue in the March 27th cabinet. At the same time it is not clear whether Knežević faced up to the possible consequence of not seeking to include the Croats and

---

[15] King Peter II, *King's Heritage*, pp. 68-69.

[16] Un Temoin, "Le Coup d'Etat de Simović," *La France Intérieure,* September and October, 1945.

[17] R. Knežević to author.

Slovenes in the cabinet. If they had not been invited, or if they had refused to serve, the Simović government might have faced civil war.

In Knežević's reasoning lies an inconsistency. He wanted a government representative of all the national groups that made up Yugoslavia—Serbs, Croats, Slovenes, and all the others. At the same time, however, he wanted to rescind the 1931 constitution, which the Croats accepted pragmatically and were willing to put up with pending modifications in their favor, and to revert to the 1921 constitution, which the Croats found completely distasteful and under which they had periodically boycotted both the cabinet and the parliament. Apparently he chose to ignore their attitude and their tactics in sending representatives to the parliament only to practice systematic obstructionism, to start a revolution, to encourage passive resistance, or to stop action designed to establish centralism.[18] After a great deal of discussion supporters of the Mirković thesis grudgingly accepted Knežević's political analysis.

Others also had ideas about the nature of the government and the composition of the cabinet. Simović wanted a government of "national salvation" with himself as prime minister, Slobodan Jovanović and Maček as vice-premiers, and Serbian Orthodox Bishop Nikolai and Roman Catholic Bishop Aksamović as ministers without portfolio. According to his plan the Slovenes would nominate two ministers, the Croats three in addition to Maček, each of the three Serbian political parties would nominate one, and the Vojvodina and Montenegro would each name one.[19] During the argument over the composition of the cabinet Simović abandoned his idea of including the two bishops. Ultimately the conspirators were able to agree on the ministers, ten of whom had served in the Cvetković government. They argued fiercely over the naming of the foreign minister. Tupanjanin, the representative of the Serb Agrarian Party and, according to Kosić, the principal agent of the British intelligence service among the Serbs, insisted on the appointment of Milan Gavrilović, then Yugoslav minister in Moscow. Kosić, who was a close friend of Simović and had collaborated with him in the organization of the *coup,* contended that their choice depended on the kind of policy they

[18] Maček, *In the Struggle for Freedom,* p. 109.
[19] Mirko M. Kosić, *Je Li 27 Mart 1941 Plaćen?* (Is March 27, 1941 Paid For?), privately printed (1950), pp. 15-17.

wanted the new minister to follow, and suggested that nominations were out of order until they decided whether they wanted peace or war.

This observation stimulated a quick poll of opinion among the conspirators. Grol of the Serb Democratic Party and Trifunović of the Radical Party came out for peace. Živković said it was impossible to think of war. Simović was for peace if it were at all possible. As they went on in this vein, Tupanjanin could restrain himself no longer. He pounded the table, his hair in disorder (he was the only man there in pajamas as if, writes Kosić, he had gone to bed that night in ignorance of what was going to happen before morning), and screamed: "What peace? This is a national revolution and when it's over there will be a national war!" This was the first time anyone had mentioned the word revolution.[20]

Despite his outburst, the majority favored peace. Then Kosić spoke up, knowing that what he was going to say would ruin his chances of participating in the new government.

If you want the Germans to trust you and to know that you are for peace, retain Cincar-Marković as foreign minister, at least until the first shock has worn off.[21]

This they rejected at once. They also barred the appointment of Gavrilović, since that would definitely mean war. There was now only one other person to consider, Momčilo Ninčić, who had been foreign minister nineteen years before. They summoned him from his home where he was recuperating from an operation. "Deathly pale and deaf as a post," he arrived to take over the most responsible portfolio in the new government.

Ninčić had been foreign minister in 1927. Since then, he had remained out of government service and had spent most of his time writing a detailed history of the Bosnian crisis of 1908. An avowed Francophile, he also served as the chairman of the Italo-Yugoslav, Germano-Yugoslav and Hungaro-Yugoslav societies. Obviously, Ninčić was everybody's friend and the perfect choice for the post to which he was now called and under the conditions which now

[20] Ibid. See also Mirko M. Kosić, Grobari Jugoslavije (Grave Diggers of Yugoslavia), privately printed (1951), p. 18.
[21] Kosić, Je Li 27 Mart 1941 Plaćen? (Is March 27 Paid For?), p. 17.

existed. Professional diplomat that he was, he believed his first task was to make the *coup* palatable to the Nazis.[22]

The conspirators now had a new government, but it was not a legitimate government. The king had not yet signed the proclamation, nor had the regents resigned.

At 7:10 that evening the royal train bearing Prince Paul and Šubašić arrived in Zemun, across the Danube from Belgrade. General Simović, who met the train, immediately escorted Prince Paul to the war ministry. There the Prince Regent, along with Stanković and Perović, signed the documents of abdication. Prince Paul and his family left at 11:50 that night for Greece.[23]

General Simović, meanwhile, reported to King Peter, who signed both the proclamation broadcast earlier that day and the act appointing Simović his prime minister. Then Peter asked the nature of the new government's internal and foreign policies. As to the domestic situation, Simović replied, he was trying to persuade Maček to enter the government. As to foreign affairs, he said, he had talked with Heeren and had assured him that the Cvetković policy toward Germany would continue; the shift in government had not been directed against Germany and the new leaders would maintain the policy of neutrality. The revolution was a matter of internal politics, he said, adding that the major deficiency of the Cvetković government was that it kept the people in "ignorance of its policy."[24]

But the world was not so rosy as Simović would have it. At the very moment that King Peter was going to bed happy with his country's "new policy of independence" the Germans were making their own plans for Yugoslavia, particularly for Croatia.

The Nazis reacted swiftly to these events. At 2:30 the afternoon of March 27th, within twelve hours after the *putschists* moved the guns

---

[22] *Ibid.*, and minutes of the council of ministers, March 27, 1941. (JBH)

[23] The *putschists* would have followed the 1903 pattern if they had murdered the Prince Regent; in fact, there was an alternative plot to kill all those responsible for the signing of the Tripartite Pact if the *coup* failed. Undoubtedly a restraining factor was the memory of British reaction to the Obrenović murder in 1903, when King Edward VII observed that there was no need for Britain to recognize a government of assassins. Not until 1906 did Great Britain recognize the Karageorgević restoration and resume diplomatic relations with the Kingdom of Serbia.

[24] King Peter II, *King's Heritage*, p. 71.

through Belgrade's quiet streets, Hitler issued his Directive 25, the order to attack Yugoslavia.[25] So far as Germany was concerned, the events of March 27th had completely altered the political situation in the Balkans. Despite all protestations of loyalty, he now considered Yugoslavia an enemy to be crushed as soon as possible.[26] He would ask Italy, Hungary, and Bulgaria to help, for the blow must be harsh, unmerciful, and lightning-quick, to dismember the Yugoslavs, frighten the Turks, and influence the Greeks. The attack on Yugoslavia would be popular with the Axis partners, particularly if he promised them territory: the Adriatic coast for Italy, the Banat for Hungary, and Macedonia for Bulgaria.[27] Furthermore, Hitler decided, he would do all he could to make the internal situation in Yugoslavia more critical by pitting the Croats against the Serbs. Although the Slovenes and Serbs had always been anti-German, he knew the Croats would come to Germany's side in this struggle. They must therefore, the Führer pointed out, have their autonomy.[28]

On the diplomatic side, Berlin instructed Heeren on March 29th to avoid Belgrade's official functions, using illness as an excuse. Nor was he to send a substitute. He was not to go to the Yugoslav foreign office to receive official communications, but to send an official representative so as to maintain the fiction of illness.[29] In Berlin, Weiszäcker ordered officials of the foreign office to feign absence if the Yugoslav minister or his staff asked for appointments. On April 2d, Ribbentrop told Heeren to reduce the size of the legation staff within twenty-four hours to four or five persons: the minister, a radio operator, a code clerk, an attaché, and a driver. When they received from Berlin the code words "Tripartite Pact" they were to destroy all secret materials and codes and to bury the wireless equipment under

[25] Halder, *Diary*, entry for March 27, 1941.

[26] "Führer Conferences on Naval Affairs, 1939-1945," in *Brassey's Naval Annual, 1948* (London: William Clowes, 1948), pp. 189-90.

[27] *IMT*, Doc. 1746-PS. The German high command recommended that Croatia become an autonomous state under Hungarian influence; that Carinthia and Styria, formerly Austrian, be reunited with the Reich; that Italy get Dalmatia, Montenegro, and the northwestern part of Yugoslavia; that Bulgaria get Macedonia; that Hungary get the formerly Hungarian sections of Yugoslavia from the frontier to the Danube, and that the German military administer the sections that had once made up old Serbia, excluding Macedonia. *USMT*, Doc. NG-3083.

[28] Führer Conferences, *supra*.

[29] *USMT*, Doc. NG-3242.

coal or in some other hiding place. As quickly as possible after that, the five remaining members of the staff were to leave Belgrade for a suitable refuge outside the city, the choice of place being left to them. In addition, Ribbentrop said, all consulates in the country except the one in Zagreb were to shut down on Thursday, April 3d. That same day a reliable member of the legation was to tell the Italian, Japanese, Hungarian, Rumanian, Bulgarian, Spanish, and Slovakian ministers (or their representatives) that in view of the increasingly tense situation the German legation had received orders to cut the size of its staff. In a manner less like an official report than a piece of information passed from one colleague to another, the German representative was to recommend that they reduce their own staffs.[30] After April 4th the Germans were to halt all Yugoslav ships within the German-Hungarian frontier of the Danube.

Hitler found Mussolini an easy partner in the new venture. The Duce was ridden by countless fears. He feared the new Yugoslav régime would attack Italy. Worse than that, he feared the new Yugoslav régime would attack Italy's forces in Greece. Over and over he called Alfieri, his ambassador in Berlin, to plead for help. The Germans must send help at once, he cried into the telephone.

But outwardly Hitler was in no hurry. Ribbentrop believed the Italians had precipitated the crisis in Yugoslavia and he was willing to let them stew for a while over the coals they themselves had fired. The trouble in Yugoslavia, said the German foreign office, was a direct consequence of Italian ineptness in Greece.[31] Hitler did not share Ribbentrop's views and on March 28th tried to quiet Mussolini's fears. He suggested that the Duce consolidate his gains in Albania, use all available forces to cover and screen the most important passes from Yugoslavia into Albania, and undertake no further operations in Albania itself. If he did this, Hitler had no doubt that "we will both achieve successes no less than the successes in Norway ..." This, he asserted, was his "unshakeable conviction."[32]

General Simović did not add to the Duce's peace of mind when

---

[30] *USMT*, Docs. NG-3319, 3248 and 3246.

[31] Simoni, *Berlin Ambassade d'Italie*, pp. 255-56. Another indication of the Duce's state of mind was his belief that Prince Paul had organized the *coup* just before Yugoslavia signed the Tripartite Pact.

[32] *IMT*, Doc. 1835-PS.

he told Mamelli, the Italian minister in Belgrade, that if German troops entered the Salonika zone it would be impossible to restrain the anger of the Yugoslavs "who were ready to sacrifice themselves and march into Albania."[33]

Nor did Simović add to Lane's peace of mind. It was he, as it turned out, who disillusioned Lane. Only a few days before, the United States minister had predicted that Yugoslavia would not face war because it bordered on both Italy and Germany; since neither of them wished to see the other in control of Yugoslavia, there could be no war. On March 27th, Lane decided not to bank on that prediction. He cabled Secretary of State Hull that the legation might be forced to destroy all codes and ciphers except the emergency Gray code.[34]

His uneasiness grew. From the beginning the Yugoslav foreign office made it plain that the new government wanted peace above all. It wanted to avoid any provocative anti-Axis acts and would appreciate Lane's cautioning his government to bear in mind the delicacy of the Yugoslav position. In his first conversation with the foreign office after the *coup* he put the same question he had put to Cvetković: What attitude did the Simović government intend to take with respect to the Tripartite Pact? The reply must have unnerved him. The Simović government had not come to any decision, he was told, and would not comment further.

He began to feel guilty. Had the United States used pressure to force Yugoslavia to take the offensive, as Britain had done? He assured Simović that the United States had never urged such a move upon the Cvetković government.

Lane then asked Simović the question he had asked of Cvetković, of Prince Paul, and of the foreign office: What did the new government intend to do about the Tripartite Pact? Simović now added to Lane's bewilderment. The new Yugoslav government wanted to avoid discussion of the pact if possible, he said. His government did not wish to denounce the pact nor would it ratify it. Since the pact was the work of his predecessor, his government was not obliged to observe terms that had not yet been ratified. Yugoslavia had no wish to provoke the Axis powers, he said. There was one thing, however,

[33] Simoni, *Berlin Ambassade d'Italie,* p. 257.
[34] *FRUS,* II (1941), 969.

that the new government would resist with force, and that was any attempt by Germany or Italy to take Salonika. Salonika was vital to the national interest, he emphasized. Nor would Yugoslavia tolerate any move that would lessen its sovereignty.

To Lane, it began to seem that somewhere along the line the Tripartite Pact's significance as the basis for the *coup* had evaporated. It was the pact that the United States and Great Britain had so vigorously protested, in Britain's case to the extent of supporting antiregency elements. Later on, in a talk with Ninčić, Lane went on trying to get a clear-cut rejection of the new tie with the Axis. Surely he must have found Ninčić's words depressing, for the new foreign minister took a legalistic approach to the matter. He said the pact could not be repudiated. Its terms provided that it would enter into effect immediately upon the affixing of the signatures. Therefore, no ratification was required.

Lane had only to consider the consequences if the government did not adhere to the pact, Ninčić went on. Not only would there be trouble with Germany but there might be a dissolution of the country, for Maček would not enter the government. The vital question, he said, was how the pact would be applied. This was still in doubt because he had not yet been able to ascertain the nature of all the secret commitments made by the Cvetković government. He was in favor of peace so long as there was no infringement of Yugoslav sovereignty.

Ninčić was unhappy about the demonstrations in the streets of Belgrade; in favoring the democracies against the Axis, the public had embarrassed the new government in its relations with Germany. As for those British broadcasts which quoted Churchill as saying that Yugoslavia had found its soul and that the *coup* was a blow to the Axis—Ninčić found them not only embarrassing but unwise. Would Mr. Lane's government please bear this in mind, he asked.

Lane, who only a short time before had reported to Washington that Yugoslav public opinion opposed the signing of the pact, now had to report that the Croats, Slovenes, and Moslems had called on the new government to adhere to it. But the Simović government was not like the Cvetković régime, he could emphatically assure the State Department; it would not give in to all demands, as Bulgaria and Rumania had done.

It is easy to see that the new government could not believe the facts confronting them. Instead, they sought evidence of some gigantic conspiracy contrived by Prince Paul and Hitler against the democracies. Despite his having just assured Lane that the Moslems, Croats, and Slovenes supported the signing of the pact and expected the new government to adhere to it, Ninčić insisted that Prince Paul had never really consulted the political leaders and therefore had not understood the feelings of the country.[35]

As for Lane, he must have had a distinct sense of *déjà vu,* and he could have found little comfort in Ninčić's replies to his questions. He probably would have felt even worse if he had known that a few hours earlier the council of ministers, on Ninčić's recommendation, had agreed not to announce a general mobilization. Instead, it had decided only to continue with preparations for the calling up of classes.[36]

Šubašić returned to Zagreb on March 29th. He reported to Maček that the Simović government would recognize all the international agreements signed by the deposed government, including the Tripartite Pact, the document that had brought the regency to its sudden, dramatic end. For all the shouting in the streets on March 27th the new government would honor the signature on the pact. For all the tanks and guns and slogans—"Better war than a pact," "Better a grave than a slave," "No war without Serbs"—Yugoslavia would not denounce its tie with the Axis or go to war for Britain.

Maček was dissatisfied with the report, particularly with Šubašić's overoptimistic prediction that Yugoslavia could avoid war with the Axis. In fact, he was so skeptical that he sent his deputy, August Košutić, to Belgrade to make a new evaluation of the situation there.

Košutić left at once and returned on March 31st much less sanguine than Šubašić had been. Yes, it was true that the new government was doing everything it could to avoid war. Vice-Premier Jovanović was going to Berlin and Minister of Foreign Affairs Ninčić to Rome in an attempt to ease the growing tension between Yugoslavia and the Axis. But, Košutić pointed out, they would gain little by these trips. There had been unpleasant incidents. For example, a mob had spat at Heeren as he returned to his home after a *Te Deum* for King Peter,

[35] *FRUS,* II (1941), 969-72.
[36] Minutes of the council of ministers, March 29, 1941. (JBH)

and he had decided to return to Berlin. Before his departure he had
told Šutej that although he would do all he could to lessen the possibility of war he could not conceal certain facts from his government,
particularly the public insult to a representative of the Reich.[37]

Maček was distraught over the future of Croatia, and furious at the
irresponsibles of Belgrade who had put the entire country in jeopardy
and endangered the lives of all Yugoslavs. In addition, a large number
of individuals calling themselves plenipotentiaries or their agents
were plaguing him with all kinds of offers from the Germans—all, he
complained, couched in the most indefinite terms.

On March 28th one named Derffler called on Maček, who urged
him to go back to Berlin immediately and find out what the officials
there thought of the Croatian independence movement. Their attitude,
he pointed out, would determine whether or not he should join the
Simović government. On March 30th, Berlin instructed Derffler to
tell Maček that he had no information as yet and to leave the impression that he would have something to tell Maček later on.[38]

According to Derffler, Maček had a "complete nervous breakdown,
because he read into this answer that no aid would be given him."

On April 1st, Ribbentrop instructed the German consulate at Zagreb:

In answer to Dr. Maček's request for our advice which has reached us by
various channels, please tell him the following.... We would strongly
advise him and other Croat leaders not to cooperate in any way with the
present Belgrade government. The fact of our giving such advice must
be strictly treated as secret. Should he follow our advice, we would remain
in touch with him. He would have to make communication secure on his
side by means of suitable intermediaries.[39]

On April 1st, a man named Malletke, with credentials from the
German foreign office, officially informed him that Germany wanted
an independent Croatia. Although this news made Maček's situation
all the more difficult, he told Malletke he would have to go to Belgrade
and join the government. He did not want to, he said, but it was the
only way to save the Croats. Serbian troops were already moving into

[37] Maček to author.
[38] USMT, Doc. NG-2449.
[39] USMT, Doc. NG-3260. The German foreign ministry asked particularly to
be informed at once of all political decisions made by the Croat leaders and to
know where they were at all times.

Croatia, making it impossible for his Home Guard to revolt against Belgrade and impossible for him to set up an independent state. Although he had asked for arms for the guard, he reminded Malletke, Germany had not supplied them. Meanwhile, the Yugoslav government had made an offer too, he disclosed. Belgrade had assured him that the king "and two other people," not named, would form an authoritarian government with the king as a figurehead. Impressed with this odd piece of information, Malletke resorted to flattery. Maček's name meant something in Germany, he said, reiterating that Germany favored a free and independent Croatia. Stressing that the Simović government was not acceptable to Germany, he said not a person in it could be trusted. He appealed to Maček to return to his "hiding place" to wait for action by Germany, and not to make the trip to Belgrade.

Maček repeated that he had to join the Simović cabinet to prevent bloodshed between the Croats and the Serbs. He was certain, he said, that he would gradually win autonomy for Croatia and be able to establish orderly relationships with Germany and Italy. He told Malletke he was just as certain he could push the Yugoslav government into declaring itself in favor of the Tripartite Pact and into offering a reparation plan [40] that would satisfy Germany under any circumstances.

When Malletke realized Maček had definitely made up his mind to go to Belgrade, he asked him not to take any new steps without obtaining approval from Berlin. Maček promised to do so.[41] He left for Belgrade the evening of April 3d.[42]

It is quite possible that Maček was playing a double-edged political game of bargaining with both sides, Berlin and Belgrade. By doing so, he would be prepared for either contingency, war or no war. The pro-German line he took with Malletke insured his position with the Nazis, and the safety of Croatia, if they attacked Yugoslavia. At the same time his pro-German tack might well have been his effort to

[40] Presumably for damage to German property and dignity during and immediately after the *putsch*.

[41] *USMT*, Doc. NG-2449.

[42] Maček to author. According to King Peter, Maček joined the cabinet on three conditions: that the Yugoslavs begin talks with the Germans, that they confirm the Serb-Croat agreement, and that they do nothing to irritate the Nazis into armed aggression. King Peter II, *King's Heritage*, p. 73.

prevent a German invasion of his country. Only the day before his conversation with the German agent, Šutej had told him that the chances of peace were slim. It was this informed opinion, Maček wrote later, that caused him to decide to go to Belgrade and enter the Simović cabinet. If he declined to enter the government it would look as if he approved Hitler's policies and plans, and he did not want the Croatian people to find themselves on the side of the Axis if there was going to be a war.

As the new rulers of Yugoslavia grasped the reality of the military and political situation into which they had thrust themselves, they rapidly adopted the same policies they had so violently condemned under the regency. From the very beginning they took on the attitudes of their predecessors. Quickly they came around to the realization that Salonika was vital to Yugoslavia as a base for the Yugoslav army. Like Cvetković, who had judged military plans by their political potentials, Simović resisted the idea of openly mobilizing the Yugoslav troops in any way that might compromise the country's position of neutrality.[43] Like Prince Paul before him, Simović also refused to let Eden come to Belgrade, for fear so obvious a move would provoke the Germans. After increased pressure from the British, who were elated over the possibility of a Balkan front, Simović did, however, consent to a secret visit from the chief of the British imperial general staff, General Sir John Dill, provided he came in civilian clothes.

As Dill talked to Simović on April 1st, it must have seemed to him that he was hearing a recording of the Anglo-Yugoslav talks in Athens only a month before. Simović, the man who led the revolt, was now saying exactly the same things Major Perišić had said then. No, Simović would not sign a military convention with the British; to do so would set off a political crisis in Yugoslavia. No, Yugoslavia was determined to take no steps that might provoke a German attack. Yes, Simović would consent to staff talks with the Anglo-Greek military so long as they did not commit the Yugoslavs.

Dill reported that he had found only confusion and paralysis

---

[43] General V. Petković, "Ko Je Kriv" ('Who Is Guilty?'), in *Iskra* (The Spark), Munich, March 1, 1951.

among Simović and his staff. They seemed to believe they had months in which to make decisions and more months in which to put them into operation.[44]

Two days later in the frontier town of Kanali south of Bitolj, General Janković, the new deputy chief of staff of the Yugoslav army, met with General Wilson and General Papagos. Eden and Dill were there to participate as needed. Quickly they learned that Simović had no knowledge whatsoever of the lack of strength of the Anglo-Greek forces and that he had assumed far greater firepower than actually existed. In addition, they found that he had authorized Janković to discuss nothing more than plans for the defense of Salonika. Since they could come to no immediate decisions on any point, they agreed to meet sometime later, in Athens.[45]

Meanwhile, the new government was taking precautions to avoid panic and preserve order. In an "order of the day" released on March 31st, Simović called on "all civilians to remain calm and to continue with their work and not be misled by rumors coming from abroad or started at home." There was no cause for alarm. The government was pursuing a friendly policy toward all neighboring states. The people of Belgrade, reading the order, began to grasp the consequences of the *coup,* for the tone was stern. It forbade them from leaving "their homes or the places where they are at present, as there is no reason for doing so." It appealed to their patriotism, stressing that the interests of the country demanded that they guard their houses and if necessary defend them at the cost of their lives "for the

---

[44] Playfair *et al., War in the Mediterranean and the Middle East,* II, 74. Also see United States Department of the Army, *German Campaigns in the Balkans (Spring, 1941),* p. 38; and Churchill, *Grand Alliance,* p. 173.

[45] Playfair *et al., War in the Mediterranean and the Middle East,* II, 74; and Papagos, *Battle of Greece, 1940-1941,* p. 330. One observer believed Simović completely taken in by the British propaganda that at least 15 British divisions and hundreds of planes would be available to the Yugoslavs as soon as they came in on the Allied side. St. John, *From the Land of Silent People,* p. 21. St. John gives a detailed picture of how a Greek journalist spread the propaganda. The official United Kingdom history of the Second World War refers to the "encouragement of British elements" given to the *coup.* Butler, *Grand Strategy,* II, 449. To what degree Mirković and Simović were influenced by their imperfect knowledge of British resources or by British representatives in Belgrade is unknown, but it is doubtful if they would have gone through with the *coup* if the British had not, early in March, put troops in Greece.

sake of the fatherland, the King and the nation." With some animus, it ordered the local authorities and the clergy, who had loudly denounced adherence to the pact, to remain at their posts under all circumstances. Then, vitiating his appeal to duty and patriotism, Simović announced that evacuation would be provided for and carried out only on specially written orders issued by the minister of the interior, who would also take "measures to prevent all unnecessary gathering of people, either for evacuation or for other purposes." It was up to the civil servants, Simović concluded his order, "to do their duty at this difficult time, to combat rumors and help keep up the morale of the people."[46]

Like the regency before it, the Simović government turned to the Russians for assistance. On April 1st, Ninčić notified Gavrilović, the Yugoslav minister in Moscow, that the Soviet chargé d'affaires had said his government was favorably inclined toward concluding a military and political pact with Yugoslavia. With that in mind, Ninčić said he was sending Colonel Božin Simić and Colonel Dragutin Savić to Moscow with instructions and full authorization for Gavrilović to sign the document.[47]

Simić and Savić arrived in Moscow on the evening of April 2d with a draft of the proposed agreement. On the 3rd they had their first conference with Andrei Vishinsky, then assistant foreign minister. He told them at once that the idea of a military pact with their country was completely new to him and that he would have to submit the proposal to Molotov for approval. He said he would give the Yugoslavs an answer the next day.

At their meeting on the 4th, Vishinsky told Gavrilović that the Soviet Union found it inconvenient to sign a military pact with Yugoslavia at that time since it would put an end to Russia's friendly relations with Germany. Furthermore, he said, to negotiate a military pact it would be necessary to know the military strength of both sides. Instead of a military pact, he offered the draft of an Accord of Friendship and Non-Aggression.

Although this was not the military pact the Yugoslavs had expected and wanted, Gavrilović and his colleagues considered accepting it

---

[46] *The Times* (London), April 1, 1941; minutes of the council of ministers, April 3, 1941. (JBH)

[47] Gavrilović to Yugoslav ministry of foreign affairs, April 4, 1941. (JBH)

because of the value of Article II. This article said that if one of the contracting parties were attacked by a third state, the other contracting party would not aid the attacker during the life of the agreement. Gavrilović believed such a pact might well be the first step toward a military alliance. In addition, Vishinsky explicitly stressed Russia's readiness to supply Yugoslavia with war materials and asked Gavrilović for a list of requirements so that the items could be delivered immediately. Vishinsky also said the Russians were thinking of instructing their ambassador in Berlin to tell the Germans that they did not want to see Yugoslavia's independence, sovereignty and integrity threatened or altered.

Gavrilović's optimism did not last long. Less than two hours after this interview, Vishinsky recalled him to the Kremlin. The Russians had changed their minds on the wording of Article II. The article no longer had the diplomatic and military possibilities it once had for the Yugoslavs. It now read: "In case one of the contracting parties should be attacked by a third state, the other contracting party will preserve its policy of neutrality and friendship."[48]

Gavrilović was upset. The change greatly weakened the pact, he said. Vishinsky pointed out that it was necessary; otherwise, the Germans might think the Soviet Union was planning to stop sending materials to them. This would involve the Soviet Union in a war with Germany at a time when the Russians were not prepared for war, said Vishinsky.

The Yugoslav representatives could not accept the change. For them, Soviet neutrality would only encourage the Germans and dishearten their own people. Gavrilović saw Vishinsky again to convey this view and to request that they postpone the signing of the pact until he had heard from Belgrade. He got little encouragement from Vishinsky, who reminded him that "that which is possible today, might not be tomorrow." He added, however, that the Yugoslavs could count on Russia's material aid in any event.

Gavrilović again expressed his surprise that the Russians had changed their minds about a military pact especially, he said, since the Soviet chargé d'affaires in Belgrade had told the Yugoslav government that Russia was willing to conclude a military and political

---

[48] Gavrilović to Yugoslav ministry of foreign affairs, April 4, 1941. (JBH)

alliance with Yugoslavia. Vishinsky denied that the Russians had given such a reply. What they had said was that they were willing to negotiate only on questions concerning the supply of military material and eventually some kind of limited agreement. Gavrilović replied that his government was positive Moscow had agreed to sign a military pact. Otherwise, there would have been no need to send a delegation with full powers, merely to sign a simple agreement of friendship and non-aggression.[49]

Since Gavrilović knew his government expected action, he told Vishinsky he would sign the agreement on two conditions: that Russia substitute for the clause on neutrality a statement that in the event Yugoslavia were atacked by a third party, friendly relations would continue to exist, and that Simić and Savić sign the treaty even though it was not within their competency to do so. Gavrilović hoped by this maneuver to make the Germans believe the pact was not an ordinary treaty of friendship, since it would differ from the usual pattern and would bear the signature of two Yugoslav army officers. Vishinsky said such a proposal was out of the question. After a good deal of wrangling, Vishinsky said he would have to report to his government. Gavrilović remained adamant.[50]

About eight o'clock on April 5th, Vishinsky telephoned Gavrilović that the papers were ready for signing. Gavrilović replied that he would not go to the Kremlin unless "that clause" had been changed. Although Vishinsky insisted the change was impossible, Gavrilović stubbornly maintained his position.

A little later Vishinsky called again. They repeated their earlier conversation almost verbatim. Then Vishinsky asked if Gavrilović would like to speak to General Simović in Belgrade. Gavrilović agreed and in ten minutes he was talking to Belgrade. The dialogue went like this:

"General Simović here."

"Where are you talking from, General?"

"Where am I talking from? What do you want to know that for?"

"Where are you, General? At home or at the office?"

"But why do you ask?"

<hr>

[49] Gavrilović to Yugoslav ministry of foreign affairs, April 4, 1941. (JBH)

[50] Gavrilović to author.

"I must know, General."

"I'm at home."

"What street is it on? What is your home number?"

"But you know very well where I live! We're neighbors!"

"Never mind that. What is your address?"

"2 Gladstone Street . . ."

"Good," said Gavrilović, convinced by this time that the call was not a Russian trick.

"What the Russians propose, sign," said the prime minister.

"I can't, General," Gavrilović replied. "I know my duty and my job."

"You must sign."

"I can't, General. Have confidence in me."

"Sign it, Gavrilović."

"I know what I'm doing, General. I can't sign this paper."

"All right. If you want an order, I order you to sign!"

"I know what I'm doing. Have confidence in me."

And that was that, Gavrilović wrote later. By the time he had ended this oddly undiplomatic exchange, it was nine o'clock.

No more than ten minutes had passed before the telephone rang again. It was Vishinsky.

"Are you coming?" he asked.

"No," said Gavrilović.

"What!"

"No, I said, I'm not coming."

Vishinsky was furious. "But you—you have an order to sign. You *must* sign!"

Gavrilović assumed the Russians had listened in on his conversation with Simović—not only the Russians but the Germans and the others, all along the line to Belgrade—but somehow he was shocked to hear Vishinsky admit it.

"I see," he answered. "But I won't sign. I can't—my hand refuses to do it."

Vishinsky, his anger out of bounds, shouted: "You *must* sign it! You must sign it now! You have an order from your prime minister."

"I do *not* have to sign it. My prime minister can dismiss me and replace me with someone else, but so long as I am here I won't sign it as it stands!"

Vishinsky slammed down the receiver.

"Now," Gavrilović wrote later, "I was alone. I can't forget those moments. 'Was I right? Was I wrong?' I kept asking myself. But somehow I felt I could not do otherwise."

Then, about half past ten, perhaps a little later, Vishinsky called again. His tone had changed, and he was extremely cordial as he said: "Do come, Mr. Gavrilović. We are waiting for you."

"I can come, but I can't sign unless that clause is changed."

"Do come, please," said Vishinsky.

When Gavrilović and his staff arrived at the Kremlin, everyone was waiting for them—Stalin,[51] Molotov, Vishinsky, and a large staff. At the end of a very large room, Gavrilović saw a small table. There lay two copies of the treaty, open for the signatures. When the introductions were over, Molotov rose, proposed that Article II be changed and then read off precisely the phraseology Gavrilović had requested. "I think," Molotov concluded, "that Dr. Gavrilović will accept this change."

"I accept it and thank you, Mr. Molotov."

"No, no, not me," Molotov quickly demurred. "Not me. Thanks go to our Comrade Stalin. *My nichego ne delaem bez nashego tovarishcha Stalina.* (We do nothing without our Comrade Stalin.)"

So Gavrilović thanked Stalin, who replied: "You were right, Mr. Gavrilović. If the clause on neutrality had remained, it would have meant that if you were attacked the Soviet Union would have washed its hands of your fate."

"I tried to explain that to Mr. Vishinsky," Gavrilović replied, "but he refused to listen."

"*Moia vina! Moia vina!*" ('My fault! My fault!') Vishinsky exclaimed as he bowed low before Stalin, his arms crossed on his breast.

It was then well into the night. While all of them waited the treaty was changed, and early in the morning of April 6th, Gavrilović, Savić, and Simić signed for the Yugoslav government and Molotov for the Soviet Union.[52]

Between the signing of the Yugoslav-Soviet treaty and the defeat of the Yugoslav armies, the Russians promised the Yugoslavs arms,

---

[51] Stalin was then only the secretary of the Communist Party of the Soviet Union.

[52] Gavrilović to author. For the text of the Soviet-Yugoslav Treaty of Friendship and Non-Aggression, see Appendix C; and *FRUS*, I (1941), 301, 311-13. Although signed on the 6th, the document is dated April 5, 1941.

munitions, and planes. To avoid complaints from the Germans, they were to be carried in Yugoslav ships. As things turned out, the Soviet authorities took no steps to carry out the promise, but waited to see what the Germans would do before making any deliveries. When Germany demanded that the Soviet Union withdraw its recognition of the Yugoslav government, the Soviet Union meekly obeyed. Vishinsky called Gavrilović to the Kremlin and orally informed him the Soviet Union no longer considered Yugoslavia existed as a political entity. No note was presented to Gavrilović.

The Soviet candle of covert resistance flickered a moment in April, 1941, and then went out. The German triumph in the Balkans and Greece had impressed the Kremlin. Appeasement was again the Soviet Union's policy.

By the afternoon of March 28th, Colonel Vauhnik's contacts in Berlin were coming to him with bits of useful information. A journalist connected with the *Deutsche Allgemeine Zeitung* reported that during a meeting of Hitler's war council the evening before, the Führer had declared that Yugoslavia was to be destroyed as a military power if the new government did not decide, instantly and unequivocally, to stand with the Germans. The same afternoon, his old friend, Doctor Sigismund Bernstorff, whispered almost the same story, with the slight difference that he had received his information from an SS group leader in the headquarters of the Gestapo. On April 1st, Vauhnik's mail contained two messages forecasting trouble for Yugoslavia within a week to ten days. That evening another warning, this time by telephone, said the attack would come in the early hours of Sunday, April 6th, and that heavy air raids would turn Belgrade to ashes and rubble.

April 6th already had meaning for Vauhnik as the date set for the launching of a German attack on Greece, from Bulgaria, to relieve Italy; he now speculated that Hitler would synchronize the offensive against Greece with a vengeful attack on Yugoslavia. Although he had wired Belgrade only a few hours before that the political division of the Wehrmacht had assured him Germany had "absolutely no hostile intentions against Yugoslavia," Vauhnik felt justified in trying to convince the Yugoslav general staff and government otherwise. Accordingly, in the early morning hours of April 2d he sent code telegrams to Belgrade via three different routes containing "the fatal news that on April 6th Yugoslavia would have to reckon with a German attack."

The night of April 2d he received still another warning, this time from an unimpeachable source. At two o'clock in the morning, while Berlin was deep in sleep, his telephone rang three times, a prearranged signal for him to pick up a message in a crack in the wall beside his garage. Slipping past the two Gestapo agents sleeping soundly in their car outside his door, he found the note: "Conference ended just now. Attack on Yugoslavia definitely fixed for April 6th. Surrounding attacks from Bulgaria in the east and Hungary in the north. May God's blessing and my sincerest wishes accompany you in this terrible ordeal." The source of the message was so reliable, so trustworthy, that he felt no need to check the information.

Nevertheless, its validity was confirmed many times over during the next few days. From the Gestapo's main office Vauhnik learned that a great number of "case workers" were on their way to the Yugoslav border. From sources in Hamburg he heard that an SS division had boarded trains for Arad, on the Rumanian-Yugoslav frontier. From friends in Bavaria he learned that a division was on its way to the frontier. Another had started through Hungary towards Yugoslavia. The information poured in at such a rate that he "had the impression the whole German population sided with the Yugoslavs." He heard that the police had received orders to put all Yugoslav citizens under surveillance and to arrest them at a given signal.

Again Vauhnik dispatched telegrams to Belgrade, which for the fifth day was silent. Vainly he tried to reach the general staff by telephone. On April 3d he sent his assistant, Major Pupis, to Belgrade by airplane with orders to report at once to the general staff and to repeat verbally the contents of the four most important telegrams. Later Colonel Vauhnik learned that all his telegrams had reached Belgrade safely only because the German intelligence service's order to withhold them had come too late. But that lucky accident was of no help, for the officials in Belgrade, convinced that their military attaché had been taken in, did not trust the telegrams. Vauhnik's last wire to Belgrade indicated that about 32 German divisions would launch an attack against both Yugoslavia and Greece. Three weeks after the occupation of Yugoslavia, Hitler disclosed in a speech that 31 divisions and 2 brigades had been ready for the attack on Yugoslavia.[53]

When Maček arrived in Belgrade the morning of April 4th, he found among the members of the cabinet a growing fear of war with Germany. Belgrade, Zagreb, and Ljubljana had just been declared open cities in case of war. All but one of his colleagues were panicky. The exception was President Simović, who assured him that the German army would break before Yugoslav resistance. But, he said, he was doing his best to avert war entirely. Maček asked him how long it would take the Germans to organize an attack against Yugoslavia. At least fourteen days, Simović estimated, if they wanted to be certain of success. On the other hand, if they were willing to risk failure, they could launch an attack with the troops now lining the Bulgarian-Yugoslav frontier.[54] He said nothing about Colonel Vauhnik's repeated warnings from Berlin that German planes, flying from Rumanian and Hungarian airfields, would bomb Belgrade the morning of April 6th. He did say, however, that Foreign Minister Ninčić would report at the cabinet meeting scheduled for the next day on his negotiations with Italian Minister Mamelli, whose government hoped to mediate the threatening conflict between Yugoslavia and Germany.[55]

As foreign minister, Ninčić had real cause for worry, for relations with Germany worsened much faster than he had expected. At the start he had not foreseen any insurmountable difficulties with Germany. He had never had any intention of repudiating the Tripartite Pact. Two days after the *coup* he had told American Minister Lane that the pact had "come into force immediately on signature. It was, in his opinion, still in effect. The new government would

---

[53] Vladimir Vauhnik, Auf der Lauer nach Hitlers Kriegsplänen (MS). (JBH) Vauhnik's source was Admiral Canaris, head of the German high command's foreign and counter intelligence office, through Major-General Hans Oster, chief assistant to Canaris. Vauhnik to author. See also, King Peter II, *King's Heritage*, pp. 74-75. Although a number of Yugoslav officers saw Vauhnik's warning cable, Minister of War General Ilić implied that he had never heard of it. General V. Petković, "Ko Je Kriv" ('Who Is Guilty?'), in *Iskra* (The Spark), Munich, March 1, 1951.

[54] Maček to author.

[55] Maček to author.

therefore honor it."[56] On the morning of April 1st, Ninčić and Simović had an appointment at eleven o'clock to assure Heeren that the new Yugoslav government planned no changes in policy. At 10:30 Heeren canceled the appointment with the explanation that Germany's policy toward Yugoslavia was now in Hitler's hands. On April 3d Ninčić notified all Yugoslav missions abroad that he had

informed the German and Italian ministers here that the Royal Government remained faithful to the principle of existing international treaties and, therefore, to the agreement of Vienna of March 25th of this year; that its chief concern was to maintain the policy of good and friendly relations with Germany and Italy; and that it will take most determined steps not to be drawn into the present conflict.[57]

Ninčić instructed the Yugoslav minister in Berlin to see officials of the German foreign office and "to offer any concessions compatible with national honor."[58] For five days, including three times on the 4th of April and once before noon of the 5th, Andrić tried to see someone—anyone—in the German foreign office, and for five days no one would see him. Desperately hoping to get a message through to the Germans, he spoke to Alfieri, the Italian ambassador, on April 4th. Andrić expressed his regret over the situation. He fervently assured Alfieri that his government was prepared to see a solution to all problems between Germany, Italy, and Yugoslavia.[59]

Meanwhile, the Italians had taken the initiative in trying to prevent a war between Yugoslavia and Germany, discreetly suggesting as a first step that Vice Premier Slobodan Jovanović come to Rome for discussions. Although they dropped the matter after the initial contact, the Yugoslavs had revived it, and on the progress of these negotiations Ninčić would report to the cabinet.[60]

Late on the afternoon of April 5th the cabinet met. Ninčić reported

[56] Arthur Bliss Lane, "Conquest in Yugoslavia," *Life*, September 15, 1941, p. 105.
[57] Circular cable from Ninčić to Yugoslav missions abroad, April 3, 1941. (JBH)
[58] Speech by Constantin Fotitch, Yugoslav minister to the United States, at the National Press Club, Washington, D.C., April 10, 1941. (JBH)
[59] *USMT*, Docs. NG 3238 and 3177. The only German foreign office representative Minister Andrić finally did see was the chief of protocol, who handed him his passport.
[60] Circular cable from Ninčić to Yugoslav missions abroad, April 3, 1941. (JBH)

that Italy was willing to intercede on Yugoslavia's behalf, on the condition that Yugoslav troops immediately occupy the Greek-Yugoslav border as a security belt preventing Greek and British troops from entering Yugoslavia. Ninčić proposed that they accept the Italian offer. Simović agreed but insisted that Yugoslav forces also occupy Salonika. This irritated Ninčić, who retorted that Simović was talking nonsense. Salonika and its hinterland were the only passage for German troops into Greece if they were to bypass Yugoslavia. Furthermore, said Ninčić, Salonika was not Yugoslav territory, and Yugoslavia would be violating its avowed declaration of neutrality, instead of using every means to preserve it, if it occupied the port.

The Yugoslavs were to deliver their reply to the Italian offer not later than seven o'clock that evening. The majority of the cabinet members favored peace and were ready to vote for the Ninčić proposal. At that point Simović took the floor and delivered a fiery speech. In it he recalled page after page of Serbian history. He saluted the bones of Serbia's militantly heroic ancestors, the battle of Kosovo, the legendary princes of early Serbia, and Serbia's epic struggle against the Turks. Maček was exasperated. To him, the speech seemed inappropriate and he said as much. Their situation was serious, he contended, and they could not develop a sound national policy by stirring up strong emotions. If Simović persisted in such remarks, said Maček, he himself would have to resign from the cabinet.[61] Urging Maček to calm down, Simović assured him they would take no definitive step before noon the next day.

The hours had slipped by and they had reached no decision. Ninčić left the room to call Mamelli and ask him to extend the deadline for their answer to the Italian offer from seven o'clock Saturday evening to noon Sunday. He returned shortly to report that Mamelli had agreed to relay their request to Rome.

But time had run out for the Simović government. At 5:15 the morning of Sunday, April 6th, German bombers flew over Belgrade. When they left, seventeen thousand Yugoslavs lay dead. During the next twelve days the Wehrmacht—with some assistance from Bulgarian, Hungarian, and Italian forces—overran the entire country. It met little real resistance from the poorly equipped, poorly deployed,

[61] Maček to author.

poorly organized, and almost completely demoralized Yugoslav army.[62]

The cabinet ministers, who fled from Belgrade when the German bombs began to fall, met later that night in the Hotel Palas in Užice, a town in western Serbia. They would try to maintain some semblance of orderly government. Kulovec, the Slovene representative, had been killed in the bombing of the capital. Maček, who chaired the meeting, announced his resignation and his intention of going back to Croatia. The ministers then decided to declare a state of emergency and to announce mobilization, to approve credits to cover expenditures created by the emergency, and to request food from the United States and Great Britain for the agriculturally deficient areas of the country and for the armed forces.

German troops had entered Skoplje, the fall of Salonika was near, and a *panzer* group was racing toward Belgrade on April 8th when the council of ministers next met in Sevojno in the west of Serbia. After hearing a report from the minister of war, General Ilić, the ministers approved a two-month salary advance for all civil servants in threatened areas and the payment of daily allowances for food amounting to 80 dinars ($1.60) for junior civil servants and 100 dinars ($2.00) for senior civil servants, along with a monthly allowance of 1,000 dinars ($20.00) for the chauffeurs and policemen who were escorting the ministers. Later that day Simović was voted a credit of five million dinars ($100,000) for political action in Albania.

By April 11th the ministers of the kingdom had moved on to Pale in Bosnia. The minutes of their crown council meeting that day reflect no awareness that Zagreb had fallen to the Germans; that an independent state of Croatia had been created with Ante Pavelić, murderer of King Alexander, as its leader; that a *panzer* corps was in forty miles of Belgrade; or that two additional German army corps had crossed the Vardar river. The ministers approved a two-month salary advance and two months leave for all evacuated civil servants and a 30-dinar ($.60) daily allowance for transportation workers; placed all silver money left behind in the capital at the

[62] "The losses sustained by the German attack forces were unexpectedly light. During the twelve days of combat the total casualty figures came to 558 men: 151 were listed as killed, 392 as wounded, and 15 as missing in action. During the XLI Panzer Corps drive on Belgrade, for example, the only officer killed in action fell victim to a civilian sniper's bullet." United States Department of the Army, *German Campaigns in the Balkans (Spring, 1941)*, p. 64.

disposal of the mayor of Belgrade for relief purposes; and approved a moratorium on debts. They also directed the minister of the interior to issue a decree forbidding civil servants and the population to leave their villages and towns. Hungry for news of the war, they then decided to invite Simović to come to Pale to see them. After that, Ninčić reported on his conversations with British diplomats who had also fled from Belgrade, and on his appeals to President Roosevelt and to Stalin for assistance.[63]

Lack of firepower, lack of equipment and material, lack of organization, lack of trained officers—all these played an important part in the defeat of Yugoslavia by a force vastly superior in men and materials. But just as deadly as its lack of armor was its lack of national unity. Without a sense of political and social cohesiveness, the country, like the army, disintegrated in the face of crisis. The marching feet of the Wehrmacht had set off the bomb that was the Serb-Croat question.

The Cvetković-Maček agreement of August, 1939, had only begun to do its work of pacification. The breach between the Serbs and Croats had lasted twenty years and few responsible members of the Yugoslav community thought the agreement could repair the damage in less than a generation. It would take at least that long to transform the Croat's hope of separatism and the Serb's tradition of centralism into the more constructive habit of working together for a united Yugoslavia. Now, almost overnight, the *coup d'état* and its consequences had caused a rupture of far greater proportions than had existed before.

Many Croats criticized the *coup* as a strictly Serb affair that endangered not only Serbia but the entire country. Many more welcomed the *coup* for that very reason because it would indeed endanger the country; it would bring the Germans into Yugoslavia and make it possible for some Croats to realize their ancient separatist dream of establishing an independent state of Croatia.

The behavior of the Yugoslav troops when they faced the enemy illustrates better than anything else the degree of Yugoslavia's political and cultural segmentation. In Slovenia and in Serbia, where native sons defended native soil, there were a few sharp engagements that

[63] Minutes of meetings of the council of ministers, April 6, 7, 8, 9, and 11, 1941. (JBH)

temporarily halted the Axis armies. In Croatia, and in areas where the troops were of mixed nationality, the story was tragically different. There were a few cases of outright treason by Croat officers. The most famous of these was the air force officer who on April 3d—three days before the invasion—flew from Belgrade to Graz, in Austria, and turned over to the Nazis a list of all airports where Yugoslav army planes were dispersed. Whole units of Croats mutinied, abandoned their positions, threw away their weapons, surrendered, or simply went home. One Croat group, in the midst of an officers' party when overrun by a German regiment, stopped the festivities long enough to surrender and then went back to their fun as if nothing untoward had happened. It was not unusual to find Croats and Serbs fighting each other instead of the Germans. Under these conditions, the Nazis had no difficulty in capturing entire units. Complete companies surrendered to German planes overhead. An entire brigade, including its commanding officer and his staff, gave up to a German bicycle company. In the drive on Zagreb the Germans took fifteen thousand prisoners, including twenty-two generals.[64]

Belgrade fell at five o'clock the afternoon of April 12th to an enterprising 1st Lieutenant Klingenberg and an SS infantry platoon. About two hours later the mayor officially handed his city over to Klingenberg and to a representative of the German foreign office interned by the Yugoslavs at the outbreak of the war and just released. In all, 254,000 Yugoslav soldiers fell into German hands during the twelve-day campaign for Yugoslavia.[65]

The three German armies that converged on Yugoslavia on April 6th were, a week later, tracking down the remnants of the Yugoslav army.[66]

As an organized body the Yugoslav army had disintegrated.

---

[64] Halder, *Diary*, entries for April 7-11, 1941; and United States Department of the Army, *German Campaigns in the Balkans (Spring, 1941)*, pp. 54, 58, 60, 63-64, and 68-69.

[65] United States Department of the Army, *German Campaigns in the Balkans (Spring, 1941)*, pp. 54 and 64.

[66] Before long small resistance groups sprang up to plague the occupying armies. By December, 1941, Hitler began to dread the possibility of fighting a subsidiary war in Yugoslavia. He told Mussolini that their military forces would have to develop a common plan to wipe out nests of insurrection in Bosnia, Serbia, and Montenegro. *Hitler e Mussolini, Lettere e Documenti*, Doc. 50.

The fall of Belgrade was imminent when the council convened in Pale on April 12th for a meeting that lasted all day. General Simović, invited the day before, was not present. The ministers continued with the business of government, ordering that the penal institutions release all prisoners sentenced under provisions of the law on the protection of the state except those convicted of espionage or treason; and that the ministries call all government workers back into service if possible, and if impossible pay them two months' salary and leave. Finally, they decreed that all 10,000 dinar notes were worthless and that all bills of smaller denominations were to be released for circulation.[67]

On Sunday, April 13th, the members of the Royal Yugoslav cabinet met for their last session on Yugoslav soil. Simović assured the ministers that the Yugoslav forces would continue to fight the Germans and that parts of Montenegro, Bosnia, Hercegovina, and Serbia would remain, at least for a few more months, in Yugoslav hands. After this unrealistic report on the military situation he suggested that the government move on to Nikšić in Montenegro. The cabinet agreed to do so and to evacuate high government officials and political leaders already in Nikšić or soon to be there.

Simović knew far more about the military debâcle than he was willing to reveal. Shortly after the cabinet meeting, he saw the king and resigned as chief of the general staff in favor of General Kalafatović. On the 13th, in his capacity as commander-in-chief of the Yugoslav army, and on behalf of the king, he told Kalafatović to arrange a truce with the Germans.[68]

The cabinet as a whole never discussed the question of capitulation and therefore never gave its approval to a decision that seems to have been made by Simović alone. When he finally discussed the capitulation with individual members of the cabinet, Simović was less than candid. As they arrived in Nikšić on the 14th and 15th, Minister of War General Ilić told them General Kalafatović had already concluded the formalities of capitulation. Simović, confirming what Ilić said, added that Kalafatović had acted without authorization either

[67] Minutes of meeting of the council of ministers, April 12, 1941. (JBH)

[68] Miha Krek to author. King Peter learned from Simović on April 13th that the army would capitulate. King Peter II, *King's Heritage*, p. 83, and the minutes of the council of ministers, April 12 and 13, 1941. (JBH)

from him or from the king. It was, said Simović, a "capitulation on the field of battle," a military and not a political act.

Before Kalafatović's representatives reached the Germans, the commanders of the Yugoslav Second and Fifth Armies asked for separate cease-fire agreements from the Germans, but the Nazis refused. They would accept only the unconditional surrender of the entire Yugoslav army as a basis for negotiation. On the 14th General Bodi and another officer, acting for General Kalafatović, approached German General von Kleist of the First Panzer Group and asked for an immediate cease-fire. Von Kleist forwarded their request to the German high command, which instructed Second Army Commander General von Weichs to take charge of the negotiations.

On the 15th, Von Weichs and his staff arrived in Belgrade and proceeded to draw up the document of unconditional surrender. When the Germans discovered Bodi lacked sufficient authority to negotiate or to sign such a document[69] they gave him a draft of the agreement, put a plane at his disposal, and told him to see to it that competent representatives came to Belgrade without delay.

Back in Nikšić, Bodi's report raised a question: Who could properly represent the Royal Yugoslav government?

Not King Peter. Unwillingly but on the advice of Gavrilo, Patriarch of the Serbian Orthodox Church, Peter and his entourage had flown to Greece on April 14th.

Not Prime Minister General Simović nor Foreign Minister Ninčić nor even General Mirković. They had followed their monarch out of the country on April 15th.

Not Maček. He had handed his resignation to Simović in Banja Koviljaca on April 7th, and had named Krnjević as his successor.

Not Jovanović nor Tupanjanin nor Grol nor Trifunović nor Ilić— they had all flown away to Athens.

No responsible political representative of the Simović government remained on Yugoslav soil. Who then could go to Belgrade? Someone remembered that former Foreign Minister Cincar-Marković might be acceptable to the Germans despite the fact he not only had no official connection with the Simović government but also was interned

[69] United States Department of the Army, *German Campaigns in the Balkans (Spring, 1941)*, pp. 63-64; and General V. Petković, "Ko Je Kriv" ('Who Is Guilty?'), in *Iskra* (The Spark), Munich, March 1, 1951.

and under guard in Brus, a village in central Serbia. They did not know that Cincar-Marković and his guards had fled from Brus when the German planes bombed Belgrade and by April 15th had managed to reach Pale. While Cincar-Marković hunted for shelter from the Germans, General Kalafatović hunted for Cincar-Marković. On the 15th, in a school house in Pale, they met.

The war was lost, Kalafatović told Cincar-Marković. King and government had fled. The army had disintegrated. Kalafatović was authorized to use his own judgment in deciding whether to carry on the war or make peace with the Germans. With the army as a fighting unit gone to the winds, there was only one thing to do: to prevent further bloodshed he would have to make peace with the invading Germans. Would Cincar-Marković help him during these last tragic moments of their country? Would he perform this final service: sign the armistice document?

Cincar-Marković listened in amazement and indignation. By what melancholy irony had it fallen to him to sign the articles of capitulation and thus cover up the follies of others? How could he sign such a document when he and the regents had followed an entirely different path trying to insure the security of the country? No! Kalafatović could not demand this onerous task of him nor could he perform it.

Kalafatović remained calm in the face of fury. He pleaded with Cincar-Marković to save what could be saved politically, and asked him to give the matter serious thought. A German officer would be arriving yet that day.

Early the following morning one of Kalafatović's officers roused Cincar-Marković and brought him to the general's quarters. There he found three Yugoslav officers and a German officer drafting the text of the armistice. Already completed were documents authorizing Cincar-Marković and General Janković, head of the operational division, to act on behalf of the supreme command and the absent Yugoslav government. By this time Cincar-Marković had accepted the necessity of signing the armistice agreement. Kalafatović, hoping that part of the country would remain unoccupied, urged Cincar-Marković to see if he could obtain for Yugoslavia the same status France had obtained after its defeat. Cincar-Marković brought the general quickly back to reality; it was all too late for negotiations of that kind, he said. Croatia had already been declared an independent state, and they could look forward to Germany's partitioning of Yugoslavia to satisfy the territorial demands of the Italians, Hungarians, and Bulgarians.

On April 16th, Cincar-Marković, General Janković, and the German officer left for Sarajevo. They spent one day there and then flew on to the ruined Yugoslav capital.

Thus, the Yugoslav high command sent Cincar-Marković, a career diplomat who had tried to keep Yugoslavia at peace, and General Janković, an army officer with a sense of duty, off to Belgrade in the German plane. There, in the former Czechoslovak legation, on behalf of the Kingdom of Yugoslavia, they signed the document of armistice on April 17th, the 12th day of the war. The armistice went into effect at noon the following day.

As it fled from the Nazis the Simović cabinet left behind a political vacuum. Its flight left to the Yugoslavs the whole of their political destiny and the remnants of their fallen army, to be reshaped by men and forces then unknown.

XI

IN RETROSPECT

The Kingdom of Yugoslavia lasted little more than two decades. Throughout its short life, marked by one crisis after another, the kingdom searched for ways of building unity within its borders and for security from outside aggression.

Many forces contributed to its disunity. Under the Wilsonian star of self-determination three national groups with divergent and often conflicting historical, administrative, and cultural backgrounds found themselves joined together in one kingdom. Their debates over the nature of the new state promptly revealed the centrifugal nature of its political forces. From the outset the conflict that raged between the Croats who argued for federalism and the triumphant Serbs who insisted on centralism warped the growth of democracy in Yugoslavia. Because the Croats would not willingly accept defeat and the Serbs would not willingly compromise in victory, the processes of constitutional government broke down. Because the major politicians and parties lacked common political traditions and could come to no agreement on the fundamentals of government, the leaders of the new state were left to run the country by force and intrigue. At no point could the institution of the monarchy successfully exercise monarchy's prime function of unifying divergent elements and bridging historic differences. The flat refusal of a substantial minority of Yugoslavs to participate in the government except on their own terms forced the crown to resort to controlled elections and coercion, rather than consensus, to administer the state.

Inevitably some of Yugoslavia's dissatisfied political parties and restless national minorities began to respond to manipulation by revisionist Bulgaria, Hungary, and Italy. In its efforts to defend itself from these predators, Yugoslavia found itself relying on outmoded diplomatic weapons: on its ties with France, on the League of Nations, and on the Little and Balkan Ententes. After a strong Germany appeared on the scene, these configurations, so carefully designed and elaborated between 1919 and 1933, no longer seemed to many nations, including the Yugoslavs, to have relevance or power.

Events set in motion by the dictatorships swept the democracies along or left them struggling in the wake. With the League's refusal to condemn the murder of their king, Mussolini's successful aggression against Ethiopia, and Hitler's occupation of the Rhineland, the Yugoslavs watched France and Britain retreat before the dictators' power, and concluded that the League and the intricate entente system offered much less protection than would specific guarantees from Italy, then the most threatening of neighbors.

After the *Anschluss,* after Munich, the Yugoslavs found themselves hemmed in by a second giant. There was no doubt in their minds now that they had been abandoned by the very states that at the peace tables of 1919 had created their country. It was clear that the great democracies of Europe had no intention of defending the integrity of Yugoslavia and the other small states which were, in effect, the children of the Peace Conference.

Germany quickly became more than an awesome neighbor. By 1938, commerce with Germany was an integral part of the Yugoslav economy. While France, Britain, and the other democracies ignored the economic factor in international politics, the Yugoslavs grew more dependent on Germany as a market for their surpluses. Failing in their search for other outlets, they reluctantly watched the Reich gain control of their agriculture, industry, and natural resources.

During the months between Munich and the German invasion of Poland, the Yugoslavs were preoccupied with disturbing domestic developments: a swift change of government and their first major attempt to negotiate the long-standing conflict between the Serbs and the Croats. Pushed toward a superficial domestic tranquillity by the knowledge that war was upon them, the two factions agreed to cooperate in running the government, and the country declared its neutrality in the quarrels of others.

But the policy was one thing, the practice another. Despite the declaration of neutrality, the Yugoslavs vainly urged the French and the British to open a Balkan front. In the fall of France they sensed a great loss, in no way offset by their long-delayed recognition of the Soviet Union. With the Italian attack on Greece, they felt the tightening of the Axis vise.

Ironically, their apprehension grew as the Greeks inflicted defeat after defeat on Mussolini's troops; despite their hope for a Greek victory, the Yugoslavs knew that each Italian setback brought nearer the day when Hitler would have to enter the Balkans to rescue his Axis partner and prevent a British landing in Greece.[1] Although the British urged the Yugoslavs and the Turks to join the Greeks in stopping the Axis, the Turks refused to fight until attacked and the Yugoslavs refused to fight without the Turks as allies and without British support on a massive scale. Neither troops nor materials were forthcoming, and the Yugoslavs held on to their neutrality, hoping for the best, trying to offset increasing pressure from Germany with new diplomatic overtures to Italy, a tactic that proved valueless.

By March, 1941, Yugoslavia was surrounded. German troops were in Rumania and Bulgaria and on the point of entering Greece. France had fallen. There was no reason to think that any help could come from the Soviet Union. As for the British, they had little to offer but advice and fighting spirit; their promises of aid sometime in the future only convinced the Yugoslavs that to abandon their neutrality was to court destruction. But as they felt increasing pressure from Hitler, strict neutrality became a state they could no longer maintain.

The objective observer would agree that the Yugoslavs had as much right to negotiate with Hitler in 1941 as did the British and the French in 1938 or the Russians in 1939. Indeed, they were in a better moral position to do so; they negotiated their own future instead of bartering away another country's territory. They accepted diplomatic embarrassment to gain time, just as Britain and France had done earlier.

While they sought to keep themselves out of the war and the Germans out of their country, the Yugoslavs also had to face the

[1] According to Liddell Hart, the British "fatuously produced German intervention in the Balkans which . . . Hitler was chary of undertaking. The reponsibility for the consequent misery that has befallen the peoples [of] Yugoslavia and Greece . . . lies heavily upon us—for losing the sense of military realities." B. H. Liddell Hart, *Why Don't We Learn from History?* (London: Allen & Unwin, 1944), p. 40.

problem of the tensions that were building up among the Serbs. Many Serbs considered the Cvetković government as unrepresentative and believed it was trying to transform Yugoslavia into a German satellite. Although their politicians, once linked in the United Opposition, realized some arrangement had to be made with the Germans, they bowed to public opinion, refused to support the government or do anything else that would injure their several parties in the eyes of the voters, and let Cvetković take the blame for coming to an agreement with the Reich. Cvetković and his ministers were fully aware of the hostility toward them before they went to Vienna to sign the Tripartite Pact; the *coup d'état* came as no surprise to them in the psychological sense. The scope of the military and civilian preparations for the *coup* was a surprise in a concrete political sense.

The *coup* itself had two distinct phases: first, the action, carried out after months of planning by a small number of officers who unquestionably believed they reflected Serb public opinion; second, the public's response to the action of these few officers. The leaders of the *coup* had many motives: some hoped to realize personal ambitions, some to bring historic Serb political parties back to power, others to express their opposition to the *Sporazum* of August, 1939, others to aid the Allies. Each felt himself attuned to Serb public opinion and each was prepared to act with it.

The people who came into the streets of Belgrade on March 27, 1941, voiced their confidence in the new government believing it would defy the Nazis and denounce the signatures on the Tripartite Pact. In this their opinion differed in no particular from Hitler's; he too assumed the Simović government would steer an anti-Nazi, pro-Allied course and hurriedly took steps to destroy it. Since he had never seriously considered invading Yugoslavia,[2] he now had to improvise plans within two weeks.

The *coup d'état* electrified and gladdened the anti-Nazi world with the sight of a people standing up to Hitler in his moment of triumph. It gave the Serbs a profound sense of national fulfillment. But when the *putsch* was over, when the "betrayers of Serbian honor" had been

[2] United States Department of the Army, *German Campaigns in the Balkans (Spring, 1941)*, p. 25; and *DGFP*, D, X, Doc. 353. See also Göring testimony, *IMT*, IX, 333; Jodl testimony, *IMT*, XV, 385-86; Keitel testimony, *IMT*, X, 523-24.

dismissed from office, the leaders of the new government had to take stock. Long before March 27th they had known the true military capacity of their country; for the purposes of the *coup* they had chosen to ignore its obvious military weaknesses. Now they were face to face with the sobering realization that to defend the honor of the Serbs they would have to defend all the Yugoslavs. They were no longer leaders of the Serbs alone; they were leaders of a country composed not only of Serbs but also of Croats and Slovenes and Bosnians and more minorities than they had ever before taken into account. In a few short hours, in the time it took to deploy troops around a few government buildings in the nation's capital and to depose a few officeholders, the new leaders of Yugoslavia found themselves transformed from Serb chauvinists into the responsible spokesmen for a multinational state whose citizens—supporters and opponents alike—expected them to defend their lives and property by keeping the Germans out of the country.

Like Cvetković before him, Simović refused to come to the aid of the British. He became acutely conscious of the military odds against his country and, like the regents, doubted the value of deliberately throwing it into a war in which its army could hold out no more than two weeks. He therefore continued the regency policy of neutrality and adherence to the Tripartite Pact and superimposed a policy of creeping mobilization, vainly hoping that one tactic or the other would prove successful in defending the country.

The short-lived political unity of Yugoslavia, reflected in the Serb-Croat agreement of 1939, could not withstand the shock of the Axis invasion. The regency had only begun to accomplish what the monarchy should have strived for years earlier—the unification of nationalities within the framework of democratic institutions. It would have taken still another generation of peace to build a democratic state and to reaffirm a strong bond of union between the monarchy and the people. It would have taken at least another generation of patriots who thought of themselves as Yugoslavs and not as Serbs or Croats or Slovenes; there were too few who thought of the whole, too many who thought of the parts. From the outset the Yugoslav state was hampered by men of limited vision and even less flexibility who revealed no capacity for working together for their common good.

After Hitler marched into Poland the world would not permit the Yugoslavs to freely choose between throwing themselves in the path of the dictators and trying to avoid a head-on collision. More than once the representatives of the great powers talked as if the future of the entire world depended solely on the degree to which the Yugoslavs were willing to sacrifice themselves. President Roosevelt put it plainly when he told United States Minister Lane:

I think we should find some means of getting across to the Prince Regent and others that the United States is looking not merely to the present but to the future, and that any nation which tamely submits on the grounds of being quickly overrun would receive less sympathy from the world than a nation which resists, even if this resistance can be continued for only a few weeks.[3]

From this distance, the regency's foreign policy—including the signing of the Tripartite Pact—seems to have been the best possible in the adverse circumstances dictated by geography, the proximity of Yugoslavia's powerful enemies, and the disinclination of the Croats and of many Slovenes for conflict with Germany.

The Yugoslav government was realistic in its analysis of German and Italian aims in the Balkans. It was realistic in its awareness of military impotence, its own and the Allies'. It was painfully conscious of the weakness and indecisiveness of the West. After the fall of France, after the rout of the British, the caretaker government saw no way of saving the country but to adopt policies of accommodation to the Axis powers. But even under those circumstances the regency, outwardly neutral, remained determinedly pro-Allied. It aided Greece when Greece was invaded. It fostered military collaboration between the Yugoslav army and the French. And for almost three years it parried the Axis thrust toward Yugoslavia.

But the Allied leaders showed very little understanding of Yugoslavia's difficult position during these years. They tried to coerce the Yugoslavs into the war. They failed to extend to Yugoslavia the patience and diplomatic restraint they showed to Sweden—despite the fact that Sweden, under conditions similar to those facing Yugo-

---

[3] Hull, *Memoirs*, II, 930.

slavia, signed an agreement with Germany permitting a steady flow of German military traffic to pass over its borders.[4]

In a larger sense, Yugoslavia provides a clear example of the small power that must continuously trim its sails to the conflicting winds stirred by the great powers. In moments of crisis, the small state is persuaded, or coerced, or patronized, sometimes even consulted, on policies of war, peace, or survival. But it never is allowed to remain aloof; great powers at war do not permit small states the luxury of neutrality or independent thinking.

The dynamics of war demanded that both the Allies and the Axis use Yugoslavia for their own purposes and then, if necessary, thrust it aside.

In 1941 Yugoslavia tried to indulge in neutrality, to ward off Germany by diplomacy alone. In doing so, it challenged the assumption, shared by all great powers, that nations with military and economic prowess invariably pursue a wise and farsighted political strategy. That the independent course plotted by the Yugoslav regency was a sound one appropriate to the circumstances, that a neutral Yugoslavia—or even one which had signed a restricted pact with Germany—could in the long run prove an asset to the Allies seem never to have entered their calculations.

After 1933 the Yugoslavs had developed a foreign policy based on freedom of diplomatic action. In 1941 they attempted to express that freedom by remaining neutral. They could successfully pursue such a policy only so long as there was a balance of power in the Balkans. In addition, they needed strong natural defenses, a mobile and well-equipped standing army, an industrial economy, and a unified people. These essentials they lacked; for them, the regency tried to substitute diplomacy. When the Balkans became a center of conflict—when the Italians moved into Greece, the British came to the aid of the Greeks, and the Germans moved into Bulgaria en route to Greece—they destroyed the balance of power which had been the keystone of Yugoslav diplomacy. Without it, the structure fell.

In January, 1940, the British had no objection to Yugoslavia's

---

[4] Sweden, with an effective army and economy, was in a stronger position to defend its version of neutrality, and could use its supply of minerals as a diplomatic weapon. Above all, Sweden was removed from the primary centers of conflict.

neutrality. They did not then believe the Germans would move into the Balkans, nor did they themselves intend to do so.

In January, 1941, it became evident that the British would honor their pledge to aid the Greeks. It became equally evident that the Germans would honor their pledge to aid the Italians. Because the Germans had more men and machines, it was also evident that they would ultimately occupy Greece. From the British point of view, therefore, Yugoslav and Turkish participation in the war did not mean immediate success for the democratic cause. It did mean, however, that the Germans, after forcing the British to withdraw from Greece, would have to use precious manpower to police large areas with hostile populations.

These calculations sharpened the moral dilemma that faced the Simović government as once it had faced the regency. Both had to make a moral decision for a nation which had little relation to the moral judgment they would have made for themselves as individuals. Both saw the issue as one of national survival. Both asked themselves if they could choose peace instead of national suicide. Both realized that their adherence to the Tripartite Pact would exact a high price in national honor and prestige abroad. Both hoped that their country, by accommodating itself to the German power within the limits of the Tripartite Pact and its accompanying guarantees, could survive today's crisis and tomorrow join the Allies.

But with the *coup* of March 27th, Yugoslavia's political fortunes were set in flux, starting a process that would be resolved years later with little credit to the political wisdom of the Western democracies and with little concern for their political peace of mind.

APPENDIX A

THE ITALO-YUGOSLAV POLITICAL AGREEMENT
OF MARCH 25, 1937

The Royal Regents in the name of H.M. the King of Yugoslavia and H.M. the King of Italy, Emperor of Ethiopia, considering that it is in the interest of their two countries as well as in that of the general peace to strengthen the bonds of sincere and lasting friendship between them and being desirous of providing a new basis for this friendship and of inaugurating a new era in the political and economic relations between the two States; persuaded that the maintenance and consolidation of a durable peace between their two countries is also an important condition for the peace of Europe; have decided to conclude an agreement . . . .

Article 1. The High Contracting Parties pledge themselves to respect their common frontiers as well as the maritime frontiers of the two States in the Adriatic and in the event that either of them might be the object of unprovoked aggression by one or more Powers, the other Party pledges to abstain from any action which might benefit the aggressor.

Article 2. In case of international complications, and if the High Contracting Parties agree that their common interests are or may be threatened, they agree to act together regarding the measures to be taken to safeguard themselves.

Article 3. In their mutual relations the High Contracting Parties reaffirm their will not to resort to war as an instrument of national policy and to resolve by peaceful means all differences or conflicts which may arise between them.

Article 4. The High Contracting Parties undertake not to tolerate in their respective territories, or aid in any way, activities directed against the territorial integrity or the existing order of the other Contracting Party, or activities of a nature that prejudices the friendly relations between the two countries.

Article 5. In order to give to their commercial relations new impetus more appropriate to the amicable relations established between their two countries, the High Contracting Parties agree to intensify and expand the present exchange of goods and services and to investigate the possibilities of closer economic collaboration. Special agreements to this end will be concluded with a minimum of delay.

Article 6. The High Contracting Parties agree that nothing in this agreement should be considered as contrary to the existing international obligations of the two countries, these obligations being public.

Article 7. The present agreement will endure for five years. If it is not denounced six months before its expiration, it will by tacit consent be prolonged year by year.

Article 8. The present agreement will be ratified. It will come into force with the exchange of ratifications. This will take place in Belgrade as soon as possible.

SUPPLEMENTARY AGREEMENT

to the Treaty of Commerce and Navigation of July 14, 1924, and to the additional agreements of April 25, 1932, January 4, 1934, and September 26, 1936, concerning the expansion of the existing exchange of goods and services and the development of general economic relations between Yugoslavia and Italy.

The Royal Regents in the name of H.M. the King of Yugoslavia and H.M. the King of Italy, Emperor of Ethiopia, in order to give their existing commercial relations a new impetus more appropriate to the cordial relations existing between their two countries; to strengthen and broaden the present exchange of goods and services on an equitable basis; to insure treatment more just and more in conformity with the above-mentioned purpose; to supervise the application of the arrangements provided for that purpose; to seek conditions for a more extensive economic collaboration; have decided to conclude an agreement . . . .

Article 1. Italy accords to Yugoslavia supplementary import quotas in addition to those provided for and established in the previous agreements. These quotas will be determined later. In order to facilitate the use of these quotas in relation to import permits, the competent authorities of the two countries will cooperate in the form and according to the procedures to be established by the Permanent Italo-Yugoslav Economic Committee provided for in Article 4 of the present agreement.

Article 2. Yugoslavia accords to Italy the right to pay by clearing accounting, for certain special goods, the quantity and value of which will be established later and for which payment is now required in foreign currency.

Article 3. The High Contracting Parties agree to grant one another equality of treatment in addition to that derived from the normal application of the most favored nation clause which is the basis of all their economic relations, so that there will be no discrimination against either country in relation to any third country or against any kind of goods.

The establishment of this equality of treatment, of its scope, of its relation to the customs system, of the goods which it concerns and of the countries to which it will apply will be entrusted to the Permanent Italo-Yugoslav Economic Committee.

Article 4. No later than one month after the present agreement comes into force, the High Contracting Parties agree to organize the Permanent Italo-Yugoslav Economic Committee provided for in the protocol of the additional agreement of April 25, 1932.

In addition to the task stated in the aforesaid protocol, the committee will supervise the application of the various stipulated provisions and continually seek ways of improving commercial exchange and of expanding economic collaboration between the two countries.

This committee is to meet at least once a year alternatively between the two countries. The first meeting will take place within three months after the present agreement comes into force.

The number of members of the committee will be established by common agreement of the two governments. It will not be necessary, however, for all members of the committee to take part in the meetings of the committee, their presence depending on the nature of the matter to be discussed.

Article 5. This supplementary agreement constitutes only the preliminary basis of a larger economic cooperation which may take the form of a closer regional agreement. The Permanent Committee will be entrusted to study the basic characteristics of this later agreement and propose its scope.

Article 6. The duration of the present agreement is tied to the Political Agreement signed today.

Article 7. The present agreement will be ratified. It will come into force with the exchange of ratifications. This will take place in Belgrade as soon as possible.

APPENDIX B

PROTOCOL OF ADHESION OF YUGOSLAVIA TO THE TRIPARTITE PACT, VIENNA, MARCH 25, 1941

The Governments of Germany, Italy, and Japan on the one hand and the Government of Yugoslavia on the other hand, through their plenipotentiaries, acknowledge the following:

Article 1. Yugoslavia adheres to the Tripartite Pact, which was signed September 27, 1940, at Berlin, between Germany, Italy, and Japan.

Article 2. Representatives of Yugoslavia will be present at conferences of commissions for common technical questions created under Article 4 of the Tripartite Pact so far as the commission deals with matters touching Yugoslavia's interests.

Article 3. The text of the Tripartite Pact is added as an annex to this protocol. This protocol is drawn up in the German, Italian, Japanese, and Yugoslav languages, each of which is authentic. The present protocol comes into effect on the day of signing.

THREE NOTES FROM GERMAN FOREIGN MINISTER RIBBENTROP TO YUGOSLAV PRIME MINISTER CVETKOVIĆ, VIENNA, MARCH 25, 1941

Mr. Prime Minister:

In the name of the German Government and at its behest I have the honor to inform Your Excellency of the following:

On the occasion of the Yugoslav adherence today to the Tripartite Pact the German Government confirms its decision to respect the sovereignty and territorial integrity of Yugoslavia at all times.

Mr. Prime Minister:

With reference to the conversations that occurred in connection with Yugoslav adherence to the Tripartite Pact I have the honor to confirm to

Your Excellency herewith in the name of the Reich Government that in the agreement between the Governments of the Axis powers and the Royal Yugoslav Government the Axis power governments during this war will not demand of Yugoslavia to permit the march or transportation of troops through the Yugoslav State or territory.

Mr. Prime Minister:

With reference to the conversations that occurred in connection with Yugoslav adherence to the Tripartite Pact, I have the honor to confirm to Your Excellency herewith in the name of the Reich Government that in the agreement between the Governments of the Axis powers and the Royal Yugoslav Government:

Italy and Germany assure the Government of Yugoslavia that, out of consideration of the military situation, they do not wish to advance, on their part, any request whatsoever regarding military assistance.

If, however, the Government of Yugoslavia, would consider, at any moment, that it is in its own interest to take part in the military operations of the powers of the Tripartite Pact, the Yugoslav Government will be free to conclude such military agreements as necessary, and with these powers themselves.

Meanwhile, I beg you to keep the preceding communication strictly secret, and to make it public only with agreement of the Governments of the Axis powers.

THE TRIPARTITE PACT BETWEEN GERMANY, ITALY, AND JAPAN, SIGNED AT BERLIN, SEPTEMBER 27, 1940

The Governments of Germany, Italy, and Japan consider it the prerequisite of a lasting peace that every nation in the world shall receive the space to which it is entitled. They have, therefore, decided to stand by and cooperate with one another in their efforts in Greater East Asia and the regions of Europe respectively. In doing this it is their prime purpose to establish and maintain a new order of things, calculated to promote the mutual prosperity and welfare of the people concerned.

It is, furthermore, the desire of the three Governments to extend cooperation to nations in other spheres of the world who are inclined to direct their efforts along lines similar to their own for the purpose of realizing their ultimate object, world peace.

Accordingly, the Governments of Germany, Italy, and Japan have agreed as follows:

Article 1. Japan recognizes and respects the leadership of Germany and Italy in the establishment of a new order in Europe.

Article 2. Germany and Italy recognize and respect the leadership of Japan in the establishment of a new order in Greater East Asia.

Article 3. Germany, Italy, and Japan agree to cooperate in their efforts on aforesaid lines. They further undertake to assist one another with all political, economic, and military means if one of the three Contracting Powers is attacked by a Power at present not involved in the European War or in the Chinese-Japanese conflict.

Article 4. With the view to implementing the present pact, joint technical commissions, to be appointed by the respective Governments of Germany, Italy, and Japan, will meet without delay.

Article 5. Germany, Italy, and Japan affirm that the above agreement affects in no way the political status existing at present between each of the three Contracting Parties and Soviet Russia.

Article 6. The present pact shall become valid immediately upon signature and shall remain in force ten years from the date on which it becomes effective.

In due time, before the expiration of said term, the High Contracting Parties shall, at the request of any one of them, enter into negotiations for its renewal.

APPENDIX C

SOVIET UNION–YUGOSLAV TREATY OF FRIENDSHIP
AND NONAGGRESSION, APRIL 5, 1941

The Presidium of the Supreme Soviet of the USSR and His Majesty the King of Yugoslavia, inspired by the friendship existing between their two countries, and convinced that the maintenance of peace is in their common interest, have decided to conclude a treaty of friendship and nonaggression . . . .

1. The two contracting parties mutually undertake to refrain from any attack on one another and to respect the independence, sovereign rights, and territorial integrity of the USSR and Yugoslavia.

2. Should either of the contracting parties be subjected to attack from a third State, the other contracting party undertakes to observe a policy of friendship toward it.

3. The present treaty is concluded for a term of five years.

If, one year before the expiration of that term, neither of the contracting parties gives notice of its desire to denounce the present treaty, it shall automatically continue in force for the subsequent five years.

4. The present treaty enters into force upon its signature. The treaty is to be ratified as quickly as possible. The instruments of ratification shall be exchanged in Belgrade.

5. The treaty is drawn up in two copies, each in the Russian and Serbo-Croat languages; the two texts have equal force.

BIBLIOGRAPHY

This is a selective bibliography. I have listed only those references that I found most helpful. No attempt has been made to list every book covering the period or every book or article consulted. The bibliography is divided into three parts. "Documents and Official Sources" includes unpublished materials such as letters and memoranda written by Yugoslav government officials and political leaders of the period, as well as my correspondence with these officials. The materials will be placed on restricted deposit in the Archives of Russian and East European History and Culture of Columbia University.

The second part consists of secondary sources, including memoirs; the third is a list of useful journals.

DOCUMENTS AND OFFICIAL SOURCES

Auswärtiges Amt. Documents on German Foreign Policy, 1918-45. Ser. C, 3 vols.; Ser. D, 11 vols. Washington, D. C.: Government Printing Office, 1949-60.

—— Documents Relatifs au Conflit Germano-Yougoslave et Germano-Grec. Berlin: Deutscher Verlag, 1941.

Butler, J. R. M. Grand Strategy. Vol. II (September 1939-June 1941). London: H. M. Stationery Office, 1957.

Ciano, Galeazzo. L'Europa Verso la Catastrofe. Verona: Mondadori, 1948.

Degras, Jane, ed. Soviet Documents on Foreign Policy, 1933-41. London: Oxford, 1953. Vol. III.

Documents Secrets du Ministère des Affaires Étrangères d'Allemagne. 3 vols. Paris: Paul Dupont, 1946. Vol. II.

Les Événements Survenus en France de 1933 à 1945. Temoignages et documents recueillis par la commission d'enquête Parlementaire. Paris: Presses Universitaire de France, 1947. Tome I.

"Führer Conferences on Naval Affairs, 1939-45," in Brassey's Naval Annual, 1948. London: Clowes, 1948.

Halder, Franz. Diary (covering the period August 14, 1939 to September

24, 1942). 6 vols. Nuremberg: Office of Chief of Council for War Crimes, Office of Military Government for Germany, 1946.

Hitler e Mussolini, Lettere e Documenti. Milan: Rizzoli, 1946.

League of Nations. Treaty Series. London: Harrison, 1920-46. Vols. VI, XII, LIV, LXVIII, CXXXIX, CXLVIII, and CLIII.

Ministarstvo Finansija. Statistika Spoljne Trgovine Kraljevine Jugoslavije za 1935, 1936 god. (Ministry of Finance. Statistics on Foreign Trade of the Kingdom of Yugoslavia for 1935 and 1936.) Belgrade: 1936, 1937.

Ministère des Affaires Étrangères du Royaume de Yougoslavie, Recueil des Traités Internationaux. Belgrade: 1934, 1935, 1936, 1937.

Ministero Degli Affari Esteri, Commissione per la Pubblicasione dei Documenti Diplomatici. I Documenti Diplomatici Italiani. Ottova Serie (Vols. XII and XIII) and Nona Serie (Vol. I). Rome: La Libreria Dello Stato, 1952, 1953, 1954.

Narodna Skupština. Stenografske Beleške (Yugoslav Parliamentary Record). Belgrade: 1935-39.

Parliamentary Debates (Hansard). House of Commons Official Reports. Fifth Series. London: H. M. Stationery Office, various dates.

Playfair, I. S. O., et al. The War in the Mediterranean and the Middle East. 2 vols. London: H. M. Stationery Office, 1954, 1955.

Službene Novine (Official Gazette). Belgrade: 1935-39.

Sontag, Raymond J., and James S. Beddie, eds. Nazi-Soviet Relations. Washington, D.C.: Department of State, 1948.

Trial of the Major War Criminals before the International Military Tribunal, Nuremberg, 1945-46. Proceedings and Documents in Evidence. Nuremberg: International Military Tribunal, 1947-49. Vols. XV-XLII.

United States Department of the Army. The German Campaigns in the Balkans (Spring, 1941). Washington, D.C.: Department of the Army, 1953.

United States Department of State. Foreign Relations of the United States, 1936-41. Washington, D.C.: Government Printing Office, various dates.

——— Peace and War, United States Foreign Policy, 1931-41. Washington, D.C.: Government Printing Office, 1943.

United States Military Tribunals. Transcript of the Trials of War Criminals before the Nuremberg Tribunals. Mimeographed documents. Washington, D.C.: Office of the Chief of Counsel for War Crimes.

Vauhnik, Vladimir. Auf der Lauer nach Hitlers Kriegsplänen (Drei Jahre als Militärattache in Berlin). Unpublished manuscript.

Woodward, E. L., and Rohan Butler, eds. Documents on British Foreign Policy, 1919-39. Ser. 2, Vols. V-VII; Ser. 3, Vols. I-VII. London: H. M. Stationery Office, 1946-60.

SECONDARY SOURCES

Alfieri, Dino. Due Dittatori di Fronte. Milan: Rizzoli, 1948.

Amery, Julian. Sons of the Eagle. London: Macmillan, 1948.

Armstrong, Hamilton Fish. The New Balkans. New York: Harper, 1926.

Badoglio, Pietro. Italy in the Second World War. London: Oxford, 1948.

Basch, Antonín. The Danube Basin and the German Economic Sphere. London: Kegan Paul, Trench, Trubner, 1944.

Beck, Joseph. Dernier Rapport; Politique Polonaise, 1926-1939. Neuchatel and Paris: Baconnière, 1951.

Beneš, Eduard. Memoirs of Dr. Eduard Beneš. London: Allen & Unwin, 1954.

Brugère, Raymond. Veni, Vidi Vichy. Vanves: Calmann-Levy, 1944.

Churchill, Winston. The Second World War. 6 vols. Boston: Houghton Mifflin, 1948, 1949, 1950. Vols. I (The Gathering Storm), II (Their Finest Hour), III (The Grand Alliance).

Ciano, Galeazzo. Ciano's Diary, 1937-38. London: Methuen, 1952.

———— Ciano's Diary, 1939-43. London: Heinemann, 1947.

Comnène, N. P. Preludi del Grande Dramma. Rome: Leonardo, 1947.

Cooper, Duff. Old Men Forget. London: Hart-Davis, 1954.

Craig, Gordon A., and Felix Gilbert, eds. The Diplomats, 1919-39. Princeton: Princeton University Press, 1953.

Crane, John O. The Little Entente. New York: Macmillan, 1931.

Donosti, Mario. Mussolini e l'Europa. Rome: Leonardo, 1945.

Eylan, Claude. La Vie et la Mort d'Alexandre Ier. Paris: Bernard Grasset, 1935.

Fisher, Allan G. B. "The German Trade Drive in South-Eastern Europe," International Affairs, XVIII (1939), 143-70.

Flandin, Pierre-Étienne. Politique Française, 1919-40. Paris: Les Éditions Nouvelles, 1947.

Fotitch, Constantin. The War We Lost. New York: Viking, 1948.

Gafencu, Grigore. The Last Days of Europe. London: Muller, 1947.

———— Prelude to the Russian Campaign. London: Muller, 1945.

Gamelin, Maurice. Servir. 3 vols. Paris: Plon, 1946, 1947. Vols. II and III.

Geshkoff, Theodore I. Balkan Union. New York: Columbia University Press, 1940.

Gregorić, Danilo. So Endete Jugoslawien. Leipzig: Goldmann, 1943.

Hagen, Walter. Die Geheime Front. Linz and Vienna: Nibelungen, 1950.

Halifax, E. F. L. W. Fulness of Days. London: Collins, 1957.

Hassell, Ulrich von. The Von Hassell Diaries, 1938-1944; The Story of the Forces against Hitler Inside Germany as Recorded by Ambassador Ulrich

Von Hassell, A Leader of the Movement. London: Hamish Hamilton, 1948.

Haumant, Emile. La Formation de la Yougoslavie. Paris: Bossard, 1930.

Henderson, Nevile. Water under the Bridges. London: Hodder and Stoughton, 1945.

Hertz, Frederick. The Economic Problems of the Danubian States. London: Gollancz, 1947.

Highley, Albert E. The Actions of the States Members of the League of Nations in Application of Sanctions Against Italy, 1935-36. Geneva: Imprimerie du *Journal de Genève*, 1938.

Hooker, Nancy Harrison, ed. Moffat Papers. Cambridge, Mass.: Harvard University Press, 1956.

Horvat, Josip. Politička Povijest Hrvatske, 1918-29 (Political History of Croatia). Zagreb: Tisak Tipografije D.D., 1938.

Hull, Cordell. Memoirs of Cordell Hull. 2 vols. New York: Macmillan, 1948. Vol. II.

Kerner, Robert J., ed. Yugoslavia. Berkeley: University of California Press, 1949.

Kerner, Robert J., and Harry N. Howard. The Balkan Conferences and the Balkan Entente, 1930-35. Berkeley: University of California Press, 1936.

Knatchbull-Hugessen, Sir Hughe. Diplomat in Peace and War. London: Murray, 1949.

Kordt, Erich. Wahn und Wirklichkeit. Stuttgart: Union Deutsche Verlagsgesellschaft, 1948.

Macartney, C. A. A History of Hungary, 1929-45. 2 vols. New York: Praeger, 1956.

—––— Hungary and Her Successors. London: Oxford, 1937.

—––— National States and National Minorities. London: Oxford, 1934.

Maček, Vladko. In the Struggle for Freedom. New York: Speller, 1957.

Machray, Robert. The Little Entente. London: Allen & Unwin, 1929.

—––— The Struggle for the Danube and the Little Entente, 1929-38. London: Allen & Unwin, 1938.

Miletich, Voucadine. Le Mouvement des Idées Constitutionelles en Yougoslavie depuis la Fin de la Grande Guerre. Paris: Rodstein, 1934.

Mondini, Luigi. Prologo del Conflitto Italo-Greco. Rome: Treves, 1945.

Moore, Wilbert E. Economic Demography of Eastern and Southern Europe. Geneva: League of Nations, 1945.

Mühlen, Norbert. Hitler's Magician: Schacht. London: Routledge, 1938.

Namier, L. B. Diplomatic Prelude. London: Macmillan, 1948.

—––— Europe in Decay. London: Macmillan, 1950.

—––— In the Nazi Era. London: Macmillan, 1952.

Ostović, P. D. The Truth about Yugoslavia. New York: Roy, 1952.

Papagos, Alexander. The Battle of Greece, 1940-1941. Athens: Scazikis, 1949.

Pasvolsky, Leo. Economic Nationalism of the Danubian States. New York: Macmillan, 1928.

Paulová, Milada. Jugoslavenski Odbor (Yugoslav Committee). Zagreb: Prosvjetna Nakladna Zadruga, 1925.

Pavelić, Ante. Aus dem Kampfe um den Selbständigen Staat Kroatien. Vienna: Holzl, 1931.

Peter II, King of Yugoslavia. A King's Heritage. London: Cassell, 1955.

Political and Economic Planning. Economic Development in S.E. Europe. London: P E P, 1945.

Rendel, Sir George. The Sword and the Olive. London: Murray, 1957.

Roatta, Mario. Otto Milioni di Baionette. Milan: Mondadori, 1946.

Royal Institute of International Affairs. The Balkan States. London: Oxford, 1936. Vol. I.

Selby, Sir Walford. Diplomatic Twilight, 1930-1940. London: Murray, 1953.

Seton-Watson, Hugh. Eastern Europe Between the Wars, 1918-41. Cambridge: Cambridge University Press, 1945.

Seton-Watson, R. W. The Balkans, Italy and the Adriatic. London: Nisbet, n.d.

Simoni, Leonardo. Berlin Ambassade d'Italie. Paris: Laffont, 1947.

St. John, Robert. From the Land of Silent People. London: Harrap, 1942.

Stadtmüller, Georg. Geschichte Südosteuropas. Munich: Oldenbourg, 1950.

Stoyanovitch, Vlastimir. Le Rapprochement Italo-Yougoslave et la Petite Entente. Paris: Bossuet, 1938.

Szembek, Jean. Journal, 1933-39. Paris: Plon, 1952.

Temperley, Harold W. V. History of Serbia. London: Bell, 1919.

Templewood, Viscount. Nine Troubled Years. London: Collins, 1954.

Tomasevich, Jozo. Foreign Economic Relations, 1918-41, in Yugoslavia, ed. by Robert J. Kerner. Berkeley: University of California Press, 1949.

—— Peasants, Politics and Economic Change in Yugoslavia. Stanford: Stanford University Press, 1955.

Toynbee, Arnold J. Survey of International Affairs, 1934, 1935 (2 vols.); 1936, 1937 (2 vols.). London: Oxford, 1937 and after.

Vucinich, Wayne S. Serbia Between East and West; the Events of 1903-8. Stanford: Stanford University Press, 1954.

Walters, F. P. A History of the League of Nations. 2 vols. London: Oxford, 1952. Vol. II.

Weinberg, Gerhard L. "Secret Hitler-Beneš Negotiations in 1936-37," *Journal of Central European Affairs*, XXVIII (1960), 366-74.

Weygand, Maxime. Mémoires; Rappelé au Service. 3 vols. Paris: Flammarion, 1950. Vol. III.

Wheeler-Bennett, John W. Munich, Prelude to Tragedy. New York: Duell, Sloan and Pearce, 1948.

Wheeler-Bennett, John W. and Stephen Heald, eds. Documents on International Affairs, 1934, 1935 (2 vols.), 1936, 1937 (2 vols.). London: Oxford, 1936 and after.

Wimmer, Lothar C. F. Expériences et Tribulations d'un Diplomate Autrichien. Neuchatel: Baconnière, 1946.

Wiskemann, Elizabeth. The Rome-Berlin Axis. London: Oxford, 1949.

Yanochevitch, Milorad. La Yougoslavie dans les Balkans. Paris: Les Éditions Internationales, 1935.

Yovanovit h, Miloutine. Le Régime Absolu Yougoslave Institue le 6 Janvier 1929. Paris: Bossuet, 1930.

JOURNALS

American Slavic and East European Review. New York
Les Balkans. Athens
Dokumenti o Jugoslavije (Documents on Yugoslavia). Paris
Hrvatska Revija (Croatian Review). Buenos Aires
Journal of Central European Affairs. Boulder, Colo.
Naša Stvarnost (Our Reality). Johannesburg
Poruka (The Message). London
Slavonic and East European Review. London

Index

Abyssinia, *see* Ethiopia

Accord of Friendship and Non-Aggression (U.S.S.R.-Yugoslavia), 276-77; text, 307

Ačimović, Milan, 121-22, 123, 124, 132

Adriatic Sea, 6, 83, 88, 168, 170; and Italy, 19, 20, 187-89, 267; islands in, 40, 172; and U.S.S.R., 178-79

Aegean Sea, 164, 178-79, 221, 230; *see also* Salonika

Africa, 31-32, 35, 36; *see also* Ethiopia; North Africa

Aggression, Lane on, 214-15

Agrarian Party, 150, 155, 169, 264

Agrarian reform, 64

Agreement, Maček-Cvetković, 154-55, 169, 175, 198-200

Agriculture, 94-95, 97, 100-2, 104, 108, 153

Aid: U.S., 159-60, 204, 225, 286; Yugoslav to Greece, 191-92; U.S.S.R. to Yugoslavia, 197-98, 206-7, 277; British to Balkans, 211-12, 220, 224, 233, 236, 286

Air force, Simović in command of, 253

Airpower, 158, 159; German, 231

Aksamović, Bishop, 264

Albania, 1, 9, 17-20 *passim*; and Italy, 12, 25, 43, 59; and Greece, 18; issue between Italy and Yugoslavia, 34, 59, 64, 68-70, 76-81, 120, 124-27, 138-39, 141, 193n, 234; Italian invasion of, 133, 137, 142-44, 153, 168; British reaction to invasion of, 146, 167; in Italian-Greek war, 181, 192, 204, 224-25; and Germany, 192, 268; and Simović, 269, 286

Alexander (Karageorgević), 7-9, 16, 18, 24-26, 87; dictatorship of, 7-8, 249, 263; and Italy, 14, 19-20, 25, 57; assassination of, 20, 25, 60, 65, 71; effects of assassination of, 26-28, 30, 32-33, 88, 90, 201; on Austria and Germany, 46n, 89, 110; policies of,

58-59, 89-90, 130, 169; on Albania, 76-77; and Pešić, 149; as regent, 248

Alexander (Obrenović), 247-48, 251, 252

Alfieri, Dino, 139, 181n, 268, 284

Algeria, 36n

Alliance system, Balkan, 9-20 *passim*; *see also* Balkan Entente; Little Entente

Allied and Associated Powers, 11

Allies, 149, 187, 195, 242; and future of Yugoslavia, 168-69, 170, 227; pressure of, on Yugoslavia, 212-13, 215-16, 220; failure of to understand Yugoslav policy, 298-300; *see also* *individual countries*

Aloisi, Baron, 27

Amery, Leopold, 241-42

Andres, Ivan, 259, 262

Andrić, Ivo, 111, 159, 184, 232-33, 255, 284

Anglo-Turkish Declaration (May, 1939), 146

Ankara, 175, 177

Anschluss, 54, 67-68, 83, 86, 89, 102, 104, 109-35, 294

Antiaircraft guns, 159

Antić, Milan, 117, 183, 219-21, 228-29, 239; and Stakić, 187, 208, 211

Anti-Comintern Pact, 147

Antimony, 103-4

Antirevisionism, 27, 29; *see also* Revisionism

Antonescu, Ion, 193, 203n, 263

Antonescu, Victor, 87

"Apis," 248, 251; *see also* Dimitrijević

Arad, 282

Aras, Rüstü, 27, 45

Armaments, 101, 103, 107, 149, 157-60, 192; and U.S.S.R., 177, 180, 197-98; to Greece, 191

Army, 156, 157-61, 285-86, 288; Serbian, and regicide, 247-52; *see also* Military questions

Assistance: technical, Greek to Yugo-

Military League (Bulgarian), 16
Minerals, 94, 95, 104, 105
Minority questions, 64, 82, 115, 116, 120, 293; *see also* Croatia; Serbia; Slovenia; Union
Mirković, Bora, 237-38n, 243, 250-59, 263-66, 290
Mobilization, 117, 168, 274; *see also* Military questions
Molotov, Vyacheslav M.: and Germany, 83n, 179, 180, 197, 231; on Balkans, 176, 178; and Tripartite Pact, 198, 237; and Yugoslav pact, 276-80 *passim*
Monarchy, failure of, 293
Monastir, 186, 187
Monastir Gap, 203
Montenegro, 1, 7, 264, 289
Morocco, 36n
Moscow, 127, 176, 276
Moslems, 1, 92, 199, 270-71
Moslem Organization, 8, 33, 123, 155
Moslem Party, 128, 198
Munich Pact, 118-19, 134
Munitions, 220; *see also* Armaments
Munitions Board, U.S., 160
Mushanov, Nikola, 16
Mussolini, Benito, 23, 39, 172-73, 181-82, 212, 230; and Paul, 13n, 62, 142; and Greece, 18, 19, 166-67; and Alexander, 19-20, 25; and France, 24, 28-32, 35, 48; and Ethiopia, 35-37, 98; and Stojadinović, 47, 86, 93, 119-20; and Eden, 49-50; Milan speech of, 57, 58; and Germany, 67, 148, 178-79, 188-89, 190, 268-69; and Albania, 133; and Croatia, 137, 140, 142; Rijeka speech of, 153; Hitler on, 195-96; to Csáky, 195-96; Stakić to, 211-12
Mutual assistance proposals, 42, 55

Nationalism, Croat, 152-53; *see also* Croatia
National Party, 126, 169
National Radical Party, 33, 34, 123n
Naval rearmament, 68-69
Navy, 43
Nazism, 49, 67; *see also* Germany; Hitler, Adolf
Nedeljković, 260-61

Nedić, Milan, 157-58, 171-72, 183-87 *passim*, 252
Nettuno convention, 64
Neuhausen, Franz, 122, 158
Neuilly, Treaty of (1919), 14, 16, 162
Neurath, Constantin, Baron von, 62, 84, 87, 100n, 106
Neutrality, 61-93 *passim*, 118-19, 144-47 *passim*, 170-201 *passim*, 224, 294-95, 299-300; and Albania, 76-77; economic aspects of, 94-108; and *Anschluss*, 112-13; and Czechoslovakia, 118; and a small state, 134-35; Heeren on, 156; "benevolent," 159; and U.S., 160, 234-35; and Bulgaria, 163; and Germany, 166, 192, 203, 210; and Italy, 167-68, 173; and Greece, 191; and Turkey, 193; great powers' views of, 212-16; Churchill on, 234; and Tripartite Pact, 237; and Simović, 266, 274; and *coup*, 297
Nikitović, Časlav, 239
Nikolai, Bishop, 264
Nikšić, 289, 290
Ninčić, Momčilo, 12, 150, 265-66, 270, 287; and Italy, 271, 285; to Gavrilović, 276; and Germany, 283-84; departure of, 290
Niš, 129
Nonaggression pacts discussed, 167, 179, 190, 207, 217
North Africa, 13n, 36n, 193
North Sea, 88
Norway, 172
Novi Sad, 104

Obrenović, Alexander, 248, 251, 252
Obrenović, Draga, 247-48
Obrenović, Milan, 247
October Revolution, 174
Official Gazette, 262
Ohrid, Lake, 153
Oil, 176, 243
Olga, Princess, 235
"Order of the Day," 275-76
Orphanos, Gulf of, 224
Orthodox Church, 174, 255; Serbian, 238, 246, 256, 264
Otranto, Strait of, 115, 236

Pabst, Willy, 232

DATE DUE

MAY 28 '65			
FEB 28 '67			
GAYLORD			PRINTED IN U.S.A.